Arbitration in the 37th America's Cup

Arbitration in the 37th America's Cup

Henry Peter (ed.)
David Tillett
Graham McKenzie
Bryan Willis
Claire Mordelet

Wolters Kluwer

Published by:
Kluwer Law International B.V.
PO Box 316
2400 AH Alphen aan den Rijn
The Netherlands
E-mail: lrs-sales@wolterskluwer.com
Website: www.wolterskluwer.com/en/solutions/kluwerlawinternational

Sold and distributed by:
Wolters Kluwer Legal & Regulatory U.S.
920 Links Avenue
Landisville, PA 17538
United States of America
E-mail: customer.service@wolterskluwer.com

ISBN 978-94-035-2969-1

e-Book: ISBN 978-94-035-2979-0
web-PDF: ISBN 978-94-035-2989-9

Photo Cover: © Ian Roman / America's Cup

Editor

Henry Peter (ed.)—Switzerland. Henry is of counsel at a large Swiss law firm (Kellerhals Carrard) and an honorary professor at the University of Geneva, where he has created and led until 2024 the Geneva Centre for Philanthropy. He specializes in corporate and sports law, fields in which he has written books and numerous articles. He often acts as arbitrator in business and sports matters. He is Vice-chairman of the Swiss Stock Exchange's Sanctions Commission, was, for almost twenty years, Vice-chairman of the Swiss Olympic Disciplinary Chamber of Swiss Sport and was, until December 2023, a member of the International Automobile Federation's Ethics Committee. He was a member of the 31st America's Cup Arbitration Panel, of the 32nd America's Cup Jury and Arbitration Panel, Chairman of the 33rd America's Cup Arbitration Panel and member of the 36th America's Cup Arbitration Panel.

Contributors

Graham McKenzie—New Zealand. Graham is a Barrister and Solicitor in New Zealand and has extensive experience as a Commercial Lawyer. He holds a Master of Laws degree from Warwick University, England, and is a Director of listed and unlisted public companies. Graham has previously been a member of the Jury and Arbitration Panel for the 32nd America's Cup and a member of the Jury of the 33rd and 34th America's Cups. He was also a member of the Arbitration Panel for the 36th America's Cup. Graham is a former Chair of the World Sailing Constitution Committee and of its Ethics Commission.

Claire Mordelet—France. Claire is a lawyer admitted to the Paris and New York bars. She is a senior associate in a large Swiss law firm (Kellerhals Carrard) and works with Henry Peter. Claire's practice focuses on domestic and international commercial arbitration, both ad hoc and institutional. She acts as counsel, arbitrator and arbitral secretary in sport and commercial matters. Claire was the Secretary of the 36th America's Cup Arbitration Panel.

David Tillett AM (Chairman)—Australia. David is a Member of the Order of Australia and was awarded the Australian Sports Medal for Services to Yachting in 2000. He has been a practising lawyer and has a long list of governance roles in sailing, including being appointed as an International Technical Official at seven Olympic Games, including three times being Chair of the International Jury. He has been an official at eight America's Cups, having been appointed as an Umpire, member of the Jury, twice as Jury Chair, and twice as Chair of the Arbitration Panel. He was a member of the World Sailing Council for eighteen years, Chair of the World Sailing Racing Rules Committee for twelve years, and was the Chairman of the World Sailing Constitution Committee for eight years. He is currently a member of the World Sailing Governance Committee and Chair of the Australian Maritime Museum/ Australian Sailing Hall of Fame. David was inducted into the South Australian Sports Hall of Fame in 2021 and has received the World Sailing Beppe Croce Trophy 2022 for "an individual who has made an outstanding voluntary contribution to the sport of sailing." David was the Chairman of the 36th America's Cup Arbitration Panel.

Bryan Willis—Great Britain. Bryan was "Rules Advisor" to the Swedish "Sverige" team in 1980, the British "Victory" team in 1983, and the Australian "Kookaburra" Defense in 1987. He was instrumental in setting up the International Sailing Federation (now World Sailing) umpiring system and the system of qualifying international umpires. Bryan was a jury member and Chief Umpire for the America's Cup in 1992, Jury Chairman and Chief Umpire in 2000 and 2003, Chairman of the combined Jury and Arbitration Panel and Chief Umpire in 2007, and a member of the Arbitration Panels in 2010 and 2013. He has been a member or chairman of no less than five Olympic Juries and many international championships. He was for many years a member of the World Sailing Racing Rules Committee, a member of the Judges Sub-committee and chaired the Race Officials Committee and the Race Management Sub-Committee. In 2018, he received the World Sailing Beppe Croce Trophy for services to sailing and in 2020 was inducted into the America's Cup Hall of Fame.

Table of Contents

Editor v

Contributors vii

List of Abbreviations xiii

Acknowledgments xvii

CHAPTER 1 Introduction 1
- 1.1 The Book 1
- 1.2 Background of the America's Cup 3
- 1.3 The Deed of Gift 3
- 1.4 The 37th America's Cup 3
  - 1.4.1 Overview of the 37th America's Cup 3
  - 1.4.2 AC37 Governing Rules 5
  - 1.4.3 AC37 Events 5
  - 1.4.4 Youth and Women's America's Cup Regattas 5
  - 1.4.5 Cost Containment and Limitations 6
  - 1.4.6 Support Vessels 6
  - 1.4.7 Crew Nationality Rules 7
  - 1.4.8 The 37th America's Cup Match 7
  - 1.4.9 AC37 Audience and Economic Impact 7
  - 1.4.10 Regatta Officials 10
- 1.5 The AC37 Arbitration Panel 11
  - 1.5.1 Composition 11
  - 1.5.2 Jurisdiction 13
  - 1.5.3 Rules of Procedure 14
  - 1.5.4 The Use of the WIPO Electronic Case Facility 14
  - 1.5.5 The Arbitration Panel's Decisions 15
- 1.6 The Future of the America's Cup 19

CHAPTER 2 The Text of the Deed of Gift 21
- 2.1 Original (Handwritten) Deed of Gift (July 8, 1857) 22
- 2.2 Current Text of the Deed of Gift 24

2.2.1 A Note by R. Steven Tsuchiya about the Current Deed of Gift 24
2.2.2 Current Text of the Deed of Gift 26
2.3 Assignment and Acceptance Agreement 30
2.3.1 A Note by R. Steven Tsuchiya about the 2017 Assignment & Acceptance Agreement 30
2.3.2 Assignment and Acceptance Agreement Executed on April 20, 2024, With Retroactive Effect as from June 26, 2017 31

CHAPTER 3 The Protocol of the 37th America's Cup 33
3.1 The Protocol of the 37th America's Cup, Incorporating Protocol Amendments 1 Through 16 (Consolidated Version Dated 25 September 2024) 33
3.2 Amendments Progressively Made to the Initial 37th America's Cup Protocol 130

CHAPTER 4 America's Cup Arbitration Panel Rules of Procedure (May 2023) 135

CHAPTER 5 Other 37th America's Cup Governing Documents 147
5.1 The World Sailing Racing Rules of Sailing – America's Cup Edition, for Use in the 37th America's Cup (v 4.07 – 25 September 2024) 147
5.2 The AC75 Class Rule (v 2.37 – 12 October 2024) 188
5.3 AC40 Class Rule (v 1.5 – 17 October 2023) 277
5.4 AC Technical Regulations (v 1.27 – 8 September 2024) 301
5.5 Race Conditions – 37th America's Cup Challenger Selection Series ("Louis Vuitton Cup Conditions") 359
5.6 Match Conditions – 37th America's Cup Match – Barcelona, Spain ("Match Conditions") 364
5.7 Sailing Instructions for the Louis Vuitton Cup Challenger Selection Series Including Amendment 8 367
5.8 Sailing Instructions for the 37th America's Cup Match Including Amendment 1 369
5.9 Documents Governing the Youth and Women's America's Cup 371
5.9.1 Youth and Women's AC Agreement (Notice of Rece – Version 15) for the 2024 Youth America's Cup and the Women's America's Cup 371

5.9.2 Sailing Instructions for the Youth and Women's America's Cup Including Amendment 8 393

CHAPTER 6 The 37th America's Cup Arbitration Panel Decisions 397

6.1 ACAP37/01 – CVS' (Luna Rossa) Request for Interpretation in Respect of 'Performance Data' and 'Competitor's Sailing Team': Decision (31 December 2022, 12.30 UT) and Amendment (11 January 2023, 12.00 NZ) 397

6.2 ACAP37/02 – CVS (Luna Rossa) Request for Relief over Allocation of AC40 Yacht to American Magic: Decision (6 March 2023, 10:50 UTC) and Amendment (6 March 2023, 22:00 UTC) 400

6.3 ACAP37/03 – SNG (ARBR) Request for Interpretation Regarding Share of AC75 Yacht Design Package: Decision (19 April 2023, 08:30 UTC) 404

6.4 ACAP37/04 – NYYC (AM) Request to Be Excused from Participation in 2nd Preliminary Regatta Held in Jeddah: Decision (28 May 2023, 14:35 UTC) 411

6.5 ACAP37/05 – SNG (ARBR) Request for Interpretation of Venue, Event and Team Bases, Regarding Retailing and Merchandising: Decision (27 August 2023, 09:10 UTC) 420

6.6 ACAP37/06 – Notice Resulting from a Report Received: Decision (14 October 2024, 14:00 UTC) 430

CHAPTER 7 The Jury Decisions 433

7.1 AC37 Jury Case 01 – Request for Redress by ITA for RR2, Race 29: Decision (10 September 2024) 433

7.2 AC37 Jury Case 02 – Jury Interpretation of 'Serious Physical Damage' and 'Action by a 3rd Party': Decision (14 September 2024) 435

7.3 Youth America's Cup Jury Case 01: Decision (18 September 2024) 437

Index 439

List of Abbreviations

AC	The America's Cup
AC31	The 31st America's Cup
AC32	The 32nd America's Cup
AC33	The 33rd America's Cup
AC34	The 34th America's Cup
AC36	The 36th America's Cup
AC37	The 37th America's Cup
AC38	The 38th America's Cup
AC31 Book	John Faire, Michael Foster, Donald Manasse, Henry Peter (ed.), David Tompkins, "*Arbitration in the America's Cup: the XXXI America's Cup Arbitration Panel and its Decisions,*" Kluwer Law, The Hague, London, New York, 2003
AC32 Book	Henry Peter (ed.), Bryan Willis, Gabrielle Kaufmann-Kohler, Graham McKenzie, Henry Menin, David Tillett, "*The 32nd America's Cup Jury and its Decisions,*" Wolters Kluwer, 2007
AC33 Book	Henry Peter (ed.), Hamish Ross, Graham McKenzie, "*The 33rd America's Cup Judicial and Arbitral Decisions,*" Wolters Kluwer, 2012
AC34 Book	Henry Peter (ed.), David Tillett, John Doerr, Josje Hofland, Graham McKenzie, Hamish Ross, Bryan Willis, "*Dispute Resolution in the 34th America's Cup,*" Wolters Kluwer, 2016
AC36 Book	Henry Peter (ed.), David Tillett, Graham McKenzie, Claire Mordelet, "*Arbitration in the 36th America's Cup - Including Additional Previously Unpublished Material,*" Wolters Kluwer, 2022

AC40 Class Rule	Class rule for the AC40 Yachts to be used in the Initial Preliminary Regattas and the Youth and Women's AC Regattas
AC75 Class Rule	Class rule for the AC75 Yachts to be used in the Final Preliminary Regatta, the CSS, the Match and/or in any other regattas sailed in AC75 Yachts
AC37 Events	The America's Cup Preliminary Regattas, the America's Cup Challenger Selection Series and the 37th America's Cup Match
ACAP37 or Arbitration Panel or Panel	The 37th America's Cup Arbitration Panel
AC Media	The Media division appointed by ACE
ACE	AC37 Event Limited
ACPI	America's Cup Properties Incorporated
AM	American Magic, representing the New York Yacht Club (NYYC)
Arbitration Panel or Panel or ACAP37	37th America's Cup Arbitration Panel
ARBR or Alinghi	Alinghi Red Bull Racing SA, representing the Société Nautique de Genève (SNG)
ARL	Athena Racing Limited, competing as INEOS Britannia
CAS	Court of Arbitration for Sport
Challenger	Yacht club whose challenge for AC37 has been accepted by the Defender
Challenger of	Royal Yacht Squadron Limited (RYS), representing Athena Racing
Competitor	Defender and/or Challenger
COR or Challenger of Record	Royal Yacht Squadron Limited (RYS), representing Athena Racing Limited, competing as INEOS Britannia
COR/D	Defender and Challenger of Record when acting together
CR	Class Rule
CSS	America's Cup Challenger Selection Series

CVS	Circolo della Vela Sicilia
Deed of Gift or Deed or DoG	Deed of Gift dated October 24, 1887, as amended
Defender	Royal New Zealand Yacht Squadron Incorporated (RNZYS), represented by Emirates Team New Zealand Limited (TNZ)
eADR	The web-based electronic alternative dispute resolution case facility created and made available by WIPO
ETNZ or TNZ	Emirates Team New Zealand Limited, representing the Defender Royal New Zealand Yacht Squadron Incorporated (RNZYS)
Events	All of the regattas that form part of AC37
HSV	Hydrogen powered vessel
INEOS Britannia or COR	INEOS Britannia, representing the Royal Yacht Squadron Limited (RYS)
Jury	World Sailing International Jury
LR or Luna Rossa	Luna Rossa Prada Pirelli Team, representing Circolo della Vela Sicilia (CVS)
Match	37th America's Cup Match, i.e., the series of races for the America's Cup between the Defender and the qualifying Challenger resulting from the CSS
Match Conditions	Conditions governing the races of the Match
NZT	New Zealand Time
OET	Orient Express Racing Team, representing Société Nautique de Saint-Tropez (SNST)
Official AC Website	Official website of AC37: www.americascup.com
Protocol	Protocol Governing the 37th America's Cup
Record or COR	Limited, competing as INEOS Britannia
RNZYS	Royal New Zealand Yacht Squadron Incorporated
RRS	World Sailing Racing Rules of Sailing
RRSAC	Racing Rules of Sailing (America's Cup Edition)
RYS	Royal Yacht Squadron Limited (Challenger of Record)

SNG	Société Nautique de Genève
SNST	Société Nautique de Saint-Tropez
TNZ or ETNZ	Emirates Team New Zealand Limited, representing the Defender Royal New Zealand Yacht Squadron Incorporated (RNZYS)
Youth and Women's AC Regattas	Youth and Women's America's Cup Regattas

Acknowledgments

The authors would like to thank **Ms. Sasha Lines** for her valuable collaboration in preparing this book. Sasha is a Corporate & Commercial Solicitor in the United Kingdom with experience in both private practice and industry. She gained her qualifications from The College of Law in Guildford, England. She also managed the logistics and operations for the British Olympic & Paralympic Sailing Teams' attendance at the Rio 2016 Olympic & Paralympic Games. Sasha was the Jury Secretary for the 32nd America's Cup assisting not only the Jury but also the Umpiring and Measurement Teams as well as the Secretary of the 37th America's Cup Arbitration Panel. She has extensive sailing and racing experience, having been a member of the British Sailing Team for many years, and subsequently has participated in the Rolex Fastnet Race, Rolex Middle Sea Race, RORC Caribbean 600 Race and sailed twice across the Atlantic Ocean.

The authors are also grateful to **Mr. R. Steven Tsuchiya** who provided what can be considered the accurate consolidated version of the Deed currently in force (reproduced at section 2.2.2 of this book) as well as an explanation thereof (section 2.2.1 below). Steven is a yachting historian and chair of the America's Cup Hall of Fame Selection Committee. He is a member of the New York Yacht Club, serving on the Club's Library, Fine Arts, and America's Cup Committees. He has contributed to preserving yachting history by designing exhibits at the Herreshoff Marine Museum and The Sailing Museum, and co-edits, with Robert Kamins, the America's Cup Bibliography at CupInfo.com, which documents over 1,000 books about the America's Cup. His latest book is the *America's Cup Deed of Gift and Related Documents* (Herreshoff Marine Museum, 2nd ed. 2025). He is also a member of the Cowan Lake Sailing Association in Wilmington, Ohio, where he races Flying Scot dinghies.

The authors would further like to extend their thanks to **Dr. Hamish Ross** who assisted Mr. R. Steven Tsuchiya with regard to determining the current text of the Deed of Gift (section 2.2 below). Hamish is a New Zealand commercial and maritime lawyer who has been an America's Cup Counsel since 1995, when he was engaged by the New York Yacht Club's challenge for America's Cup before being General Counsel for Team Alinghi SA when SNG won the Cup in 2003 and in 2007, as well as in its 2010 defense. He served during the 34th America's Cup in 2013 as General Counsel for America's Cup Race Management, was an adviser to the Defender in the 35th America's Cup and was Counsel for American Magic, the New York Yacht Club challenge in the 36th America's Cup as well as advising other interested parties.

Hamish is a member of the America's Cup Hall of Fame Selection Committee. His doctoral thesis[1] was dedicated to the America's Cup Deed of Gift, and he writes widely on America's Cup history and legal issues. Hamish has contributed to the AC36 Book in providing unpublished documents and Court decisions regarding the Deed of Gift as well as in drafting commentaries in that regard (*see* AC36 Book, pp. 75-76, p. 83 and p. 101). He restores and races classic wooden yachts and was one of the founders and now Patron of the New Zealand Classic Yacht Association.

1. The America's Cup Deeds of Gift (The University of Auckland, 2017); https://researchspace.auckland.ac.nz/handle/2292/37021.

CHAPTER 1 Introduction

1.1 THE BOOK

This book is the sixth of a series of books compiling and making available decisions rendered during all (but one)[2] editions of the America's Cup since 2020, as well as supporting materials. Kluwer Law International and Wolters Kluwer Law & Business have indeed already published five books in the same series about the 31st, the 32nd, the 33rd, the 34th and the 36th editions of the America's Cup, respectively entitled "*Arbitration in the America's Cup: the XXXI America's Cup Arbitration Panel and its Decisions*,"[3] "*The 32nd America's Cup Jury and its decisions*,"[4] "*The 33rd America's Cup judicial and arbitral decisions*,"[5] "*Dispute resolution in the 34th America's Cup*"[6] and "*Arbitration in the 36th America's Cup—Including Additional Previously Unpublished Material*."[7]

The America's Cup is one of the most important sporting competitions in the world. It is also the oldest sporting competition in existence, now more than 170 years old. Like all sporting events, it raises a series of issues, including sometimes litigation cases regarding issues which might arise again during other America's Cup editions, or which can be of interest beyond the sport of sailing. What happens in the America's Cup can in fact be of general interest to the sport and arbitration communities in general.

2. Upon decision of the Defender, for confidentiality reasons no book was published regarding the 35th America's Cup. The book concerning the 36th America's Cup decisions ("Arbitration in the 36th America's Cup—Including Additional Previously Unpublished Material") also included the Protocol of the 35th America's Cup as well as a few comments regarding the 35th America's Cup, including about the dispute resolution arrangements set out in such Protocol and about the 35th America's Cup Arbitration Panel appointment and jurisdiction.
3. John Faire, Michael Foster, Donald Manasse, Henry Peter (ed.), David Tompkins, Kluwer Law, 2003. This book is referred to herein as the "AC31 Book."
4. Henry Peter (ed.), Bryan Willis, Gabrielle Kaufmann-Kohler, Graham McKenzie, Henry Menin, David Tillett, Wolters Kluwer, 2007. This book is referred to herein as the "AC32 Book."
5. Henry Peter (ed.), Hamish Ross, Graham McKenzie, Wolters Kluwer, 2012. This book is referred to herein as the "AC33 Book."
6. Henry Peter (ed.), David Tillett, John Doerr, Josje Hofland, Graham McKenzie, Hamish Ross, Bryan Willis, Wolters Kluwer, 2016. This book is referred to herein as the "AC34 Book."
7. Henry Peter (ed.), David Tillett, Graham McKenzie, Claire Mordelet, Wolters Kluwer, 2022. This book is referred to herein as the "AC36 Book."

But until the first book of this series was published by Kluwer in 2003, the decisions rendered by state courts or arbitration bodies in the various editions of the Cup were not collected nor, in any event, preserved in their final version, and were therefore often difficult to locate if needed for reference. In other words, irrespective of their possible "binding effect," regrettably, no case law was at hand. Sometimes very interesting decisions and the rationale thereof were thus not available to further America's Cup arbitration panels nor to the arbitration sports community at large. The aim of this book is to continue collecting and making available all arbitration decisions rendered during the America's Cup editions.

In summary, this book contains the following documents:

- The (current version of the) Deed of Gift.
- The Protocol of the 37th America's Cup and the amendments made thereto.
- The America's Cup Arbitration Panel Rules of Procedure (May 2023).
- Other documents governing the 37th America's Cup edition: The World Sailing Racing Rules of Sailing—America's Cup Edition, for use in the 37th America's Cup (Version 4.07—September 25, 2024); the AC75 Class Rule (Version 2.37—October 12, 2024); the AC40 Class Rule (Version 1.5—October 17, 2023); the AC Technical Regulations (Version 1.27—September 8, 2024); the Race Conditions—37th America's Cup Challenger Selection Series ("Louis Vuitton Cup Conditions"); the Match Conditions—37th America's Cup Match—Barcelona, Spain ("Match Conditions"); the Sailing Instructions for the Louis Vuitton Cup Challenger Selection Series Including amendment 8; the Sailing Instructions for the 37th America's Cup Match Including amendment 1.
- The documents governing the Youth and Women's America's Cup: the Youth and Women's America's Cup Agreement (Notice of Race—Version 15) for the 2024 Youth America's Cup and the Women's America's Cup; the Sailing Instructions for the Youth and Women's America's Cup, including amendment 8.
- All 37th America's Cup Arbitration Panel Decisions.
- All 37th America's Cup Jury Decisions.

Besides compiling these documents, the authors have deemed it useful to start the book with this introduction in which, after briefly providing some historical background, they explain and comment on what they considered are the most important and peculiar issues pertaining to the 37th America's Cup and what can be learnt for the future editions of the America's Cup.

1.2 Background of the America's Cup

The story of the Cup has been summarized in the previous books of this series. The authors refer to these books with that regard,[8] as well as, *inter alia*, to the following books: Ian Dear, *The America's Cup: An Informal History*, New York: Dodd, Mead, 1980; Bob Fisher, *An Absorbing Interest: The America's Cup—A History 1851-2003*, Wiley, 2011; Gérard A. Jaeger, C'era una volta la Coppa America, Longanesi, 2007; Gary Jobson, La Coupe de l'America, 1893-1937, L'album d'Edwin Levick, photographe; Van de Velde, 2000; Dr. Hamish Ross, The America's Cup Deeds of Gift, Thesis, The University of Auckland, 2017; R. Steven Tsuchiya, America's Cup Deed of Gift and Related Documents, Herreshoff Marine Museum, second edition, 2025.

1.3 The Deed of Gift

Chapter 2 of the Book shows the handwritten version of the original Deed of Gift dated July 8, 1857 (2.1 *infra*). It also contains what can be considered the current text of the Deed of Gift. This text (2.2.1 *infra*) as well as a brief explanation thereof (2.2.2 *infra*) have been written by R. Steven Tsuchiya with the assistance of Dr. Hamish Ross.

Following extensive research carried out by R. Steven Tsuchiya, it has become apparent that there is still uncertainty regarding the current text of the Deed of Gift (Deed or DoG). This concerns both the original text and its successive amendments. Chapter 2 of this book—in section 2.2.1—which R. Steven Tsuchiya kindly accepted to write with Dr. Hamish Ross' assistance, explains the hurdles he had to overcome and submits what he considers should be the accurate consolidated version of the Deed currently in force (*see* below section 2.2.2). In another section of Chapter 2 (section 2.3.1), R. Steven Tsuchyia provides useful explanations about the Deed of Assignment and Acceptance.

1.4 The 37th America's Cup

1.4.1 Overview of the 37th America's Cup

The Royal New Zealand Yacht Squadron Incorporated was the Defender (D), represented by Emirates Team New Zealand (ETNZ or TNZ), and the Challenger of

8. *See* in particular AC31 Book, pp. 2 et seq.; AC32 Book, pp. 2 et seq.; AC33 Book, pp. 2 et seq.; AC34 Book, pp. 3 et seq., AC36 book, pp. 3-5.

Record (COR) was The Royal Yacht Squadron Limited, represented by INEOS Britannia. A Protocol was agreed between them, dated November 15, 2021, allowing other yacht clubs to enter a Challenger Selection Series.

Besides the Challenger of Record, the other challengers which accepted to take part to this edition of the Cup were Circolo della Vela Sicilia (CVS) (represented by Luna Rossa Prada Pirelli Team (Luna Rossa)), Société Nautique de Genève (SNG) (represented by Alinghi Red Bull Racing SA (Alinghi or ARBR)), Société Nautique de Saint-Tropez (SNST) (represented by Orient Express Racing Team (OET)) and the New York Yacht Club (NYYC) (represented by American Magic (AM)).

In addition to the Protocol, there were other documents governing the event, namely the AC75 Class Rules, the Racing Rules of Sailing (America's Cup version) (RRS AC), the Match Conditions, the AC Technical Regulations, and the Sailing Instructions for the 37th America's Cup Match. These, together with other documents which the authors have deemed relevant for future reference, are reproduced in their entirety in this book.

To run the event, the Defender incorporated a limited liability company named AC37 Event Limited (ACE). ACE was responsible for organizing and managing the commercial rights of the event and for implementing the decisions of the Defender and Challenger of Record acting together (COR/D).

The AC75 yachts used during the 37th America's Cup proved to be faster than the first generation of AC75s. With suitable conditions, it was not unusual for them to exceed 50 knots, and the highest speed recorded during the 37th America's Cup was 55.5 knots on board Ineos Britannia. The following speeds show the evolution of the AC yachts' performances between 2020 and 2024.[9] Notable high speeds actually recorded in racing were in fact:

- 49.1 kn (90.9 km/h; 56.5 mph) by Te Rehutai (ETNZ) (in 15 and 19 kn of wind being 28 and 35 km/h or 17 and 22 mph) on December 17, 2020.
- 50.25 kn (93.06 km/h; 57.83 mph) by Britannia (INEOS Britannia) during day 4 of the Prada Cup January 23, 2021.
- 53.31 kn (98.73 km/h; 61.35 mph) by Patriot (American Magic) during day 1 of the Prada Cup Semifinals (in breeze gusting up to 22 kn (41 km/h; 25 mph)) on January 29, 2021.
- 55.2 kn (102.2 km/h; 63.5 mph) by Luna Rossa (Luna Rossa Prada Pirelli) during day 3 of the Louis Vuitton Cup Final on September 29, 2024.
- 55.5 kn (102.8 km/h; 63.9 mph) by Britannia (INEOS Britannia) during day 5 of the Louis Vuitton Cup Final on October 1, 2024.

On October 20, 2024, ETNZ won the 37th America's Cup over a tough Challenger INEOS Britannia (*see* section 1.4.8 hereunder).

9. https://en.wikipedia.org/wiki/AC75.

1.4.2 AC37 GOVERNING RULES

Pursuant to Article 33.1 of the Protocol, the rules governing the 37th edition of the America's Cup were, which are all included in the present book:

(a) the Deed of Gift (but excluding the Preliminary regattas and the Challengers Selection Series);
(b) the Protocol of the 37th America's Cup;
(c) the AC75 Class Rule, the AC40 Class Rule and the AC Technical Regulations;
(d) the Race Conditions;
(e) the Racing Rules; and
(f) the Sailing Instructions.

1.4.3 AC37 EVENTS

Two initial preliminary regattas (which all Challengers were required to attend) were held in the AC40 class yachts in Jeddah, Saudi Arabia (November 29-December 2, 2023) and in Vilanova i La Geltrú, Spain (September 14-17, 2023). The final Louis Vuitton Preliminary Regatta was held in Barcelona between August 20 and 25, 2024, where all six Competitors sailed their AC75 yachts.

The Louis Vuitton Cup Round Robin Series commenced on August 29 and ran until September 11, 2024. It was also sailed in the AC75 yachts. The races that Emirates Team New Zealand participated in did not carry any points.

The Louis Vuitton Challenger Selection Series semi-final was between Luna Rossa Prada Pirelli Team and Alinghi Red Bull Racing, on the one hand, and between INEOS Britannia and NYYC American Magic, on the other. The French entry, Orient Express Racing Team, did not qualify for the semi-final after the Round Robin series.

The final of the Louis Vuitton Challenger Selection Series was scheduled between September 26 and October 7, 2024. It was a tightly fought series between Luna Rossa Prada Pirelli and INEOS Britannia, with the winner being INEOS Britannia by 7 race wins to 2.

1.4.4 YOUTH AND WOMEN'S AMERICA'S CUP REGATTAS

Article 22.2 of the Protocol provided that ACE was responsible for developing and publishing a one-design class rule; this led to the AC40 yacht. Each Competitor was required to purchase at least one AC40 yacht.

In an enlightened innovative development and for the first time, with a view to continuing the development of the America's Cup as the premier event in the sport of sailing, in addition to the AC37 events, Youth and Women's America's Cup regattas were held in the new one-design AC40 class of yachts. These were held between September 10 and October 13, 2024.

Under Article 9.2(b) of the Protocol, each Competitor (including the Defender and all Challengers) was required to make available their AC40 yachts for use by teams competing in the Youth and Women's AC regattas. No charter fee was payable. In addition, six other teams from different Nations were invited to participate in each of these regattas.

Other than with regard to the obligation to provide AC40 yachts under the Protocol, the Arbitration Panel had no jurisdiction over the youth and women competing at those regattas.

The winners of both the Youth and the Women's AC40 regattas were from the Luna Rossa Prada Pirelli Team.

1.4.5 COST CONTAINMENT AND LIMITATIONS

In order to limit costs, under Article 24 of the Protocol, each Competitor was entitled to build only one new AC75 hull. Also, the AC Technical Regulations contained various restrictions regarding both the number and modification which could be made to various components on the yachts. Under Article 24.2 of the Protocol, there were also restrictions on when AC75 yachts could be sailed.

The usual "construction in country" requirements were contained in Article 26 of the Protocol.

1.4.6 SUPPORT VESSELS

With a view to promoting sustainable equipment, under Article 31 of the Protocol, each Competitor was required to use a minimum of two hydrogen-powered support vessels (HSVs) at the Match venue to support its on-water race operations. The minimum specifications included a top speed of 50 knots, the capacity to carry six people, 169 kW of hydrogen fuel cell power, and the capability to fully foil at boat speeds of 24 knots and above.

There were a number of technical issues, and some Competitors regarded the HSVs as less than successful.

1.4.7 CREW NATIONALITY RULES

In the perspective of the provision in the Deed of Gift pursuant to which the America's Cup is a "friendly competition between countries," Article 30.1 of the Protocol required that 100% of the crew members of all AC75 yachts be nationals of the country of the yacht club that the Competitor represented. Such a requirement included any crew member to hold, as of March 17, 2021, a valid passport of the country of the yacht club that the Competitor represented. This requirement was regarded as contentious by some Competitors and may be subject to further debate or challenge in the context of AC38 if the rule is maintained.

1.4.8 THE 37TH AMERICA'S CUP MATCH

The 37th America's Cup Match was held on the waters off Platja de Barceloneta from August 19 to October 19, 2024. It saw the continued use of the AC75 foiling monohull class of boat that had first been used in the 36th America's Cup held in Auckland, New Zealand in 2021. During its 37th edition, the design competition at the forefront of sailing technology has continued to be a major element of the America's Cup.

Pursuant to the Protocol, the winner of the 37th edition of the America's Cup was the winner of a best-of-13 race series. In total, nine races were sailed. During Race 9, which took place on Day 6 (October 19, 2025), Emirates Team New Zealand won the 37th America's Cup after an epic final showdown in Barcelona against the Challenger of Record, INEOS Britannia, in a single race that ebbed and flowed from the outset but ultimately saw the Kiwis secure victory by 37 seconds.

On-site in Barcelona, there were three "Race Village areas" which included several large television screens providing commentary in both English and Spanish. Most saw it as a commercial success and a step up from the COVID-19-affected AC36.

1.4.9 AC37 AUDIENCE AND ECONOMIC IMPACT

It is common for studies to be carried out in association with each edition of the America's Cup, analyzing the economic impact it has had on the area in which it has been held. In order to measure the effects that the 37th America's Cup had on Barcelona and Catalonia, it has been proposed to carry out three different studies, complementary to each other, each focusing on a specific dimension of the impact generated. The conduct of these studies has resulted in three reports issued by the University of Barcelona and the Barcelona Capital Nàutica Foundation (FBCN): (i) an

"Ex post economic impact study" Report, based on real data, the aim of which is to provide the maximum quantitative information, following the Input-Output methodology, estimating the economic activity generated by the America's Cup;[10] (ii) a "Qualitative and quantitative social assessment" Report;[11] and (iii) a "Qualitative Analysis and Arrival" Report.[12]

The Economic Impact Report has revealed that Barcelona benefited from a EUR 1.03 billion economic boost from hosting the 37th America's Cup.[13] Here are some key findings appearing in the Reports, as summarized by Yacht Life Racing:[14]

> A total of 1.068 team members were present in Barcelona across six America's Cup teams, 12 Puig Women's, and 12 UniCredit Youth America's Cup teams. 11 AC40 foiling yachts were built for the Preliminary Regattas in Vilanova i la Geltrú and Jeddah, the UniCredit Youth America's Cup and the Puig Women's America's Cup and it was named "Boat of the Year" by World Sailing.
>
> 20.677 young people reached through the 37th America's Cup via the various educational programs such as the FBCN's "Programa Educatiu La Navegació al Segle XXI, Un Repte Tecnològic," the city council's "VIU LA VELA" program and the America's Cup Trophy Tour regattas.
>
> The event was attended by 244 superyachts, injecting a spend of EUR 35 million into the local economy.

The Economic Impact Report also found that there was a total gross brand exposure value of EUR 1,367 billion for all of the brands, sponsors and host venue

---

10. Jordi Suriñach and Esther Vayá (dir), Rosina Moreno, José Ramón García and Javier Romaní, Report entitled "Impacte econòmic de la 37a Copa Amèrica de Vela, Barcelona 2024" (i.e., Economic Impact of the 37th America's Cup, Barcelona 2024), Published in March 2025; https://www.barcelonacapitalnautica.org/wp-content/uploads/2025/03/Report-1-Impacte-Economic_.pdf.
11. Jordi Suriñach and Esther Vayá (dir), Rosina Moreno, José Ramón García and Javier Romaní, Report entitled "Valoració social qualitativa de la 37a Copa Amèrica de Vela, Barcelona 2024" (i.e., Qualitative and Quantitative Social Assessment, Barcelona 2024), Published in March 2025; https://www.barcelonacapitalnautica.org/wp-content/uploads/2025/03/Report-2-Impacte-social.pdf.
12. Jordi Suriñach and Esther Vayá (dir), Rosina Moreno, José Ramón García and Javier Romaní, Report entitled "Anàlisi qualitativa de la 37a Copa Amèrica de Vela, Barcelona 2024" (i.e., Qualitative Analysis and Arrival), Published in March 2025; https://www.barcelonacapitalnautica.org/wp-content/uploads/2025/03/Report-3-Llegat_.pdf.
13. Jordi Suriñach and Esther Vayá (dir), Rosina Moreno, José Ramón García and Javier Romaní, Report entitled "Impacte econòmic de la 37a Copa Amèrica de Vela, Barcelona 2024" (i.e., Economic Impact of the 37th America's Cup, Barcelona 2024), Published in March 2025, pp. 46 et seq.; *see also* https://www.nzherald.co.nz/sport/sailing/americas-cup/americas-cup-brings-near-2-billion-positive-economic-impact-to-barcelona-study-finds/M63D3CQAAZGGJOPEEZEHMYSBJU/.
14. https://www.yachtracinglife.com/what-do-barcelonas-big-numbers-mean-for-the-future-of-the-americas-cup/https://www.sail-world.com/news/284121/EURO1billion-payday-for-Barcelona-from-AC37.

associated with the 37th America's Cup, i.e., a 64% increase from the 36th America's Cup.

The 37th America's Cup created the equivalent of 12,872 jobs in Barcelona. Ninety per cent of the 380 different event suppliers and providers were locally based businesses.

The volunteer program called "Team B" quickly became the beating heart of the event, with 2,300 volunteers, 78% being local residents.

The official America's Cup E-Sports game was downloaded over a hundred times. There were eight Grand Finalists invited to Barcelona from seven different countries, and the "Gamer to Sailor" initiative took the winning two gamers racing in the AC40s.

Sustainability and contributing to the Barcelona Blue Economy were a priority, and nine hydrogen-powered foiling chase boats were constructed and used across team and event operations, which eliminated 78,000 litres of fuel from on-water operations and reduced 181.531 kgs of CO_2 emissions.

The Reports also found that 1.8 million visitors were counted over the fifty-nine days across all event sites on and off the water including more than 460,000 attendees who came to Barcelona specifically for the event. Three event sites totaling 32,000 sqm provided free viewing. The spectator attendance provided strong support from each of the countries represented in the regattas. Of the total of 382,989 estimated attendees on ground at the Barcelona Harbour, 65.9% were foreigners, followed by those living in the city of Barcelona (20.6%), by those from the rest of the province of Barcelona (8.5%), by those from the rest of Spain (8.5%) and, lastly, by those from the rest of Catalonia (1.5%).

The Report also revealed that the regatta was well-watched around the world. A total of 954 million viewers were assessed, topping the global audience of 941 million that had made the Auckland 2021 regatta the then-most-watched America's Cup ever. A reported 37% growth in dedicated audience from the New Zealand-hosted event was reported.[15]

As far as media coverage was concerned, 11.182 hours of global broadcast coverage; 9.6 million hours of watch time on YouTube; social media viewership increased by 235% compared to the previous edition. Broadcast coverage included 29 broadcast contracts in 210 territories, live or featured broadcasts on YouTube and Facebook in 239 territories, and agreements with major news agencies such as Reuters, AFP, CNN and other accredited media.[16] As many as 1,512 media articles were written and over 250,000 photo images were downloaded by the media from the America's Cup photo library.

---

15. https://www.nzherald.co.nz/sport/sailing/americas-cup/americas-cup-brings-near-2-billion-positive-economic-impact-to-barcelona-study-finds/M63D3CQAAZGGJOPEEZEHMYSBJU/.
16. *Ibid.*, p. 64.

The objective to bring the sport of sailing and the America's Cup to a huge audience was considered achieved.

1.4.10 REGATTA OFFICIALS

Articles 42 through 47 of the Protocol deal with the Regatta Officials. These are, respectively, the Regatta Director (Articles 42.1 and 43.1) and the "other Regatta Officials" (Article 42.2). The other Regatta Officials are, respectively, the Measurement Committee (Articles 42.2(a) and 44.1), the Rules Committee (Articles 42.2(b) and 44.2), the Umpires (Articles 42.2(c) and 45), the World Sailing International Jury (Jury)(Article 42.2(d)) and "such other regatta officials and/or staff (Article 42.2(e)) requested by the Regatta Director as reasonably necessary in meeting the purpose and intent set out in the introduction of this Protocol."

The appointor(s), the terms of engagement and the role of these respective Regatta Officials, their tasks, responsibilities, authorities, powers and jurisdiction are described in detail in the Protocol.

The Protocol provided for an identity overlap between the Umpires and the members of the Jury as all the core Umpires were qualified International Judges and could therefore be used to make up an ad hoc International Jury needed to hear any particular case. In fact, the Jury was "comprised of Umpires who have been appointed under Article 42.2(c) [of the Protocol]," where 42.2(c) provides that the Umpires are the persons "as may be reasonably required to umpire the races comprising each Event, including a chief umpire." Article 45, entitled "Umpires and Jury," provided that "the Umpires and Jury shall be responsible for ...," including "umpiring the racing," "interpreting the Racing Rules" and "undertaking the actions for which the Jury has responsibility under the AC Technical Regulations and art. 47.3."

Article 47.2, entitled "Decisions," is an interesting provision providing that "All decisions of the Regatta Director, Measurement Committee, Rules Committee, Umpires and the Jury that are taken in good faith within their proper authority and/or jurisdiction as prescribed in and/or contemplated by the Rules in each case shall not be subject to any review or appeal unless otherwise expressly provided in this Protocol." This was obviously aiming at establishing a system where the decisions of these respective bodies were final. One could wonder to which extent this solution would achieve its purpose, since it requires any decision: (i) to be "taken in good faith" (which might induce an unsatisfied party to challenge a decision on that basis); (ii) to be taken "within their proper authority and/or jurisdiction" (which might be another angle of attack in view of the number of bodies involved with a risk of overlap between their real or alleged authority or jurisdiction) and, but maybe above all; (iii) because it is a well-established principle in sports law that, with only a few exceptions, decisions may always be challenged at least once in front of a true arbitration body or, in the absence thereof, of a Court. This was not tested during

AC37 but might be in the future if the same solution is adopted in forthcoming editions of the Cup.

The Rules Committee was solely and exclusively responsible for all matters relating to the interpretation of the Class Rule (Article 44.2(a) of the Protocol) and the Umpires and International Jury were responsible for interpreting the Racing Rules (Article 45 of the Protocol).

Article 67.3 of the Protocol provided in particular that the Arbitration Panel was to resolve all matters of interpretation of the Protocol and Rules and, generally, all disputes arising between the Defender, the Challenger of Record and the Challengers, "*other than those concerning the Racing Rules or the Class Rules.*" The Arbitration Panel had thus no jurisdiction to interpret or resolve matters under the Racing Rules and the Class Rule.

The 37th America's Cup Umpires and Jury Members were Richard Slater (AUS) (Chief Umpire), Miguel Allen (POR), Arnaud Mante (FRA), Craig Mitchell (GBR), and Sofia Truchanowicz (POL).

For the first time, there were no Umpires on the water. All decisions were made in an Umpires' booth ashore. This was a room containing electronic equipment monitoring the precise location of the Competitors' yachts.

There were three Jury Decisions, which are all reproduced in this book. Two regard the America's Cup competition and one the Youth America's Cup.

1.5 The AC37 Arbitration Panel

With regard to dispute resolution, the solution adopted by the Protocol was much the same as had been used for the 36th edition, with an Arbitration Panel which had jurisdiction to deal with: (i) any disputes arising out of the Protocol; and (ii) all Rule 69 matters under the RRS AC.

1.5.1 COMPOSITION

In accordance with Article 67 of the Protocol, the Arbitration Panel was composed of three members. One was nominated by the Royal New Yacht Squadron Incorporated as Defender, and another by the Royal Yacht Squadron Limited as Challenger of Record. The Chairman was appointed by the mutual agreement of the Defender and Challenger of Record.

The three selected members were David Tillett (Chairman), Graham McKenzie appointed by the Defender, and Bryan Willis appointed by the Challenger of Record. In addition, pursuant to its Rules of Procedure (Article 1.5), Sasha Lines was appointed as Panel Secretary. All three members had previously worked together on various America's Cups. They had extensive AC knowledge and an excellent working relationship.

Here is a short biography of each of the three members of the 36th America's Cup Arbitration Panel and of its Secretary:

David Tillett AM (Chairman)—Australia. David is a Member of the Order of Australia and was awarded the Australian Sports Medal for Services to Yachting in 2000. He has been a practising lawyer and has a long list of governance roles in sailing, including being appointed as an International Technical Official at seven Olympic Games, including three times being Chair of the International Jury. He has been an official at eight America's Cups, having been appointed as an Umpire, member of the Jury, twice as Jury Chair, and twice as Chair of the Arbitration Panel. He was a member of the World Sailing Council for eighteen years, Chair of the World Sailing Racing Rules Committee for twelve years, and was the Chairman of the World Sailing Constitution Committee for eight years. He is currently a member of the World Sailing Governance Committee and Chair of the Australian Maritime Museum /Australian Sailing Hall of Fame. David was inducted into the South Australian Sports Hall of Fame in 2021 and has received the World Sailing Beppe Croce Trophy 2022 for "an individual who has made an outstanding voluntary contribution to the sport of sailing." David was the Chairman of the 36th America's Cup Arbitration Panel.

Graham McKenzie—New Zealand. Graham is a Barrister and Solicitor in New Zealand and has extensive experience as a Commercial Lawyer. He holds a Master of Laws degree from Warwick University, England, and is a Director of listed and unlisted public companies. Graham has previously been a member of the Jury and Arbitration Panel for the 32nd America's Cup and a member of the Jury of the 33rd and 34th America's Cups. He was also a member of the Arbitration Panel for the 36th America's Cup. Graham is a former Chair of the World Sailing Constitution Committee and of its Ethics Commission.

Bryan Willis—Great Britain. Bryan was "Rules Advisor" to the Swedish "Sverige" team in 1980, the British "Victory" team in 1983, and the Australian "Kookaburra" Defense in 1987. He was instrumental in setting up the International Sailing Federation (now World Sailing) umpiring system and the system of qualifying international umpires. Bryan was a jury member and Chief Umpire for the America's Cup in 1992, Jury Chairman and Chief Umpire in 2000 and 2003, Chairman of the combined Jury and Arbitration Panel and Chief Umpire in 2007, and a member of the Arbitration Panels in 2010 and 2013. He has been a member or chairman of no less than five Olympic Juries and many international championships. He was for many years a member of the World Sailing Racing Rules Committee, a member of the Judges Sub-committee and chaired the Race Officials Committee and the Race Management Sub-Committee. In 2018, he received the World Sailing Beppe Croce Trophy for services to sailing and in 2020 was inducted into the America's Cup Hall of Fame.

Sasha Lines (Secretary)—Great Britain. Sasha is a Corporate & Commercial Solicitor in the United Kingdom with experience in both private practice and industry. She gained her qualifications from The College of Law in Guildford, England. She also managed the logistics and operations for the British Olympic & Paralympic Sailing Teams' attendance at the Rio 2016 Olympic & Paralympic Games. Sasha was the Jury Secretary for the 32nd America's Cup, assisting not only the Jury but also the Umpiring and Measurement Teams. She has extensive sailing and racing experience, having been a member of the British Sailing Team for many years, and subsequently has participated in the Rolex Fastnet Race, Rolex Middle Sea Race, RORC Caribbean 600 Race and sailed twice across the Atlantic Ocean.

1.5.2 JURISDICTION

The Arbitration Panel's jurisdiction was set out in Article 67.3 of the Protocol, namely:

> **67.3 Jurisdiction and penalties**
>
> Subject always to the terms of Articles 47.2 and 67.5, the Arbitration Panel shall have the following powers:
>
> (a) to resolve all matters of interpretation of the Protocol and Rules (excluding the Racing Rules or the Class Rules) except where expressly excluded in the provisions of such documents and Rules and including, where necessary, the determination of the facts relevant to the matter of interpretation;
> (b) to resolve disputes (other than those concerning the Racing Rules or the Class Rules) between the Defender and the Challenger of Record;
> (c) to resolve disputes (other than those concerning the Racing Rules or the Class Rules) between the Defender and an individual Challenger when the Challenger of Record 65 expresses in writing to the Defender its agreement that the issue be resolved by the Arbitration Panel;
> (d) to resolve disputes (other than those concerning the Racing Rules or the Class Rules) between individual Challengers when one of those Challengers so requests, or between an individual Challenger and the Challenger of Record;
> (e) to resolve disputes between ACE and a Competitor;
> (f) to resolve any disagreement between the Defender and the Challenger of Record in respect to the Race Conditions under Article 34;
> (g) to determine the appropriate penalty under Reconnaissance;
> (h) to resolve disputes under an ACPI license agreement;
> (i) to impose penalties in support of decisions made by ACE and/or the Regatta Director when it reasonably considers such penalties to be necessary to enforce the relevant Rules;

(j) to resolve any other matters which it is given jurisdiction to determine by agreement of COR/D;
(k) to impose penalties as considered necessary by the Arbitration Panel; and/or
(l) to mediate at the request of the parties (or at its own instigation) any dispute it considers appropriate for mediation. Such mediation is to be undertaken by a single member of the Arbitration Panel who will be chosen by the Arbitration Panel at its sole discretion. The member chosen to mediate shall thereafter not be precluded or excluded from further involvement in the dispute should the mediation be unsuccessful and therefore followed by a regular dispute.

1.5.3 RULES OF PROCEDURE

Article 67.14(a) of the Protocol provided for the Arbitration Panel to establish and publish its own Rules of Procedure; they are included in this book (Chapter 4). These Rules were very similar to the Rules issued during the 36th America's Cup. They worked to the satisfaction of all parties during this edition of the Cup which suggests that they can now be considered well established for any further edition of the America's Cup.

One of the improvements made to the Rules of Procedure was that, in addition to the traditional "Full Arbitration Panel Process," Article 67.14(b) included a provision pursuant to which the Arbitration Panel was to establish a fast-track process. Although the Panel did receive requests for the fast-track process to be implemented, it was considered that the particular cases could not be fairly resolved under accelerated proceedings as the balance of interest between the need to urgently get to a decision and due process principles did not justify it in the circumstances. Tight procedural deadlines were however set to ensure that decisions were made by the Arbitration Panel as timely as possible and decisions published very promptly.

1.5.4 THE USE OF THE WIPO ELECTRONIC CASE FACILITY

As in the 36th America's Cup, the Arbitration Panel used a customized version of the web-based electronic alternative dispute resolution case facility (e-ADR) created by the World Intellectual Property Organization (WIPO). WIPO e-ADR aimed to facilitate the conduct of cases by enabling parties and ACAP to efficiently share and access case-related information through a single and secure portal. More information about WIPO and the main features of the WIPO e-ADR system are set out in pages 41 to 43 of the AC36 Book as well as on WIPO's website at https://www.wipo.int/amc/en/eadr/wipoeadr/.

Unfortunately, on the occasion of the 37th America's Cup, the use of WIPO e-ADR was not finalized until after Cases 1 to 4 had been completed. These were handled by conventional email. WIPO e-ADR was used for Cases 5 and 6.

1.5.5 THE ARBITRATION PANEL'S DECISIONS

Only six cases were dealt with by the Arbitration Panel during the 37th America's Cup. This was the smallest number of cases that any of the Arbitration Panel members had experienced in any America's Cup they had been involved in. This is probably attributable to the fact that the Defender and the Challenger of Record were able to resolve most matters amicably between themselves, and that other technical issues were dealt with by the Measurement Committee and the Rules Committee.

Only one case (Case *ACAP37-05*) was referred to mediation. The mediation did however not get past the first meeting between the parties since it immediately appeared that there was no prospect of agreement; the case was thus referred back to the full Arbitration Panel for determination.

Below is a short summary of each of the six cases. The full reproduction of each ACAP decision can be found further on in this book under Chapter 6.

Case ACAP 37-001

This case started with an application made by Circolo della Vela Sicilia/Luna Rossa Challenge dated December 7, 2022, requesting an interpretation of Article 24.3 of the Protocol with respect to "performance data" and a "Competitor's sailing team."

Following the filing of the application, the Defender and the Challenger of Record agreed to amend Article 24.3 of the Protocol. Based thereon, the Defender and the Challenger of Record submitted that "*the outcome of the amended Article is that Team Members who are not members of the Sailing Team are permitted to sail on third party Surrogate Yachts as individuals, but Article 24.3(c) prohibits the Competitor (and in particular members of its design team) from receiving any performance data which emanates from such sailing. They further submitted that by sailing on a yacht a person does not automatically obtain performance data. They therefore concluded that sailing on a Surrogate Yacht by a non Sailing Team member is permitted.*"[17]

The decision, issued on December 31, 2022, was that the Protocol changes[18] clarified the points raised in Luna Rossa's application and did not appear to result in ambiguity. It was also decided that any further questions would need to be the subject of another application, setting out specific facts with reference to the amended wording of the Protocol.

17. §8 of the Decision.
18. As published on December 19, 2022.

Case ACAP 37-002

This case started with an application made by Circolo della Vela Sicilia/Luna Rossa Challenge filed on February 26, 2023. The Applicant submitted that the Challenger New York Yacht Club (NYYC)/American Magic (AM) had, on February 24, 2023, announced on its social media channels the receipt of an AC40 Yacht and that the receipt by AM of such AC40 Yacht was in violation of the priority order expressly set out by the Protocol and constituted a material unfair competitive advantage for AM. Luna Rossa requested the Arbitration Panel to impose appropriate orders and penalties to redress the alleged breach of the Protocol.

It appeared that AM and Alinghi Red Bull Racing SA had agreed to exchange their allocated AC40 Yachts. AM submitted that nothing in the Protocol forbade transferring the property of any AC40 Yacht.

The Panel found that ACE had met its obligations under Article 22.2(d) of the Protocol to allocate the AC40 Yachts in the required order of priority and that the contract arrangements made between AM and ARBR did not alter ACE's AC40 Yacht Hull allocation and did not constitute a breach of the Rules.

Case ACAP 37-003

This case started with an application filed on April 1, 2023 by Société Nautique de Genève/Alinghi Red Bull Racing SA requesting an interpretation of several articles of the Protocol relating to the sharing of an AC75 yacht design package. The applicant was of the opinion that the Defender may be (or had, or was in the process of) selling (or otherwise sharing) to Orient Express Team (OET) the complete design, engineering, manufacturing 3D models and 2D drawings, and all related information of the Defender's AC75 yacht which was going to be raced by the Defender in the 37th America's Cup (the "Design"). The applicant also requested that the Panel clarify whether an AC75 yacht built by OET as per the Design of the Defender should be deemed a "Surrogate Yacht" as defined in Schedule 1 of the Protocol and as contemplated by the America's Cup Technical Regulations.

The Arbitration Panel noted that Article 67.10 of the Protocol is broad in its terms and has the effect of requiring applicants to file an application within ten days as from when the applicant was or could reasonably have been aware of the circumstances justifying the application. This was to apply to what may be considered "interpretive" applications as well as "factual" applications.

A press release had been published on the 37th America's Cup website on February 2, 2023, drawing attention to an agreement between ETNZ and OET. The press release referred to "a technological agreement" having been established between ETNZ and OET and further referred to "a fantastic opportunity which makes it possible to erase the debt in time induced by a late entry which places the French on equal terms against talented competition." The press release further referred to securing the fact that OET would be competitive, and that "this partnership technology includes a latest generation design package from which we will work and build our own AC75 made in France. This partnership allows us to start on equal terms with the other Challengers."

Such statement made it clear that a substantial design package was being provided, such that the information was in the public arena so that any Competitor could have made an application relating to the same. The applicant was thus either aware or could reasonably have been aware of sufficient circumstances on which to make an application. Accordingly, the Arbitration Panel considered that the ten-day time limit within which an application should have been lodged had started to run on or about February 2, 2023 and that, therefore, elapsed when the application had been filed.

Notwithstanding the above, the Panel noted that the applicant, in its Response and Observations, had acknowledged that the "Protocol contains no limitations on share of design or freedom of designers to work for more than one Competitor."

The applicant also raised the issue of the ramifications and implications of such a case. The Panel considered that it was not for the Panel to comment with regard to ramifications or implications deriving from the wording of the Protocol.

Finally, the Panel took the view that the conduct referred to did not constitute individual Reconnaissance or co-ordinated testing as referred to in the Protocol. Should such breaches be considered in fact to occur, this could be the subject of a separate application.

Case ACAP 37-004

The New York Yacht Club / American Magic filed an application seeking orders: (i) to be excused from participating in the Second AC37 Preliminary Regatta in Jeddah; (ii) to exclude the application of Article 10.2 of the Protocol; and (iii) for no penalty to be imposed for such lack of participation. The applicant submitted that it had reasonable and genuine safety concerns in participating in any of the AC37 Events.

The application was dismissed. In the Panel's view, as currently drafted, the Protocol was clearly providing that it was only COR/D which had the power to excuse a competitor from an AC37 Event. The Panel was not entitled under the Protocol to make the orders sought in the application. COR/D was required to make such decision on "reasonable grounds" in accordance with the Protocol, which is a subjective test. COR/D had not yet made a decision. When COR/D would have made a decision on whether or not to excuse AM from participation in the Second AC37 Preliminary Regatta in Jeddah, if AM still considered such decision to be not in accordance with the Protocol, AM could have made a new application to the Panel.

Equally, Article 10.2(a)(i)(B) of the Protocol entitled COR/D to apply to the Panel "to impose such financial penalty it considers appropriate" should COR/D not have excused AM from attending the Second AC37 Preliminary Regatta in Jeddah. What is "appropriate" was within the Panel's discretion.

Case ACAP 37-005

This application was filed by Société Nautique de Genève/Alinghi Red Bull Racing, requesting mediation and seeking an interpretation of Article 53.1(a) and several definitions of the Protocol with regard to "Venue Merchandising."

Since it immediately appeared that there was no prospect of agreement between the parties, the case was referred back to the full Arbitration Panel for determination.

ACAP's decision was that the Protocol itself did not prohibit Competitors from having their own shops at their Team Bases, nor did it prohibit Competitors from selling at their Team Bases their team's merchandise to their guests and to the guests of sponsors. However, under Article 53.1(a) of the Protocol, only ACE's approved retailers and concessionaires were authorized to carry on any retailing or merchandising activities at any Venue. Any such activities therefore required ACE's approval of the retailer/concessionaire, and Article 53.1 of the Protocol conferred on ACE an absolute discretion to authorize retailers and concessionaires to carry out such activities. It was noted that an authorization had been sought by the applicant from ACE and that it had been declined.

Accordingly, the Arbitration Panel decided that the applicant was not entitled to the declaration sought.

Case ACAP 37-006

On October 13, 2024, the Arbitration Panel received a report by email claiming that misconduct (inappropriate language) had occurred by Sir Ben Ainslie, a helm on INEOS Britannia, in contravention of RRS AC Rule 69, at the conclusion of Race 3 in an on-water post-race interview. The Arbitration Panel also noted that Peter Burling, an Emirates Team New Zealand helm, had also used inappropriate language as their boat crossed the finish line of that race.

The Arbitration Panel considered that Sir Ben Ainslie's words (in particular "F*****g W*****r") were made when he clearly believed the interview had been completed and he was off-air. The Arbitration Panel also noted that neither AC Media nor the America's Cup Event Authority had received a complaint about the words used by Sir Ben Ainslie or by Peter Burling.

Accordingly, the Arbitration Panel considered that, in the particular circumstances, the inappropriate language used did not breach RRS AC Rule 69.1(a) and that the Panel was therefore not obliged to report the matter for further investigation to the Event Disciplinary Investigation Officer (EDIO) under World Sailing Disciplinary Code 35.4.3. The Arbitration Panel considered there was a threshold test to be satisfied before they were required to report the matter to the EDIO, and that, in this particular case, that test was not satisfied. The broadcast had not caused widespread offence and had not brought the sport into disrepute.

The Arbitration Panel however reminded all those competing in the 37th America's Cup Match that what they say on board may be broadcast live and that they have an obligation not to commit misconduct.

Several comments can perhaps be made with regard to this case:

- In case of misconduct, the standard Racing Rules of Sailing confer jurisdiction to a "protest committee." In the specific case of the AC37, the protest committee is the International Jury (drawn from the Umpire team). The AC version of the Racing Rules of Sailing (RRS AC) confers jurisdiction for misconduct matters on the Arbitration Panel.
- The EDIO role was introduced by World Sailing through a World Sailing Regulation that requires the Judicial Board to appoint a person at Major International Events to investigate, at the event, complaints of misconduct. This followed concerns being expressed by the Court of Arbitration for Sport in a previous America's Cup misconduct case [*Dirk de Ridder v. ISAF*, CAS 2014/A/3630] pursuant to which, under the then applicable Racing Rules of Sailing, the protest committee was the sole body which would receive a report, investigate such report, issue a notice (if appropriate), call a hearing, and then decide the matter before them.
- The EDIO therefore has the responsibility to investigate a matter in case they receive a report, and, in such hypothesis, determine if further action is required, including whether to charge a person with misconduct. In such a case, the EDIO shall disclose to the Arbitration Panel all relevant (favorable and/or unfavorable) information it has gathered and present to the Arbitration Panel the allegation of misconduct against the competitor. The Arbitration Panel shall then have jurisdiction to adjudicate the matter. This represents a substantial change to procedures.

1.6 The Future of the America's Cup

On November 8, 2024, the Royal New Zealand Yacht Squadron accepted a Notice of Challenge for the 38th America's Cup (AC38) from the Royal Yacht Squadron Limited, represented by INEOS Britannia. Pursuant to a statement published on the 38th America's Cup website on November 8, 2024, the following has been agreed between the Defender and the Challenger of Record:

(a) the class of yacht shall be the AC75 and each team will be restricted to building one new AC75 for AC38;
(b) the existing Crew Nationality rule contained in the AC37 Protocol will be retained, with the Emerging Nations provisions to be reviewed;

(c) it is intended that the AC38 Match will be held within three years following the completion of the AC37 Match. This is however subject to any adjustment needed in relation to the hemisphere in which the AC38 Match is to be sailed. The Venue will be announced by the Defender within eight months of the final race of the AC37 Match, and the Protocol will be published as soon as practicable within that period;
(d) the following restrictions shall apply to the sailing and testing of the AC75 and AC40 yachts to be used in AC38:
   - no sailing of AC75 yachts for a period of twelve months from the date of the final race in the AC37 Match is permitted, except when participating in any Preliminary Regattas which may be organized with a dispensation of that requirement for the earlier sailing of AC75s by new teams;
   - a limit on the total number of sailing days in AC75 yachts will be introduced;
(e) investigations and, where appropriate, measures will be implemented in order to reduce costs, including a budget cap and carbon cap for teams. A strategy will be worked on to further commercialize the America's Cup;
(f) there is an intention to increase the number of Preliminary Regattas to provide more regular racing during the AC38 cycle, including a mixture of AC40 & AC75 racing, with both fleet racing and match racing formats being considered for the AC40s and AC75s;
(g) both the Defender and the Challenger of Record are committed to building on the success of the AC37 Women's and Youth America's Cup events.

Article 23 of the Protocol governing the 37th America's Cup provided that "in order to promote competition and sustainability," each Competitor was to sign a Deed of Participation pursuant to which the AC75 yacht class would be retained during AC38 in both the Challenger Selection Series and the Match. To what extent this undertaking may be enforceable during the 38th America's Cup, should it be challenged, is yet to be determined.

The Protocol governing the 38th America's Cup was published on August 12, 2025.[19] The AC75 Class Rule and Technical Regulations applicable to the 38th America's Cup have been published on September 11, 2025.[20]

Henry Peter
David Tillett, AM
Bryan Willis
Graham McKenzie
Claire Mordelet
September 2025

19. https://www.americascup.com/files/m26244_FINAL-PROTOCOL-12-AUGUST-2025.pdf.
20. https://www.americascup.com/files/m26296_2025-09-09-AC75-Class-Rule-V301.pdf.

CHAPTER 2 The Text of the Deed of Gift

This chapter includes a copy of the handwritten version of the original Deed of Gift dated July 8, 1857 (2.1 *infra*). It also contains what can be considered the current text of the Deed of Gift. This text (2.2.2 *infra*) as well as a brief explanation thereof (2.2.1 *infra*) have been written by R. Steven Tsuchiya with the assistance of Dr. Hamish Ross.

In addition, the authors have deemed it useful to include the "Assignment and Acceptance Agreement" which has been executed by The Golden Gate Yacht Club and The Royal New Zealand Yacht Squadron on April 17-20, 2024, with retroactive effect as from June 26, 2017 (2.3.2 *infra*), as well as a brief explanation thereof written by R. Steven Tsuchiya (2.3.1 *infra*). Pursuant to such Agreement, The Royal New Zealand Yacht Squadron became the trustee, agreed that the laws of the State of New York would apply, and that, further, the Courts of the State of New York would have jurisdiction with regard to any amendment or interpretation of the Deed of Gift.

2.1 Original (Handwritten) Deed of Gift (July 8, 1857)

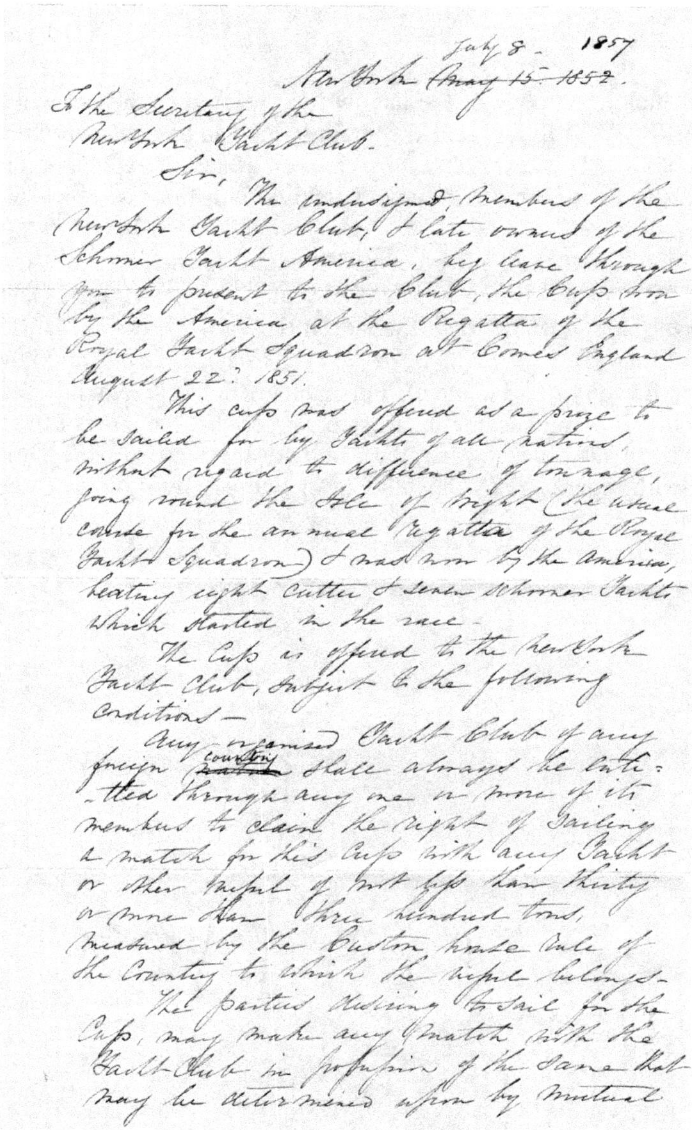

New York ~~May 15 1852~~ July 8 - 1857.

To the Secretary of the
New York Yacht Club.

Sir,

The undersigned, members of the New York Yacht Club, & late owners of the Schooner Yacht America, beg leave through you to present to the Club, the Cup won by the America at the Regatta of the Royal Yacht Squadron at Cowes England August 22d 1851.

This cup was offered as a prize to be sailed for by Yachts of all nations, without regard to difference of tonnage, going round the Isle of Wight (the usual course for the annual regatta of the Royal Yacht Squadron) & was won by the America, beating eight cutter & seven schooner Yachts which started in the race.

The Cup is offered to the New York Yacht Club, subject to the following conditions—

Any organised Yacht Club of any foreign ~~nation~~ country shall always be entitled through any one or more of its members to claim the right of sailing a match for this Cup with any Yacht or other vessel of not less than thirty or more than three hundred tons, measured by the Custom house rule of the Country to which the vessel belongs.

The parties desiring to sail for the Cup, may make any match with the Yacht Club in possession of the same that may be determined upon by mutual

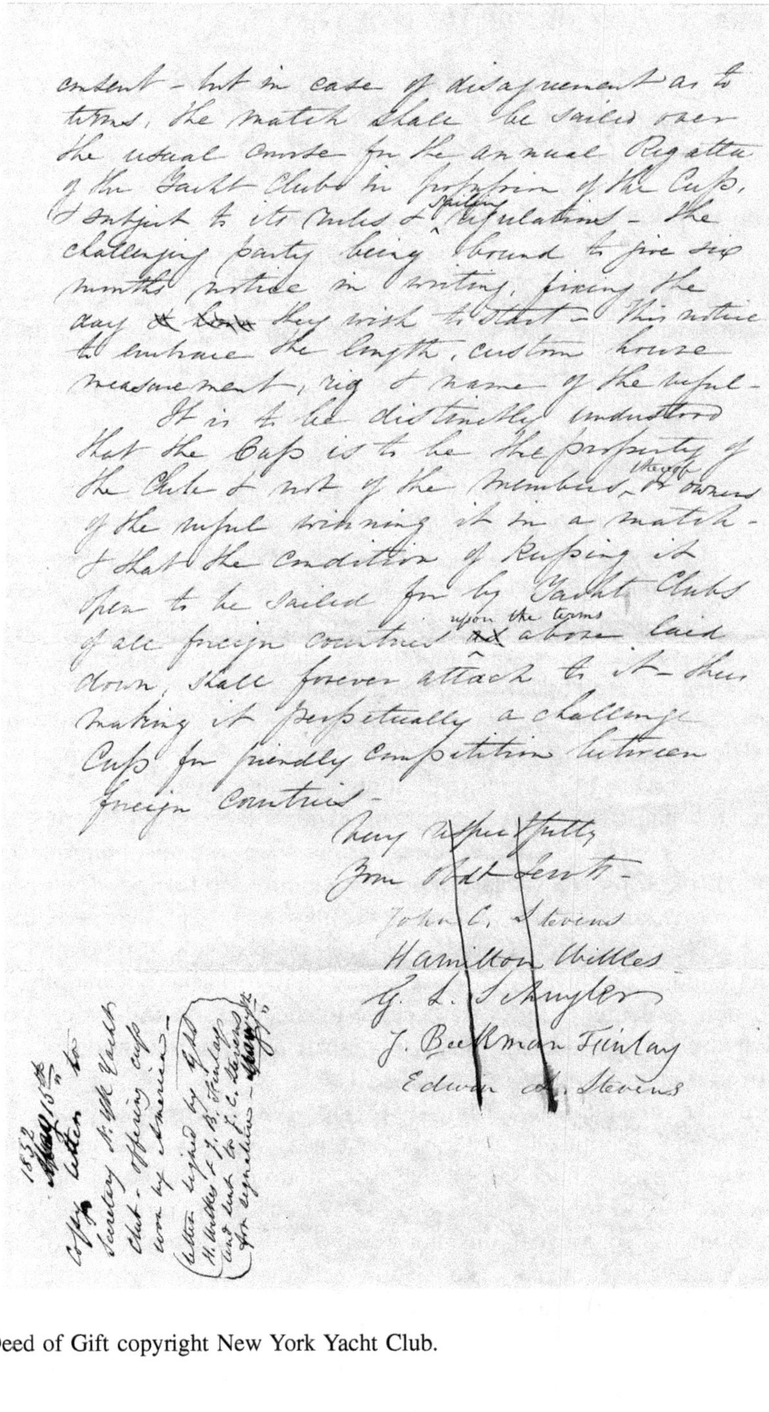

content - but in case of disagreement as to terms, the match shall be sailed over the usual course for the annual Regatta of the Yacht Club in possession of the Cup, & subject to its Rules & Sailing Regulations - the challenging party being bound to give six months notice in writing, fixing the day they wish to start - This notice to embrace the length, custom house measurement, rig & name of the vessel -

It is to be distinctly understood that the Cup is to be the property of the Club & not of the members thereof or owners of the vessel winning it in a match - & that the condition of keeping it open to be sailed for by Yacht Clubs of all foreign countries upon the terms above laid down, shall forever attach to it - thus making it perpetually a challenge Cup for friendly competition between foreign countries -

Very respectfully

Your Obdt Servts -

John C. Stevens

Hamilton Wilkes

G. L. Schuyler

J. Beekman Finlay

Edwin A. Stevens

1857 July 8th copy letter to Secretary N.Y. Yacht Club - offering cup won by America - (letter signed by G. L. S., H. Wilkes & J. B. Finlay and sent to J. C. Stevens for signature)

Credit: Deed of Gift copyright New York Yacht Club.

2.2 Current Text of the Deed of Gift

2.2.1 A NOTE BY R. STEVEN TSUCHIYA ABOUT THE CURRENT DEED OF GIFT

2024 Transcription of the Current Deed of Gift

The current Deed of Gift is the Third Deed of Gift (executed on October 24, 1887), acknowledging the amendments ordered by the New York State Supreme Court on December 17, 1956, and April 5, 1985. However, most—if not all—of the published versions of the current Deed of Gift contain typographical errors, ranging from omissions of irregular verbs to significant errors (e.g., the word "part" used instead of "party").

In 2024, I prepared a new transcription of the current Deed of Gift to reduce the propagation of errors. The following steps were taken to ensure the utmost accuracy.

First, the Third Deed of Gift was transcribed from the original typewritten, signed, and sealed document archived at the New York Yacht Club, preserving every detail, including the distinctive punctuation style in the body of the Deed and the signatures. My colleague Robert Kamins and I jointly proofread the transcription several times over the course of a month. The differences between the transcription and the original are superficial. The transcription uses the Adobe Caslon Pro typeface, while the original employs a monospace typeface from the typewriter on which it was written. The transcription features justified margins, with no words divided; the original has ragged right margins, with a dozen words divided.

Second, because the original document features the seals of George L. Schuyler and the New York Yacht Club, these seals were digitally reproduced in the transcription. In all previous transcriptions, including the first one (published by the Club on October 28, 1887), the seals were not shown; instead, they were described as "[Seal of the New York Yacht Club.]" and "[L.S.]." The New York Yacht Club seal in the transcription is displayed right side up for clarity; on the original, the embossed seal is rotated 90 degrees clockwise because the neck of the embossing tool was too short to stamp it right side up. Schuyler's seal in the transcription is a silhouette created from a photograph of the actual seal.

Third, the amendments from 1956 and 1985 were incorporated into the transcription. For example, I deleted the sentence, "Vessels selected to compete for this Cup must proceed under sail on their own bottoms to the port where the contest is to take place," and replaced the word "sixty-five" with "forty-four" to reflect the 1956 amendment. To prevent misinterpretations and other errors, I relied on the official copies of the New York State Supreme Court's orders (Index No. 12696/56 and Index No. 4615/85) that authorized the amendments. Although the 1956 order is directed solely at the New York Yacht Club, it is assumed—and practice indicates—that the order applies to the trustee, successors, and assigns.

Finally, the statement, "as amended by orders of the Supreme Court of the State of New York dated December 17, 1956, and April 5, 1985," was inserted in the first paragraph, following the practice started by the New York Yacht Club in 1956 and continued by the Royal Perth Yacht Club in 1985.

This accurate transcription was published in my book, *America's Cup Deed of Gift and Related Documents* (Herreshoff Marine Museum/America's Cup Hall of Fame, 2024). The book's chief purpose is to showcase high-resolution images of primary sources related to the Deed of Gift, including all three Deeds of Gift (1857, 1882, and 1887), the court orders, George Schuyler's manuscripts, the New York Yacht Club's interpretative resolutions, and many other documents.

2025 Transcription of the Current Deed of Gift

The transcription of the Deed of Gift in this book (*see* below section 2.2.2) is the 2024 transcription *with additional edits* suggested by my colleague, Dr. Hamish Ross. He informed me that the New York State Supreme Court's amendment orders did not direct the trustee to change the text of the Deed of Gift (the Third Deed of Gift, executed in 1887). Instead, the orders directed the trustee to modify only how the Deed would be administered. For instance, in 1956, the Court ordered the New York Yacht Club to administer the America's Cup "*as if* (emphasis mine) said Deed of Gift included no provision requiring yachts or vessels competing for the America's Cup to sail, on their own bottoms, to the port where the contest is to take place, and *as if* (emphasis mine) the minimum load water-line length of the competing yachts or vessels of one mast was thereby required to be forty-four (44) feet."

Heeding Ross's advice, the transcription in this book maintains the complete text of the Third Deed of Gift, executed in 1887, with the amendments indicated in brackets or strikethrough text. The primary reason for this is to preserve every word of the 1887 text for interpretative purposes in determining the Donor's intent.

Finally, Ross suggested that I not include the statement, "as amended by orders of the Supreme Court of the State of New York dated December 17, 1956, and April 5, 1985." He argues that this statement (added by the New York Yacht Club in 1956 and revised by the Royal Perth Yacht Club in 1985) is not technically appropriate because, as mentioned above, the Court did not order the trustee to change the text of the Deed of Gift.

2.2.2 CURRENT TEXT OF THE DEED OF GIFT

This DEED OF GIFT made the twenty-fourth day of October, one thousand eight hundred and eighty-seven, Between GEORGE L. SCHUYLER as sole surviving owner of the Cup won by the yacht America at Cowes, England, on the twenty-second day of August, one thousand eight hundred and fifty-one, of the first part, and THE NEW YORK YACHT CLUB, of the second part, WITNESSETH:

THAT the said party of the first part, for and in consideration of the premises and of the performance of the conditions and agreements hereinafter set forth by the party of the second part, has granted, bargained, sold, assigned, transferred and set over, and by these presents does grant, bargain, sell, assign, transfer and set over unto the said party of the second part, its successors and assigns, the Cup won by the schooner yacht America at Cowes, England, upon the twenty-second day of August, 1851. To Have and To Hold the same to the said party of the second part, its successors and assigns, IN TRUST NEVERTHELESS for the following uses and purposes: -

This Cup is donated upon the condition that it shall be preserved as a perpetual challenge cup for friendly competition between foreign countries.

Any organized yacht Club of a foreign country, incorporated, patented, or licensed by the legislature, admiralty or other executive department, having for its annual regatta an ocean water course on the sea, or on an arm of the sea, or one which combines both, shall always be entitled to the right of sailing a match for this Cup, with a yacht or vessel propelled by sails only and constructed in the country to which the challenging Club belongs, against any one yacht or vessel constructed in the country of the Club holding the Cup.

The competing yachts or vessels, if of one mast, shall be not less than ~~sixty-five~~ [forty-four] feet[1] nor more than ninety feet on the load water line; if of more than one mast, they shall be not less than eighty feet nor more than one hundred and fifteen feet on the load water line.

---

[1] On December 17, 1956, the New York State Supreme Court, with the consent of the New York State Attorney General, ordered (Index No. 12696/56) the New York Yacht Club, as trustee of the America's Cup, to administer the Cup as if the Deed of Gift required that the minimum load water-line length of competing yachts or vessels with one mast was forty-four feet.

The challenging Club shall give ten months' notice in writing naming the days for the proposed races; but no race shall be sailed in the days intervening between November first and May first [if the races are to be conducted in the Northern Hemisphere; and no race shall be sailed in the days intervening between May 1st and November 1st if the races are to be conducted in the Southern Hemisphere.][2] Accompanying the ten months' notice of challenge, there must be sent the name of the owner and a certificate of the name, rig and following dimensions of the challenging vessel, namely, length on load water line; beam at load water line, and extreme beam; and draught of water; which dimensions shall not be exceeded; and a custom-house registry of the vessel must also be sent as soon as possible. ~~Vessels selected to compete for this Cup must proceed under sail on their own bottoms to the port where the contest is to take place.~~[3] Centreboard or sliding keel vessels shall always be allowed to compete in any race for this Cup, and no restriction nor limitation whatever shall be placed upon the use of such centreboard or sliding keel, nor shall the centreboard or sliding keel be considered a part of the vessel for any purposes of measurement.

The Club challenging for the Cup and the Club holding the same may by mutual consent make any arrangement satisfactory to both as to the dates, courses, number of trials, rules and sailing regulations, and any and all other conditions of the match, in which case also the ten months' notice may be waived.

---

[2] On April 5, 1985, the New York State Supreme Court, with the consent of the New York State Attorney General, ordered (Index No. 4615/85) "that the Deed of Gift is amended, and the trust established pursuant to the Deed of Gift shall hereafter be administered, as if, following the phrase 'no race shall be sailed in the days intervening between November 1st and May 1st", there were added the following language: 'if the races are to be conducted in the Northern Hemisphere; and no race shall be sailed in the days intervening between May 1st and November 1st if the races are to be conducted in the Southern Hemisphere.'"

[3] On December 17, 1956, the New York State Supreme Court, with the consent of the New York State Attorney General, ordered (Index No. 12696/56) the New York Yacht Club, as trustee of the America's Cup, to administer the Cup as if the Deed of Gift included no provision requiring yachts or vessels competing for the Cup to sail, on their own bottoms, to the port where the contest is to take place.

In case the parties cannot mutually agree upon the terms of a match, then three races shall be sailed, and the winner of two of such races shall be entitled to the Cup. All such races shall be on ocean courses, free from headlands, as follows: the first race, twenty nautical miles to windward and return; the second race, an equilateral triangular race of thirty-nine nautical miles, the first side of which shall be a beat to windward; the third race, (if necessary), twenty nautical miles to windward and return; and one week day shall intervene between the conclusion of one race and the starting of the next race. These ocean courses shall be practicable in all parts for vessels of twenty-two feet draught of water and shall be selected by the Club holding the Cup; and these races shall be sailed subject to its rules and sailing regulations so far as the same do not conflict with the provisions of this deed of gift, but without any time allowances whatever. The challenged Club shall not be required to name its representative vessel until at the time agreed upon for the start, but the vessel when named must compete in all the races; and each of such races must be completed within seven hours.

Should the Club holding the Cup be for any cause dissolved, the Cup shall be transferred to some Club of the same nationality, eligible to challenge under this deed of gift, in trust and subject to its provisions. In the event of the failure of such transfer within three months after such dissolution, said Cup shall revert to the preceding Club holding the same, and under the terms of this deed of gift. It is distinctly understood that the Cup is to be the property of the Club, subject to the provisions of this deed, and not the property of the owner or owners of any vessel winning a match.

No vessel which has been defeated in a match for this Cup can be again selected by any Club as its representative until after a contest for it by some other vessel has intervened, or until after the expiration of two years from the time of such defeat. And when a challenge from a Club fulfilling all the conditions required by this instrument has been received, no other challenge can be considered until the pending event has been decided.

AND the said party of the second part hereby accepts the said Cup subject to the said trust, terms and conditions, and hereby covenants and agrees to and with said party of the first part that it will faithfully and fully see that the foregoing conditions are fully observed and complied with by any contestant for the said Cup during the holding thereof by it; and that it will assign transfer and deliver the said Cup to the foreign yacht Club whose representative yacht shall have won the same in accordance with the foregoing terms and conditions, provided the said foreign Club shall by instrument in writing lawfully executed enter with said party of the second part into the like covenants as are herein entered into by it, such instrument to contain a like provision for the successive assignees to enter into the same covenants with their respective assignors, and to be executed in duplicate, one to be retained by each Club, and a copy thereof to be forwarded to the said party of the second part.

IN WITNESS WHEREOF, the said party of the first part has hereunto set his hand and seal, and the said party of the second part has caused its corporate seal to be affixed to these presents and the same to be signed by its Commodore and attested by its Secretary, the day and year first above written.

In the presence of
H.D. Hamilton

George L. Schuyler

The New York Yacht Club
by Elbridge T Gerry,
Commodore.

John H Bird
Secretary

2.3 Assignment and Acceptance Agreement

2.3.1 A Note by R. Steven Tsuchiya about the 2017 Assignment & Acceptance Agreement

The Deed of Gift's penultimate paragraph directs a trustee of the America's Cup, who has lost a match for the Cup, to transfer the trophy to the winning yacht club through an "instrument in writing." This instrument, known as the "Assignment & Acceptance," ensures that the winning yacht club, as the new trustee of the Cup, adheres to the terms and conditions of the Deed. Additionally, the Deed requires that the New York Yacht Club (NYYC), as the Cup's original trustee, receive a copy of each Assignment & Acceptance (A&A). There have been six transfers of the Cup: in 1983, 1987, 1995, 2003, 2010, and 2017.

In December 2023, NYYC Commodore Paul M. Zabetakis initiated an effort to ensure the Club had all six copies of the A&A. Commodore Zabetakis enlisted my help (as we were both going to begin our term on the America's Cup Committee in January 2024). We soon discovered that the Club had copies of all the A&As except for one: the 2017 agreement between the Golden Gate Yacht Club (GGYC), which lost the Cup to the Royal New Zealand Yacht Squadron (RNZYS) in the 35th America's Cup Match. As it turned out, neither GGYC nor RNZYS could locate copies of the A&A. I contacted Dr. Hamish Ross regarding this matter, and he did not have a copy either; he suspected that the two Clubs may not have executed one.

At the start of the New Year, this issue became a significant project for NYYC's America's Cup Committee, chaired by Ex-Commodore Philip A. Lotz. Ex-Commodore Zabetakis (his term had ended in 2023) took the lead in urging GGYC and RNZYS to complete an A&A, as they either had not executed one or had lost their copies. Ex-Commodore William H. Dyer Jones, Senet S. Bischoff (who also chairs the Club's Legal Advisory Committee), and I assisted Zabetakis.

Hamish Ross informed me that RNZYS might have considered changing the A&A's applicable law from the jurisdiction of New York to New Zealand, which could have delayed the execution of the A&A had it not already been carried out. Since 1983, each A&A has required the trustee to submit any proceedings for amending or interpreting the terms and conditions of the Deed of Gift to the courts of the State of New York.

I insisted that there are two reasons for maintaining the New York court system as the judiciary to resolve matters related to the Deed of Gift. First, the Deed of Gift requires "successive assignees to enter into the *same covenants* (emphasis mine) with their respective assignors ..." The first A&A (1983) established the covenant that the judiciary be the New York court system, and every successive A&A (1987, 1995, 2003, and 2010) has honored this requirement. Second, the New York court system is relatively reliable and fair. While New Zealand's court maintains a similar quality, changing the Applicable Law would set an undesirable precedent; a future yacht club that wins the Cup may be domiciled in a country with a less reliable court system.

The Committee agreed. To ensure this, Bischoff and I drafted an execution-ready A&A for GGYC and RNZYS. On January 29, Zabetakis emailed both clubs with the draft of the A&A and followed up on March 21. GGYC and RNZYS accepted the New York courts as the jurisdiction in the Applicable Law clause; however, they added a new clause: "3. It is agreed that the effective date of this Assignment and Acceptance Agreement was June 26, 2017." June 26, 2017, marked RNZYS's victory in the 35th America's Cup Match. RNZYS Vice Commodore Gillian Williams and GGYC Commodore Maurice Quillen signed the A&A on April 17 and April 20, 2024, respectively.

2.3.2 ASSIGNMENT AND ACCEPTANCE AGREEMENT EXECUTED ON APRIL 20, 2024, WITH RETROACTIVE EFFECT AS FROM JUNE 26, 2017

Assignment and Acceptance Agreement

This Assignment and Acceptance is made by and between the GOLDEN GATE YACHT CLUB (the "GGYC") and the ROYAL NEW ZEALAND YACHT SQUADRON (the "RNZYS").

The yacht, Aotearoa, as representative of the RNZYS, won the 35th America's Cup (the "Cup") on June 26, 2017 in accordance with the terms and conditions of a deed of gift dated October 24, 1887, between George L. Schuyler and the New York Yacht Club (the "NYYC"), as amended by orders of the Supreme Court of the State of New York dated December 17, 1956, September 20, 1984 and April 5, 1985, ("Deed of Gift").

This Assignment and Acceptance Agreement now formally records certain terms on which the Cup was handed over to RNZYS by GGYC.

The parties hereto agree that:

(1) Assignment. The GGYC has assigned and transferred the Cup to the RNZYS on the condition that the RNZYS shall hold the Cup, in trust, in accordance with the terms and conditions of the Deed of Gift.
(2) Acceptance. The RNZYS has accepted the Cup subject to the said trust and to the terms and conditions of the Deed of Gift and covenants and agreed that it will:
    (a) faithfully and fully see that the conditions of the Deed of Gift are fully observed and complied with by any contestant for the Cup during the holding thereof by it; and

(b) assign, transfer and deliver the Cup to the foreign Yacht Club whose representative yacht shall have won the same in accordance with the terms and conditions of the Deed of Gift, provided that said foreign yacht club shall, by instrument in writing lawfully executed, enter with the RNZYS into the like covenants as are herein entered into by it, such instrument to contain a like provision for the successive assignors, and such instrument to be executed in duplicate, with one counterpart to be retained by each club and a copy thereof to be forwarded to the NYYC.

(3) It is agreed that the effective date of this Assignment and Acceptance Agreement was June 26, 2017.

(4) Applicable law. The parties hereto further agree that, the Trust under which the Cup is held having been created under the laws of the State of New York, and having been amended as aforesaid by order of the Supreme Court of the State of New York, the terms and conditions of the Deed of Gift shall be governed by, and construed in accordance with, such laws, and any proceeding for the amendment or interpretation of such terms and conditions shall be brought before the courts of the State of New York.

IN WITNESS WHEREOF, the parties have caused this instrument to be executed by their duly authorized officers as of the date first above written.

THE GOLDEN GATE YACHT CLUB

By: ______________________________

Commodore Maurice Quillen

Date: April 20, 2024

THE ROYAL NEW ZEALAND YACHT SQUADRON

By: ______________________________

Vice Commodore Gillian Williams

Date: April 17, 2024

Chapter 3 The Protocol of the 37th America's Cup

3.1 The Protocol of the 37th America's Cup, Incorporating Protocol Amendments 1 Through 16 (Consolidated Version Dated 25 September 2024)

THE PROTOCOL GOVERNING THE 37TH AMERICA'S CUP
The Royal New Zealand Yacht Squadron Incorporated

and

Royal Yacht Squadron Limited
15 November 2021

Contents

PART A: INTERPRETATION
1. Interpretation

PART B: EVENT STRUCTURE
2. **Defender and Challenger of Record**
3. **America's Cup Event Authority**
4. **Competitor Forum**

PART C: EVENT FORMAT
5. **AC37 Events**
6. **America's Cup Preliminary Regattas**
7. **America's Cup Challenger Selection Series**
8. **Match**
9. **Youth and Women's America's Cup Regattas**
10. **Requirement to Race**
11. **Postponement / Cancellation**

PART D: COMPETITORS
12. **Challenger of Record**
13. **Entry of Further Challengers**
14. **Entry Process**
15. **Entry Fees**
16. **Preliminary Regattas Entry Fees**
17. **Performance Bond**
18. **Defender Payments**
19. **Shared costs**
20. **Failure to pay Entry Fees or Shared Costs**
21. **Withdrawal of Challenge**

PART E: YACHTS/CREW
22. **Yachts**
23. **Class of Yacht for AC38**
24. **Cost containment and limitations**
25. **Shrouding**
26. **Constructed in country**
27. **Customs house registry**

28. **Transport and Logistics**
29. **Crew Restrictions**
30. **Crew Nationality**
31. **Support Vessels**
32. **Television and technical equipment on-board**
PART F: RULES
33. **Rules**
34. **Race Conditions**
35. **Sailing Instructions**
36. **Wind Limits**
37. **Racing Areas and courses**
38. **Participation in other regattas**
39. **Sports betting**
40. **Meteorological and Oceanographic Data**
41. **Reconnaissance**
PART G: REGATTA OFFICIALS
42. **Appointment of Regatta Officials**
43. **Regatta Director**
44. **Measurement Committee and Rules Committee**
45. **Umpires and Jury**
46. **World Sailing**
47. **Rules and Decisions**
PART H: COMMERCIAL RIGHTS
48. **Overview**
49. **Branding and Advertising**
50. **Special Events**
51. **Team Bases**
52. **Signage**
53. **Merchandising**
54. **Entertainment**
55. **Security**
56. **Air Space**
57. **Water Space**
58. **Team Information**
59. **Anti-ambush obligations**
PART I: MEDIA RIGHTS
60. **ACE Media Rights**
61. **Competitor Media Rights**

62. **Media commitments and public appearances**
63. **Official Documentary**
64. **Electronic Games and Board Games**
65. **Digital Media – Websites, Social Media and Applications**
PART J: AMERICA'S CUP PROPERTIES INCORPORATED
66. **America's Cup intellectual property**
PART K: GENERAL PROVISIONS
67. **Arbitration Panel**
68. **Protocol Amendments**
69. **Compliance with Applicable Laws and Regulations**
70. **Costs and Expenses to compete**
71. **Liability and Indemnity**
72. **Applicability**
73. **Insurance Requirements**
Schedule 1: Definitions
Schedule 2: Notice of Challenge

This **Protocol Governing the 37th America's Cup** is made on 15 November 2021

between	**(1)**	**The Royal New Zealand Yacht Squadron Incorporated**
and	**(2)**	**Royal Yacht Squadron Limited**

Introduction

A. The Royal New Zealand Yacht Squadron Incorporated ("**RNZYS**"), having defended the 36th America's Cup, holds the silver trophy known as the America's Cup in accordance with the terms of a Deed of Gift dated 24 October 1887 (the "**Deed of Gift**").
B. On 17 March 2021, immediately following the final race of the 36th America's Cup, RNZYS received and accepted a notice of challenge for the 37th America's Cup from Royal Yacht Squadron Racing Limited in accordance with the Deed of Gift.
C. Royal Yacht Squadron Racing Limited changed its name to Royal Yacht Squadron Limited ("RYS") on 24th March 2021.
D. RYS, having submitted the first valid notice of challenge for the 37th America's Cup has been appointed as the initial Challenger of Record.
E. RNZYS and RYS believe that a form of protocol is a desirable way of mutually consenting to various items that, in accordance with the Deed of Gift, may be

agreed between the yacht club holding the America's Cup and the yacht club challenging for the America's Cup.

F. Accordingly, RNZYS and RYS now record in this Protocol (the "**Protocol**") the arrangements they have mutually agreed for and in respect of the 37th America's Cup ("**AC37**") in accordance with the terms of the Deed of Gift.

G. In this Protocol COR/D have sought to continue the development of the America's Cup as the premier event in the sport of sailing, consistent with the provisions of the Deed of Gift, so as to:
   a. maintain the balance between sailing and design;
   b. keep the America's Cup at the forefront of technology;
   c. endeavour to increase the number of Competitors involved in the America's Cup;
   d. increase public engagement with the America's Cup;
   e. cut the cost of design, production and operations of AC75 Yachts; and
   f. maintain the value of the existing fleet of AC75 Yachts.

It is agreed as follows

PART A: INTERPRETATION

1. Interpretation

1.1 Definitions

In the interpretation of this Protocol, defined terms used herein shall have the meanings set out in Schedule 1.

1.2 Interpretation

In the interpretation of this Protocol:

(a) the use of the words "including", "include", "in particular", "for example" and similar words or expressions shall be construed as illustrative and shall not imply any limitation to the words following such expression;
(b) unless the context otherwise requires, words importing the singular include the plural and vice versa and words importing any gender include any gender;
(c) the **Introduction** forms part of this Protocol;
(d) the headings to the Articles of this Protocol are for convenience only, have no legal effect and shall not be taken into account in the construction or interpretation of this Protocol;
(e) no rule of construction will apply to the disadvantage of a Person on the basis that that Person put forward this Protocol or any part of it;

(f) any obligation in this Protocol on a party not to do something includes an obligation not to agree or allow that thing to be done; and
(g) references to writing include any modes of reproducing words in a legible and non- transitory form.

1.3 Conflicting documents

In the event of a conflict between any provision or provisions of this Protocol and any other document, other than the Deed of Gift, the terms of this Protocol shall prevail.

1.4 Official dictionary

The official language of this Protocol is English. Unless separately defined in Schedule 1, the meaning of any word used in this Protocol and any document governing the whole or any part of AC37 shall be determined by reference to the Oxford English Dictionary as it exists (as at the date of this Protocol) in the official online dictionary available at www.oed.com (or such later official website of the Oxford English Dictionary).

1.5 Articles / Schedules

In the interpretation of this Protocol, a reference to an **Article** or **Schedule** is a reference to an article of or schedule to this Protocol.

1.6 Dates and times

Unless otherwise specified, all dates and times referenced in, or in any communications pursuant to, this Protocol are the dates and times in New Zealand time ("**NZT**").

1.7 Meanings

In the interpretation of this Protocol, the words "shall", "must" and "will" are mandatory; and the word "may" is permissive.

PART B: EVENT STRUCTURE

2. Defender and Challenger of Record

2.1 Role of the Defender

(a) The Defender has responsibility for meeting its obligations under the Deed of Gift and this Protocol.
(b) RNZYS has appointed Team New Zealand Limited ("**TNZL**") as its Representative Team to defend the America's Cup in AC37 on its behalf and to organise

the delivery of all of the Events that will comprise AC37. **SEE PROTOCOL AMENDMENT 8**

(c) In this Protocol, RNZYS and TNZL are together referred to as the "**Defender**".

2.2 Role of the Challenger of Record

(a) RYS, having submitted the first valid notice of challenge for the 37th America's Cup, has been appointed as the initial challenger of record and is responsible for:
   (i) acting as the single point of communication between the Challengers and the Defender in relation to matters covered by this Protocol; and
   (ii) meeting its obligations under the Deed of Gift and this Protocol.

(b) RYS has appointed Athena Racing Limited ("**ARL**"), competing as INEOS Britannia, as its representative team that will challenge for AC37 on its behalf. **SEE PROTOCOL AMENDMENT 8**

(c) In this Protocol, RYS and ARL are together referred to as the "**Challenger of Record**".

2.3 Role of COR/D

(a) In this Protocol, when acting together the Defender and the Challenger of Record shall be referred to as "**COR/D**".

(b) The responsibilities of COR/D are as prescribed in this Protocol.

3. America's Cup Event Authority

3.1 Appointment

The Defender has incorporated a New Zealand registered company, AC37 Event Limited ("**ACE**"), for the purpose of fulfilling the event management obligations under this Protocol.

*3.2 **Responsibilities of ACE***

(a) ACE has the sole responsibility to:
   (i) organise and manage the format and commercial rights of AC37; and
   (ii) implement the decisions and instructions of COR/D in relation to the Rules; as provided in this Protocol.

(b) More specifically, ACE shall be responsible for:
   (i) establishing and implementing the timing and format of AC37 and the Events consistent with the terms of this Protocol;
   (ii) working with the Defender to select the Host City(ies) and Venue(s) for each of the Events and reaching any agreement(s) with the relevant authorities in each case;

(iii) the development, protection, management and exploitation of the commercial and media rights referred to in Parts H and I of this Protocol;
(iv) endeavouring to ensure that the objectives set out in Paragraph G of the Introduction to this Protocol are met for AC37;
(v) endeavouring to raise funds, to meet its costs of AC37;
(vi) promoting AC37 and the Events;
(vii) the delivery of an independent and professional on-water racing operation for each Event in accordance with COR/D instructions (where required under this Protocol);
(viii) recruitment and training of on-water event officials;
(ix) race management logistics in accordance with COR/D instructions; and
(x) other obligations specifically given to ACE under this Protocol.

4. Competitor Forum

4.1 Constitution and purpose

ACE shall establish and maintain a Competitor Forum as a consultative body only for the purpose of regular consultation and communication with all Competitors.

4.2 Meetings of the Competitor Forum

(a) Meetings of the Competitor Forum shall be held:
(i) at least once every one hundred and twenty (120) days for the duration of this Protocol (as scheduled by ACE); and
(ii) on an ad hoc basis at the request of COR/D, ACE or the Regatta Director (on reasonable notice under the circumstances).
(b) Meetings of the Competitor Forum shall be attended by:
(i) up to three representatives from each Competitor;
(ii) the appropriate personnel from ACE; and
(iii) the Regatta Director (once appointed).
(c) A Competitor that is:
(i) in default of any payment obligation referred to in Article 20;
(ii) (subject to Article 4.2(d)) eliminated from the AC37 competition;
(iii) disqualified from participation in the AC37 competition;
(iv) otherwise ineligible to participate in Events; or
(v) no longer a Competitor by reason of the withdrawal of its challenge or otherwise;

will not be entitled to attend a meeting of the Competitor Forum.
(d) If the Challenger of Record is eliminated during or at the end of the Challenger Selection Series but continues in its role as Challenger of Record, it may continue to take part in meetings of the Competitor Forum.

(e) Once appointed, Competitor Forum meetings will be chaired by the Regatta Director who will be responsible for setting the agenda at each meeting. Prior to the appointment of the Regatta Director, the agenda shall be set and meetings will be chaired by a person agreed by COR/D.
(f) Where a matter requires the attendance of additional persons, the Regatta Director may request and/or allow additional expert representatives (including from Competitors) that are relevant to that agenda item only.
(g) Meetings of the Competitor Forum may be held in person, by telephone or other audio/visual link-up.
(h) ACE, acting on the instructions of the Regatta Director, shall promptly provide Competitors with details of agenda items to be discussed at a Competitor Forum meeting.
(i) The Competitor Forum shall act as a consultative body only and decisions of the Competitor Forum shall not be binding on any party except in relation to a vote under Article 22.1(c), in which case the voting requirement of that Article shall apply.

PART C: EVENT FORMAT

5. AC37 Events

The following events will form the regattas to determine the yacht club that will become the holder of the 37th America's Cup:

(a) the America's Cup Preliminary Regattas;
(b) the America's Cup Challenger Selection Series; and
(c) the 37th America's Cup Match; (together, the "**AC37 Events**").

6. America's Cup Preliminary Regattas

(a) The intention of COR/D is for ACE to stage up to three (3) America's Cup Preliminary Regattas (the "**Preliminary Regattas**"). At the date of this Protocol, it is intended that:
    (i) up to two of these Preliminary Regattas may be held at venues different to that of the Match Venue (the "**Initial Preliminary Regattas**"); and
    (ii) the final Preliminary Regatta would be held at the Match Venue, immediately prior to the CSS (the "**Final Preliminary Regatta**").
(b) After consultation with COR/D, ACE will publish:
    (i) the Host City and Venue for each Initial Preliminary Regatta; and
    (ii) the period scheduled for completion of each Preliminary Regatta (the "**Preliminary Regatta Racing Period**");

at least six (6) months prior to the first race of the relevant Preliminary Regatta, except that the above details for the 2023 Initial Preliminary Regattas will be published by 30 April 2023. **SEE PROTOCOL AMENDMENT 9**

(c) It is currently anticipated that each of the Initial Preliminary Regattas will be conducted over a period of up to ten (10) days, including two weekends and additional practice days during the week.

(d) COR/D will publish the format, scoring and Preliminary Regatta Conditions for each Preliminary Regatta at least one (1) month prior to the first race of the relevant Preliminary Regatta.

(e) ACE, in consultation with the Regatta Director and COR/D, shall prescribe event logistics and other relevant considerations for each Preliminary Regatta as soon as practicable following finalisation of the Venue for each Preliminary Regatta.

(f) Competitors shall race in:
  (i) AC40 Yachts for the Initial Preliminary Regattas; and
  (ii) AC75 Yachts for the Final Preliminary Regatta.

7. America's Cup Challenger Selection Series

7.1 Overview

The America's Cup Challenger Selection Series ("**CSS**") shall comprise:

(a) a Round Robin stage;
(b) a Semi-Finals stage; and
(c) a Finals stage.

7.2 Format

Each stage of the CSS shall be completed in accordance with the CSS Conditions which shall include the following agreed principles:

(a) each race shall be a match race between two (2) boats;
(b) the Racing Area shall be the same as for the Match;
(c) the winner of each race scores one (1) point, the loser scores no points;
(d) all Competitors shall comply with the Racing Rules and Sailing Instructions;
(e) an abandoned race is not a completed race;
(f) the Defender will be eligible to compete in the Round Robin stage but not the Semi- Final or Final stages of the CSS;
(g) COR/D may, at any time prior to the commencement of any stage of the CSS, in consultation with the Regatta Director and the Competitor Forum, agree to alter the CSS Conditions and/or the Racing Rules, and such changes shall be implemented by ACE;

(h) changes to the Sailing Instructions shall be at the discretion of the Regatta Director with the agreement of COR/D and in consultation with ACE; and
(i) Competitors shall race in yachts that comply with the AC75 Class Rule.

7.3 Round Robin stage

(a) The Round Robin stage shall consist of a double round robin and the Regatta Director shall use best efforts to ensure that both round robins are completed.
(b) Each Competitor will face each other Competitor once during each round of the Round Robin stage. A round robin will only be considered to be completed and scored if all scheduled races between the Challengers in that round robin have been completed. If only the first of the two round robins is completed, then scoring from races in the partially completed round robin shall not count and only the Challenger scoring in the first round robin (excluding races between a Challenger and the Defender) shall apply when determining qualification for the Semi-Finals under Article 7.4(a).
(c) Seeding for the Round Robin stage of the CSS will be based on the final overall standing of each Competitor in the combined scoring of the first two Preliminary Regattas conducted in 2023. **SEE PROTOCOL AMENDMENT 12**
(d) If, at the completion of the Round Robin stage, Challengers are tied for first or last place in the Challenger point scoring (excluding all races between a Challenger and the Defender), then the Regatta Director shall endeavour to schedule a sail off before resorting to any other method of breaking the tie. **SEE PROTOCOL AMENDMENT 11**

7.4 Semi-Finals stage

(a) The top four (4) placed Challengers in the Round Robin stage of the CSS shall qualify to compete in the Semi-Finals stage of the CSS. In determining the top four (4) Challengers, the results from all races during the Round Robin stage between a Challenger and the Defender will be ignored.
(b) The top placed Challenger in the Round Robin stage shall choose its opponent for the Semi-Finals stage of the CSS. The remaining two (2) Challengers shall race each other in a separate Semi-Final.
(c) The winner of each Semi-Final shall be the first Challenger to score at least five (5) points after applying any penalties.
(d) If there are less than four (4) Challengers in the Round Robin stage of the CSS, there shall be no Semi-Finals stage and the top two (2) placed Challengers therein shall qualify for the Final Stage of the CSS. In determining the top two (2) Challengers, the results from all races during the Round Robin stage between a Challenger and the Defender will be ignored.

7.5 Final stage

The winner of each Semi-Final shall compete against each other in the Final stage. The winner of the Final stage will be the first Challenger in the Final stage to score at least seven (7) points after applying any penalties. The Challenger that wins the Final stage shall qualify to compete against the Defender in the Match. If for any reason the winner of the Final stage is ineligible or unable to compete as the challenger against the Defender in the Match, then the next highest placed Challenger that is eligible and able shall be the challenger in the Match.

7.6 Venue and dates

(a) The CSS shall be held at the Match Venue during the CSS Racing Period.
(b) The precise dates determining the CSS Racing Period shall be published by ACE (in consultation with COR/D) not less than twelve (12) months prior to the first scheduled race in the Match.
(c) COR/D may, in consultation with ACE and the Regatta Director, adjust the race day schedule within the CSS Racing Period to meet circumstances such as prevailing weather at the Venue and the intention to maximise weekend racing.

7.7 Preference for sail-off

The Regatta Director shall use best efforts to ensure that each of the Semi-Finals and Final stages of the CSS are completed without having to resort to tie-breaks other than a sail-off.

8. Match

8.1 Venue and dates

(a) The 37th America's Cup Match ("**Match**") will be contested between the Defender and the winner of the CSS.
(b) The Match Venue and the approximate dates for the Match (the "**Match Racing Period**") shall (unless otherwise agreed by COR/D) be announced by the Defender on or before 31 March 2022.
(c) The precise dates determining the Match Racing Period and the race schedule shall be announced by ACE on or before 30 November 2022.
(d) The dates of the Match Racing Period and the preceding CSS Racing Period shall both be scheduled between the months of August and October 2024 (inclusive). This timing will either be confirmed or adjusted by COR/D in conjunction with the Match Venue announcement depending upon such factors as the hemisphere in which the selected Match Venue is located. **SEE PROTOCOL AMENDMENT 1**

8.2 Format

The Match will be completed in accordance with the Match Conditions which shall include the following agreed principles:

(i) each race shall be a match race between two (2) boats;
(ii) the winner of each race scores one (1) point, the loser scores no points;
(iii) the winner of the Match will be the first Competitor to score at least seven (7) points after applying any penalties;
(iv) the Challenger and the Defender shall comply with the Racing Rules and the Sailing Instructions;
(v) an abandoned race is not a completed race;
(vi) changes to the Sailing Instructions shall be at the discretion of the Regatta Director with the agreement of COR/D and in consultation with ACE;
(vii) Competitors shall race in yachts that comply with the AC75 Class Rule;
(viii) if no Challenger is eligible and able to compete in the Match as at the scheduled start date of the Match Racing Period, the Defender will be declared the winner of the Match; and
(ix) if the Defender is ineligible or unable to compete in the Match as at the scheduled start date of the Match Racing Period, the Challenger which is eligible to compete in the Match under Article 7.5 shall be declared the winner of the Match.

9. Youth and Women's America's Cup Regattas

9.1 Event details

(a) In addition to the AC37 Events, in order to help promote the goals set out in Paragraph G of the Introduction to this Protocol, ACE intends to hold or approve one or more youth regattas and one or more women's regattas as additional regattas in association with the America's Cup (the "**Youth and Women's AC Regattas**").
(b) Competitors will be required to participate in the final for each of the Youth and Women's AC Regattas and may also but shall not be required to participate in earlier or qualifying Youth and Women's AC Regattas (if any).
(c) Full details of the Youth and Women's AC Regattas, including race conditions, commercial conditions (including entry fee), eligibility restrictions for crew and the venue shall be set out in the Youth and Women's AC Agreement which will be released by ACE (after consultation with COR/D) no later than 30 June 2023.
(d) Third party yacht clubs that are not Competitors may, at the discretion of ACE, be permitted to enter the Youth and Women's AC Regattas.
(e) Subject to Article 11.1(a), it shall be a condition of eligibility for the AC37 Events that Competitors sign the Youth and Women's AC Agreement and compete in the

final regatta for each of the Youth and Women's AC Regattas, representing the country of its yacht club. It is intended that crew members aged 25 years and under on the date of the first race of the Match shall be eligible to compete in the youth regattas. There shall be no age restriction for the women's regattas. The crew nationality requirements in Article 30.1(b) shall also apply to the Youth and Women's AC Regattas.

9.2 Class of Yacht

(a) The Youth and Women's AC Regattas shall be sailed with four (4) crew in the AC40 Yachts supplied to Competitors under Article 22.2(b).
(b) Each Competitor will be required to make available the AC40 Yacht that it purchases from ACE (or its nominated manufacturer) under Article 22.2, for use by other teams competing in the Youth and Women's AC Regattas. In the event that a Competitor acquires more than one AC40 Yacht under Article 22.2, ACE may require that such Competitor supplies all of its AC40 Yachts (such request to depend on the number of entries in each regatta and the number of AC40 Yachts available for use). Such AC40 Yachts shall be supplied to ACE in a condition that is fully compliant with the AC40 Class Rule, and free of any branding and with one set of new unbranded sails.
(c) There shall be no charter fee payable by ACE for the use of the AC40 Yachts under Article 9.2(b), however ACE, as the organising authority for both regattas, will be responsible for insurance, maintenance and upkeep (fair wear and tear excepted) of each AC40 Yacht during the period of each regatta. ACE shall be responsible for meeting the costs of any repairs, removal of event branding and shall deliver the yacht(s) back to each Competitor at the relevant Venue as soon as practicable after the conclusion of the relevant regatta. Transport of each AC40 Yacht to and from the Venue of each Youth and Women's AC Regatta shall be at the cost of the Competitor. Further details will be outlined in the Youth and Women's AC Agreement.
(d) Each Competitor shall also provide the following with its AC40 Yacht for the duration of each Regatta, including each Practice and Race Day:
    (i) not less than six batteries (including spares) and not less than two chargers;
    (ii) a suitable chase boat and experienced driver or drivers to be the primary support chase boat for the Competitors AC40 Yacht at all times, no matter which Competitor's crew is at various times sailing the particular AC40 Yacht. **SEE PROTOCOL AMENDMENT 11.**

10. Requirement to Race

10.1 Requirement to race

Competitors shall participate in:

(a) all AC37 Events; and
(b) the final regatta for each of the Youth and Women's AC Regattas (if it is held);
subject to the discretion of COR/D to excuse any Competitor pursuant to Article 10.2.

10.2 Penalties for breach

(a) Unless COR/D (in consultation with the Regatta Director) is satisfied on reasonable grounds that a failure to comply with Article 10.1 was due to unintended damage, circumstances beyond the reasonable control of the Competitor and/or reasonable and genuine safety concerns of the Competitor, then:
  (i) in the event that a Competitor fails to compete in any AC37 Event in which it is required to compete under Article 10.1:
    (A) the Arbitration Panel shall impose the points penalties set out in Clause 10.2(b) on the Competitor; and
    (B) COR/D may apply to the Arbitration Panel for it to impose such financial penalty it considers appropriate having regard to the nature and manner of the breach; and
  (ii) in the event that a Competitor fails to compete in the final regatta for each of the Youth and Women's AC Regattas, COR/D may apply to the Arbitration Panel for it to impose such financial penalty it considers appropriate having regard to the nature and manner of the breach.
(b) For each failure to compete in an AC37 Event:
  (i) where the failure is by a Challenger, the Challenger will be docked one (1) point in every ongoing or remaining stage of the CSS and the Match;
  (ii) where the failure is by a Defender, the Defender will be docked one (1) point in the Match;
subject to a maximum of three (3) docked points per Competitor.

11. Postponement / Cancellation

11.1 Initial Preliminary Regattas / Youth and Women's AC Regattas

(a) If for any reason it becomes impossible or unfeasible or uneconomic for ACE to hold either the Youth and Women's AC Regattas and/or one or both of the Initial Preliminary Regattas, including but not limited to force majeure or the failure or inability of the host entity/city/country to abide by their agreement with ACE, or insufficient numbers of AC40 Yachts being available for use, ACE, having consulted the Competitor Forum, COR/D and the Regatta Director, may postpone and/or relocate, or cancel, such event or events.
(b) ACE, in consultation with COR/D, shall provide no less than sixty (60) days' notice to Competitors of any rescheduled Initial Preliminary Regatta or any final

Youth and Women's AC Regatta. Such notice shall include all details necessary to enable Competitors' participation in accordance with COR/D's instructions and this Protocol.

(c) If ACE fails, or is unable, to provide the notice required under Article 11.1(b), Competitors shall not suffer any sanction under Article 10.2 if they are unable to attend the rescheduled Event. In the event of cancellation of one or both of the Initial Preliminary Regattas, ACE shall refund each Competitor a proportion of the entry fees it has paid for such Preliminary Regattas but only to the extent that ACE has not spent, or irrevocably committed to spend, such entry fees in organising the relevant event.

11.2 Final Preliminary Regatta / CSS / Match

(a) If for any reason it becomes impossible or unfeasible or uneconomic for ACE to hold the whole or any part of the Final Preliminary Regatta and/or the CSS and/or the Match, including but not limited to force majeure or the failure or inability of the host entity/city/country to abide by their agreement with ACE in each case, ACE may, with COR/D's agreement (COR/D having taken due consideration of any contractual commitments to which ACE is subject), select an alternative Host City and/or Venue and/or dates for the affected part of the Final Preliminary Regatta and/or the CSS and/or Match (as applicable), provided that ACE shall give Competitors as much notice as reasonably practicable in the circumstances both that a change to the Host City, Venue and/or dates are being considered and of the new Host City, Venue and/or dates once selected.

(b) If the Match is to be rescheduled, it shall take place during the next available Northern or Southern Hemisphere sailing period as prescribed by the Deed of Gift (depending on the Venue for such rescheduled Match) and COR/D shall liaise in good faith to agree if any other consequential changes to this Protocol, the Class Rules and/or the AC Technical Regulations would be necessary or desirable.

PART D: COMPETITORS

12. Challenger of Record

12.1 Appointment of initial Challenger of Record

RYS, together with its representative team INEOS Britannia, has been appointed as the initial Challenger of Record, having submitted the first notice of challenge to RNZYS for AC37 that met the requirements of the Deed of Gift and RNZYS having accepted such challenge. **SEE PROTOCOL AMENDMENT 8**

12.2 Withdrawal of challenge

(a) The initial Challenger of Record shall remain in the position of Challenger of Record (even if eliminated from the CSS) unless it withdraws its challenge for AC37.
(b) If the Challenger of Record withdraws its challenge, then the Defender shall promptly appoint one of the other remaining Challengers as the new Challenger of Record, such appointment to be at the sole discretion of the Defender.

13. Entry of Further Challengers

13.1 Entry Period

(a) Subject always to Articles 13.1(b) and 13.3 below, the Defender shall be entitled, at its discretion, to accept Additional Challenges for AC37 where the Notice of Challenge (in each case) is received by the Defender pursuant to Article 14.1 from 00:00 NZT on 1 December 2021 through until 23:59 NZT on 31 July 2022 (the "**Entry Period**").
(b) No Additional Challenge shall be reviewed by the Defender during the period commencing on 17:00 NZT on 22 December 2021 and ending on 00:00 NZT on 16 January 2022, but any such Additional Challenges shall still be reviewed in the order of their receipt.
(c) The Defender shall be entitled, at its discretion, to reject any Additional Challenge but only after consultation with the Challenger of Record.

13.2 Late entries

(a) Subject always to Articles 13.2(b) and 13.3 below, late challenges for AC37 may be accepted by the Defender following the close of the Entry Period ("**Late Challenge**"), provided that:
    (i) such Late Challenge is submitted in accordance with Article 14.1 by no later than 31 May 2023;
    (ii) the Late Challenger:
        (A) provides each of the documents prescribed in Article 14.1;
        (B) pays the fees prescribed in Articles 15.1 and 15.3; and
        (C) pays the Late Entry fees prescribed in Article 15.4.
(b) The Defender must consult with the Challenger of Record before accepting any Late Challenge that is submitted after 30 September 2022.
(c) The Defender will promptly:
    (i) publish all accepted Late Challenges, together with the date on which they were accepted; and

(ii) confirm with the Challenger of Record when all payments due from the Late Challenger under Article 15 have been received.

(d) A Late Challenger is not entitled to participate in the Competitor Forum and its consent will not be required to any proposed change to the Class Rules until all fees payable by it, as referred to in Article 20, have been paid to ACE in full.

13.3 Restrictions

Additional Challenges and Late Challenges will only be accepted if:

(a) they comply with Articles 14.1 and 14.2; and
(b) the Additional Challenger or Late Challenger meets the qualification requirements of this Protocol and the Deed of Gift for a challenging yacht club.

13.4 List and order of Challengers

Following the close of the Entry Period, the Defender shall publish a list of accepted Challengers received during the Entry Period and the order in which their Notices of Challenge were received by the Defender, and thereafter keep the list updated to include any accepted Late Challenges and withdrawals.

14. Entry Process

14.1 Submission of Notice of Challenge

All Additional Challenges and Late Challenges for AC37 must include a Notice of Challenge in the form set out in Schedule 2 and a Deed of Participation, in each case duly completed and signed, and must be submitted to the Defender:

(a) by email to the Defender at russell.green@emiratesteamnz.com, with a copy to ayoung@rnzys.org.nz,
(b) with the originals to be received by the Defender within ten (10) days at:

The Royal New Zealand Yacht Squadron
181 Westhaven
Drive Westhaven
Marina Auckland
1011
New Zealand

14.2 Review of Notices of Challenge

(a) The Defender will review and accept Additional Challenges and Late Challenges for AC37 in the order that the challenges are received. If the Defender is satisfied that a challenge is valid and that the challenging yacht club meets the requirements of this Protocol and the Deed of Gift, the Defender will advise the challenging yacht club and will provide written confirmation of the bank details for payment of the fees prescribed in Article 15.

(b) The Defender will not accept an Additional Challenge or Late Challenge from a yacht club which cannot demonstrate, to the Defender's satisfaction, that it meets the following requirements as at the date of the Notice of Challenge:
   (i) it must be incorporated, patented or licensed by the legislature, admiralty or other executive department of its country;
   (ii) it must hold an annual regatta on an ocean water course of the sea or on an arm of the sea;
   (iii) it must have been in existence for a minimum of three years prior to the date of the Notice of Challenge;
   (iv) it must have a membership of at least 200 members;
   (v) it must be financially supported by a majority of its membership on a pro-rata basis;
   (vi) it must operate as a yacht club and have objectives consistent with the furtherance of yachting activities; and
   (vii) it must be a member of its national sailing authority.

(c) The Defender may in its discretion allow any challenging yacht club a period of up to two (2) weeks after being so notified by the Defender to correct any deficiencies in its Notice of Challenge or provide requested follow-up information, during which period that challenger shall not lose its priority date in the list of challengers. At the end of such period, if the deficiencies have not been corrected and/or the requested follow-up information has not been provided, the Notice of Challenge shall be deemed not accepted.

14.3 Challenge Representative

When submitting its challenge, each yacht club shall nominate a challenge representative who will be the sole person authorised to receive and issue official communications from and to the Defender for the entire duration of AC37 and associated events (the **"Challenge Representative"**). A yacht club may replace at any time its Challenge Representative by giving prior written notice to COR/D, ACE and, once appointed, the Regatta Director.

15. Entry Fees

15.1 Initial Entry Fees

Each Challenger shall pay the initial Entry Fees to the Defender as follows:

(a) a first instalment of US$1,000,000 (one million United States dollars) by wire transfer direct to the bank account nominated by ACE (the "**ACE Account**") by no later than seven (7) days following the written confirmation of acceptance of the challenge provided by the Defender pursuant to Article 14.2 (the "**First Instalment**"); and
(b) a second instalment of US$1,250,000.00 (one million two hundred and fifty thousand United States dollars) by wire transfer direct to the ACE Account by 1 September 2022 (the "**Second Instalment**"),
(together, the "**Initial Entry Fees**"), each such payment to be non-refundable.

15.2 Election to pay the Second Instalment of the Initial Entry Fee in instalments

(a) A Challenger may elect to pay the Second Instalment of the Initial Entry Fee (in accordance with the payment instructions provided in Article 15.1(b)) in the following four (4) deferred instalments, provided that the total amount payable will be increased to US$1,400,000.00 (one million four hundred thousand United States dollars):
    (i) US$350,000 (three hundred and fifty thousand United States Dollars) by no later than 1 September 2022;
    (ii) US$350,000 (three hundred and fifty thousand United States Dollars) by no later than 1 October 2022;
    (iii) US$350,000 (three hundred and fifty thousand United States Dollars) by no later than 1 December 2022; and
    (iv) US$350,000 (three hundred and fifty thousand United States Dollars) by no later than 1 February 2023;
(b) If any Challenger elects to pay the Second Instalment in instalments pursuant to Article 15.2(a) above, then:
    (i) it shall not be entitled to participate in the Competitor Forum; and
    (ii) its consent will not be required to any proposed change to the Class Rules;
    until such Challenger has paid the Second Instalment to ACE in full.

15.3 Additional Entry Fees

In addition to the Initial Entry Fees above, each Challenger will be required to pay the following additional payments in order to participate in AC37:

(a) **ACPI contribution:** the sum of US$25,000 (twenty-five thousand United States Dollars) by wire transfer direct to the nominated bank account of ACPI, as a non-refundable contribution to ACPI's costs (in accordance with Article 66.2 below) to help protect the America's Cup trademarks, such amount to be payable at the same time as the First Instalment is due;

(b) **Website contribution:** the sum of US$150,000 (one hundred and fifty thousand United States Dollars) by wire transfer direct to the ACE Account, as a non-refundable contribution towards ACE's costs in hosting and maintaining the Official AC Website (which will include Competitor specific sections) and the Official AC Social Media Channels, such amount to be payable at the same time as the First Instalment of the Initial Entry Fees are due; and

(c) **Performance Bond:** by 1 September 2022, provide a valid and binding performance bond of US$1,000,000 (one million United States Dollars) to assure the Challenger's participation in AC37, and compliance with this Protocol, as further described in Article 17,

together, the "**Additional Entry Fees**").

15.4 Late Entry Fees and Payment

(a) In addition to the Entry Fees, all Late Challengers shall pay a late entry fee calculated at the rate of US$100,000 per month (or part thereof) from 1 August 2022 up until the date the Late Challenge is received by the Defender (the "**Late Entry Fees**").

(b) Late Entry Fees, Additional Entry Fees, Preliminary Regatta Fees and Retrospective Shared Costs (as defined in Article 19(d)) shall be paid by Late Challengers to ACE in full at the same time as the First Instalment.

(c) Where the Late Challenge is submitted after 1 September 2022, the Second Instalment shall be paid by the Late Challenger in full to ACE at the same time as the First Instalment in the increased amount set out at Article 15.2(a). Where such Late Challenger elects to pay the Second Instalment in deferred instalments under Article 15.2(a), the Late Challenger must pay all those instalments which are due and payable as at the date of acceptance of their Challenge.

16. Preliminary Regattas Entry Fees

(a) In addition to the Initial Entry Fees, Additional Entry Fees and Late Entry Fees set out in Article 15 of this Protocol, each Challenger shall pay to ACE the sum of US$200,000 (two hundred thousand United States dollars) for each Preliminary Regatta (the "**Preliminary Regatta Fees**"). Each payment will be due no later than two (2) months before the start date for the relevant Preliminary Regatta Racing Period. Such payments shall be non-refundable, paid by wire transfer direct to the ACE Account and shall be applied to the payment of any costs associated with the relevant Preliminary Regatta.

(b) Preliminary Regatta Fees must be paid by all Challengers regardless of whether they are able to take part in any or all Preliminary Regattas for whatever reason (including by reason of force majeure).

17. Performance Bond

17.1 Form

The Performance Bond described in Article 15.3(c) may be provided either:

(a) in cash by wire transfer direct to the segregated Performance Bond bank account nominated by ACE for such purposes (details to be provided upon request); or
(b) by way of a standby letter of credit (with a term expiring no earlier than 180 days after the final race of the Match) issued by a bank approved by ACE in the form approved by ACE at its sole discretion. In the event that the financial condition of the issuer bank changes in any materially adverse way, as determined by ACE in its sole discretion, the Competitor shall within fifteen (15) days of written notice from ACE obtain a replacement standby letter of credit from an issuer bank and in the form approved by ACE.

17.2 Return of balance

Subject always to Article 21(c), the balance of a Challenger's Performance Bond held by ACE will be returned not later than sixty (60) days after the Challenger has discharged all of its obligations in relation to AC37 to the reasonable satisfaction of ACE. ACE shall take best endeavours to make such determination as quickly as possible after the date on which the relevant Challenger ceases participation in AC37, and shall provide all information reasonably requested by such Challenger in the event that the Performance Bond is not returned in full.

17.3 Maintaining Performance Bond

In the event that a Challenger forfeits any or all of its Performance Bond, the Challenger shall immediately provide a renewed (or new) Performance Bond for the full US$1,000,000 (one million United States Dollars). If the full amount of the total Performance Bond is not timely reinstated following any forfeiture (in whole or in part), the Challenger shall cease to be eligible for AC37, including for any entitlements as a Challenger under the Rules, and shall be disqualified from further participation in AC37 by ACE.

17.4 Extension

If the CSS and/or the Match is postponed, ACE may require each Challenger to maintain the Performance Bond on the same terms, except that the Performance Bond period shall be extended to one hundred and eighty (180) days after the last re-scheduled race of the Match.

18. Defender Payments

In recognition of the commitment made by the Defender to provide the financial resources to deliver the Events, the Defender will not be required to make a further contribution by way of Entry Fees or Performance Bond.

19. Shared costs

(a) In addition to the payment of the Entry Fees by the Challengers under this Protocol, all Competitors shall be required to contribute on an equal basis to the costs of the following joint initiatives:
  (i) the joint weather programme (of a scale similar to AC36), as detailed in Article 40;
  (ii) the Joint Recon Programme as detailed in the AC Technical Regulations; and
  (iii) any other joint arrangements that are agreed to by COR/D from time to time, (together, the "**Shared Costs**").

(b) COR/D shall agree on the costs and providers in respect of each joint initiative.

(c) Each Competitor will be required to contribute an equal amount towards the Shared Costs, such amounts to be payable by each Competitor to ACE in advance or arrears (as determined by COR/D) in accordance with the budget for the relevant joint initiative as determined by Article 19(b).

(d) Late Challengers will be required to pay a full share of Shared Costs, including such share of any Shared Costs they would have incurred up to the date of acceptance of their challenge if their challenge had been submitted within the Entry Period, ("**Retrospective Shared Costs**"), at the same time as they pay their Entry Fees. ACE shall credit Retrospective Shared Costs received from Late Challengers to other Competitors proportionately so as to ensure all Shared Costs are shared equally.

20. Failure to pay Entry Fees or Shared Costs

(a) A Challenger shall pay the applicable Initial Entry Fees, Additional Entry Fees, Late Entry Fees, Preliminary Regatta Fees and their portion of any Shared Costs in full as a condition precedent to its eligibility to compete in the Preliminary Regattas and CSS.

(b) If a Challenger fails to pay when due any applicable fees referred to in Article 20(a), or the Defender fails to pay when due any Shared Costs, then if such default is not remedied within seven (7) days following issue of a demand for remedy by ACE or COR (and unless otherwise agreed by COR/D):
  (i) the penalty for such default shall be exclusion from AC37 Events upon application to the Arbitration Panel by either or both of the Challenger of Record or the Defender (at its sole discretion), except that a failure to pay the

First Instalment on time (which is subsequently remedied) will only result in the following penalties for the defaulting Challenger:
(A) if remedied before the end of the Entry Period, a late payment fee of five thousand US Dollars (US$5,000) per day that the Challenger remains in default (up to a maximum of one hundred thousand US Dollars (US$100,000); or
(B) if not remedied before the end of the Entry Period, the defaulting Challenger shall be considered a Late Challenger subject to the requirements of Articles 13.2 and 15.4; and
(ii) during the period the Competitor is in default of payment, that Competitor may not:
(A) exercise any of its rights granted under this Protocol (and for the avoidance of doubt this shall mean that the AC75 Class Rule may be amended during the relevant period without the consent of that Competitor); and
(B) participate in the joint initiatives referred to Article 19.

21. Withdrawal of Challenge

(a) A Challenger may withdraw by written notice to the Defender. All rights of a Challenger under the Rules shall cease immediately upon confirmation of receipt of that Challenger's withdrawal by the Defender.
(b) A Challenger that withdraws from AC37 in accordance with the terms of this Protocol has no obligation to fulfil those requirements of Articles 15, 16 and 19 that are not required to have been performed as of the effective date of the Challenger's withdrawal.
(c) Subject to Article 21(b), in the event that a Challenger withdraws before it is eliminated in the CSS, such withdrawal will result in the forfeiture of its Performance Bond (if such bond has been provided at the time that the Challenger has withdrawn).

PART E: YACHTS/CREW

22. Yachts

22.1 AC75 Class Rule

(a) COR/D shall publish Version 2 of the AC75 Class Rule in conjunction with this Protocol (the "**AC75 Class Rule**").

(b) Only yachts complying with the AC75 Class Rule will be eligible to compete in the Final Preliminary Regatta, the CSS and the Match.
(c) The AC75 Class Rule cannot be amended or replaced other than as specifically allowed in the AC Technical Regulations.

22.2 AC40 Yachts

(a) ACE (with support from the Defender) shall be responsible for developing and publishing as soon as practicable a one-design class rule for AC40 Yachts (the "**AC40 Class Rule**"), which shall be the yachts used for the Initial Preliminary Regattas and the Youth and Women's AC Regattas ("**AC40 Yacht**"). The AC40 Class Rule cannot be amended or replaced other than as specifically allowed in the AC Technical Regulations. ACE shall keep COR fully informed during the development of the AC40 Class Rule and give due consideration to input from COR. The AC40 Yacht is still in design phase but based on current estimates the price of an AC40 Yacht package will not exceed the sum of US$1.85 million (excluding the cost of sails and running rigging which will be purchased separately). If however, due to factors outside the control of ACE such as increases in the cost of materials caused by supply constraints or similar circumstances the price does increase beyond US$1.85 million, then ACE shall provide a full breakdown of all costs, supported by financial information capable of being audited.
(b) Each Competitor shall purchase at least one AC40 Yacht from ACE (or its nominated manufacturer) which shall be supplied to the Competitor to a standard specification mandated by ACE with compliant componentry and equipment so that the yacht is capable of receiving an AC40 class certificate in accordance with the AC40 Class Rule.
(c) The terms and conditions under which each Competitor will purchase an AC40 Yacht from ACE (or its nominated manufacturer) will be set out in a separate standardised purchase agreement to be entered into between ACE (or its nominated manufacturer) and each Competitor. The purchase price of each AC40 Yacht shall be identical for each purchaser for all AC40 Yachts ordered before 31 March 2022 and thereafter shall be no less than the amount paid by Competitors who have ordered AC40 Yachts before 31 March 2022.
(d) Competitors will be allocated their AC40 Yachts in the following order of priority:
  (i) the Defender;
  (ii) the Challenger of Record;
  (iii) each remaining Challenger in the order in which their challenges were accepted by the Defender in accordance with the list published pursuant to Article 13.4; and then
  (iv) third parties that are not Competitors.

(e) Outside the period of the Initial Preliminary Regattas and the Youth and Women's AC Regattas, Competitors will be entitled to use their AC40 Yacht as a test yacht, including the utilisation of componentry that is not compliant with the AC40 Class Rule (subject to the restrictions outlined in that rule), provided that the AC40 Yacht is returned to an AC40 Class Rule compliant condition for each Initial Preliminary Regatta and Youth and Women's AC Regatta. Any changes required to bring the AC40 Yacht back to a condition that is compliant with the AC40 Class Rule will be at the cost of the relevant Competitor.

22.3 AC Technical Regulations

(a) COR/D shall publish the "**AC Technical Regulations**" at the same time that the AC75 Class Rule is published under Article 22.1.
(b) In addition to complying with the relevant Class Rule, each Competitor must ensure compliance with the AC Technical Regulations.
(c) The AC Technical Regulations may only be amended in accordance with the provisions of the AC Technical Regulations.

23. Class of Yacht for AC38

23.1 In order to promote competition and sustainability, amongst other things, in AC38, as a condition of its eligibility to compete in AC37:

(a) each of the Challenger of Record and the Defender shall sign a copy of the Deed of Participation; and
(b) each Competitor shall submit a signed copy of the Deed of Participation to the Defender with its Notice of Challenge in accordance with Article 14.1;
subject always to the terms of the Deed of Gift.

23.2 The Deed of Participation shall include the following conditions:

(a) if a Competitor wins the Match and becomes the next holder of the America's Cup, the AC75 Yacht class will be retained for AC38 and both the challenger series and the match for AC38 will be contested in AC75 Yachts;
(b) all Competitors agree not to challenge for or defend AC38 in any class of yacht that is not compliant with the version of the AC75 Class Rule as at the date of the final race of the AC37 Match, or agreed developments which do not alter the fundamental concept of the AC75 Class as a 75-foot LOA Bermudan sloop rigged foiling monohull;
(c) an acknowledgement that damages for breach of the Deed of Participation shall not be an adequate remedy and that any and all of the other parties thereto shall be entitled to an injunction to restrain a breach of the deed by any other party;

(d) an obligation to pay liquidated damages of twenty million US Dollars (US$20,000,000) (or the maximum sum which may otherwise be permitted by applicable law) into a bank account nominated by COR/D to be shared equally between the non-breaching parties to the Deed of Participation;
(e) an obligation not to:
  (i) assist any third parties to compete in;
  (ii) procure any third party to compete in; or
  (iii) procure any third party to assist any of the parties to compete in,
  AC38 in any class of yacht which is not an AC75 Yacht; and
(f) an obligation on parties to procure that the sailing teams representing them in AC37, together with all members of the sailing teams' management boards and sailing crew agree not to compete in, or attempt to enter, AC38 in any class of yacht which is not an AC75 Yacht.

24. Cost containment and limitations

The following provisions shall apply as conditions of eligibility for all Competitors in AC37:

24.1 Components

(a) Each Competitor shall only be entitled to build a maximum of one (1) new AC75 Hull during AC37.
(b) The AC Technical Regulations will contain restrictions on the number of, and modifications to, components that can be used on:
  (i) an AC75 Yacht; and
  (ii) any other sailing yacht (or platform towed to simulate a sailing yacht) that exceeds 6 metres LOA that is capable of producing design or performance information for use either directly or indirectly in the design, construction or sailing of an AC75 Yacht.

24.2 Sailing limitations

(a) Each Competitor may only sail one AC75 Yacht at a time.
(b) The periods specified in Articles 24.2(c) and 24.2(d) below ("**Non-Sailing Periods**") are based on the Match being sailed in June 2024 and are subject to change by COR/D if the timing of the Match changes as a result of the location of the selected Match Venue (including the hemisphere in which the selected Match Venue is located). The finalised dates for Non-Sailing Periods will be published by 30 July 2022. **SEE PROTOCOL AMENDMENT 2**
(c) Subject to the exception specified in Article 24.2(f), no Competitor shall sail an AC75 Yacht during the following periods:

(i) from 17 March 2021 until 17 September 2022. **SEE PROTOCOL AMENDMENT 4**

(d) No Competitor shall sail either an AC75 Yacht or an AC40 Yacht (whether or not in Class Rule compliant mode) from 1 July 2023 to 31 October 2023 except at the Match Venue. This prohibition shall not apply to any Preliminary Regatta held during this period outside the Match Venue. **SEE PROTOCOL AMENDE-MENT 4**

(e) Any of the Challenger of Record, the Defender or the Regatta Director may apply to the Arbitration Panel to impose such penalty as it determines appropriate for any breach of Clauses 24.2(c) or (d) including, but not limited to:

(i) financial penalties and extension of the next Non-Sailing Period for the breaching Competitor by one (1) week for each day (or part of a day) that such Competitor has sailed during a Non-Sailing Period; and

(ii) in the case of repeated breaches, exclusion from all subsequent AC37 Events.

(f) As an exception to the restrictions above, if a New Competitor purchases a Version 1 AC75 Yacht, such New Competitor will be entitled to sail that Version 1 AC75 Yacht for a maximum of 20 Sailing Days between 17 June 2022 and 17 September 2022 subject to the provisions of the AC Technical Regulations.

(g) Each Competitor shall provide the Regatta Director (if appointed, otherwise ACE) with a declaration of compliance following the expiry of the relevant Non-Sailing Periods set out in Articles 24.2(c) and (d) above and all Notices of Challenge filed under Article 14.1 shall also include a declaration undertaking to comply with the requirements of Article 24.2 as applicable.

(h) There shall be no sailing or testing of AC75 Yachts, AC40 Yachts, Surrogate Yachts or LEQ12 yachts (or any combination thereof) in a coordinated manner with other Competitors or third parties except:

(i) when participating in scheduled AC75 Yacht racing or AC40 Yacht racing during AC37 Events; or

(ii) when participating in Official Training or Official Practice, in each case to be designated as such by the Regatta Director, during periods to be specified by ACE in consultation with the Regatta Director; or

(iii) when participating in official pre-regatta TV testing sessions as requested by AC Media; or

(iv) when eligible crews are training in AC40s for the Youth and Women's AC Regattas in Barcelona from 1 August 2024 provided that no crew member who has been declared under Article 30.5(a) shall participate in such training and no crew member who participates shall subsequently be eligible to race on an AC75 in the Final Preliminary Regatta, the Challenger Selection Series or the Match. **SEE PROTOCOL AMENDMENT 11**

(i) The following shall be considered sailing in a "coordinated manner" for the purposes of Article 24.2(h) above:

   (i) yachts sailing within 400 metres of each other on the same approximate heading for more than 20 seconds;
   (ii) yachts rounding shared practice marks within 30 seconds of each other; or
   (iii) non-compliance with the Sailing Instructions or such other guidelines issued by the Regatta Director from time to time.

(j) Subject to Article 24.2(e), the Regatta Director (when appointed) shall be responsible for managing and monitoring the permitted and prohibited sailing under this Article 24.2.

24.3 Surrogate Yachts

No Competitor shall:

(a) acquire, sail or test any Surrogate Yacht; or
(b) allow any Sailing Team member to sail on board any Surrogate Yacht. This prohibition shall not apply to a Sailing Team member who is eligible to sail in either the Youth America's Cup Regatta or the Women's America's Cup Regatta but is not eligible to race or otherwise permitted to sail on an AC75 Yacht; or **SEE PROTOCOL AMENDMENT 12**
(c) obtain any performance data from a third party sailing any Surrogate Yacht.
The determination as to whether a yacht is a Surrogate Yacht or not shall be the sole responsibility of the Rules Committee (when appointed) whose decision shall be final. For the avoidance of doubt, the Rules Committee (once appointed) may consider breaches of this Article 24.3 which occurred prior to its appointment and apply appropriate penalties retrospectively. The restrictions in Article 24.3(b) above may be waived if COR/D, in its sole discretion, determines that it would be equitable for all Competitors and in the interests of AC37 to do so. **SEE PROTOCOL AMENDMENT 8**

Interpretation Note: In order to avoid any ambiguity as to the operation of Article 24.3 that may have existed prior to Amendment 08, the restrictions on Sailing Teams sailing onboard a Surrogate Yacht set out in this Article shall only apply from the date of publication of Amendment 08 onwards and the Protocol shall be interpreted accordingly. ***SEE PROTOCOL AMENDMENT 8***

24.4 Testing limitations

No Competitor shall carry out fluid dynamic testing of designs, at any scale, in any controlled environment such as a wind tunnel, cavitation tunnel, towing tank or manoeuvring basin. Any fluid dynamic testing of designs can only be undertaken in the open air and on open water, subject to the restrictions of this Article 24. This restriction does not apply to the calibration of sensors in a controlled environment. **SEE PROTOCOL AMENDMENT 2**

24.5 Class limitations

(a) The Class Rules shall detail all limitations which may include, but not be limited to, the incorporation of one design and/or standard single manufacturer elements; restrictions on materials, components and equipment; restrictions on construction techniques; and sail restrictions ("**Limitations**").
(b) The interpretation, calculation and enforcement of the Limitations and the determination on the compliance or not with such Limitations shall be the sole responsibility of the Rules Committee whose decision shall be final. Any measurement required by the Rules Committee to make a decision under this Article shall be carried out on its behalf by the Measurement Committee.

25. Shrouding

The AC Technical Regulations shall specify criteria in relation to shrouding of a Competitor's yachts.

26. Constructed in country

(a) In respect of an AC75 Yacht that is constructed after 17 March 2021, the Deed of Gift requirement that the yacht of a challenging yacht club be constructed in the country of the challenging yacht club, and the yacht representing the yacht club holding the America's Cup be constructed in the country of such yacht club, shall be deemed to be satisfied by the lamination or another form of construction of the Hull in such country. Replaceable bows and sterns, materials, tooling and other components and hardware used in or during the lamination or other form of construction of the Hull may be obtained from any country. In order to ensure compliance with this Article the following provisions shall apply:
    (i) a Competitor shall arrange in a timely manner for a member of the Measurement Committee to inspect the Hull at the place of construction to determine whether the Hull has been constructed in accordance with this Article and, if this rule is met, the Measurement Committee shall certify it as per its findings ("**Constructed in the Country Certificate**"). Such a certificate by the Measurement Committee shall be final;
    (ii) for the avoidance of doubt, the fabrication, acquisition or use of any component, materials or resources used to complete an AC75 Yacht may be sourced without restriction as to their country of origin, place of fabrication, assembly, construction or development, but any such component, materials or resources must nevertheless comply with the AC75 Class Rule; and
    (iii) the repair, modification or replacement of any part of an AC75 Yacht that has received the Constructed in the Country Certificate may be undertaken in any country.

(b) In respect of a Version 1 AC75 Yacht, the Deed of Gift requirement that the yacht of a challenging yacht club be constructed in the country of the challenging yacht club shall be deemed to be satisfied if the modifications to such yacht required to enable it to comply with the AC75 Class Rule are carried out in such country and the yacht is relaunched and sailed in that country. It shall be the responsibility of the Competitor to satisfy the Measurement Committee that it has complied with these requirements in a manner to be specified by the Measurement Committee.

27. Customs house registry

Competitors need not provide a customs house registry of any AC75 Yacht or AC40 Yacht.

28. Transport and Logistics

(a) Competitors shall arrange, at their own cost, transport of their yachts and associated equipment to each Venue.
(b) Each Competitor shall comply with all requirements published by the Regatta Director for the handling and the mooring of AC75 Yachts and AC40 Yachts in any Venue.

29. Crew Restrictions

A person who has crewed on a Competitor's yacht during the CSS shall not crew on any other Competitor's yacht while it competes in a race in an AC37 Event, except with the consent of all Competitors still competing in the AC37 Events at that time.

30. Crew Nationality

30.1 Nationality rules

In an effort to better maintain the provision in the Deed of Gift for "*Friendly competition between foreign countries*", the following nationality rules shall apply:

(a) for all racing in the Preliminary Regattas, the CSS and the Match, 100% of the crew sailing each yacht in each race shall be nationals of the country of the yacht club that the relevant Competitor represents; and
(b) for all racing in the Youth and Women's AC Regattas, 100% of the crew sailing each yacht in each race shall be nationals of the country of the yacht club that the Competitor (if participating) or yacht represents. If ACE accepts teams from other countries (not represented by the Competitors) for the Youth and Women's AC Regattas, 100% of the crew of those teams sailing each yacht in each race shall be nationals of the country of the yacht club that the team represents. Article 30.3 shall also apply to a team competing in the Youth and Women's AC Regattas.

30.2 Nationality criteria

For the purposes of Article 30.1, a crew member shall be deemed to be a "national" of a country if they satisfy any one (or more) of the following criteria:

(a) such crew member held a valid passport (or other valid proof of citizenship accepted by ACE) of the country of the yacht club that the Competitor represents as at 17 March 2021; or
(b) such crew member was physically present in the country of the yacht club that the Competitor represents (or acting on behalf of such yacht club at the venue for AC36) for a total of 548 days between (but excluding) 17 March 2018 and 18 March 2021. If a crew member is present in the country for only part of a particular day, that day will be counted as a full day.
(c) Upon application by a Competitor, COR/D may, at its discretion, partially waive the requirements of Article 30.2(b) for a particular crew member who they are satisfied was unable to fully comply with those requirements only due to circumstances created by the COVID 19 pandemic and/or an absence from the country of such Competitor's yacht club competing in sailing regattas with such Competitor. It shall be the responsibility of the Competitor making the application to provide sufficient evidence in support of the application to enable COR/D to make its decision. **SEE PROTOCOL AMENDMENT 8**

30.3 Emerging Nations

(a) A Challenger or prospective team who has advised the Defender of their intention to challenge for AC37 (a "**Prospective Challenger**") may apply to COR/D for:
    (i) a ruling that the country of the yacht club will be considered as an Emerging Nation for the purposes of this Article 30; and
    (ii) a dispensation from the crew nationality requirements of Article 30.1 to allow a specific number of approved non-nationals to compete as crew on the Competitor's AC75 Yacht or AC40 Yacht.
(b) Such applications shall be determined by COR/D in its sole discretion.
(c) If a country is approved as an Emerging Nation by COR/D, the number of non-nationals approved to compete on the yacht of that Challenger will be determined by COR/D based on the following factors:
    (i) the experience (including America's Cup racing) and skill level of the Challenger's or Prospective Challenger's Sailing Team; **SEE PROTOCOL AMENDMENT 8**
    (ii) the experience and skill level of each non-national sailor either engaged or whom the Challenger or Prospective Challenger proposes to engage for AC37; and
    (iii) other relevant circumstances of the Challenger or Prospective Challenger.

(d) Approvals under this Article will be given for specific sailors and may be amended or reviewed by COR/D, at their sole discretion at a later date upon application by a Competitor if there is a change of personnel or a change in other relevant circumstances.
(e) It shall be the responsibility of COR/D to ensure that the decisions made under this Article are as far as possible equitable in relation to other Competitors.

30.4 Disputes

Any disputes relating to this Article 30 will be resolved by the Arbitration Panel Fast Track Process.

30.5 Declarations

(a) Each Competitor shall submit to COR/D a declaration setting out the names, passport details and details of compliance with one of the nationality criteria set out in Article 30.2 for those persons in their organisation who will be eligible and may be crew sailing on the Competitors yacht in a race during the Final Preliminary Regatta, the CSS and the Match. Such declaration must be submitted to COR/D:
  (i) by 30 June 2024 for those persons engaged by the Competitor on or before that date; and
  (ii) not more than 10 days after the date of engagement for any person that is engaged after 30June 2024.
(b) COR/D shall promptly provide copies of each declaration provided under Article 30.5(a) to all Competitors.
(c) A person whose name and details have been properly submitted to COR/D within a declaration under Article 30.5(a) shall be deemed eligible to sail as a crew member on the relevant Competitors yacht during racing in the Final Preliminary Regatta, CSS and the Match, unless there is a challenge to that person's eligibility during the period that is 10 days following the date on which notification was provided to all Competitor's under Article 30.5(b).
(d) Where a challenge to a person's eligibility is made during the period specified in Article 30.5(c), such challenge shall be resolved by the Arbitration Panel Fast Track Process under Article 30.4 of the Protocol. **SEE PROTOCOL AMENDMENT 11**

31. Support Vessels

(a) The Racing Rules agreed under Article 33.1(d) shall contain requirements in relation to team support vessels based on rule 87 of the Racing Rules of Sailing America's Cup Version for AC36 together with any additions or amendments agreed by COR/D.

(b) As outlined in the COR/D Notice to Competitors dated 31 May 2022, each Competitor will be required to employ a minimum of one (1) hydrogen powered vessel ("**HSV**") at the Match Venue to support its on-water race operations, such HSV to be at least 10m LOA.

(c) All HSVs shall be capable of achieving a cruise speed of 25 knots under hydrogen fuel cell power alone with no other source of power other than hydrogen fuel cell and batteries. The general minimum specification for an HSV is:
   (i) a range of 75nm at an average speed of 25 knots;
   (ii) a duty cycle corresponding to two back-to-back AC75 Yacht race distances at AC75 Yacht VMG speeds directly up and down the course;
   (iii) a top speed of 50 knots;
   (iv) a length of 10m LOA;
   (v) capacity for 6 people including the driver plus two hundred and fifty kilograms (250kg) of additional payload;
   (vi) 160kw of hydrogen fuel-cell power, supplemented by batteries; and
   (vii) capability to fully foil at a boat speed of 24 knots and above.

(d) In order to further the promotion of the America's Cup and showcase the technology and its sustainability benefits in the media coverage of the event, Competitors will be required to have one (1) HSV inside the race course boundaries in locations specified by the Regatta Director from the time of the warning signal for any race in which their yacht is competing until the completion of such race.

(e) Competitor's HSVs must be operational and located at the Match Venue from the start of the Final Preliminary Regatta until the conclusion of a Competitor's racing in the Challenger Selection Series or Match. If at any time an HSV is out-of-service and not operational then an exemption may be obtained from the Regatta Director.

(f) When a Competitor's HSV is operational, that Competitor's entire support boat fleet will be restricted to a maximum of the one (1) HSV on the course and four (4) additional non-hydrogen powered support vessels operating in the Racing Area. On race days the Competitor's entire support boat fleet dedicated to supporting the Competitor's AC75 in the Racing Area will be restricted as follows:
   (i) one (1) HSV in the Flag area to be permitted on the racecourse during racing as instructed by the Regatta Director;
   (ii) three other team support vessels inside the Flag Area, two on the side of the racecourse from which the Competitor's Race yacht enters the prestart area and one on the other side; and
   (iii) one additional support vessel operating in the Racing Area. **SEE PROTOCOL AMENDMENT 11**

(g) Subject to compliance with this Article 31, Competitors are not required to use an HSV as their primary support vessel for racing.

(h) Each Competitor shall be entitled to purchase one or more 10 metre HSVs from ACE (or its nominated manufacturer) under agreements similar in structure to the purchase of the AC40 Yachts under Article 22.2. The price of a 10 metre HSV shall not exceed two million New Zealand Dollars (NZ$2 million). If however, due to factors outside the control of ACE such as increases in the cost of materials caused by supply constraints or similar circumstances the price does increase beyond two million New Zealand Dollars (NZ$2 million), then ACE shall provide a full breakdown of all costs, supported by financial information capable of being audited, to all Competitors.

(i) If a competitor chooses to purchase HSVs from ACE (or its nominated manufacturer) in accordance with Article 31(h), the purchase agreement shall include a statement setting out HSV service requirements, warranty obligations and provisions that ACE (or its nominated manufacturer) will make to ensure the Competitor's HSVs remain operational including trained staff at the Match Venue to assist in servicing such HSVs.

(j) A Competitor may also elect to construct its own HSV providing it meets the specifications in Article 31(c). **SEE PROTOCOL AMENDMENT 3**

32. Television and technical equipment on-board

32.1 Equipment

(a) While racing in the AC37 Events, or when sailing in the Racing Area within three (3) weeks prior to any AC37 Event, the AC40 Yachts, AC75 Yachts, support boats and crew of each Competitor shall carry and operate such television, audio, biometric, navigation and associated telemetry systems and/or other equipment as may be required by AC Media, in consultation with the Regatta Director. The amount and placement of such equipment shall be consistent for all Competitors. The precise requirements shall be communicated to each Competitor through the issue of a Media Equipment Specification notice, to be issued by AC Media no later than a date to be agreed by COR/D. Such Media Equipment Specification notice shall not require the Competitors to take any action which would constitute a breach of any applicable data privacy laws with respect to employees, contractors, customers and other persons connected with them.

(b) All equipment installed under Article 32.1(a) will be provided, paid for and owned by AC Media (or its appointed production partner) and each Competitor agrees to return such equipment to AC Media in good working order within 10 days of such Competitor's final participation in the AC37 Events. Each Competitor agrees not to make any modifications to such equipment so that it operates in the manner intended by AC Media.

(c) Each Competitor will use reasonable efforts to obtain adequate all risks insurance cover for the replacement value of all equipment installed under Article 32.1(a) for the period such equipment is under the Competitor's control. In the event that a Competitor damages or loses such equipment during the period that it has been installed on a Competitor's yacht, support boat or crew member (or is otherwise under the Competitor's control), such Competitor will be liable to AC Media for the replacement value of such damaged or lost equipment provided that such liability shall only apply if the relevant insurance policies do not cover the damage or loss incurred.

32.2 Access

(a) Subject to applicable privacy laws, Competitors shall give AC Media full access to all equipment installed under Article 32.1(a) and its output during AC37 Events as determined by AC Media, in consultation with the Regatta Director, and communicated in advance to the Competitors. Competitors shall fully co-operate with AC Media with regards to the installation, operation and maintenance of all such on-board equipment.

(b) AC Media will act in an independent manner and be responsible for ensuring that adequate measures are put in place (including confidentiality agreements with relevant production partners and technical/hardware measures) so that:
   (i) performance information of individual yachts is not available to any other Competitor, other than such information that is available to the public; and
   (ii) all data is processed in accordance with applicable privacy laws.

(c) Each Competitor shall have reasonable access to all recorded data from equipment installed on their own yachts under Article 32.1(a) and AC Media shall use reasonable efforts to fulfil all requests by Competitors for such data, taking into account AC Media's own operational priorities.

32.3 Telemetry

As required by AC Media for media purposes, Competitors shall provide telemetry data from their competing yachts in all AC37 Events as further specified in the Class Rules.

32.4 Event officials

AC Media, in consultation with the Regatta Director, may require official event boats to carry television and technical equipment and personnel during the AC37 Events. Such equipment may be used to capture still and moving images that may be exploited by AC Media in accordance with Part I of this Protocol.

32.5 Voice communications system

COR/D will prescribe an on-board voice communications system which shall be the sole on- board voice communications system on Competitors' yachts on race days for all AC37 Events. Details of this system will be published by AC Media as part of the Media System and associated Media Equipment specifications according to dates in the AC75 Class Rule and the forthcoming AC40 Class Rule. **SEE PROTOCOL AMENDMENT 5**

32.6 Frequencies

In consultation with AC Media, the Regatta Director shall assign radio frequencies for use by Competitors, Regatta Officials and AC Media during the AC37 Events.

32.7 Open data

From the date that the equipment detailed in Article 32.1 is operational as provided for therein through the last race of the Match, whenever an AC75 Yacht or AC40 Yacht of any Competitor is racing in an Event, AC Media shall make the data that is generated by AC Media's equipment and sensors pursuant to Article 32.1 available to the public provided that, in so doing, it complies with all applicable data privacy laws.

32.8 Ownership

All data and information of whatever nature, and for whatever purpose, produced by the television, audio and other electronic equipment carried on yachts and/or crew under this Article 32 shall be the property of the respective Competitor, who shall subject to all applicable data privacy laws:

(a) grant sole rights to use such data and information for any lawful purpose to ACE for the duration of AC37; and
(b) following the end of AC37, a non-exclusive right to use such data and information for any lawful purpose to ACPI in accordance with Article 60.5.

PART F: RULES

33. Rules

33.1 Governing Rules

AC37 shall be governed by:

(a) the Deed of Gift (but excluding the Preliminary Regattas and CSS);
(b) this Protocol;

(c) the AC75 Class Rule, the AC40 Class Rule and the AC Technical Regulations;
(d) the Race Conditions;
(e) the Racing Rules; and **SEE PROTOCOL AMENDMENT 11**
(f) the Sailing Instructions; (together, the "**Rules**").

33.2 Priority of Rules

Unless otherwise provided, the documents referred to in Article 33.1 shall have precedence in the order the documents are listed. Any conflict between the provisions of such documents shall be resolved in favour of the document first listed.

34. Race Conditions

34.1 Match Conditions

(a) COR/D will agree upon, circulate to the Competitors and publish the Match Conditions on the Official Noticeboard not later than 30 June 2023 or such other date agreed by COR/D.
(b) The Match Conditions shall:
  (i) address all issues COR/D reasonably consider necessary to ensure that the Match is completed in accordance with this Protocol; and
  (ii) reflect the principles set out in Article 8 above.
(c) COR/D will use all reasonable endeavours to resolve any differences between them as to the terms of the Match Conditions through amicable negotiation within ten (10) working days of being informed of such difference by the other party, failing which the matter shall be resolved by the Arbitration Panel Fast Track Process.

34.2 CSS Conditions

(a) COR/D will agree upon, circulate to the Competitors and publish the CSS Conditions on the Official Noticeboard not later than 30 November 2023 or such other date agreed by COR/D.
(b) The CSS Conditions shall:
  (i) address all issues COR/D reasonably consider necessary to ensure that the CSS is completed in accordance with this Protocol; and
  (ii) be identical to the Match Conditions, subject to necessary changes to achieve the principles set out in Article 7 above.
(c) COR/D will use all reasonable endeavours to resolve any differences between them as to the terms of the CSS Conditions through amicable negotiation within ten (10) working days of being informed of such difference by the other party, failing which the matter shall be resolved by the Arbitration Panel Fast Track Process.

34.3 Preliminary Regatta Conditions

(a) COR/D will agree upon, circulate to the Competitors and publish the Preliminary Regatta Conditions on the Official Noticeboard not later than one month before the date of the first scheduled race in each Preliminary Regattas
(b) The Preliminary Regatta Conditions shall:
   (i) address all issues COR/D reasonably consider necessary to ensure that the Preliminary Regattas are completed in accordance with this Protocol; and
   (ii) be identical to the Match Conditions, subject to necessary changes to achieve the principles set out in Article 6 above.
(c) COR/D will use all reasonable endeavours to resolve any differences between them as to the terms of the Preliminary Regatta Conditions through amicable negotiation within ten (10) working days of being informed of such difference by the other party, failing which the matter shall be resolved by the Arbitration Panel Fast Track Process.

35. Sailing Instructions

(a) The Sailing Instructions for the CSS and the Match shall be issued by the Regatta Director after consultation with COR/D, not later than one month before the first scheduled race in the CSS.
(b) The Sailing Instructions for the Preliminary Regattas will be issued by the Regatta Director after consultation with COR/D no later than two weeks before the first scheduled race of each Preliminary Regatta.

36. Wind Limits

36.1 The permitted TWS range referred to in Article 36 is between 6.5 knots and 21 knots.

36.2 The TWS referred to in Article 36 shall be determined as follows:

(a) the wind shall be measured with wind measuring devices at two locations:
   (i) in the vicinity of the start line, approximately 5.7 meters above the water on each of the start line marks (the two start line devices); and
   (ii) in the vicinity of the windward gate approximately 5.7 meters above the water on each of the windward gate marks (the two windward gate devices);
(b) the wind on each measuring device at each position shall be filtered with a left sided 30 second rolling average using 1 Hz samples;
(c) the measurements shall be corrected to represent the TWS relative to the water with the correction being based on the forecasted tidal currents in the area where the race course is located, using a procedure and tidal current forecast published by the Regatta Director; and

(d) if any wind measuring device is considered unreliable by the Regatta Director, it shall be removed from the selection pool.

36.3 The warning signal for a race of the Final Preliminary Regatta, the Louis Vuitton Cup CSS or the Match shall not be given if:

(a) the Regatta Director considers the sea state unsuitable;
(b) there are no reliable devices in the vicinity of the windward mark;
(c) there are no reliable devices in the vicinity of the start line;
(d) during the period between nine minutes and four minutes before the scheduled start, the TWS measured at any time on any start line gate device, and the TWS measured at any time (not necessarily the same time) on any windward gate device falls outside the permitted TWS range; or
(e) during the period between five minutes and four minutes before the scheduled start, both windward gate devices are reliable and the TWS measured at any time (not necessarily the same time) on both windward gate devices falls outside the permitted TWS range.

36.4 If at any time any condition in 36.3 is met, the Regatta Director shall reset the start of the wind measurement period and delay the scheduled start time accordingly.

36.5 ***[Note: Article deleted with effect from 20 September 2024]*** **SEE PROTOCOL AMENDMENT 16**

37. Racing Areas and courses

37.1 Announcement of Racing Areas and course details

(a) ACE (in consultation with the Regatta Director if appointed) shall announce the Racing Areas for the AC37 Events as follows:
  (i) for the Preliminary Regattas, by no later than the date that is two months before the first scheduled race of each Preliminary Regatta; and
  (ii) for the CSS and the Match, by no later than 30 November 2022;
(b) The course details for each AC37 Event shall be included in the applicable Sailing Instructions issued by the Regatta Director under Article 35.

37.2 Course configuration

Unless otherwise agreed by COR/D and stated in the Sailing Instructions, the course used for all races in AC37 Events shall comprise a windward and leeward configuration with an upwind start.

37.3 Changes to Racing Areas

Once announced, COR/D may subsequently agree to amend any Racing Area following consultation with the Regatta Director provided that the Racing Area for the Semi-Finals and Final of the CSS will always be the same as the Racing Area for the Match. The Sailing Instructions shall be promptly updated to reflect any agreed changes.

37.4 Equal access to course

(a) During the Semi-Finals and Final stages of the CSS, access to the course at the Venue of the Match shall be managed by the Regatta Director to ensure that, during the time of the day when racing in the Match is scheduled, access shall be shared equally between the Challengers and the Defender with the intention that if either has exclusive access then the other is allowed the same period of exclusive access.
(b) On the CSS Final race days this will achieved by the Defender being granted periods of access inside the closed race course before, between and after the CSS races (some of these periods may be non-exclusive) as specified by the Regatta Director after consultation with COR/D. **SEE PROTOCOL AMENDMENT 16**
(c) The Regatta Director may refuse access to the course under this Article 37.4 if, in his reasonable opinion, racing would be delayed, interrupted or cancelled as a result of allowing such access.
(d) The Regatta Director, after consultation with the Jury, shall determine appropriate sanctions for any breach of this Article 37.4 by any Competitor.

38. Participation in other regattas

Competitors and/or their respective Sailing Teams shall not participate, without the prior written approval of ACE (not to be unreasonably withheld), in any non-Event regatta for foiling monohull yachts that is presented in a way that is or could be perceived to be an ambush of any Event, or that is presented or held out to be part of any Event, or infringes the trademark rights of ACPI (and Competitors shall cooperate with ACPI in enforcing ACPI's rights on any non-Event regatta organiser). **SEE PROTOCOL AMENDMENT 8**

39. Sports betting

Competitors, their Team Members and all event officials engaged by or on behalf of ACE shall not participate (either directly or indirectly) at any time in any sports betting or related activity with respect to the whole or any part of AC37, including:

(a) accepting a bribe or agreeing to improperly influence the result, progress, conduct or any other aspect of a race in any Event; and/or

(b) placing, accepting, laying or otherwise entering into any bet (or soliciting, inducing and/or authorising another party to do so) with any other party in relation to the result, progress, conduct or any other aspect of any race in any Event.

40. Meteorological and Oceanographic Data

40.1 Common weather programme

Subject to Article 19(b), COR/D will, as soon as practicable, implement a common programme for the collection of wind, sea state and associated data in the Racing Area of the Match. Such information shall be made available to all Competitors on a shared cost basis as set out in Article 19.

40.2 Restrictions on collection of data

As a consequence of the above and in order to save campaign costs, Competitors shall not (and will not procure others on their behalf to) collect weather, wind, sea state or sea current instrument data relevant to Match Venue after it has been announced, except:

(a) as explicitly permitted in the Class Rules;
(b) from personal observation from land or on the water, where personal observation excludes the use of any measurement equipment such as handheld anemometers, GPS or floating markers, and excludes timing or measuring drift;
(c) for data that is publicly and readily available to all Competitors, the subscription to which costs less than US$50 per month;
(d) from wind measuring equipment on a crane situated at or adjacent to a Competitor's Team Base; or
(e) when the data becomes available through competition in an event or regatta organised by a recognised yacht club, using World Sailing rules and in yachts of classes existing as at 17 March 2021 (such as TP52's or F50s/Sail GP), or yachts which held valid IRC or ORC certificates as at 17 March 2021, or other rating yachts from time to time approved by COR/D.

In this case, Competitor's Team Members can participate in these events, and use wind data measured and collected on the competing yacht's instrument system, along with data available to all competitors from the race organisers, providing that data is used only for the purpose of that specific regatta by the Team Member (i.e. it is not used or distributed more widely by the Competitor, and is not transferred to any devices that are used within the Competitor's America's Cup campaign). This specific permission only applies for data collected for a period of five days prior to the morning of the scheduled first race, until the end of the final scheduled race. No other wind data collected during this period can be used unless it is publicly available. **SEE PROTOCOL AMENDMENT 7**

40.3 Data used for forecasts and modelling

Competitors may only obtain forecasts, models and/or model generated data relating to weather, wind, sea state or sea current data relevant to any Racing Area provided that:

(a) all measured data used is collected in compliance with this Article 40; and,
(b) this Article 40 shall not restrict the Competitors' right to purchase and use historic data relating to the Match Venue that is commercially available to the public and collected prior to the date which is six (6) months before the first scheduled race of the Match.

41. Reconnaissance

41.1 Joint Recon Programme

(a) As a campaign cost reduction measure, COR/D has mutually agreed to cooperatively implement a centralised reconnaissance programme for all teams for the reconnaissance of all Competitors' AC75 Yachts, AC40 Yachts and LEQ12 yachts including both on-land and on-water imagery (the "**Joint Recon Programme**"). The operational conditions for the Joint Recon Programme are specified in the AC Technical Regulations.
(b) The intent of the Joint Recon Programme is to reduce the costs that Competitors would otherwise be spending on their individual recon activities and to help grow the audience of the America's Cup in the lead up to and during the AC37 Events.
(c) Such Joint Recon Programme shall be made available to all Competitors on a shared cost basis and each Competitor will be required to provide a suitable support boat (capable of keeping up with an AC75 Yacht) for use by the relevant recon team assigned to that relevant Competitor.
(d) It is intended that such content will be made available to AC Media who will exploit such content in the manner set out in Part I of this Protocol in order to provide updates to the general public as to what developments each Competitor is pursuing. AC Media may also make requests for specific photographs, videos or interviews with Team Members.

41.2 Prohibited activities

Competitors are prohibited from engaging in any of the following in an attempt to gain information about another Competitor:

(a) any on-water and on-land reconnaissance outside of the Joint Recon Programme, except as permitted under the AC Technical Regulations;
(b) any illegal act;
(c) the use of eavesdropping devices;
(d) accessing correspondence, electronic communications or communication frequencies or channels allocated to other Competitors or used by other Competitors via a commercial service provider;
(e) the unauthorised entry into any computer system;
(f) interception of information emanating from telemetry, instruments, computers, etc.;
(g) without the prior consent of the affected Competitor, use of satellites, drones, aircraft, and/or other means of flight to observe or record from above another Competitor's yacht;
(h) the acceptance of any information from a third party that a Competitor is prohibited from obtaining directly; and
(i) obtaining positional data about another Competitor's yacht via electronic means, other than from publicly available sources.

41.3 Non-interference

(a) Except when participating in any Official Training, Official Practice or as part of any Event (or other permitted regatta), or with the prior consent of the affected Competitor, Competitors shall not intentionally, irresponsibly or unreasonably impede, disrupt or otherwise interfere with another Competitor's yacht when such yacht is sailing, whether or not for the purpose of observing it in an attempt to gain information about the affected (or any other) Competitor.
(b) ACE, in consultation with the Regatta Director, shall issue a safety protocol governing the operation of all Competitors' support boats within a Racing Area. Such safety protocol will include a penalty regime which shall apply for any breaches of that protocol and will involve instant fines for minor infringements and the right for ACE to apply to the Arbitration Panel to seek a further penalty for more serious infringements, including points deductions where appropriate.

41.4 Accredited media

The terms of this Article 41 shall not restrict the lawful and permitted activities of any media organisation/representative accredited by AC Media, provided such media organisation/representative shall not, other than by way of public dissemination through a Media Organisation, provide to any Competitor any information that a Competitor is prohibited from obtaining directly.

PART G: REGATTA OFFICIALS

42. Appointment of Regatta Officials

42.1 Appointment of Regatta Director

COR/D shall jointly appoint (and may agree to remove and replace) an independent Regatta Director for AC37 (the "**Regatta Director**"). The Regatta Director shall be engaged by ACE on behalf of COR/D and will perform the functions set out in more detail in Article 43.1.

42.2 Appointment of other Regatta Officials

Additional Regatta Officials for AC37 shall be jointly appointed by COR/D (who may agree to remove and replace such officials) and engaged by ACE on behalf of COR/D as follows:

(a) a Measurement Committee, which shall include a chief measurer and not less than two (2) other members, as further described in Article 44.1;
(b) a Rules Committee, which shall comprise three (3) members, as further described in Article 44.2;
(c) Umpires (to be appointed in consultation with World Sailing) as may be reasonably required to umpire the races comprising each Event, including a chief Umpire, as further described in Article 45;
(d) a World Sailing International Jury (to be appointed in consultation with World Sailing) comprised of Umpires who have been appointed under Article 42.2(c) above; and
(e) such other regatta officials and/or staff requested by the Regatta Director as are reasonably necessary in meeting the purpose and intent set out in the Introduction of this Protocol.

42.3 Terms of engagement for Regatta Officials

The structure and terms of engagement of the Regatta Officials shall be agreed between ACE and COR/D, taking into account the overriding principles of the qualification, experience and capability of each candidate, independence of the Regatta Officials, cost efficient management, reporting and compliance, and relevant jurisdictional issues. ACE shall enter into an agreement with the relevant Regatta Official, subject to any amendments requested by the Regatta Official and approved by COR/D.

42.4 Neutral management

The Regatta Officials, while complying with the Rules shall not unreasonably favour the interests of any Competitor over another.

43. Regatta Director

43.1 Role of the Regatta Director

The Regatta Director shall:

(a) be responsible for the conduct of all racing at each Venue for each Event, including the management of the Racing Areas, course and Flag Areas;
(b) be responsible for ensuring that all races at the Venue for each Event are conducted in a professional and timely manner pursuant the terms of the Rules;
(c) be responsible for the co-ordination of the activities of the other Regatta Officials to run the races comprising each Event in a professional manner that is consistent with the purpose and intent of this Protocol and with the obligations and commercial requirements of ACE;
(d) co-operate with ACE on all issues such as schedules for Events, management of the Racing Area, the course and/or the Flag Areas and other commercial requirements;
(e) in consultation with COR/D, issue (and/or amend) the Sailing Instructions for the Preliminary Regattas, the CSS and the Match;
(f) have the authority to publish regulations regarding the conduct of racing and the management of the Racing Area, the course and/or the Flag Areas, provided that such regulations are consistent with the terms of the Rules, which regulations shall be binding on Competitors in accordance with their terms;
(g) be responsible for the management and monitoring of the permitted and prohibited sailing by Competitors referred to in Article 24.2 including the authority:
    (i) in consultation with COR/D, to publish regulations including compliance guidelines, which shall be binding on Competitors and a schedule of fines for minor breaches of the published regulations; and
    (ii) to apply to the Arbitration Panel to assess the penalty for a breach by a Competitor which the Regatta Director considers, in his sole discretion, to be more than minor; and
(h) have all such other powers as may be necessary or appropriate to fulfil his responsibilities as prescribed in and/or contemplated by the Rules,
(i) be responsible for receiving and assessing reports from the Measurement Committee of non-compliance with the AC75 Class Rule or the AC Technical Regulations;

(i) by a yacht after its Measurement Certificate has been withdrawn and then acting in accordance with AC Technical Regulations 6.4 and 6.5; or
(ii) by a Competitor whilst racing or otherwise and then acting in accordance with Article 47.3, **SEE PROTOCOL AMENDMENT 15**

provided always that the Regatta Director shall have no authority and/or jurisdiction in respect of the separate responsibilities of ACE, the Measurement Committee, the Rules Committee, the Umpires, the Jury and/or the Arbitration Panel as prescribed in and/or contemplated by the Rules.

44. Measurement Committee and Rules Committee

44.1 Role of the Measurement Committee

The Measurement Committee shall be solely and exclusively responsible for all matters relating to:

(a) the measurement of AC75 Yachts under the AC75 Class Rule;
(b) the issue or withdrawal of an AC75 class certificate for an AC75 Yacht in accordance with the requirement of the AC75 Class Rule following the procedures set out in the AC75 Class Rule;
(c) the measurement of AC40 Yachts under the AC40 Class Rule;
(d) the issue or withdrawal of an AC40 class certificate for an AC40 Yacht in accordance with the requirement of the AC40 Class Rule following the procedures set out in the AC40 Class Rule;
(e) the certification of compliance with the construction in country requirement and issue the relevant Constructed in the Country Certificate; and
(f) the monitoring of Competitors whilst racing for compliance with the AC75 Class Rule and the AC Technical Regulations;
(g) the notification to the Regatta Director of a Competitor's non-compliance with the AC75 Class Rule or the AC Technical Regulations;
(h) any other matter which it is given jurisdiction under this Protocol, the AC40 Class Rule and/or the AC75 Class Rule. **SEE PROTOCOL AMENDMENT 15**

44.2 Role of the Rules Committee

The Rules Committee shall be solely and exclusively responsible for all matters relating to:

(a) the interpretation of the Class Rules as applicable, according to the provisions of the relevant Class Rule;
(b) the determination of whether or not any yacht constitutes a Surrogate Yacht, based on information provided by the Measurement Committee; and

(c) to resolve any other matter which it is given jurisdiction under the Protocol and/or the Class Rules.

44.3 Interpretations

Unless otherwise stated in the Class Rules, the Rules Committee shall have no authority to amend any of the Rules but may issue interpretations of the Class Rules according to the procedures that will be detailed in the Class Rules.

44.4 Delegation

One or more measurers or rules officials may carry out measurement, inspection or other duties on behalf of the Measurement Committee or Rules Committee (as applicable).

44.5 Costs

Members of the Rules Committee and Measurement Committee shall be engaged by ACE on an agreed retainer basis. In addition, they shall be paid an agreed hourly rate for their services involving the interpretation of the Class Rules or other tasks requested by the Competitors. The retainer and hourly fees shall be agreed between ACE (on behalf of COR/D) and the relevant committee. The hourly fees incurred shall be recovered on a user pays basis from the Competitors, as ordered by the Rules Committee.

44.6 Jurisdiction

(a) The Rules Committee and the Measurement Committee will, within their respective jurisdictions, both be responsible for determining whether a yacht meets the relevant Class Rule.
(b) If there is any conflict between the Rules Committee and the Measurement Committee in relation to jurisdiction or otherwise it will be the sole responsibility of the Rules Committee to determine the matter.

45. Umpires and Jury

The Umpires and Jury shall be responsible for:

(a) umpiring the racing in each of the Events, with primary responsibility to make the on-water decisions about infringements under the Racing Rules; and
(b) interpreting the Racing Rules with any such interpretation requiring the agreement of the chief Umpire and two other Umpires; and
(c) undertaking the actions for which the Jury has responsibility for under the AC Technical Regulations and Article 47.3. **SEE PROTOCOL AMENDMENT 15**

46. World Sailing

(a) ACE shall conclude any necessary arrangements with World Sailing for the sanctioning of AC37, consistent with the purpose and intent of this Protocol. Costs of such sanctioning are included within the Entry Fees.
(b) The terms of this Protocol shall prevail over the terms of any arrangements with World Sailing and, other than the Regatta Officials (if applicable), no staff and/or appointed representatives of ACE shall be subject to any present or future rules, regulations or other jurisdiction of World Sailing and/or its member national authorities for or in respect of the whole or any part of AC37.

47. Rules and Decisions

47.1 Rules

The Regatta Director, Measurement Committee, Rules Committee, Umpires and the Jury shall comply with the Rules to the extent required for them to perform their respective obligations under this Protocol.

47.2 Decisions

All decisions of the Regatta Director, Measurement Committee, Rules Committee, Umpires and the Jury that are taken in good faith within their proper authority and/or jurisdiction as prescribed in and/or contemplated by the Rules in each case shall not be subject to any review or appeal unless otherwise expressly provided in this Protocol.

47.3 Non-Compliance by a Competitor with the Class Rule

On receiving a report from the Measurement Committee of a Competitor's non-compliance with the AC75 Class Rule or the AC Technical Regulations whilst racing or otherwise, but which does not involve the compliance of a yacht or the validity of its Measurement Certificate, the Regatta Director shall review the Measurement Committee report and request further investigation if necessary. As a result, if the Regatta Director determines the non-compliance is:

(a) unintentional and unlikely to have impacted the outcome of a race, the Regatta Director may give a warning or refer it to the Jury which, in consultation with the Regatta Director, may impose a fine on the Competitor; or
(b) intentional, or could have impacted the outcome of a race, refer it to the Jury which, in consultation with the Regatta Director, may:
    (i) disqualify the yacht from the race or races during which the non-compliance occurred, but such disqualification shall be limited to the races in which that

yacht competed on the day the Measurement Committee report was received; or

(ii) if the non-compliance does not occur whilst racing impose one or more penalty points which shall be deducted from the Competitors score in the AC37 Event Stage in respect of which the non-compliance occurs. **SEE PROTOCOL AMENDMENT 15**

PART H: COMMERCIAL RIGHTS

48. Overview

48.1 Commercial rights of ACE

To allow ACE to raise funds to organise, deliver and manage AC37 and to reduce the financial risks on ACE, all commercial rights in and in relation to the whole and/or any part of AC37 on a worldwide basis and any revenues or other value-in-kind arising from the exploitation thereof shall be vested in ACE in accordance with the terms of this Protocol and shall be managed by ACE pursuant to Article 3.1 and this Part H. Such commercial rights shall include (without limitation):

(a) sponsorship and other rights of association in connection with the whole and/or any part of AC37;
(b) broadcast production and distribution and other media rights in connection with the Events (including still images, moving images, gaming, data, telemetry and animations in whatever medium or technology);
(c) Event branding and advertising;
(d) Event merchandising and brand licensing (in coordination with ACPI);
(e) Event hospitality and related consumer and corporate experiences;
(f) Event ticketing, entertainment (including public screenings, live performances and any concert series);
(g) food and beverage concessions;
(h) host venue rights in connection with the whole and/or any part of each Event (in conjunction with the Defender);
(i) super yacht berthage and associated services; and
(j) such other commercial rights and fundraising opportunities in connection with the whole and/or any part of AC37 as ACE may identify from time to time, including those commercial rights and opportunities in line with recent editions of the America's Cup.

Nothing in this Article 48.1 (or otherwise in this Protocol) shall affect the rights and/or obligations conferred or imposed by the constitution of ACPI.

48.2 Granting of rights by Competitors

Each Competitor hereby transfers to the maximum extent allowed by law, the commercial rights related to their participation in the Events to ACE, in order to allow for the smooth and efficient exercise of the above commercial rights by ACE.

48.3 Commercial rights of Competitors

Each Competitor shall have the right to exploit any and all commercial rights, on a worldwide basis and any revenues or other value-in-kind arising from or in respect of its participation as a Competitor on and subject to the terms of the Rules. This does not include the commercial rights pursuant to Article 48.1. Such commercial rights shall include (without limitation):

(a) sponsorship and other rights of association in connection with the whole and/or any part of the Competitor;
(b) media rights in connection with the Competitor's campaign for AC37 (including still images, moving images, audio files, electronic print, data and animations in whatever medium or technology), but not (unless approved by ACE in writing in advance acting reasonably) in connection with the Events or otherwise in conflict with Event-related activities;
(c) the Competitor's branded merchandising and brand licensing;
(d) the Competitor's hospitality and related consumer and corporate experiences;
(e) the Competitor's promotional and public relations events which do not conflict with or otherwise undermine Event-related activities;
(f) the Competitor's public entertainment activities which do not conflict with or otherwise undermine Event-related activities; and
(g) such other commercial rights and fundraising opportunities in connection with the whole and/or any part of the Competitor's team activities as may be identified from time to time;

in each case being on and subject to the terms of the Rules.

48.4 Event title sponsor conflicts

In order to avoid any conflict of interest, no Competitor shall be entitled to engage as a sponsor, or advertise or promote an association with, a title/naming sponsor of any of the AC37 Events (for example by the inclusion of such sponsor's name in the name of a team, yacht or other similar promotion) without the prior approval in writing of ACE. The giving of any such approval shall be at the sole discretion of ACE, having taken into account whatever matters it thinks fit, and may include conditions to ensure that the title/naming sponsor's association with an individual Competitor does not either conflict with the contractual rights and responsibilities of its event sponsorship or in any way affect the fairness of competition or the promotion of the event for all other Competitors.

49. Branding and Advertising

49.1 Title/presenting sponsors

In the event that ACE announces a title or presenting sponsor for the whole or any part or parts of any Event, Competitors (and their Team Members) and Regatta Officials shall always use and reference the proper official title and official logo in each case as prescribed by ACE.

49.2 Brand Manual

(a) Branding and Advertising, for the whole or any part of any Event, including, without limitation, on Competitors and their Team Members, Regatta Officials, AC75 Yachts, AC40 Yachts, support boats, official boats, Team Bases and clothing, shall always comply and respect the brand manual (the "**Brand Manual**") which will be published as soon as practical but no later than 28 February 2023 by ACE. **SEE PROTOCOL AMENDMENT 8**
(b) Such Brand Manual may be updated by ACE from time to time in consultation with the Competitor Forum.

49.3 Branding on Yachts

Subject to Article 49.4 below, Competitors may display Advertising or other branding anywhere on their AC75 Yachts and/or AC40 Yachts, except:

(a) in the areas reserved for the official logo of the AC37 Events or title sponsor of the Events, marked "ACE area" as prescribed in the Class Rules and confirmed in the Brand Manual;
(b) in the areas on the mainsail marked "country flag of Competitor" in the Brand Manual, where each Competitor shall display the national flag of the country of the yacht club that the Competitor represents, to be included on both sides of the mainsail, in such form as prescribed in the Class Rules and confirmed in the Brand Manual; and
(c) that no AC75 Yacht shall have a name that constitutes Advertising, unless such name is approved by ACE in advance.
(d) from 29 July 2024 until the date of the last race of the Match, the Official Event Logos as prescribed in the Branding Manual (updated by Event Authority Notice No. 38) shall be displayed on the mainsails and jibs of an AC75 Yacht at all times whilst sailing including training, participating in TV testing, Official Practice or Official Training, or racing in the AC37 Events. **SEE PROTOCOL AMENDMENT 13**

49.4 Branding restrictions

No Competitor may display as Advertising or other branding anywhere on its yachts, on the clothing of its Team Members and/or otherwise in any Venue:

(a) any name, logo, brand, products and/or services relating to the tobacco industry;
(b) any name, logo, brand, products and/or services of a Media Organisation (unless otherwise with the prior approval of ACE not to be unreasonably withheld); and/or
(c) any offensive, obscene, abusive, defamatory and/ or illegal image or other content.

Additionally, should the advertising of a specific product category significantly limit and/or jeopardize the TV and media coverage of the Events - or be in breach with local applicable regulations - then ACE shall have the authority at its sole discretion to require the relevant Competitor(s) to remove such advertising.

49.5 Team Member clothing

(a) Subject always to the terms of Article 49.4 and save in respect of the Youth and Women's AC Regattas for which Article 49.5(b) below shall apply, each Competitor may display Advertising on the clothing of its Team Members and shall display on one
    (1) sleeve of all Team Member clothing a Challenger or Defender patch with the Event logo for AC37 and with the national flag and burgee of the challenging yacht club in the form and with free space around the patch as shall be prescribed in the Brand Manual;
(b) The team clothing (including crew helmets and caps) of each Competitor for the Youth and Women's AC Regattas (and any branding, colour, design scheme and the display of an Event patch and/or Advertising thereon) shall comply with specifications prescribed in the Brand Manual.

50. Special Events

50.1 Organisation of Special Events

ACE has the exclusive right to organise and manage the following Special Events:

(a) formal presentation of the Competitors' yachts and crew at the beginning of each Event;
(b) public display of Competitors' yachts at specific locations and times during each Event;
(c) opening and closing ceremonies for each Event;

(d) press conferences comprising more than one (1) Competitor during each Event;
(e) Event-related social events;
(f) Event-related prize giving ceremonies; and
(g) other Event-related special events as may reasonably be advised by ACE,

unless otherwise agreed by ACE. ACE may delegate by agreement the organisation and management of Special Events to third parties, including Competitors, sponsors and other commercial partners.

50.2 Mandatory participation

All Competitors are required to participate in Special Events as prescribed by ACE with at least three (3) days prior notice, with the number and identity of their Team Members to be reasonably specified by ACE in consultation with the Competitor Forum. If for any reason the three (3) days prior notice is unable to be given, then Competitors shall only be expected to use reasonable efforts to participate in that particular Special Event.

50.3 Calendar of Special Events

(a) To prevent conflicts, ACE will publish and keep updated a calendar of Special Events. Competitors shall advise ACE of any significant event they intend to host, and shall not schedule any events that will conflict with any Special Events.
(b) Competitors shall only be required to use reasonable efforts to attend events which are added to the calendar of Special Events on less than three (3) clear days' notice.

51. Team Bases

51.1 Overview

Each Competitor shall occupy a Team Base in a temporary space allocated by ACE, from which each Competitor shall conduct its sailing operations at the Venue of each Event for the duration of each Event (dates as prescribed by ACE). Team Bases may not be of equal size or prominence, and some facilities may be required to be shared.

51.2 Allocation

Team Bases shall be allocated for each Venue in the following order of priority:

(a) the Defender;
(b) the Challenger of Record; and

(c) one base for each of the remaining Challengers in the order in which their challenges were accepted by the Defender in accordance with the list published pursuant to Article 13.4.

51.3 Lease and/or Licence

(a) Where required by ACE, a Competitor shall enter into a lease and/or licence agreement with ACE or the relevant Host City prior to taking possession of the temporary space allocated for its Team Base in any Venue. Such lease and/or licence will set out the terms and conditions under which each Competitor will occupy their Team Base, including any fee to be paid by each Competitor.
(b) If practical, ACE shall use reasonable endeavours to procure that applicable rental payments or licence fees to be paid by Competitors are secured at a discounted rate, based on the prevailing market rate applicable to the relevant site before any development by the Competitors.

51.4 Construction

Unless otherwise agreed by ACE in writing, Competitors shall be responsible to organise, manage and meet all costs of construction of their facilities, as follows:

(a) all Team Bases shall comply with the architectural guidelines to be advised by ACE or the Host City, including guidelines regarding height, construction materials, impact on surrounding areas and overall exterior appearance, and the positioning of piles and floating docks on any water space;
(b) unless otherwise provided under the relevant lease or licence agreement specified in Article 51.3, each Competitor shall dismantle all improvements and/or installations made by or on behalf of the Competitor in the location of its Team Base or otherwise within any Venue within of the later of ninety (90) days after the last race of the Match and the relevant date for such action in the relevant lease or licence agreement; and
(c) each Competitor shall restore the area to the state and condition it was in prior to any improvements and/or installations made by or on behalf of that Competitor.

51.5 Occupation through the Match

Until the conclusion of the last race of the Match, all Competitors shall:

(a) continue to occupy and operate their Team Base in the Match Venue; and
(b) not disassemble, dismantle or pack up their Team Base, AC75 Class Yacht, support vessels and/or other assets and equipment in any area visible to the public.

51.6 Safety of Batteries

(a) Any lithium-ion or lithium polymer yacht batteries brought on to a Team Base must be stored and charged within a commercially supplied fire-safe cabinet designed for the purpose of storing and charging lithium batteries. The cabinet shall be:
   (i) appropriate for the energy capacity and quantity of batteries stored or charged within it; and
   (ii) approved by ACE, acting under the guidance of a battery supplier or other person who has relevant expertise.
(b) From the date of the Protocol amendment incorporating this requirement, each Competitor shall endeavour to source such a cabinet as soon as possible and shall place an order for the supply of a suitable cabinet within two weeks. Until such a cabinet is obtained, Competitors may continue to store and charge batteries in a secure location and shall ensure adequate monitoring systems are in place.
(c) Within this Article, a *yacht battery* is:
   (i) any Epsilor battery, whether supplied, required or otherwise, used on an AC75, AC40 or other vessel;
   (ii) any other battery with an energy capacity exceeding 100Wh, unless exempted by paragraph 51.6 (d).
(d) The following batteries are exempt from the requirements of this Article:
   (i) Batteries supplied with, or as accessories to unmodified commercial products, such as cars, e-bikes, scooters and drones;
   (ii) Batteries installed in powered vessels that have been built to meet the safety criteria of CE, Lloyds, Veritas, DNV, RINA or other recognised standards body. **SEE PROTOCOL AMENDMENT 10 AND AMENDMENT 14**

52. Signage

52.1 Team Base brand guidelines

All branding / signage on or within Team Bases shall comply with the Brand Manual.

52.2 Flags on Team Bases

Each Competitor shall display at their Team Base throughout each Event the national flag of the country of their challenging yacht club in accordance with the Brand Manual.

52.3 Flags on support boats

Each Competitor shall display throughout each Event on each of their support boats and spectator boats the national flag of the country of their challenging yacht club in accordance with the Brand Manual.

53. Merchandising

53.1 Venue merchandising

(a) Only ACE's approved retailers and concessionaires are authorised to carry on any retailing or merchandising activities at any Venue.
(b) ACE shall ensure that the facility selling team merchandise of Competitors shall be afforded a prominent location and presence within each Venue.
(c) ACE's appointed retailers and concessionaires shall be entitled to sell team merchandise for each Competitor and Competitors shall ensure that they or their merchandising suppliers sell their team merchandise to ACE's appointed retailers and concessionaires at favourable prices and terms to be agreed between the parties.
(d) Competitors shall use reasonable endeavours to ensure sufficient quantities of its team merchandise are produced to meet ACE's retailers' reasonable requirements.
(e) ACE's appointed retailers and concessionaires shall endeavour to stock a representative selection of each Competitor's team merchandise.

53.2 Intellectual property

Competitors shall give consent and shall procure written consent from the owners of all trademarks and other intellectual property used in or depicted on their team merchandising so as to permit the sale by ACE and its appointed retailers and concessionaires of such merchandising.

53.3 Promotions

Competitors shall not distribute promotional products or samples in any Venue without the prior written approval of ACE (not to be unreasonably withheld).

53.4 Restrictions

No Competitor shall use in its merchandising any image taken of racing during any Event which depicts any other Competitor unless with the prior written approval of ACE, except where such use is incidental and is less than twenty per cent (20%) of the total content of the product.

54. Entertainment

ACE shall have the exclusive right to organise and manage all public entertainment at each Venue. ACE may exercise this right in any manner at its sole discretion, including by contracting the organisation, management and provision of public entertainment at the Venues to third parties.

55. Security

Subject to and in full compliance with the laws and/or other lawful directives of the competent (relevant) government authorities, Competitors (and their respective Team Members (as applicable)) and all Regatta Officials shall comply with security measures adopted by ACE for or in respect of the whole or any part or parts of AC37. Competitors shall assist security personnel appointed by ACE and/or provided by the Host City. Competitors shall be responsible for the security of their Team Bases, their competing yachts, support boats, spectator boats and all other equipment and assets of the Competitor and their respective Team Members (as applicable).

56. Air Space

Subject to and in full compliance with the laws and/or other lawful directives of the competent (relevant) government authorities, all air space above each Venue during each Event shall be under the control and direction of ACE. Competitors and their sponsors or other commercial partners or authorised agents shall not contest or use the air space for any purpose without the prior approval of ACE.

57. Water Space

57.1 Control of water space

Subject to and in full compliance with the laws and/or other lawful directives of the competent (relevant) government authorities, the Racing Area at each Event shall be under the control and direction of ACE. ACE shall delegate its control of the Racing Area to the Regatta Director.

57.2 Spectator vessels

ACE shall optimize the opportunities for accredited spectator vessels in the Racing Area during Events, with priority to a limited number of nominated Competitor supporters, ACE and its commercial partners and then the competing Competitors. Without the prior approval of ACE, Competitors shall not provide spectator vessel services to the general public at any Venue during any Event.

58. Team Information

Each Competitor shall timely provide ACE with such information regarding the Competitor and its Team Members as ACE may reasonably request.

59. Anti-ambush obligations

(a) A Competitor (and each of their Team Members) must not engage in any form of unauthorised promotional, advertising or commercial activity ("**Ambush Marketing**") which:

    (i) associates a commercial brand with the Events (as opposed to the Competitor's participation in the Events); or
    (ii) has the effect, in the reasonable opinion of ACE, of conferring the status of a commercial partner of the Events on a person who is not a commercial partner of the Events.

(b) Each Competitor agrees that in participating in AC37:
    (i) it will use reasonable endeavours to eliminate or neutralise any Ambush Marketing, including in respect of any brands or logos of a third party that is not a commercial partner of the Events or any Competitor and is displayed during the Events; and
    (ii) when it becomes aware of any Ambush Marketing, it will consult with and provide reasonable assistance to ACE in taking all necessary steps to eliminate or neutralise such Ambush Marketing.

PART I: MEDIA RIGHTS

60. ACE Media Rights

60.1 Event-related media rights

(a) Pursuant to Article 3.2(b)(iii) of this Protocol, ACE will be responsible for the development, protection, management and exploitation of the media rights related to AC37 and the Events.

(b) Accordingly, all rights in and to any audio, visual and/or digital content and data collected by or on behalf of ACE during the course of or in connection with the whole or any part or parts of the Events or the lead up to the Events (including any still and moving, virtual or digital images and any content generated by other technologies) shall vest solely and exclusively in ACE which shall, at its sole discretion, be entitled to use, assign, transfer, licence and/or otherwise exploit any such rights in and to the applicable content and data.

(c) ACE will establish a media division consisting of independent contractors appointed by ACE ("**AC Media**") who will be responsible for exercising ACE's media rights and responsibilities under this Protocol, including the delivery of the broadcast and media production (including the race management system), social media and other media related activities for AC37, and having the responsibility to deal with each Competitor on media matters in an independent and confidential manner vis a vis all other Competitors and ACE itself.

(d) As at the date of this Protocol, it is intended that AC Media shall exploit such media rights through the production of global broadcast feeds, magazine programmes, preview and review shows, behind the scenes documentary programmes, clips and features, digital and social media content and news content.

AC Media may appoint one or more production and distribution partners to assist with its delivery of such AC37 media coverage.

(e) To assist AC Media with the production of the broadcast and media coverage of AC37, Competitors shall:

  (i) provide access as reasonably required by AC Media, following consultation with the Competitor, for AC Media and/or its licensees or authorised agents to take or record still and/or moving images of Competitors, including (but not limited to) its representative team training and sailing, and conducting interviews with its Team Members, during or outside the periods of Events; and

  (ii) carry and allow the unhindered operation of the television and technical equipment on board their AC75 Yachts, AC40 Yachts, support vessels and crew as specified in Article 32.

(f) In addition, AC Media and its appointed production and distribution partners shall be given priority choice of location at all open media events and mixed zones organised by or hosted by any Competitor.

60.2 Releases

(a) Broadcasting and digital

  (i) All Competitors acknowledge, and shall (subject to applicable data privacy laws) obtain written acknowledgements and releases from all of their Team Members, sponsors, licensees and other commercial partners, that AC Media, its licensees and its authorised agents, including its authorised broadcasters and other content providers, shall be entitled, without payment of fees to any Person including Competitors or any of their Team Members, sponsors, licensees or other commercial partners, to reproduce, broadcast, transmit, print, publish and/or disseminate worldwide in any medium the names, logos, images, likenesses, voices and any data of Competitors, their yachts and other vessels, their Team Members, sponsors, licensees or other commercial partners and/or burgee for the purposes of broadcasting or otherwise transmitting the whole or any part or parts of any Event or Events in any medium, live or by way of delayed coverage, and in the distribution, exploitation, advertising and promotion of such coverage of the Event(s).

  (ii) AC Media may also include the names and/or logos of ACE's sponsors, licensees and/or other commercial partners within any Event-related broadcast or transmission.

(b) Promotion and advertising

  (i) All Competitors acknowledge, and shall obtain written acknowledgements and releases from all of their Team Members, sponsors, licensees and other commercial partners, that ACE and its authorised agents, sponsors, licensees, other commercial partners and any Host City, shall be entitled, without payment of fees to any Person including Competitors or any of their Team Members, sponsors, licensees and other commercial partners to reproduce, print, publish or disseminate worldwide in any medium the names, logos, images, likenesses and voices of Competitors, their yachts and other vessels, their Team Members, sponsors, licensees and other commercial partners and/or burgee within audio and/ or visual (still and/ or moving) images for the purposes of promoting and advertising the Event(s) and the official merchandising activities of ACE (and/or its appointed retailers, licensees and/or concessionaires) in connection with the whole or any part or parts of AC37, provided that neither ACE nor its authorised agents, sponsors, licensees, other commercial partners or Host Cities place an undue prominence on any single Competitor in connection therewith (except with the approval of such Competitor).

(ii) ACE may also include the names and/or logos of ACE's sponsors, licensees and/or other commercial partners in any of its promotion, advertising and merchandising.

(c) Biometric Data

(i) Competitors shall own all biometric data recorded in relation to Sailing Team members. Subject to compliance with applicable data privacy laws, Competitors shall make selected biometric performance data available free of charge to AC Media for use in global broadcast feeds, magazine programmes, preview and review shows, behind the scenes documentary programmes, clips and features, digital and social media content and news content. **SEE PROTOCOL AMENDMENT 8**

(ii) Competitors, ACE and AC Media shall enter into separate data sharing agreements governing the use and processing of Team Member personal data.

60.3 Media access restrictions

Except with the prior approval of AC Media in any case (which AC Media may grant or withhold at its sole discretion), a Competitor:

(a) shall not exclude any accredited media from any media event related to the whole or any part or parts of AC37;

(b) may not enter into any exclusive arrangement with any Media Organisation that has the effect of preventing access by any media authorised by AC Media;

(c) shall not provide or permit any media access (excluding AC Media and its appointed production partners) to its competing yacht (being a yacht participating in any given race day of an Event) and/or any of its crew and/or any of its other yachts, tenders and/or chase boats, during the period commencing thirty (30) minutes before the first scheduled race of each race day and ending thirty (30) minutes after the final scheduled race of that race day during any Event;

(d) shall not undertake any media activities that creates any scheduling or other conflict with any of AC Media's media, commercial and/or promotional activities; and

(e) shall not provide or permit media access to telemetry information of or related to its competing yacht or the competing yachts of any other Competitors on any race day during any Event.

60.4 Media Accreditation

AC Media will publish the procedures and conditions governing media access during the Events (the "**Media Accreditation Conditions**") by no later than the date that is three (3) months before the date of the first race of each AC37 Event.

60.5 Post-AC37

(a) Upon the date that is ninety (90) days following the final race of AC37, all such rights and related intellectual property that remain vested in, and are capable of being assigned by, AC Media (on behalf of ACE) at that time (including both physical and digital copies of any content), shall be assigned by AC Media (on behalf of ACE) to ACPI and shall subsequently form part of the property of the America's Cup to be held in trust for the benefit of all future trustees.

(b) Subject to Article 60.5(a), after a period of one month following the conclusion of the Match, each Competitor shall retain the right to use still and moving images of their participation in those events, provided such use is in a historical context only.

60.6 Obligations of AC Media

(a) AC Media shall act as neutral custodians of the America's Cup media channels and build awareness and exposure for all Competitors, partners and sponsors for the continued growth of the event and the sport of sailing.

(b) AC Media shall continue to cover all aspects of the Event, both on and off the water in a fair, accurate and balanced way.

(c) In performing activities pursuant to this Protocol, ACE shall procure that AC Media uses all reasonable efforts to ensure such activities do not:

    (i) hinder, interrupt or prevent Competitors, ACE, Regatta Officials and/or the Arbitration Panel in relation to their participation in AC37;

    (ii) damage the reputation of any Competitor (or its commercial partners), Team Members, ACE (or its commercial partners), Regatta Officials and/or the Arbitration Panel or otherwise; and/or

(iii) disclose or publish any Competitor information the disclosure or publication of which damages, or might reasonably be considered likely to damage, the competitive position of any Competitor in AC37. This restriction shall not apply to any information published as authorised by the Joint Recon Programme under Article 41.

61. Competitor Media Rights

61.1 Use by Competitors and their sponsors of still and/or moving images

(a) Competitors and their sponsors may use still and/or moving images of their own yachts and crews taken or recorded by them at any time, on and subject to the terms of this Protocol, in particular the restrictions contained in Article 61.2 below.
(b) Where any other Competitor or its yacht or Team Member also appear in such images, they shall first obtain the written approval of any other Competitor depicted, except where such appearance is incidental and is less than twenty per cent (20%) of the total image. Such approval is intended to also be the approval of all sponsors and suppliers of the relevant Competitor depicted in the approved image.
(c) Each Competitor may also submit requests to AC Media for the prior written approval by AC Media pursuant to Article 60.1 for any specific use by the Competitor on its own official Competitor platforms, on a royalty-free basis, of up to one hundred and twenty (120) seconds per day of still and/or moving images of its yacht and crew that have been recorded by or on behalf of AC Media. Prior to granting any approval AC Media may amend such terms and conditions of such use at its sole discretion.

61.2 Use of moving images recorded during the Racing Window

(a) In addition to AC Media and its authorised licensees, only a Competitor's internal media team ("**Competitor's Media Team**") may record moving images of their own yachts and crew racing during the time period commencing thirty (30) minutes before the first scheduled race and ending thirty (30) minutes after the final scheduled race of each race day during any Event (the "**Racing Window**").
(b) Except with the prior approval of AC Media, each Competitor shall ensure that all other media personnel that are contracted by or on behalf of or affiliated to any Competitor and/or their sponsors or other commercial partners shall not record any moving images during the Race Window.
(c) Competitors, their sponsors and other commercial partners may not without AC Media's prior written approval, sell, broadcast, stream or otherwise publicly distribute (or allow to be distributed) any moving images of any Competitor's yachts or crew recorded by the Competitor during the Racing Window.

(d) Each Competitor agrees to make available to AC Media (for use by AC Media and/or its broadcaster partners) any moving images of its or any other Competitor's yachts and/or crew recorded by the Competitor's Media Team during the Racing Window.

61.3 Not create misleading impression of status

All Competitors shall ensure their own use and the use by any of their sponsors or other commercial partners of any image does not create a misleading impression as to a sponsorship or association with any Event or Events. In particular, to prevent any misleading impression as to the status of the sponsor or other commercial partner, any Competitor's sponsor or commercial partner using Event-related images shall always include a clear statement as to its designation as sponsor or commercial partner of a particular Competitor.

61.4 Competitors' photographers

(a) Photographers contracted to provide photographic services to Competitors and/or their sponsors or other commercial partners must obtain accreditation from AC Media (on and subject to the Media Accreditation Conditions imposed by AC Media under Article 60.4) and will be bound at all times and comply with the provisions of such Media Accreditation Conditions.
(b) AC Media may withdraw the accreditation of a Competitor's photographer for failure to comply with the Media Accreditation Conditions imposed by AC Media, in which case such photographer shall not be further engaged by a Competitor at any Venue or in respect of any Event for the remainder of AC37.

61.5 Competitors' media units

(a) Except with the prior approval of AC Media, each Competitor shall ensure that both its own Competitor Media Team and all other media personnel contracted by or on behalf of or affiliated to any Competitor and/or their sponsors or other commercial partners:
   (i) shall obtain accreditation from AC Media (on and subject to the Media Accreditation Conditions imposed by AC Media under Article 60.4);
   (ii) shall not record any moving images of any racing during any Event from the air; and/or
   (iii) shall not record moving images anywhere within any Venue, except for:
      (A) images of its yachts and/or any of its crew and/or any of its other tenders and/or chase boats whilst afloat within the Venue on any day in which such yachts are not participating in an Event and/or at any time on an Event race day other than as is restricted pursuant to Article 61.2 above;

(B) within the Team Base of the Competitor for the purposes of its own team media and promotions; and/or

(C) within such designated areas of the Venue and at such times as may be permitted pursuant to the Media Accreditation Conditions imposed by AC Media (including, without limitation, at official press conferences and within the designated media mixed zone);

provided always that such media activities shall not create any scheduling or other conflict with any of AC Media's media, commercial and/or promotional activities.

(b) AC Media may withdraw the accreditation of any media personnel contracted by or on behalf of or affiliated to any Competitor and/or their sponsors or other commercial partners for failure by such party to comply with the above conditions or the Media Accreditation Conditions imposed by AC Media, in which case such media personnel shall not be further engaged by a Competitor or their respective sponsors or other commercial partners at any Venue or in respect of any Event for the remainder of AC37.

62. Media commitments and public appearances

62.1 Crew comments for broadcast

Competitors shall ensure that prior to and after racing in all Events, crew on their competing yachts shall be available to provide brief comments for the broadcast and other AC Media programming.

62.2 Penalty for profanity

In the event that a Team Member of a Competitor swears or undertakes any profane conduct that is captured on any live broadcast by AC Media's licensed broadcasters, AC Media will be entitled to seek reimbursement from that Competitor of up to one hundred per cent (100%) of any financial penalty imposed on AC Media by any of AC Media's licensed broadcaster(s) or other commercial partner. The amount shall be payable to AC Media and, if not timely paid, the Competitor shall forfeit the amount from its Performance Bond.

62.3 Media commitments and public appearances

(a) Competitors will be required to provide Team Members to attend certain Event related media commitments and public appearances at each AC37 Event. Such commitments may include pre and post-race public appearances within the Venue, official post-race press conferences and interviews with media at the media mixed zone.

(b) The precise media and public appearance requirements for each AC37 Event will be discussed by COR/D and published by ACE at the same time that the calendar of Special Events is issued under Article 50.3.
(c) AC Media may require specific Team Members from each Competitor to attend such public and media commitments, including sailing personnel who will be on-board each competing yacht that day or other personnel requested by the host broadcaster.
(d) Each Competitor will not make available in advance to the media any Team Members who will be attending a press conference arranged by AC Media on that day, unless approved by AC Media.

63. Official Documentary

(a) In order to broaden the reach and appeal of both the America's Cup and the sport of sailing, AC Media intends to produce a documentary programme and/or series and/or film(s) that will document the preparation and participation of each Competitor in the lead up to and during the AC37 Events (the "**Official Documentary**"). It is intended that the Official Documentary will provide audiences with behind the scenes access to each Competitor and allow the public to gain a better understanding of what goes into an America's Cup campaign.
(b) In order to provide for the production and distribution of the Official Documentary, each Competitor agrees that AC Media and its production partners, licensees and other commercial partners may use still and moving images of the whole or any part or parts of any Event and any other images taken by or on behalf of AC Media, its authorised broadcaster(s) and other media as well as the name, logo and yacht branding of any Competitor to compile, produce, market, sell and distribute the Official Documentary without restriction, except that it is understood that the Official Documentary shall be packaged and marketed as an AC37 and/or Event-specific product, either as an individual product or as a series.
(c) In the event that AC Media proceeds with the Official Documentary, it will appoint one or more third party production partners to implement the production and distribution of the Official Documentary. Such third parties will remain editorially neutral vis-à-vis AC Media and each Competitor, and the relevant agreements with such third parties will include customary protections to maintain the confidential information of each Competitor.
(d) AC Media shall in, consultation with COR/D, develop the terms and conditions under which its production partners shall be provided access to the Team Bases, Team Members and team equipment of each Competitor to enable AC Media, its production partners, licensees and other commercial partners to create and capture content that will be included in the Official Documentary. Such terms and conditions shall be contained within a Competitors Notice to be issued by COR/D by 31 October 2022 or such other date agreed by COR/D. It is also intended that

content generated as part of the Joint Recon Programme may be included in the Official Documentary. **SEE PROTOCOL AMENDMENT 5**

(e) Consultation with each Competitor as to the use of footage filmed through the access granted by that Competitor to a production partner appointed by AC Media will be undertaken in accordance with the Editorial Review Process specified in the Competitors Notice issued by COR/D under Article 63(d). AC Media will assign final editorial control over the Official Documentary to its appointed production partner.
SEE PROTOCOL AMENDMENT 6

(f) To protect the exclusivity of the Official Documentary, each Competitor agrees that it will not release or publish a similar 'behind the scenes' style documentary project until at least six (6) months following the last race of the Match, except with the prior written approval of AC Media. **SEE PROTOCOL AMENDMENT 6**

64. Electronic Games and Board Games

(a) All Competitors acknowledge and agree, that AC Media and its authorised agents, licensees and other commercial partners, shall be entitled, without payment of fees to any Person including Competitors or any of their Team Members, sponsors, licensees and other commercial partners, to reproduce, publish or disseminate worldwide the names, logos, images, likenesses and voices of Competitors, their yachts and other vessels, their Team Members, sponsors, licensees and other commercial partners and/or burgee within audio and/or visual (still and/or moving) images in order to produce, market, sell and distribute any digital, electronic, fantasy and/or board games of the America's Cup without restriction, provided that all such electronic or board games shall be packaged and marketed as an AC37 and/or Event-specific product, either as an individual product or as a series.

(b) Each Competitor agrees that it will not produce its own digital, electronic, fantasy and/or board game in connection with its involvement in AC37, except with the prior written approval of AC Media.

(c) In the Event that AC Media decides to produce any electronic or board game under Article 64(a), AC Media may reasonably require that each Competitor provides specific Team Members to participate in activations and promotions relating to the game (subject to payment of associated reasonable expenses).

65. Digital Media – Websites, Social Media and Applications

65.1 Intent of this Article

The intent of this Article 65 is to lay the framework for substantially growing the digital media audience of the Events and the Competitors for the benefit of:

(a) AC37 and the Events, including by ensuring better content for both the Official AC Website, the Official AC Social Media Channels and the Official AC App (together the "**AC Digital Channels**");
(b) the Competitors, including by increasing exposure for their own team content and enabling them and their commercial partners to connect with fans through customised digital campaigns on their own Official Competitor Websites; and
(c) future editions of the America's Cup and the sport of sailing.
To achieve the intentions outlined in this Article 65.1, AC Media will act as the neutral custodian of the AC Digital Channels during AC37 in a similar manner to how the channels were operated during AC36.

65.2 Official America's Cup Website

All Competitors acknowledge and agree that the sole and exclusive official website of AC37 shall be produced and hosted by or on behalf of AC Media under the domain www.americascup.com (the **Official AC Website**).

65.3 Official Competitors Websites

(a) Within three (3) months following the close of the Entry Period (or as reasonably required by AC Media in respect of any Late Challenger), each Competitor and its Team Members shall use an official Competitor website (each, an "**Official Competitor Website**") built and hosted by or on behalf of AC Media under the domain of the Official AC Website as their sole and exclusive digital presence.
(b) For the purposes of Article 65.3(a), "sole and exclusive digital presence" means any internet website (including blogs and online stores) and/or application software and/or any other digital technology platform, other than any presence on third party branded and operated social media platforms (such as Facebook, Twitter, Instagram, Flickr, Pinterest, TikTok, Snapchat and YouTube).
(c) Each Official Competitor Website will be operated as follows:
    (i) **URL access:** Each Official Competitor Website may also be initially accessed via an automatic redirection from the Competitor's own domain name, URL or proxy.
    (ii) **Blogs:** Each Official Competitor Website may have a blog or blog pages set up as sub-site(s) of its official website such that each sub-site is also hosted by and linked as a sub-site of the Official AC Website.

(iii) **Merchandise store:** Each Official Competitor Website may have an online merchandise store set up as sub-site of its official website such that the sub-site is also hosted by and linked as a sub-site of the Official AC Website.
(iv) **Content updates:** Each Competitor is responsible for timely updating all content on its Official Competitor Website via the content management system designated by AC Media, such that AC Media may elect to use and exploit (and reformat, where necessary) such content, including on the Official AC Website.
(v) **Space on americascup.com:** AC Media shall timely provide each Competitor with as much space within the Official AC Website as the Competitor reasonably requires for its Official Competitor Website.
(vi) **Branding and content:** Subject always to the terms of the Rules, each Competitor shall have exclusive control of both the branding and 'look and feel' of, and all content within, its Official Competitor Website within the Official AC Website.
(vii) **Analytics:** AC Media shall share analytics and relevant visitor / user data for each Official Competitor Website with that (but not with any other) Competitor in each case.
(viii) **Contribution to hosting and maintenance costs:** Each Competitor shall pay the website contribution fee to AC Media in accordance with Article 15.3(b).

65.4 Official America's Cup Social Media Channels

(a) All Competitors acknowledge and agree that the official social media channels for AC37 (the "**Official AC Social Media Channels**") shall be produced and hosted by or on behalf of AC Media on the following platforms: Facebook, YouTube, Instagram, Twitter, LinkedIn, TikTok and may include any other platforms not currently being utilised or not currently created.
(b) AC Media may (but will not be required) at its sole discretion share, post, publish or otherwise distribute any story, photo, video, news item or other digital media content about a Competitor, their Team Members, sponsors or other commercial partners that have appeared on a Competitors social media channel or online in any form such as a blog, vlog or news bulletin. For the avoidance of doubt, this Article will not require AC Media to share or post all content produced by or on behalf of a Competitor.
(c) AC Media will work with Competitors on a case by case basis to provide exposure for each Competitor's commercial partners on the Official AC Social Media Channels. Each Competitor acknowledges that AC Media will retain ultimate control as to what content is shared or posted and that whether a piece of content is shared or posted will depend on its relevance, authenticity and greater value to

the America's Cup community and whether there is any conflict with any AC Media commercial partner.

(d) Competitors agree to provide AC Media with a high level content and production rollout plan on a monthly basis to ensure that the social media content plan for AC37 is as full and robust as possible and to help with resources and production if required.

65.5 Official America's Cup App

Each Competitor acknowledges and agrees that AC Media will have the right to produce and host the sole and exclusive official digital application of AC37 and the Events (the "**Official AC App**").

65.6 Competitor produced content requirements

(a) Within three (3) months following the close of the Entry Period (or as reasonably required by AC Media in respect of any Late Challenger), each Competitor will be required to produce a minimum amount of AC37 related content per month for its own digital channels. This requirement is for a minimum amount of content and is not meant to be onerous for each Competitor. The intention with these requirements is to ensure that each Competitor's digital channels and the AC Digital Channels as a whole can continue to grow and engage fans in the lead up to AC37.

(b) The minimum amount of content that each Competitor will be required to produce is as follows:
   (i) a minimum of two (2) minutes of video per month, either as a single two (2) minute video or multiple shorter videos that add up to two minutes in aggregate; and
   (ii) a minimum of one (1) written article per month (between roughly 500 – 1000 words in length.

(c) The content above shall be produced in consultation with AC Media's Social Media and Digital Manager and may be shared on the AC Digital Channels in accordance with Article 65.

(d) The focus of the content above should be in line with the major calendar/campaign moments at the point in time they are created, such as crew training/selection, boat launches, first sailing, event preparations and race day countdowns.

65.7 Non-America's Cup content

The terms of this Article 65 do not apply to content that is not related in any way to the America's Cup, such as content from or related to other, non-America's Cup events in which a Competitor and/or its Team Members may be participating in accordance with the Rules.

65.8 AC Digital Channels post AC37

Upon the date that is ninety (90) days following the final race of AC37, all rights and content related to the AC Digital Channels that are capable of being assigned by ACE at that time (including passwords, content and followers, subject to applicable law), shall be assigned by ACE to ACPI and shall subsequently form part of the property of the America's Cup to be held in trust for the benefit of all future trustees.

PART J: AMERICA'S CUP PROPERTIES INCORPORATED

66. America's Cup intellectual property

66.1 Responsibility

ACPI shall continue to have the sole responsibility for exploiting and managing the intellectual property owned by the America's Cup, as set out in more detail in this Part J. Such responsibilities shall include (without limitation):

(a) holding and maintaining the intellectual property vested in the America's Cup;
(b) exploiting and licensing out the America's Cup intellectual property; and
(c) protecting and enforcing the America's Cup intellectual property on a worldwide basis.

66.2 ACPI contribution

As set out in Article 15.3(a), each Competitor shall pay the sum of US$25,000 (twenty-five thousand United States Dollars) to ACPI as a non-refundable contribution towards ACPI's costs associated with the maintenance of ACPI and the creation and maintenance of America's Cup trademarks and other intellectual property held or to be held by ACPI. Such contribution does not create any rights in ACPI or constitute a licence or right to use any trademark or other intellectual property except as separately provided in Article 66.3.

66.3 ACPI Licence Agreement

Each Competitor shall execute a licence agreement with ACPI relating to the America's Cup trademarks in such form as ACPI may reasonably require. Any dispute as to the terms of that agreement shall be subject to resolution by the Arbitration Panel.

66.4 Use of America's Cup trademarks

No Competitor may use any America's Cup trademarks unless / until the Competitor has executed a licence agreement with ACPI authorising the use of America's Cup trademarks as set out in Article 66.3 above.

66.5 Removal of America's Cup trademarks

Competitors shall remove any America's Cup trademark or other intellectual property owned by ACPI that is affixed to its yacht or equipment prior to selling, leasing or otherwise parting with such yacht or equipment to any Person that is not a Competitor, or otherwise promptly following the end of AC37.

66.6 Control of ACPI

A Competitor winning the America's Cup in the Match shall take control of ACPI in accordance with the terms of the Pre-incorporation Agreement dated October 1, 1986 and the constitution of ACPI.

PART K: GENERAL PROVISIONS

67. Arbitration Panel

67.1 Constitution and chairman

An America's Cup Arbitration Panel ("**Arbitration Panel**") made up of three (3) members shall be established to adjudicate disputes under this Protocol.

The three members of the Arbitration Panel shall be appointed as follows:

(a) The Defender and the Challenger of Record shall each nominate one member (and his or her deputy if at any time this is considered necessary due to the unavailability of the nominated member).
(b) The third member, who shall be the Chairman of the Arbitration Panel, shall be appointed by the mutual agreement of COR/D, or failing such agreement, by the two members initially nominated under Article 67.1(a) above. If at any time it is considered necessary to appoint a deputy due to the unavailability of the Chairman, such appointment shall also be by the mutual agreement of COR/D or failing such agreement, by the two members initially nominated under Article 67.1(a) above.
(c) When a nominated member or the Chairman is not available to sit, he or she will be replaced by his or her deputy.

67.2 Criteria for selection

Criteria for selection of all members of the Arbitration Panel shall include:

(a) they may be a resident or citizen of any country (including those participating in AC37) whether or not the country has a significant interest in the dispute or issue;
(b) they shall possess knowledge of America's Cup history and the Deed of Gift;
(c) they shall possess good general knowledge of yacht racing and yacht clubs; and
(d) they shall possess a judicial temperament with good judgement and be known to be fair-minded.

67.3 Jurisdiction and penalties

Subject always to the terms of Articles 47.2 and 67.5, the Arbitration Panel shall have the following powers:

(a) to resolve all matters of interpretation of the Protocol and Rules (excluding the Racing Rules or the Class Rules) except where expressly excluded in the provisions of such documents and Rules and including, where necessary, the determination of the facts relevant to the matter of interpretation;
(b) to resolve disputes (other than those concerning the Racing Rules or the Class Rules) between the Defender and the Challenger of Record;
(c) to resolve disputes (other than those concerning the Racing Rules or the Class Rules) between the Defender and an individual Challenger when the Challenger of Record expresses in writing to the Defender its agreement that the issue be resolved by the Arbitration Panel;
(d) to resolve disputes (other than those concerning the Racing Rules or the Class Rules) between individual Challengers when one of those Challengers so requests, or between an individual Challenger and the Challenger of Record;
(e) to resolve disputes between ACE and a Competitor;
(f) to resolve any disagreement between the Defender and the Challenger of Record in respect to the Race Conditions under Article 34;
(g) to determine the appropriate penalty under Reconnaissance;
(h) to resolve disputes under an ACPI licence agreement;
(i) to impose penalties in support of decisions made by ACE and/or the Regatta Director when it reasonably considers such penalties to be necessary to enforce the relevant Rules;
(j) to resolve any other matters which it is given jurisdiction to determine by agreement of COR/D;
(k) to impose penalties as considered necessary by the Arbitration Panel; and/or
(l) to mediate at the request of the parties (or at its own instigation) any dispute it considers appropriate for mediation. Such mediation to be undertaken by a single member of the Arbitration Panel who will be chosen by the Arbitration Panel at its sole discretion. The member chosen to mediate shall thereafter not be precluded or excluded from further involvement in the dispute should the mediation be unsuccessful and therefore followed by a regular dispute.

67.4 Penalties

Subject always to the terms of Articles 47.2 and 67.5, the Arbitration Panel shall have the following powers:

(a) to impose penalties in respect of such matter that the Arbitration Panel believes to be just and equitable having regard to the nature and manner and effect of the circumstances, including any one (1) or more of the following:
   (i) censure and/or retraction;
   (ii) fine, not to exceed US$1,000,000 (one million United States Dollars) in any case unless otherwise prescribed in this Protocol;
   (iii) order a partial or full forfeiture of a Challenger's Performance Bond;
   (iv) order a loss of existing or future points, scores or races;
   (v) award points or races to another Competitor;
   (vi) disqualify a Competitor from any race, series, Event or Events;
   (vii) order a reduction in the number of sails permitted to be used by a Competitor in any Event or Events;
   (viii) order the suspension or expulsion of any Team Member from AC37 or from any Event or Events; and/or
   (ix) such other action as the Arbitration Panel may deem appropriate in the circumstances.

(b) to fix or determine the fee payable in relation to any application made to the Arbitration Panel; and

(c) to fix or determine the costs in respect of any application payable by an applicant or a party directed to be served with an application, including the imposing of costs as a penalty for frivolous or vexatious claims or imposing the costs to the losing party.

67.5 No jurisdiction

Unless otherwise agreed by the parties to the dispute (on terms that the Arbitration Panel shall approve), the Arbitration Panel shall not have any jurisdiction to resolve disputes between:

(a) RNZYS and TNZL;
(b) RYS and ARL/INEOS Britannia
(c) any other Competitor and its Representative Team; **SEE PROTOCOL AMENDMENT 8**
(d) RNZYS and ACE;
(e) ACE and any of its staff or other appointed representatives concerning their employment or other contractual relationship with ACE;
(f) any Competitor and any of its Team Members; and/or
(g) any of:

(i) on the one hand, any Competitor, ACE and/or any Regatta Official; and
(ii) on the other hand, any Person that is not bound by this Protocol, such as (but not limited to) any Host City, Venue Authority, sponsors, broadcasters, suppliers and/or other commercial partners.

67.6 Quorum and meetings

The quorum for meetings of the Arbitration Panel shall be all three (3) members for all matters. Meetings of the Arbitration Panel may be held in person, by telephone or other audio/visual link-up or by email. Each Arbitration Panel member shall be entitled to one (1) vote. Decisions shall be made by a majority of votes.

67.7 Engagement

The members of the Arbitration Panel shall be paid a retainer plus an agreed hourly rate for their services as approved by ACE and be reimbursed for their approved travel and out of pocket expenses. The costs so incurred shall be recovered on a user pays basis from the parties involved, as ordered by the Panel.

67.8 Replacement

(a) The Defender and/or the Challenger of Record shall have the right at any time to replace their respective Arbitration Panel members (and/or their deputies, if any), in the event of death, illness, loss of mental faculties, resignation or any other reason which, in the view of the respective entity which appointed the particular member, makes them unable or unwilling to exercise their powers and/or functions under this Article.
(b) COR/D or, failing mutual agreement between COR/D, the two members of the Arbitration Panel appointed by the Defender and the initial Challenger of Record, shall have the power to replace the third member of the Arbitration Panel (and/or their deputy, if any) mutually appointed by them at any time in the event of death, illness, loss of mental faculties, resignation, or for any other reason which, in the view of those two members who appointed that third member, makes that third member (and/or their deputy, if any) unable or unwilling to exercise their powers and/or functions under this Article.

67.9 Presence at Events

The Arbitration Panel shall not be required to be present at the Youth and Women's AC Regattas or the Preliminary Regattas, but they may be present at the Venue at times during the CSS and the Match in a manner to be agreed with COR/D.

67.10 Application time limits

An application to the Arbitration Panel shall be filed within ten (10) days from when the applicant was or could reasonably have been aware of the circumstances justifying the application, unless:

(a) a shorter time limit is specified in the applicable Rules; or
(b) the Arbitration Panel extends this time limit when it is satisfied that there is good reason to do so, taking into account the desire to expedite disputes and to avoid parties from storing up potential applications.

67.11 Application fee

Application fees shall be as specified in the Rules of Procedure issued by the Arbitration Panel under Article 67.14.

67.12 Confidentiality

(a) As a matter of principle, the proceedings before the Arbitration Panel shall be transparent with all the decisions of the Arbitration Panel to be published. The Arbitration Panel may however decide otherwise in its discretion if exceptional circumstances so justify.
(b) Despite Article 67.12(a), all proceedings before the Arbitration Panel shall be confidential from the time of the filing of an application until the time of the publication of a decision by the Arbitration Panel and Competitors shall not disclose or disseminate information in relation to the proceedings beyond that contained in the decision of the Arbitration Panel.
(c) The Arbitration Panel may issue or withdraw an order for confidentiality as it considers just and equitable. The Arbitration Panel will only grant such an order in exceptional circumstances. If, following an application for confidentiality, the Arbitration Panel decides that it will not grant such an order, the Arbitration Panel will advise the relevant Party, who may elect to withdraw any evidence or submission (in such a case, the withdrawal shall occur within not more than 48 hours, unless the Arbitration Panel decides otherwise) or to proceed without confidentiality.

67.13 Award of costs

The Arbitration Panel may award costs to be paid by one or more parties as the Arbitration Panel considers just and equitable. These may include the costs and expenses of the Arbitration Panel and/or the costs and expenses of any other parties.

67.14 Rules of procedure and Arbitration Panel Fast Track Process

(a) Promptly following its appointment (and prior to taking jurisdiction or authority over any matter), the Arbitration Panel, in consultation with COR/D, shall establish and publish its rules of procedure consistent with the rules of natural justice and due process (and consistent with the Rules) ("**Rules of Procedure**") which shall apply to all proceedings of the Arbitration Panel.

(b) As part of its Rules of Procedure, the Arbitration Panel shall establish the Arbitration Panel Fast Track Process based on the following principles:
   (i) the first stage of any Arbitration Panel proceedings shall be the Arbitration Panel Fast Track Process;
   (ii) when submitting any matter to the Arbitration Panel, a party ("**the Applicant**") shall:
      (A) submit the matter by way of a dedicated email address established by the Arbitration Panel for that purpose;
      (B) include a reasonably detailed summary of the basis for its submission and any requested remedy or ruling; and
      (C) provide electronic copies of its submission to ACE and all other Competitors (in each case to email addresses nominated by the Competitors and ACE for such purpose);
   (iii) ACE and any other Competitors may submit observations regarding the matter to the Arbitration Panel (using the email address referred to in Article 67.14(b)(ii)(A) above) within three (3) days of receiving the Applicant's submissions;
   (iv) the Arbitration Panel shall use all reasonable endeavours to reach a decision on the matter, based on submissions received, within five (5) working days of the end of the period referred to in 67.14(b)(iii) above; and
   (v) such decision is final and binding in accordance with Article 67.18 and will be notified to the Competitors and ACE promptly by way of their nominated email addresses.

(c) If the Arbitration Panel reasonably considers that:
   (i) additional information, further submissions, expert advice or oral evidence is required in order to resolve the Applicant's matter, and/or
   (ii) that such matter is not suitable for resolution by the Arbitration Panel Fast Track Process;

   it may give notice (via the email addresses referred to in Article 67.14(b)(ii)(C)) to ACE and the Competitors that such matter will proceed to a full Arbitration Panel meeting in accordance with the procedure referred to in Article 67.14(a).

67.15 Counsel and experts

The Arbitration Panel may, other than as part of Arbitration Panel Fast Track Process, seek expert assistance, engage independent counsel and/or technical experts to assist the Arbitration Panel and to provide legal and/or technical advice from time to time. Costs of engagement shall be agreed with the proposed counsel and approved by ACE and the Arbitration Panel.

67.16 Previous decisions

The Arbitration Panel shall not be bound by decisions from any previous America's Cup but may take into account such decisions when making any determination.

67.17 Purpose and intent

In making its decisions, the Arbitration Panel shall always give effect to the purpose and intent of this Protocol as set out in Recital G of the Introduction.

67.18 Decisions final and binding

All decisions and/or awards of the Arbitration Panel taken in good faith within their proper authority and/or jurisdiction as prescribed in and/or contemplated by the Rules shall be final and binding on all parties and shall not be subject to any review or appeal. Neither ACE nor any Regatta Official shall have any jurisdiction over any decision, ruling, interpretation and/or other act of the Arbitration Panel taken in good faith within the Arbitration Panel's proper authority and/or jurisdiction as prescribed in and/or contemplated by the Rules.

67.19 Language

All proceedings of the Arbitration Panel shall be in English.

67.20 Arbitration agreement

(a) The Arbitration Panel shall act as an arbitration body.
(b) The legal seat of the Arbitration Panel is Auckland, New Zealand. However, the Arbitration Panel may carry out actions that fall within its jurisdiction at any Venue, or other places that it deems appropriate, or by correspondence, e-mail or other means of communication at a distance, including but not limited to ECAF (Arbitration Panel Electronic Case Facility) or other similar electronic device.
(c) Proceedings of the Arbitration Panel shall be governed by the laws governing arbitration proceedings at the seat of the Arbitration Panel, the Rules of Procedure to be drafted under Article 67.14 and by the New York Convention of 1958 on the Recognition and Enforcement of Arbitral Awards.

(d) When permitted by the laws governing arbitration proceedings at the seat of the Arbitration Panel, the Rules of Procedure shall prevail. The Arbitration Panel shall act fairly and impartially and shall provide equal treatment and a fair opportunity to be heard given the circumstances in which the decision must be made.

67.21 Resort to courts prohibited

A Competitor shall not resort to any court or other tribunal where the Arbitration Panel has jurisdiction, except that nothing in this Article 67.21 or otherwise in this Protocol shall in any way limit the right of any Competitor to initiate proceedings or suit in relation to:

(a) any proceedings against a third party that is not a Competitor, ACPI, and/or ACE (or any of ACE's staff or appointed representatives, including any Regatta Official);
(b) any loss or damage to physical property or person;
(c) any person who is alleged to be in breach of any confidentiality undertaking or restrictive covenant entered into with any Competitor; or
(d) the enforcement of contractual or property or other rights not based on or derived from any of the Rules.

A Competitor that breaches this Article 67.21 shall cease to be eligible for the whole or any part or parts of AC37 and for any entitlements under the Rules.

67.22 Consent to exclusive jurisdiction

If resort to a court of competent jurisdiction is permitted to resolve any dispute and/or issue arising out of this Protocol, each Competitor, including each of its Team Members, submits and each of the Indemnified Parties submits any such proceedings to the exclusive jurisdiction of any New Zealand court and agrees to any such proceedings being brought there. The laws of New Zealand, without giving effect to its principles of conflicts of law, shall be applied to resolve any such proceedings.

68. Protocol Amendments

(a) This Protocol may be amended at any time with the agreement of both the Defender and the Challenger of Record, including where the Protocol is required to be amended in order to meet the requirements of any authority having jurisdiction over the Deed of Gift. As an exception to this provision, Article 22.1(c) and this Article 68(a) shall not be amended.
(b) If for any reason, including force majeure, the CSS or the Match is postponed or cancelled under Article 11, the Defender and Challenger of Record will agree to

amend the Protocol to provide alternative arrangements for such cancelled or postponed event(s). If the Defender and Challenger of Record are unable to agree upon such alternative arrangements, the matter shall be referred to the Arbitration Panel for resolution.

(c) If this Protocol is changed pursuant to Article 68(a) after a challenge for AC37 has been received by the Defender but before the Defender has accepted or rejected such challenge, the Prospective Challenger may withdraw its challenge by written notice to the Defender within two (2) calendar days of being notified of the Protocol change, in which case all monies paid by the Prospective Challenger with its challenge shall be refunded in full. If the Prospective Challenger does not withdraw its challenge within the two (2) calendar days, its challenge for AC37 shall be considered to have been made under the revised Protocol.

69. Compliance with Applicable Laws and Regulations

Competitors shall comply with all applicable laws and legally binding regulations of any city, state, national or other governmental authority having jurisdiction over the whole or any relevant part of AC37.

70. Costs and Expenses to compete

Unless otherwise provided under the Rules, each Competitor's costs and expenses for competing in the Event shall be its sole and exclusive responsibility.

71. Liability and Indemnity

71.1 Structural testing

For and on behalf of itself and its Team Members, a Competitor understands, acknowledges and agrees that:

(a) it is solely and wholly responsible for assessing the structural integrity and safety of its AC75 Yacht and any of its test yachts other than its AC40 Yacht (and their components), whether or not in compliance with its applicable Class Rule or the AC Technical Regulations in any case;
(b) following delivery of its AC40 Yacht, it is solely and wholly responsible for assessing the maintenance requirements of its AC40 Yacht (and its components) and for determining whether it is in a proper and safe condition to sail; and
(c) none of RNZYS, TNZL, RYS, ARL, INEOS Britannia, ACE, ACPI, any Regatta Official and/or the Venue Authorities (the "**Indemnified Parties**") warrants or guarantees the safety in general, or the structural integrity in particular, of the whole or any part of any of the Competitor's yachts (and their components), including any AC75 Yacht and/or AC40 Yacht, whether or not the yacht complies with its applicable Class Rule or the AC Technical Regulations in any case.

71.2 Competitor responsibility for own safety

A Competitor, for itself and on behalf of its Team Members, expressly understands and agrees that safety is of paramount importance while testing, training, sailing and/or racing any of a Competitor's boats or yachts (including, but not limited to, any AC75 Yacht and/or AC40 Yacht).

71.3 Participation at own risk

Consistent with the principle articulated at Articles 71.1 and 71.2, a Competitor has sole discretion to determine whether or not it is safe to test, train, sail, and/or race on any given day. Therefore, each Competitor, for itself and on behalf of its Team Members, also expressly understands and agrees that in taking part in the whole or any part of AC37 it does so at its own risk and responsibility and further agrees to the detailed exculpation and indemnity provisions in Article 71.4.

71.4 Exculpation and indemnity

(a) To the fullest extent permitted by law, a Competitor hereby waives and releases any and all Claims against each and all of the Indemnified Parties, and agrees to protect, indemnify and hold harmless the Indemnified Parties from and against any and all Claims, in each case arising directly or indirectly out of or in any way connected with:
   (i) the acceptance of the Competitor's entry to participate in the whole or any part of AC37;
   (ii) the Competitor's participation in the whole or any part of AC37, which includes attendance and participation in Events and/or designing, constructing, testing, sailing and/or racing any yacht (including an AC75 Yacht and/or AC40 Yacht), whether or not pursuant to the terms of the Rules in each case; and/or
   (iii) any failure by the Competitor and/or any of its Team Members in the observance or performance of any of the terms, covenants or conditions of the Rules.

(b) The terms of this Article 71.4 shall be enforceable regardless of the joint or concurrent, active or passive, negligence of any of the Indemnified Parties, regardless of whether liability without fault is imposed or sought to be imposed on any of the Indemnified Parties, and except to the extent that the whole or any part of it is void or otherwise unenforceable under applicable law in effect or, or validly retroactive to, the date of this Protocol. The Competitor's indemnification obligation hereunder shall begin from the first notice that any Claim is or may be made.

(c) The terms of these exculpation and indemnity provisions in this Article 71.4 shall not apply to any proceedings relating to the Rules and decisions that fall under the Jurisdiction of the Arbitration Panel and detailed above in Article 67.

71.5 Defence

A Competitor specifically acknowledges and agrees that it has an immediate and independent obligation to defend the Indemnified Parties from Claims that actually or potentially fall within the scope of the provisions of Article 71.4, even if the allegations are or may be groundless, false or fraudulent. The Competitor's obligation to defend shall arise at the time any Claim is tendered to the Competitor by any of the Indemnified Parties and shall continue at all times thereafter.

71.6 No liability for postponement / cancellation

None of the Indemnified Parties shall be liable for any losses, damages, injury, loss of profits, loss of prospective profits, consequential damages, penalties or inconvenience, whether direct or indirect, however arising, as a result of the postponement or cancellation of the whole or any part of AC37 due to any event, occurrence or circumstances whatsoever, including acts of God, terrorism, war, government intervention or regulation, public health (including for the avoidance of doubt the COVID-19 pandemic), environmental conditions, strikes, lock-outs, other industrial acts, lack of funding or support, or any other force majeure circumstance.

71.7 Legal advice

By signing this Protocol in the case of the Defender and the Challenger of Record, or by submitting a Notice of Challenge in the case of any other Challenger, each Competitor specifically acknowledges and confirms that it was represented by counsel who explained the consequences of the terms of this Article 71, or that Competitor had ample opportunity to consult with counsel, but declined to do so.

71.8 Survival

The terms of this Article 71 shall survive the expiration or earlier termination of this Protocol.

71.9 Enforcement

The Arbitration Panel shall not have jurisdiction to interpret and/or enforce the terms of this Article 71. The enforcement of any of the provisions of, and the resolution of any disputes regarding, this Article 71 shall be determined by a court of competent jurisdiction in accordance with Article 67.22.

72. Applicability

This Protocol applies throughout the world from the time it is published until the completion of the last race of the Match provided that the sailing restrictions set out in Article 24.2 shall be retrospectively applied as from the 17 March 2021.

73. Insurance Requirements

73.1 Insurances required of Competitors

Subject to the remainder of this Article 73, each Competitor shall, at its expense, obtain and maintain in full force and effect from a date to be agreed by COR/D through the remainder of its participation in the whole or any part of AC37 the following minimum required levels of insurance coverage:

(a) Protection and Indemnity Insurance, with a primary limit of not less than US$1,000,000 (one million United States Dollars) per occurrence, covering property damage, personal injury and excess collision/towers liability coverage caused by or occurring on any and all of its yachts/vessels (including operated, owned, chartered and borrowed/loaned). Such protection and indemnity coverage shall also provide first party liability of transportation, wages, maintenance and cure for all Team Members regardless of nationality or country of registration of the yachts/vessels;
(b) Marine Comprehensive General Liability Insurance, with a primary limit of not less than US$1,000,000 (one million United States Dollars) per occurrence, including coverage for contractual liability, independent contractors, broad form property damage, personal injury, products and completed operations, fire damage and legal liability. This policy must also cover non-owned and for-hire vehicles and all mobile equipment or unlicensed vehicles, such as forklifts. This policy must further cover non- owned vessel liability, charter legal liability, and wharfingers legal liability (these particular coverages may also be obtained through a mono-line insurance product with the same liability limits);
(c) Business Automobile Liability Insurance, with limits not less than US$1,000,000 (one million United States Dollars) per occurrence combined single limit for bodily injury and property damage, including coverage for owned, non-owned and hired automobiles, as applicable;
(d) Bumbershoot Excess Liability Coverage, of US$10,000,000 (ten million United States Dollars) excess to each of the:
  (i) Protection and Indemnity coverage required pursuant to Article 73.1(a);
  (ii) Marine Comprehensive General Liability required pursuant to Article 73.1(b); and
  (iii) Business Automobile Liability coverage required pursuant to Article 73.1(c);

(e) Pollution Liability Insurance, either by endorsement to the appropriate insurances listed above in this Article 73.1, or by separate insurance, in the amount of not less than US$5,000,000 (five million United States Dollars), as provided for under any other state law or municipal law that may be applicable at each Venue;
(f) Medical, personal accident, death or dismemberment coverage, including emergency medical treatment, for all of its Team Members in amounts and of a type appropriate for the country in which the particular Team Member is located from time to time whilst working for the Competitor; and
(g) any other insurance coverage, that may be required by applicable laws in the jurisdiction in which any Event takes place.
ACE may by written notice to Competitors alter these requirements to meet the applicable laws and regulations in the country of each Venue where an Event is being conducted.

73.2 Claims-made policies

Should any of the insurances required pursuant to Article 73.1 be provided under a claims- made form, the Competitor shall maintain such coverage continuously throughout AC37 and, without lapse, for three (3) years beyond the end of the last Event, to the effect that, should occurrences during the term of AC37 give rise to claims made after the end of AC37, such claims shall be covered by such claims-made policies.

73.3 Annual aggregate limit

Should any of the insurances required pursuant to Article 73.1 be provided under a form of coverage that includes a general aggregate limit or provides that claims investigation or legal defence costs be included in such aggregate limit, such annual aggregate limit shall be not less than double the applicable occurrence limits specified in Article 73.1.

73.4 Additional insureds

Each of the liability policies required pursuant to Article 73.1 shall include a waiver of subrogation in favour of, and shall be endorsed to name as additional insureds, each of RNZYS, TNZL, RYS, ARL, ACE, any Regatta Official, and/or the Venue Authorities and/or their respective directors, officers, employees, elected and appointed officials, representatives, agents advisors and/or contractors in each case (as applicable). These additional insured and waiver of subrogation requirements may be met by a blanket endorsement or other endorsement(s) at least as broad as ISO 2010 combined with ISO 2037, providing coverage to the additional insureds for both ongoing and completed operations.

73.5 Primary and non-contributory

All insurance policies required pursuant to Article 73.1 shall be endorsed to provide that such insurance is primary to any other insurance available to the additional insureds with respect to claims covered under the policy and that insurance applies separately to each insured against whom claim is made or suit is brought, but the inclusion of more than one insured shall not operate to increase the insurer's limit of liability.

73.6 Insurance rating

All insurance policies required pursuant to Article 73.1 shall be issued by an insurance company or companies, each with a general policy rating of not less than A- and a financial class of VIII or better, as determined by the latest edition of the Best's Insurance Guide published by A.M. Best Company Inc. or its equivalent.

73.7 Proof of insurance

Upon request by ACE, each Competitor shall promptly provide reasonably acceptable evidence that policies complying with the requirements of this Article 73 have been issued or renewed and are in force, with payment in full of all premiums.

73.8 Other

Neither RNZYS, TNZL, RYS, ARL, INEOS Britannia nor ACE shall have any obligation or liability to provide or maintain any insurance coverage (including health care or workers' compensation coverage) for any Competitor or its Team Members.

Execution

Executed as an agreement.

Dated this 15th day of November 2021

THE ROYAL NEW ZEALAND YACHT SQUADRON INCORPORATED

by Aaron Young, Commodore

ROYAL YACHT SQUADRON LIMITED

by Robert M. Bicket, Chairman

Schedule 1: Definitions

In the interpretation of this Protocol, defined terms used herein shall have the following meanings for all purposes:

AC36 means the 36th America's Cup;

AC37 means the 37th America's Cup;

AC37 Events means the regattas that will determine the next holder of the America's Cup, being the Preliminary Regattas, the CSS and the Match;

AC38 means the 38th America's Cup;

AC40 Class Rule means the class rule for the AC40 Yachts to be used in the Initial Preliminary Regattas and the Youth and Women's AC Regattas, including all amendments to, interpretations of and rulings regarding such class rule and the relevant sections of the AC Technical Regulations;

AC40 Yacht means the one-design yachts that will be supplied by ACE (or its nominated manufacturer) under Article 22.2 and that will compete in the Initial Preliminary Regattas and the Youth and Women's AC Regattas;

AC75 Class Rule means the version of the class rule for the AC75 Yachts published by COR/D in accordance with Article 22.1(a), to be used in the Final Preliminary Regatta, the CSS, the Match and/or in any other regattas sailed in AC75 Yachts (if any), including all amendments to, interpretations of and rulings regarding such class rule and the relevant sections of the AC Technical Regulations;

AC75 Yacht means a yacht that complies with or could comply with the AC75 Class Rule, and shall include for the avoidance of doubt any Version 1 AC75 Yacht;

AC Media means the division of ACE consisting of contractors appointed by ACE to be responsible for the delivery of the broadcast and media production (including the race management system), accreditation, social media and other media related activities for AC37, and having the responsibility to deal with each Competitor in an independent and confidential manner vis a vis all other Competitors and ACE itself;

AC Technical Regulations means the technical regulations agreed and published by COR/D under Article 22.3.

ACE means AC37 Event Limited being the entity incorporated pursuant to Article 3.1 and includes any subsidiary or entity nominated by ACE to perform ACE's obligations under this Protocol;

ACE Account means the bank account administered on behalf of ACE to fund the event organisation and management operations of ACE under this Protocol;

ACPI means America's Cup Properties Incorporated, a company incorporated in the State of New York, United States of America, the holder of America's Cup trade mark registrations and the licensor of those marks;

Additional Challenge means any challenge for AC37 submitted by any yacht club during or after the Entry Period;

Additional Challenger means any a yacht club that submits an Additional Challenge;

Additional Entry Fees has the meaning given to that term in Article 15.3;

Advertising means the display of, and/or reference to, a name, design, logo, symbol, slogan, description and/or depiction (or a variation or distortion thereof in any case), or any other feature, in each case that promotes, endorses or otherwise identifies a company, organisation, product, service, brand or idea, except that the following do not constitute **Advertising** for the purposes of this definition:
(a) the name and/or national flag of the country of the yacht club that the Competitor represents;
(b) the name and/or burgee of the yacht club that the Competitor represents;
(c) the number of the yacht;
(d) the name of the skipper of the yacht; and/or
(e) the name and/or logo of a Competitor, provided such logo is the sole and exclusive property of the Competitor or a closely related person or entity and does not incorporate or closely resemble another trade mark that is used commercially other than a mark licensed for use by that Competitor by ACPI;

Arbitration Panel means the panel appointed pursuant to Article 67.1, as further described in Article 67;

Arbitration Panel Fast Track Process means the fast track process referred to in Article 67.14;

Arbitrator means a member of the Arbitration Panel;

ARL means Athena Racing Limited, competing as INEOS Britannia, being RYS' Representative Team in AC37; **SEE PROTOCOL AMENDMENT 8**

Brand Manual has the meaning given to that term in Article 49.2;

Challenge Representative means the person nominated in accordance with Article 14.3;

Challenger means a yacht club whose challenge for AC37 has been accepted by the Defender, and the Representative Team for such yacht club in AC37. For the avoidance of doubt, Challenger includes the Challenger of Record; **SEE PROTOCOL AMENDMENT 8**

Challenger of Record means RYS and INEOS Britannia, RYS' Representative Team in AC37; **SEE PROTOCOL AMENDMENT 8**

Claims means any and all liabilities, losses, injuries, losses, costs, claims, proceedings, judgments, settlements, damages, liens, fines, penalties, expenses, lawyer's fees, consultant's fees, court costs and investigation and remediation costs whatsoever, including direct and vicarious liability of any kind;

Class Rules means the AC75 Class Rule, the AC40 Class Rule and the AC Technical Regulations;

Combined Projected Appendage Area means the total combined surface area of all foils, wings, rudders or other components on a vessel designed to produce hydrodynamic lift, as projected to a waterline plane of the vessel, where projected shall have the meaning given by the AC Technical Regulations; **SEE PROTOCOL AMENDMENT 2**

Competitor means the Defender and/or a Challenger, as the context requires;

Competitor Forum means a forum of Competitors that may meet from time to time in accordance with Article 4;

Constructed in the Country Certificate has the meaning given to that term in Article 26(a)(i);

COR/D means the Challenger of Record and the Defender when acting together;

CSS means the America's Cup Challenger Selection Series, being the series of races to determine the Challenger that will compete against the Defender in the Match;

CSS Conditions means the conditions governing the races of the CSS, as referred to in Article 34.2;

CSS Racing Period: means the period allowed for completion of the CSS as referred to in Article 7.6;

Deed of Gift means the deed dated October 24, 1887 between George L. Schuyler and the New York Yacht Club regarding a silver cup won by the schooner yacht 'America' at Cowes, England on August 22, 1851;

Deed of Participation means the deed referred to in Article 23.2 which shall be signed by each Competitor and submitted to the Defender;

Defender means RNZYS and TNZL;

Emerging Nation means a country which:
(a) has never had a yacht club be the holder of the America's Cup Trophy;
(b) has not submitted one or more challenges for the America's Cup since the final race of the 30th America's Cup Match; or

is otherwise considered by COR/D to be an Emerging Nation for the purpose of Article 30.3;

Entry Fees means the Initial Entry Fees, the Additional Entry Fees and the Preliminary Regatta Fees;

Entry Period has the meaning given to it in Article 13.1;

Events means all of the regattas that form part of AC37, being the AC37 Events, the Youth and Women's AC Regattas and all other regattas held by or on behalf of ACE as part of AC37;

Final Preliminary Regatta means the Preliminary Regatta that shall be held at the Match Venue prior to the CSS;

First Instalment has the meaning given to it in Article 15.1(a);

Flag Area means the area or areas adjacent to the course as prescribed by ACE and managed by the Regatta Director for the exclusive use by vessels with accreditation flags;

Generation 1 Foiling Chase Boats means motorised chase boats (including HSVs) launched prior to 1st April 2022, owned and operated by Competitors which have a Combined Projected Appendage Area of 0.3 m2 or greater; **SEE PROTOCOL AMENDMENT 2**

Generation 2 Foiling Chase Boats means motorised chase boats (including HSVs) launched on or after 1st April 2022, owned and operated by Competitors which have a Combined Projected Appendage Area of 0.3 m2 or greater; **SEE PROTOCOL AMENDMENT 2**

Host City means the city hosting any Event or Events as announced by ACE in each case;

HSV has the meaning given to it in Article 31(b);

Hull shall have the meaning ascribed in the AC75 Class Rule;

Indemnified Parties means RNZYS, TNZL, RYS, ARL, INEOS Britannia, ACE, ACPI, any Regatta Official and/or the Venue Authorities and/ or their respective directors, officers, employees and/or contractors in each case (as applicable);

Initial Entry Fees has the meaning given to that term in Article 15.1;

Initial Preliminary Regattas means the first two Preliminary Regattas that may be held during AC37 that will be contested in AC40 Yachts;

Joint Recon Programme has the meaning given to that term in Article 41.1;

Jury means a World Sailing International Jury that has been appointed under Article 42.2(c), as further described in Article 45;

Late Challenger means a yacht club which submits an Additional Challenge after the Entry Period and **Late Challenge** shall refer to all such late Additional Challenges;

LEQ12 yacht has the meaning given to it in the AC Technical Regulations;

Limitations has the meaning given to that term in Article 24.5(a);

LOA means the length of the vessel overall, measured parallel to the waterline, including all fittings that will be used when sailing in the Events such as rudder struts and bowsprits and with the rudder at zero (0) degrees yaw angle;

Match means the series of races for the 37th America's Cup between the Defender and the qualifying Challenger resulting from the CSS;

Match Conditions means the conditions governing the races of the Match as referred to in Article 34.1;

Match Racing Period: means the period allowed for completion of the Match as referred to in Article 8.1;

Match Venue means the Venue at which the Match will take place;

Measurement Committee means the committee appointed pursuant to Article 42.2(a), as further described in Article 44;

Media Organisation means an organisation whose business, in whole or in part, is the dissemination of information to the public (or to any section of the public) in any form by any means;

New Competitor means a Competitor which has its status as such approved by ACE in consultation with COR/D. In determining whether to give such approval, ACE will consider the extent to which the yacht club and/or its representative team and/or any of its key personnel (sailors or otherwise) participated in any capacity with a team in AC36;

Notice of Challenge means a Notice of Challenge submitted in accordance with Article 14 by Additional Challengers and Late Challengers in the form set out in Schedule 2;

NZT means New Zealand Time;

Official AC Website has the meaning given to it Article 65.2;

Official Competitor Website has the meaning given to it in Article 65.3;

Official Noticeboard means the official noticeboard established as a separate section on the Official AC Website;

Official Practice means practice racing designated under Article 24.2(h) which is conducted on a course at a Venue under the supervision of the Regatta Director immediately prior to an AC37 Event or one of its stages;

Official Training means practice racing (but not testing) designated under Article 24.2(h) which is conducted by the teams laying their own marks on courses identical in configuration to official AC37 Event race courses;

Performance Bond means the performance bond to be provided and maintained by each Competitor pursuant to Article 15.3(c) and Article 17;

Person means any natural person, corporation (including any business trust), limited liability entity, partnership, joint venture or any other entity or association, or governmental or other political subdivision or agency;

Preliminary Regattas means the America's Cup Preliminary Regattas, being the series of preliminary regattas to be held as part of AC37 as referred to and further described in Article 6;

Preliminary Regatta Conditions means the conditions governing the races of the Preliminary Regattas as referred to in Article 34.3;

Preliminary Regatta Fees has the meaning given to that term in Article 16;

Preliminary Regatta Racing Period means the period scheduled for completion of each Preliminary Regatta as published by ACE under Article 6(b);

Prospective Challenger has the meaning given to that term in Article 30.3(a);

Protocol means this Protocol Governing the 37th America's Cup and all attachments, schedules and appendices hereto, including as the same may be amended from time to time in accordance with its terms;

Race Conditions means the Match Conditions, the CSS Conditions and the Preliminary Regatta Conditions;

Racing Area means the area within which courses will be set for any Event or Events as determined by ACE;

Racing Rules means the Racing Rules of Sailing America's Cup Edition to be used for AC37, as agreed and adopted by COR/D in consultation with World Sailing to be administered and enforced by the Umpires and the Jury, as developed and published pursuant to Article 33.1;

Regatta Director means the person appointed pursuant to Article 42.1, as further described in Article 43.1;

Regatta Officials means:
(a) the Regatta Director;

(b) the Measurement Committee;
(c) the Rules Committee;
(d) the Umpires and Jury;
(e) the Arbitration Panel; and
(f) any other regatta officials and/ or other staff appointed pursuant to Article 42.2(e);

Representative Team means, in respect of any Competitor, the professional yachting team representing such Competitor in AC37 and/or the Events including all of its Team Members; **SEE PROTOCOL AMENDMENT 8**

Retrospective Shared Costs has the meaning given to that term in Article 19(d);

RNZYS means the Royal New Zealand Yacht Squadron Incorporated;

Rules means those rules governing AC37 listed in Article 33.1;

Rules Committee means the committee appointed pursuant to Article 42.2(b), as further described in Article 44;

Rules of Procedure has the meaning given to it in Article 67.14(a);

RYS means Royal Yacht Squadron Limited;

Sailing Day means a day on which a Competitor's AC75 Yacht is launched and sailed or towed.

Sailing Instructions means those instructions issued by the Regatta Director in accordance with Article 35;

Sailing Team means, in respect of any Competitor, those Team Members who are employed, personally contracted or otherwise engaged by its Representative Team as sailing crew for its LEQ12 Yachts, AC40 Yachts and AC75 Yachts (specifically excluding any other Team Members who may be present on a yacht but do not participate as sailing crew members); **SEE PROTOCOL AMENDMENT 8**

Second Instalment has the meaning given to it in Article 15.1(b);

Shared Costs has the meaning given to that term in Article 19(a);

Special Event means any event described or contemplated in Article 50.1;

Surrogate Yacht means:
(a) any sailing yacht, motorised vessel or towed platform which exceeds 6 metres LOA that has one or more of the following design characteristics:
   (i) a monohull design with canting T-foils;
   (ii) a foil with one or more adjustable flaps; or
   (iii) a sail which has two sail skins similar to the design requirements set out in the AC75 Class Rule; or

(a2) any sailing yacht, motorised vessel or towed platform which exceeds 6 metres LOA that is designed, built, modified or tested for the purpose of evaluating design or performance characteristics to be applied to an AC75 Yacht or LEQ12 Yacht; or **SEE PROTOCOL AMENDMENT 8**

(b) any foiling monohull design, or derivative of a design, which is either created with an intention of establishing a class or circuit for the design, or is promoted as such, the first example of which has been or will be launched after 17 March 2021,

but excluding:

(c) any AC75 Yacht or LEQ12 Yacht owned and operated by a Competitor, subject to the Components limitations and modifications specified in the AC Technical Regulations;

(d) yachts of classes existing as at 17 March 2021 or yachts which held valid IRC or ORC certificates as at 17 March 2021 or other rating yachts from time to time approved by COR/D, provided they are used only for participation in and preparation for their in-class or rating racing whether they are one design, subject to a rating rule or governed by other class restrictions;

(e) any AC40 Class Yacht for which all of the components listed in AC40 Class Rule 12.4 are *in class* components; **SEE PROTOCOL AMENDMENT 11**

(f) Generation 1 Foiling Chase Boats and Generation 2 Foiling Chase Boats provided that:

   (i) hydrodynamic surface shall have the meaning given by the AC Technical Regulations;

   (ii) each of a Competitor's Generation 1 Foiling Chase Boats must have identical, immutable hydrodynamic surface geometry to all of that Competitor's other Generation 1 Foiling Chase Boats;

   (iii) each of a Competitor's Generation 2 Foiling Chase Boat must have identical, immutable hydrodynamic surface geometry to all of that Competitor's other Generation 2 Foiling Chase Boats;

   (iv) a Competitor must declare the combined projected appendage area and the unloaded appendage hydrodynamic surface geometry of any Generation 1 Foiling Chase Boats or Generation 2 Foiling Chase Boats they launch to the Measurement Committee, and such a declaration shall be within 48 hours of any such vessel's first launch, or within 7 days of the appointment of at least one member of the Measurement Committee, whichever is later;

   (v) the declaration of the hydrodynamic surface geometry to the Measurement Committee shall include the position and orientation of each appendage with respect to the vessel and its design waterline plane; and

(vi) the hydrodynamic surface geometry of that vessel shall not be modified after the declaration to the Measurement Committee, except for:

(A) rotation of parts such as flaps where the axis of rotation is approximately in the span wise direction of that appendage and rudders to control the vessel when in use, and disassembly for maintenance when not in use.

(B) one modification of the hydrodynamic surface geometry which is required for safe operation of the vessel and only if the Measurement Committee has approved the change. The Competitor requesting the change shall document the details and reasons for the proposed change to the Measurement Committee who shall publish these documents to all Competitors. The Measurement Committee shall consider responses from Competitors when reviewing the requested modification.

(g) Motorised chase boats owned and operated by Competitors which have a combined projected appendage area of less than 0.3 m2; **SEE PROTOCOL AMENDMENT 2**

Team Base means facilities in a Venue occupied by a Competitor during an Event, as further described in Article 51.1;

Team Members means, in respect of any Competitor, all of its sailors, senior management and other staff who are team members from time to time;

TNZL means Team New Zealand Limited, RNZYS' Representative Team in AC37; **SEE PROTOCOL AMENDMENT 8**

Umpires means the umpires appointed pursuant to Article 42.2(c), as further described in Article 45;

Venue means the venue for any Event in the applicable Host City, comprising the Team Bases, public areas, all berthage areas, water space, airspace, Racing Areas and all other areas:

(a) controlled by or on behalf of ACE pursuant to its arrangements with the Venue Authorities for the Event; and/or

(b) designated as part of the venue for the Event pursuant to ACE's arrangements with the Venue Authorities for the Event (whether or not controlled by or on behalf of ACE);

Venue Authorities means the Host Cities and other Persons with which ACE contracts for the availability and use of the Venues for the Events;

Version 1 AC75 Yacht means an AC75 Yacht that was constructed and launched prior to 17 March 2021 for the purposes of AC36;

Week means a period of seven (7) calendar days starting on a Monday and ending on the following Sunday.

Youth and Women's AC Agreement means the agreement referred to in Article 9.1(c) setting out the conditions under which the Youth and Women's AC Regattas shall be held and which shall be signed by all Competitors as a condition of eligibility to compete in AC37 Events in accordance with Article 9.1(e) and by any third party wishing to enter the Youth and Women's AC Regattas under Article 9.1(d).

Youth and Women's AC Regattas means the series of races referred to in Article 9 to be arranged in accordance with the terms of the Youth and Women's AC Agreement.

Schedule 2: Notice of Challenge

Challenger Form per Article 14.1

TO: The Royal New Zealand Yacht Squadron

181 Westhaven Drive Westhaven Marina Auckland 1011

New Zealand

Attention: The Commodore

By hard copy, and email to: russell.green@emiratesteamnz.com, with a copy to ayoung@rnzys.org.nz

1. I, [insert Full Name] am the [Commodore or state office with authority] of the [insert name of yacht club] of [insert country] (the **Challenger**) and I am duly authorised as a representative of such yacht club to deliver this Notice of Challenge to you for and on behalf of the Challenger.
2. The Challenger by this Notice hereby challenges for the 37th America's Cup (including its constituent events) in accordance with the Protocol Governing the 37th America's Cup dated 15 November 2021 (the **Protocol**). The Challenger hereby agrees to be bound by and undertakes to comply with, and hereby agrees to procure that all of its Team Members (as such term is defined in the Protocol) shall comply with, the terms of the Protocol and all other rules referred to therein.
3. The Challenger is a qualified yacht club under the terms of the Deed of Gift of the America's Cup dated 24 October 1887 to challenge for the 37th America's Cup.
4. Attached to this Notice of Challenge is:
   (a) a copy of the Challenger's certificate of incorporation, patent or license or other document evidencing the incorporation, patent or license of the Challenger.
   (b) details of the Challenger's annual regatta on the sea or arm of the sea demonstrating the Challenger meets the obligations in the Deed of Gift.

(c) a certificate duly issued by the authorised representative of the yacht club in which it is affirmed that the yacht club:
   (i) has been in existence for a minimum of three years;
   (ii) maintains a membership of at least 200 members;
   (iii) is financially supported by a majority of its membership on a pro-rata basis;
   (iv) operates as a yacht club and has objectives consistent with the furtherance of yachting activities; and
   (v) is a member of the national sailing authority of its country.

(d) a certificate by the national sailing authority of the country of the yacht club affirming that the yacht club is a member of such national sailing authority.

5. On behalf of the Challenger, I hereby declare that the Challenger:
   (a) accepts that it will be bound by the terms of the Deed of Gift, the Protocol (including in particular, but without limitation, the express terms of Articles 48.4 (Event title sponsor conflicts), 71 (Liability and Indemnity) and 73 (Insurance Requirements) thereof) and all other rules referred to in the Protocol;
   (b) accepts that it will be bound by the terms of the Deed of Participation;
   (c) for and on behalf of its Team Members (as such term is defined in the Protocol), accepts that its Team Members will be bound by the terms of the Protocol and all other rules referred to therein;
   (d) has complied with, and will at all times comply with the terms of the Deed of Gift, the Protocol and all other rules referred to in the Protocol;
   (e) shall procure that its Team Members (as such term is defined in the Protocol) will at all times comply with the terms of the Protocol and all other rules referred to therein;
   (f) agrees to submit solely and exclusively to the respective jurisdictions of ACE and the Regatta Officials, in each case as prescribed in the Protocol;
   (g) shall procure that its Team Members (as such term is defined in the Protocol) will submit solely and exclusively to the respective jurisdictions of ACE and the Regatta Officials, in each case as prescribed in the Protocol;
   (h) has complied, and will continue to comply, with the sailing limitations specified in Article 24.2; and
   (i) acknowledges and agrees (for and on behalf of itself and its Team Members) that no decisions or actions of ACE and the Regatta Officials, in each case, shall be subject to appeal or be referred to any court, tribunal or other authority or body for review in any manner except as may be expressly permitted by the terms of the Protocol.
6. The Challenger will be represented by [insert name of representative sailing team] in AC37.

7. All communications and notices are to be sent to:

   [Insert the Address, email and telephone details of both the yacht club and the representative sailing team with the names of contact persons]

DATED this [insert date of notice] at [insert location]

Signed for and on behalf of the **Challenger**

By [insert name and title]

____

Signature

Accompanying checklist:

- Copy of the Challenger's certificate of incorporation, patent or license referred to at paragraph 4(a) above.
- Details of the Challenger's annual regatta on the sea or an arm of the sea referred to at paragraph 4(b) above.
- Certificate of compliance issued by the Challenger referred to at paragraph 4(c) above.
- Certificate issued by the national sailing authority of the Challenger's referred to at paragraph 4(d) above;
- Duly signed Deed of Participation.

3.2 Amendments Progressively Made to the Initial 37th America's Cup Protocol

Version	Amendment	Date	Article	Summary
Pro v16	16	25/9/24	37.3(b)	Equal course access
			36.5	Wind limits for Youth and Women's AC deleted from Protocol
Pro v15	15	2/9/24	43.1(i)	Regatta Director responsible for receiving and assessing reports of non- compliance for AC75 CR
			44.1	Measurement Committee responsible to report issues of non- compliance to Regatta Director
			45	Jury responsible act in issues of AC75 non- compliance
			47.3	New rule regarding processes for some AC75 non- compliance
Pro v14	14	17/8/24	36	Wind measurement
			51	Yacht battery
-	13	16/7/24	49.3	Requirement for Mainsail and Jib logos
Pro v12	12	3/7/24	7.3	Change Preliminary Regattas used for seeding
			24.3	Surrogate yacht - Youth and Women's team member exclusion
-	11	28/5/24	7	Description of CSS Round Robin stage and scoring
			9	Youth and Women's AC - What Competitors are required to supply
			24	Sailing Limitations - exceptions
			30	Crew nationality - declarations
			31	Support boat restrictions

Version	Amendment	Date	Article	Summary
			33	Swap (d) and (e) in rules precedence
			Def	Change to definition of 'surrogate yacht'. Add an exclusion
-	10	22/5/24	51	Team Bases. New Article regarding safety of batteries
Pro v9	9	17/3/23	6(b)	New date for announcing Preliminary Regattas. Note, initial notice was corrected. see here
Pro v8	8	19/12/22	2.1(b)	Clarification to role of TNZL. Remove reference to sailing team.
			2.2(b)	Clarification to role of ARL. Remove reference to sailing team.
			12.1	Remove reference to sailing team in first line.
			24.3	Change to surrogate yacht article.
			30.2(c)	New article - ability for OR/D to partially waive nationality criteria due to COVID 19 circumstances.
			30.3(c)(i)	Capitalize the word 'Sailing Team' to refer to new definition.
			38	Capitalize the word 'Sailing Teams' to refer to new definition.
			49.2	Date for the publication of the brand manual changed to 28 February 2023.
			60.2(c)(i)	'Sailing team performance' shall be replaced with 'Sailing Team members'.
			67.5(c)	'Sailing team' shall be replaced with 'Representative Team'
			Def	New defined term - ARL

Version	Amendment	Date	Article	Summary
			Def	Change to definition of 'Challenger'
			Def	Change to definition of 'Challenger of Record'
			Def	Change to definition of 'Surrogate Yacht'
			Def	Change to definition of 'TNZL'
			Def	New defined terms: 'Representative team' and 'Sailing team'
			24.3	Clarification regarding restrictions contained in Article 24.3
Pro v7	7	25/10/22	40.2(e)	Allowance for team members to collect weather data when participating in bona fide regattas.
-	6	25/10/22	63(e)	Footage filmed consultation as per Editorial Review Process.
			63(f)	time period changed from 3 months to 6 months.
Pro v5	5	22/9/22	32.5	Standard on-board voice communication systems.
			63(d)	Date of publication of T&C's for Documentary access to be published by 31 October 2022.
Pro v4	4	23/7/22	24.2(c)	Delete 24.2(c)(ii).
			24.2(d)	Replace article regarding no sailing periods.
-	3	12/7/22	31	Change to Support Vessels.
-	2	6/7/22	24.2	Change date for finalising Non-Sailing Periods to 30 July 2022.
			24.4	Restriction not to apply to calibration of sensors in a controlled environment.

Version	Amendment	Date	Article	Summary
			42.1	Amend reference.
			Sch 1	New definition - 'Combined projected appendage area'.
				Add new definition to 'Generation 1 Foiling Chase Boats'.
				Add new definition to 'Generation 2 Foiling Chase Boats'.
				Amend definition of 'Surrogate Yacht'.
				Amend reference in definition of 'Regatta Director'.
-	1	29/3/22	8.1(d)	Dates for Match and CSS racing periods August to October 2024.
Pro v0	-	15/11/21	-	Signed Protocol.

Source: Table published on the AC37 website.

CHAPTER 4 America's Cup Arbitration Panel Rules of Procedure (May 2023)

These Rules of Procedure of the America's Cup Arbitration Panel ("**Arbitration Panel**") for the 37th America's Cup are established pursuant to Article 67 of the Protocol governing the 37th America's Cup, as amended (the "**Protocol**"), for all matters within the Arbitration Panel's jurisdiction under the Protocol.

1. DEFINITIONS

The definitions contained in the Protocol shall apply in addition to the following:

1.1. **Applicant** means any Party filing an Application in accordance with these Rules of Procedure and entitled to do so pursuant to the Protocol.

1.2. **Application** means a written request for a decision by the Arbitration Panel in relation to a dispute, a request for interpretation, or any other submissions about a matter within the Arbitration Panel's jurisdiction under the Protocol.

1.3. **Arbitration Panel Chairman** means the Chairman of the Arbitration Panel as appointed in accordance with Article 67.1 (b) of the Protocol.

1.4. **Arbitration Panel Fast Track Process** means the fast track process referred to in Article 67.14 of the Protocol.

1.5. **Arbitration Panel Secretary** means the person who may be appointed by the Arbitration Panel to handle administrative matters for the Arbitration Panel.

1.6. **Bank Account** means the bank account as will be indicated from time to time by the Arbitration Panel.

1.7. **Claimant** means the same as Applicant and is the term that may be used in eADR.

1.8. **Documentation** means any written material or physical evidence filed in relation to any matter before the Arbitration Panel.

1.9. **eADR** means the Arbitration Panel Electronic ADR Case Facility made available by the Arbitration and Mediation Center of the World Intellectual Property Organization (WIPO Center).

1.10. **Observer** means a person permitted by the Arbitration Panel to observe the conduct of a hearing, in accordance with these Rules of Procedure.

1.11. **Party** means any person or entity over whom the Arbitration Panel has jurisdiction under Article 67.3 of the Protocol and Paragraph 5.12 of these Rules of Procedure.

1.12. **Protocol** means the Protocol governing the 37th America's Cup dated 15th November 2021, as amended from time to time.
1.13. **Racing Rules** mean the current Racing Rules as agreed and adopted by COR/D in consultation with World Sailing referred to in Article 33.1(d) of the Protocol.
1.14. **Service Address List** means a list of the email addresses advised to the Arbitration Panel Chairman and/or to the Arbitration Panel Secretary by the Parties and which shall be the list of persons registered to use eADR.
1.15. Unless otherwise defined in these Rules of Procedure, words with capital letters refer to the terms defined in the Protocol.
1.16. References to "Paragraphs" are to paragraphs of these Rules of Procedure.

References to Articles are to articles of the Protocol.

2. JURISDICTION

2.1. The Arbitration Panel shall have the powers foreseen in Article 67.3 of the Protocol.

3. LEGAL SEAT – LAW GOVERNING 37TH AMERICA'S CUP PROCEEDINGS – LANGUAGE

3.1. The legal seat of the Arbitration Panel is Auckland, New Zealand. However, the Arbitration Panel may carry out all the actions which fall within its jurisdiction at any Event or Venue of the America's Cup or its Preliminary Regattas or in any other place it deems appropriate, or by correspondence, e-mail or other means of communication at a distance, including but not limited to eADR or other similar electronic devices.
3.2. The Arbitration Panel proceedings shall be governed by these Rules of Procedure, by the New Zealand Arbitration Act 1996 and by the New York Convention of 1958 on the Recognition and Enforcement of Arbitral Awards. Whenever acceptable under the New Zealand Arbitration Act 1996, these Rules of Procedure shall prevail. In all instances, the Arbitration Panel shall act fairly and impartially and shall provide equal treatment and a fair opportunity to be heard given the circumstances in which the decision must be made.
3.3. The Arbitration Panel proceedings shall be in the English language. Unless otherwise agreed by the Arbitration Panel, evidence in a language other than English shall be translated into English by an independent qualified translator or such other translator approved by the Arbitration Panel, the costs of such translator to be borne by the Party producing such evidence.

4. COMMUNICATIONS

4.1. Each Party shall advise the Arbitration Panel Chairman and each of the Panel members of up to five (5) email addresses and up to two (2) physical addresses for service of documents. Each Party shall be responsible for keeping the Arbitration Panel Chairman and each of the Panel members as well as the Arbitration Panel Secretary advised of any additional addresses (up to the maximum number permitted from time to time) or changes to them.

4.2. Parties shall use the relevant eADR (once established) for all filings of, and access to, all Documentation under these Rules of Procedure, except:

4.2.1. Matters pertaining to confidentiality (see Paragraph 7 herein);

4.2.2. Matters otherwise directed by the Arbitration Panel.

Should circumstances prevent a Party from using eADR for filing or accessing Documentation, other than as described in Paragraph 4.5, it shall seek directions from the Arbitration Panel Chairman.

All Arbitration Panel notices concerning pending matters will be filed on eADR, unless the Arbitration Panel decides otherwise.

The Arbitration Panel and all other participants of eADR will use eADR only for its above-described purpose. In particular, eADR participants will not share access information with any unauthorized parties and will not obtain unauthorized access to non-eADR data or systems.

4.3. The Arbitration Panel and the Parties on the Service Address List will receive an eADR email notice of any filing made using eADR.

4.4. Matters, such as physical items, which cannot be filed through eADR, shall be delivered or couriered to the Arbitration Panel Chairman at the address referred to in Paragraph 4.6.2.

4.5. Communications to the Arbitration Panel, other than those required to be made through eADR, shall unless otherwise advised by the Arbitration Panel Chairman be addressed:

4.5.1. By email to the Arbitration Panel Chairman (dtillett54@gmail.com) and to the two other members of the Arbitration Panel (gmackconsulting@gmail.com, bryanwillis@gmail.com) and to the Panel Secretary (sasha.lines@gmail.com);

or, when sending by email is not possible,

4.5.2. By courier or hand delivery to the Arbitration Panel Chairman: David Tillett AM

75/33 Colley Terrace
Glenelg SA 5045

or such other address as may be advised by the Arbitration Panel Chairman.

4.6. Time limits:

4.6.1. The time limits fixed under the Protocol and these Rules of Procedure shall begin from the day after that on which a notification or communication is received.
4.6.2. Upon application on justified grounds and after consultation with the other Party (or Parties), the Arbitration Panel Chairman may extend any time limit if the circumstances so warrant and provided that the initial time limit has not already expired.
4.6.3. The Arbitration Panel may, upon application on justified grounds, suspend ongoing arbitration proceedings for a limited period of time.
4.6.4. All time periods and references in the Protocol or in any directions issued by or on behalf of the Arbitration Panel Chairman or ACAP37 shall be deemed to be working days in New Zealand time, unless otherwise stated in such Protocol or directions.

5. INITIATION OF PROCEEDINGS / PROCEDURE FOR APPLICATIONS

5.1. Applications
Prior to filing an Application with the Arbitration Panel, the Applicant / Claimant (hereinafter the Applicant) shall pay a non-refundable application fee to the Bank Account in the sum of 10,000 Euro (ten thousand Euros) per initiating Application.
5.2. Any Applicant may file a written Application on eADR, with attachments if appropriate. In doing so such Party shall be deemed to have affirmed the jurisdiction of the Arbitration Panel.
5.3. Prior to filing a written Application on eADR, the Applicant shall notify the Arbitration Panel and the Panel Secretary by email, of their intention to file such Application. The Panel Secretary will liaise with WIPO Center to establish a new case on eADR and allocate a case number. Once this has been done, the Panel Secretary will notify the Applicant by email and the Applicant may then proceed to file their Application in accordance with paragraph 5.2 above.
5.4. The Application shall include:
5.4.1. A statement as to:
5.4.1.1. whether the Applicant considers that the matter is suitable for resolution by the Arbitration Fast Track Process;
5.4.1.2. the basis for the Arbitration Panel's jurisdiction;
5.4.1.3. a reasonably detailed summary of the basis for its Application/submission; and
5.4.1.4. the remedy, ruling or other order sought; and
5.4.2. Proof of payment of the Application Fee referred to in Paragraph 5.1.
5.5. Any Application to the Arbitration Panel shall be filed in accordance with the requirements of Article 67.10.
5.6. Observations

5.6.1 Any Party may submit on eADR observations regarding the matter within 3 working days of receiving the eADR email notice of an Application in accordance with Paragraph 4.3.

5.6.2 The Applicant may then submit on eADR a response to the observations within 2 further working days of the deadline referred to in paragraph 5.6.1.

5.6.3 In its discretion the Panel may determine different time periods to apply in paragraphs 5.6.1 and/or 5.6.2 above.

5.7. Arbitration Fast Track Process

5.7.1. As soon as practicable after receiving the Application in accordance with Paragraphs 5.2, 5.4 and 5.5, the Arbitration Panel shall decide:

(i) whether or not the matter is suitable for resolution by the Arbitration Panel Fast Track Process; or (ii) whether or not any additional evidence, further submissions, expert advice or oral evidence is required in order to resolve the Applicant's matter.

If the Arbitration Panel decides to proceed with the Fast Track Process, it shall use all reasonable endeavours to publish its decision within 5 working days of the deadline referred to in Paragraph 5.6.2.

5.7.2. The Arbitration Panel may issue further directions for additional information or submissions, or advise the estimated date in which a decision will be reached if it is not within the 5 working day period.

5.7.3. The provisions of Paragraph 15 shall apply to the decision that is issued.

5.8. Full Arbitration Panel Process

In the event that the Panel determines that an Application either: (i) is not suitable for resolution by the Arbitration Panel Fast Track Process; or (ii) requires any additional evidence, further submissions, expert advice or oral evidence in order to resolve the Applicant's matter, and that it will proceed under the Full Arbitration Panel Process, it will issue such directions it considers appropriate which shall include if the matter is to proceed on paper only, or with an oral hearing.

5.9. In respect of any Application, a Party is deemed to have waived the issue of lack of jurisdiction of the Arbitration Panel unless such Party raises the issue within its initial filing.

5.10. The Arbitration Panel has absolute discretion to answer hypothetical questions but only in exceptional circumstances and only when it decides that a decision on the question is in the best interests of AC37.

5.11. Upon filing with the Arbitration Panel any observation or application stating that the filing Party intends to cause a third party to participate in the arbitration, that Party shall simultaneously provide a copy of its observation or application to the third party. The Arbitration Panel shall fix a time limit for such party to state its position on its participation and file an observation with the Arbitration Panel.

5.12. If a third party wishes to participate as a Party to any arbitration proceedings, it shall file an application to this effect with the Arbitration Panel, together with the reasons therefor within 1 (one) working day after the arbitration has become known to the intervenor, provided that such application is filed prior to the decision being given. The Arbitration Panel shall communicate a copy of this application to the Parties and fix a time limit for them to express their position on the participation of the third party and to file, to the extent applicable, an observation.

5.13. A third party may participate in the arbitration only if the Arbitration Panel considers its participation as a Party necessary for the resolution of the arbitration proceedings and the Arbitration Panel shall determine the terms and conditions under which the third party shall participate in the proceedings.

6. ORAL HEARINGS

6.1. Any Party to an arbitration may request an oral hearing and suggest the location thereof in its Application or its observations. In such a case, it shall give the reasons for such request and for such location.

6.2. The Arbitration Panel will always have discretion to decide whether an Application will be determined by an oral hearing and, as the case may be, where and when such hearing shall take place, or on documents only.

6.3. In the event of an oral hearing, the Arbitration Panel Chairman will confirm the date, time and place of the hearing and will advise the manner in which the hearing will be conducted. The Arbitration Panel may, from time to time, adjourn a hearing, on its own volition or at the request of a Party.

6.4. With the prior approval of the Arbitration Panel and subject to its directions, a Party may withdraw or amend its Application, submissions or observations.

7. CONFIDENTIALITY

7.1. As a matter of principle: (i) as between the Parties, the proceedings before the Arbitration Panel will be transparent and confidential; and (ii) all Arbitration Panel decisions will be published. The Arbitration Panel may however decide otherwise in its discretion if exceptional circumstances so justify in which case it will publish such decision with reasons.

7.2. The Arbitration Panel may issue or withdraw an order for confidentiality as it considers just and equitable. The Arbitration Panel will only grant such an order in exceptional circumstances. If, following an Application for confidentiality, the Arbitration Panel decides that it will not grant such an order, the Arbitration Panel will advise the relevant Party, who may elect to withdraw any evidence or submission (in such a case, the withdrawal shall occur within not more than

48 hours, unless the Arbitration Panel decides otherwise) or to proceed without confidentiality.

8. WRITTEN APPLICATIONS, SUBMISSIONS AND OBSERVATIONS

8.1. Subject to Paragraph 7.1 all Applications, submissions and observations and evidence before the Arbitration Panel shall be available to each Party on the relevant eADR system or through any other communication means as determined by the Arbitration Panel and notified to all Parties.

8.2. Other than that which is permitted in Paragraph 16.1 and subject to Paragraph 7.1, all proceedings before the Arbitration Panel shall be confidential from the time of the filing of an Application until the time of the publication of a decision by the Arbitration Panel and the Parties shall not disclose or disseminate information in relation to the proceedings beyond that contained in the decision of the Arbitration Panel.

9. ORAL HEARINGS RECORDINGS

9.1 The Arbitration Panel may, from time to time, decide that a stenographic or other record of the hearing be organized, on its own volition or at the request of a Party. The costs of such a record will be shared by the Parties unless otherwise ordered by the Arbitration Panel.

10. REPRESENTATIVES/OBSERVERS AT ORAL HEARINGS

10.1. Each and any Party as well as ACE, the Defender and Challenger of Record may appoint up to 2 representatives who will be permitted to represent their interest at oral hearings. The Arbitration Panel may permit additional representatives at any time.

10.2. Each and any Party as well as ACE, the Defender and the Challenger of Record may appoint up to two Observers who will be permitted to observe at oral hearings. The Arbitration Panel may alter the number of Observers at any time and may permit additional Observers.

10.3. As a matter of principle, media observers will not be permitted to attend any oral hearing, unless authorized by the Arbitration Panel following submissions by the Parties.

10.4. The Arbitration Panel may order that a hearing, or any part thereof, shall be held in private and may impose other conditions with respect to each Party and Observers that it deems appropriate.

10.5. Unless otherwise directed by the Arbitration Panel, Observers shall not make public the Applications, submissions or observations, or any of the evidence, documentary or otherwise prior to the publication of the Arbitration Panel decision and only then to the extent contained in such decision.

11. ORAL EVIDENCE / PROCEDURE FOR APPLICATION

11.1. At an oral hearing, any Party or any Party whom the Arbitration Panel has invited to file submissions may, to the extent the Application touches on matters within their area of responsibility, present oral testimony through witnesses if so decided by the Arbitration Panel. Witnesses shall be subject to examination by any Party who has a direct interest in the outcome of the matter and by the Arbitration Panel.

11.2. The Arbitration Panel may order the appearance of witnesses and may compel such appearance through application of the New Zealand Arbitration Act 1996.

11.3. When permitted by the Arbitration Panel, witnesses may testify by remote video or such other means as the Arbitration Panel directs.

11.4. When the Arbitration Panel permits the use of written statements from a witness at an oral hearing, the Arbitration Panel may direct that the witness shall be made available for examination by any Party who has a direct interest in the outcome of the matter and by the Arbitration Panel.

11.5. Witnesses will not be required to give evidence under oath however, the Chairman shall invite such persons to tell the truth, subject to the sanctions of perjury or other disciplinary sanctions.

11.6. If a person who has given a written statement is not available for examination at the hearing or through a remote system authorised by the Arbitration Panel, the Arbitration Panel will consider the statement but give such weight to it as the Arbitration Panel determines appropriate in the light of submissions made in opposition to it.

11.7. After the hearing, no further submission or argument may be made or evidence produced, unless requested or authorized by the Arbitration Panel.

12. PROCEDURAL DIRECTIONS

12.1. The Arbitration Panel will give such directions as it considers appropriate and fair to the Parties to facilitate the resolution of the Application.

12.2. Any directions issued by the Arbitration Panel will have the status as if they were Rules of Procedure.

13. PROVISIONAL REMEDIES

13.1. Upon the request of a Party in any proceeding pending before the Arbitration Panel, the latter may make an order for provisional or interim relief, including the stay of the effects of a decision under challenge. In agreeing to these Rules of Procedure, in compliance with the Protocol, the Parties expressly waive their right to request such relief from other authorities.

13.2. Upon the filing of an Application for interim or preliminary relief, the Arbitration Panel Chairman shall advise each Party of the Application and invite each Party to express its position within a time limit to be fixed in consideration of the circumstances. In the case of utmost urgency, the interim or preliminary relief may be issued without first hearing any other Party, provided that each Party is offered the opportunity to be heard at the earliest possible time thereafter. An order for interim or preliminary relief will cease to be effective whenever the Arbitration Panel so decides, but at the latest upon issuance of the Arbitration Panel's final decision.

13.3. An order granting interim or preliminary relief:

13.3.1. Shall not be appealable;

13.3.2. May be conditional upon the provision of security;

13.3.3. Shall be made for the minimum period necessary; and

13.3.4. In any event, shall survive only until such time as the relevant arbitration is finally decided.

13.4. When deciding whether to award interim or preliminary relief, the Arbitration Panel shall consider whether the relief is necessary to protect the Applicant from irreparable harm, whether the Applicant is likely to succeed on the merits, and whether the interests of the Applicant outweigh those of any other Party, or of others who participate in any capacity in the America's Cup.

14. COSTS AND PENALTIES

14.1. Referring to Article 67.7 of the Protocol, the fees and expenses of the members of the Arbitration Panel and the Panel Secretary (including the retainer and the agreed hourly rate for their services) as well as any other proceedings related costs (as determined by the Arbitration Panel) shall be recovered on a user pay basis from the Parties involved, as ordered by the Arbitration Panel. The Arbitration Panel shall determine an amount payable on each Application by the Parties to satisfy the retainer recovery obligation referred to in Article 67.7.

14.2. In addition to the application fee provided for in Paragraph 5.1, if the Arbitration

Panel shall consider it appropriate it may order costs or security to be paid in advance of any further step of the proceedings (e.g. oral hearing or the matter being determined).

14.3. Pursuant to Article 67 of the Protocol, the Arbitration Panel shall, whenever appropriate in its award, fix or determine the costs in respect of any Application that are to be payable by any Party, including imposing costs as a penalty for frivolous claims or imposing the costs to the losing Party. The Arbitration Panel shall do so as it considers just and equitable, having regard to all relevant matters which may include:

14.3.1. The outcome of the Application;

14.3.2. The reasons for the decision;

14.3.3. Whether the decision is of universal application or for the benefit of a significant number of Competitors, AC37 or the Events generally;

14.3.4. The conduct of the Parties prior to and during the Application or any hearing, including procedural conduct which may include obstructive or delaying conduct;

14.3.5. Whether the Application related solely to the Racing Rules and only required a relatively straightforward application of the Racing Rules, and if so it would normally result in no award of costs; and

14.3.6. Whether the decision has the effect of providing an interpretation or compliance with the documents referred to in Article 33.1 of the Protocol.

14.4. The Arbitration Panel may also impose such penalties as it considers appropriate, which may include penalties in accordance with Article 67.4 of the Protocol. Where no penalty is specifically provided for in respect of a breach of any of the provisions of the Protocol, the Conditions, the Deed of Gift or previous decisions of the Arbitration Panel, the Arbitration Panel shall determine and impose such penalty as it considers appropriate having regard to the nature and manner of the particular breach. Pursuant to Article 67.4 of the Protocol, the Arbitration Panel may determine the penalty for failure to make any payment fixed or determined by it. The penalty may include the forfeiture of the Performance Bond.

14.5. In determining the amount to be recovered from each of the Parties involved, whether by way of costs or penalties, the Arbitration Panel shall credit the relevant Party with the amount of the application fee that was paid by such Party in accordance with Paragraph 5.1 and any other advance made on costs in accordance with Paragraph 14.2.

14.6. The Arbitration Panel will whenever possible give the opportunity to relevant Parties to provide their views on any order or award for costs or any penalty that may be imposed.

14.7. Each Party shall bear the costs of its own witnesses, experts and interpreters, unless otherwise determined by the Arbitration Panel.

14.8. Any amount to be paid by a Party, including an application fee (see Paragraph 5.1), security (see Paragraph 13.3), an advance on costs (see Paragraph 14.2), a final costs determination (see Paragraph 14.3) or a penalty (see Paragraph 14.4), shall be paid into the Bank Account.

15. DECISIONS

15.1. The Arbitration Panel shall rule on each matter placed before it in accordance with the Deed of Gift and the Protocol, using the merits, general principles of law and the rules of law the application of which it deems appropriate. The Arbitration Panel will use all reasonable endeavours to act in a time and cost- efficient manner on all such matters.

15.2. Decisions of the Arbitration Panel will be in writing and will contain reasons. Before the written decision is published, a summary of the decision may be given orally or in writing at the conclusion of an Application or a hearing. Decisions will be published without restriction unless the Arbitration Panel determines that, for reasons of confidentiality in terms of Paragraph 7, publication of a decision should be restricted in such manner as the Arbitration Panel considers appropriate.

15.3. In the event that a decision is not unanimous, any dissenting member of the Arbitration Panel has the right to be identified and have such dissent published with the Arbitration Panel decision. The dissenting opinion will be appended to the Arbitration Panel decision.

15.4. On its own initiative, the Arbitration Panel may correct a clerical, computational or typographical error, or any errors of similar nature contained in the award, provided that such correction is done within thirty (30) days of the date of such award. Any application of a Party for a correction of a clerical, computational or typographical error must be made within thirty (30) days of the receipt of the eADR email notice of a decision given in accordance with paragraph 4.3. The Arbitration Panel shall then grant the other Parties such time as it considers appropriate to submit any comments thereon. The decision to correct the award shall take the form of an addendum and shall constitute part of the award.

15.5. All decisions and/or awards of the Arbitration Panel taken in good faith within their proper authority and/or jurisdiction as prescribed in and/or contemplated by the Rules shall be final and binding on all Parties and shall not be subject to any review or appeal, unless the Arbitration Panel, in its sole discretion and based on new evidence, so decides.

15.6. The Arbitration Panel shall not be bound by decisions from any previous America's Cup but may take into account such decisions when making any determination.

16. DISSEMINATION OF INFORMATION

16.1. In addition to what is foreseen in Paragraphs 8.2 and 10.5 above, the Parties may only disseminate information issued by the Arbitration Panel or having a direct or indirect relation with the activities or proceedings conducted by the Arbitration Panel in accordance with directions from the Arbitration Panel Chairman.

16.2. As a matter of principle, the Parties shall not disseminate information issued by the Arbitration Panel or having a direct or indirect relation with the activities or proceedings conducted by the Arbitration Panel, in particular to the media.

17. AMENDMENTS

These Rules of Procedure may be amended or revoked at any time by the Arbitration Panel following consultation with the COR/D.

18. SUBMISSION TO THE ARBITRATION PANEL

By filing an Application, submission or observation with the Arbitration Panel, a Party agrees to be bound by these Rules of Procedure, as amended from time to time.

19. EFFECTIVE DATE

These Rules of Procedure have been drafted by the Arbitration Panel and approved by COR/D.

David Tillett, Chairman

Arbitration Panel members: Graham McKenzie, Bryan Willis

CHAPTER 5 Other 37th America's Cup Governing Documents

5.1 THE WORLD SAILING RACING RULES OF SAILING – AMERICA'S CUP EDITION, FOR USE IN THE 37TH AMERICA'S CUP (V 4.07 – 25 SEPTEMBER 2024)

RRS
AC

RACING RULES OF SAILING – AMERICA'S CUP EDITION

Version 4.07

The Racing Rules of Sailing, America's Cup Edition has been approved by World Sailing for use in the 37th America's Cup. This America's Cup Edition v4 replaces the Racing Rules of Sailing in their entirety including all Appendices. These rules include changes approved by World Sailing in accordance with Regulation 28.1.3.

World Sailing
Special Event

INTRODUCTION

Terminology A term used in the sense stated in the Definitions is printed in italics or, in preambles, in bold italics (for example, *racing* and ***racing***).

Each of the terms in the table below is used in *The Racing Rules of Sailing* with the meaning given.

Term	*Meaning*
Competitor	A person who races or intends to race in the event.
Class Authority	The Rules Committee as appointed pursuant to Article 42.2(b).
Jury	The World Sailing International Jury, or Arbitration Panel as applicable under rule 69, appointed for AC 37.
Race committee	The Regatta Director and any other person performing a race committee function.
Racing rule / RRS	A rule in *The Racing Rules of Sailing America's Cup Edition v4*.
Vessel	Any boat or ship not competing in a race.
Boat	An AC75 class boat or an AC40 class boat (as applicable) competing in a race of AC 37 and the crew on board.

Other words and terms are used in the sense ordinarily understood in nautical or general use.

World Sailing Regulations The World Sailing regulations on: Eligibility, Anti-Doping, and Disciplinary are referred to in the definition *Rule*. The regulations that apply as a *rule* are published on the World Sailing website.

Cases and Calls Only Cases that are adopted by the jury or Calls adopted by the umpires are recognized as authoritative interpretations of these *Racing Rules of Sailing America's Cup Edition.*

Rule Numbering This edition of the rules has kept the original numbering of the World Sailing *Racing Rules of Sailing* (where possible) to aid reference to those rules.

DEFINITIONS

In interpreting these ***rules****, the definitions in Schedule 1 of the Protocol shall apply. Defined terms within the class rule shall apply unless a different definition is stated below. A term used as stated below is shown in italic type or, in preambles, in* ***bold italic*** *type.*

Abandon To *abandon* a race means to stop *racing* and not score the race.

Boundary The line that marks the limits of the *racing* area as designated via the *RO Comms*.

Capsize A boat is *capsized* when her masthead is in the water.

Clear Astern* and *Clear Ahead; Overlap One boat is *clear astern* of another when her *platform border* is behind a line abeam from the aftermost point of the other boat's media post. The other boat is *clear ahead*. They *overlap* when neither is *clear astern*. However, they also *overlap* when a boat between them *overlaps* both.

Conflict of Interest A person has a *conflict of interest* if he

(a) may gain or lose as a result of a decision to which he contributes,
(b) may reasonably appear to have a personal or financial interest which could affect his ability to be impartial, or
(c) has a close personal interest in a decision.

Fetching [deleted]

Finish A boat *finishes* when after being completely on the course side, any part of its *platform border* crosses the finishing line from the course side after completing any penalties. However:

(a) a boat has not *finished* if she continues to *sail the course*;
(b) in a match race, when penalties are cancelled under rule 44.4(c) after one or both boats have *finished*, each shall be recorded as *finished* when it crossed the line;
(c) in a fleet race, when a boat crosses a finishing line while still taking a penalty, or receives a penalty after finishing, and the boat does not complete the penalty and then crosses the finishing line, she has *finished* (but shall be scored as calculated by rule 44.4(g)).

Keep Clear A boat *keeps clear* of a right-of-way boat

(a) if the *keep clear border*s do not intersect,
(b) if the right-of-way boat can sail her course with no need to take avoiding action and,
(c) if the right-of-way boat can also change course in both directions without its *keep clear border* immediately intersecting the *keep clear border* of the *keep clear* boat.

Keep Clear Border A symmetrical polygon that touches the:

AC40	AC75
• aft point on the media post, • 2.000 m outboard of the transom corners, perpendicular to the LCP, • 2.000 m outboard of the maximum beam of 5.415 m, perpendicular to the LCP, at the foil arm region (6.278 m and 6.890 m forward of TRP), perpendicular to the LCP, and • 2.000 m outboard from 12.963 m forward of TRP, perpendicular to the LCP.	• aft point on the media post, • 2.000 m outboard of the transom corners, perpendicular to the LCP, • 2.000 m outboard of the maximum beam of 8.006 m, perpendicular to the LCP, at the foil arm region (10.000 m and 12.000 m forward of TRP), perpendicular to the LCP, and • 2.000 m outboard from 22.893 m forward of TRP, perpendicular to the LCP.

Note: LCP and TRP as defined in the applicable class rule

Leeward* and *Windward A boat's *leeward* side is the side that is or, when she is head to wind, was away from the wind. The other side is her *windward* side. When two boats on the same *tack overlap*, the boat on the *leeward* side of the other is the *leeward* boat. The other is the *windward* boat.

Mark An object the sailing instructions require a boat to leave on a specified side, a race committee vessel surrounded by navigable water from which the starting or finishing line extends, and an object intentionally attached to the object or vessel. However, an anchor line is not part of the *mark*.

Mark-Room *Room* for a boat to sail no farther from the *mark* than needed to sail her *proper course* to round or pass the *mark*, and *room* to pass a *finishing mark* after *finishing*.

Obstruction An object that a boat could not pass without changing course substantially, if she were sailing directly towards it and one of her hull lengths from it. An object that can be safely passed on only one side, a *boundary*, and any object, area or line so designated by a *rule* are also *obstructions*. However, a boat *racing* is not an *obstruction* to other boats unless they are required to:

(a) *keep clear* of her and the other boats are not approaching the starting line to *start* on opposite *tacks*; or
(b) avoid her under rule 22.

A vessel under way, including a boat *racing*, is never a continuing *obstruction*.

OCS A boat is *OCS* when at her starting signal any part of her *platform border* is determined at that time to be on the course side of the starting line or one of its extensions.

Overlap See ***Clear Astern* and *Clear Ahead; Overlap*.**

Party A *party* to a hearing is

(a) for a *protest* hearing: a protestor, a protestee;
(b) for a redress hearing: a boat requesting redress or for which redress is requested; a boat for which a hearing is called to consider redress under rule 60.3(b);
(c) for a redress hearing under rule 62.1(a): the body alleged to have made an improper action or omission;
(d) a person against whom an allegation of a breach of rule 69.1(a) is made; a person presenting an allegation under rule 69.2(e)(1);
(e) a support person subject to a hearing under rule 60.3(d) or 69; any boat that person supports; a person appointed to present an allegation under rule 60.3(d).

However, the Jury is never a *party*.

Platform Border A symmetrical polygon that touches the:

AC40	AC75
• aft point on the media post, • the transom corners, • the maximum beam of 5.415 m, perpendicular to the LCP, at the foil arm region (6.278 m and 6.890 m forward of TRP), and • 12.963 m forward of TRP	• aft point on the media post, • the transom corners, • the maximum beam of 8.006 m, perpendicular to the LCP, at the foil arm region (10.000 m and 12.000 m forward of TRP), and • 22.893 m forward of TRP

Note: LCP and TRP as defined in the applicable class rule

Postpone A *postponed* race is a race delayed before its scheduled start but may be started or *abandoned* later.

Proper Course A course a boat would choose in order to sail to the next *mark*, or *finish*, on the leg they believe they are on as soon as possible in the absence of the other boats referred to in the *rule* using the term. A boat has no *proper course* before her starting signal.

Protest An allegation made under rule 61.2 by a boat, the Regatta Director or the Jury that a boat has broken a *rule*.

Racing A boat is *racing* from her preparatory signal until she *finishes* and clears the finishing line and *marks* or retires, or until the race committee signals that *racing* is stopped.

RO Comms The communication system(s) provided by race management for boats and race officials when on the water consisting of

(a) information displayed on the RMS displays on each boat;
(b) light signals emitting from race management supplied equipment on each boat;
(c) information transmitted over the race management supplied radio;
(d) the clock on the sides of the Race Committee Signal Vessel;
(e) data supplied via the Media System Telemetry in accordance with the Class Rules;
Any communication listed above constitutes communication to a boat.

Room The space a boat needs in the existing conditions, including space to comply with her obligations under the rules of Part 2 and rule 28.3, while maneuvering promptly in a seamanlike way.

Rule (a) The *rules* in this book, including the Definitions, Introduction, preambles and the rules of relevant appendices, but not titles;

(b) The World Sailing Regulations on: Eligibility Code (Regulation 19); Anti-Doping Code (Regulation 21); and Disciplinary, Appeals and Review Code (Regulation 35);
(c) [deleted]
(d) the Class Rule;
(e) [deleted]; and
(f) the race conditions and sailing instructions.
(g) [deleted]

Sail the Course A boat *sails the course* when:

(a) she *starts*;
(b) a string representing her track until she *finishes*, when drawn taut,
    (1) passes each *mark* of the course for the race on the required side and in the correct order (including the starting marks),
    (2) touches each *mark* designated in the sailing instructions to be a rounding mark, and
    (3) passes between the *marks* of a gate from the direction of the course from the previous *mark*; then
(c) she *finishes*.

Scoring Distance is when one boat completed at least four legs and has complied with rule 28.1 up to that point. Sailing Instructions may change the number of legs required for the *scoring distance* in a Preliminary Regatta or a Youth and Women's AC Regatta.

Start A boat *starts* when:

(a) her *platform border* having been entirely on the pre-start side of the starting line at or after her starting signal, any part of her *platform border* crosses the starting line from the pre- start side to the course side*;* or
(b) having crossed the starting line from the pre-start side to the course side been identified as *OCS*, she completes a penalty for *OCS.*
(c) having been on or near the starting line at or after the starting signal, the boat is *OCS* but is not penalised as OCS.

Support Person Any person who provides, or may provide, physical or advisory support to a competitor, including any coach, trainer, manager, team staff, medic, paramedic or any other person working with, treating or assisting a competitor in, or preparing for, the competition.

Tack, Starboard* or *Port A boat is on the *tack, starboard* or *port*, corresponding to her *windward* side.

Windward See ***Leeward* and *Windward*.**

Zone The area

(a) within the radius of 60 meters around the signal mast on the marks;
(b) around *obstructions* (other than a *boundary*) within a distance of 60 meters;
(c) from the *boundary* within a distance of 115 meters in a match race and 90 meters in a fleet race; and
(d) around a boat *racing* or vessel within the course, when the boats are at that *obstruction*. A boat is in the *zone* when any part of her *platform border* is in the *zone*.

BASIC PRINCIPLES

SPORTSMANSHIP AND THE RULES

Competitors in the sport of sailing are governed by a body of *rules* that they are expected to follow and enforce. A fundamental principle of sportsmanship is that when a boat breaks a *rule* and is not exonerated she will promptly take an appropriate penalty or action, which may be to retire.

ENVIRONMENTAL RESPONSIBILITY

Participants are encouraged to minimize any adverse environmental impact of the sport of sailing.

PART 1

FUNDAMENTAL RULES

Races shall be umpired.

1 SAFETY

1.1 Helping Those in Danger

A boat, competitor or *support person* shall give all possible help to any person, boat, or vessel in danger.

1.2 Life-Saving Equipment and Personal Flotation Devices

A boat shall carry adequate life-saving equipment for all persons on board. Crew equipment requirements in these *racing rules* prescribe the minimum required. Each crewmember is individually responsible for wearing personal equipment adequate for the conditions.

1.3 First Aid Training

While *racing*, at least 50% of the crew on board a boat must have completed a recognized First Aid / CPR course. The Youth or Women's America's Cup regattas may increase this percentage via the Notice of Race.

2 FAIR SAILING

Competitors shall comply with the *rules* and act at all times in compliance with recognized principles of sportsmanship and fair play. A boat may be penalized under this rule only if it is clearly established that these principles have been violated. The penalty shall be a disqualification that is not excludable. When *racing*, a boat need not take a penalty unless signalled to do so by an umpire.

3 DECISION TO RACE

The responsibility for a boat's decision to participate in a race or to continue *racing* is hers alone.

4 ACCEPTANCE OF THE RULES

4.1 (a) By participating, or intending to participate, in an event conducted under the *rules*, each competitor agrees to accept the *rules*.

(b) A *support person*, by providing support, agrees to accept the *rules*.

4.2 A competitor agrees on behalf of their *support persons* that such *support persons* are bound by the *rules*.

4.3 Acceptance of the *rules* includes agreement:

(a) to be governed by the *rules*;

(b) to accept the penalties imposed and other action taken under the *rules*, subject to the appeal and review procedures provided in them, as the final determination of any matter arising under the *rules*;

(c) with respect to any such determination, not to resort to any court of law or tribunal not provided for in the *rules*; and

(d) for a competitor to ensure that their *support persons* are aware of the *rules*.

4.4 The person in charge of each boat shall ensure that all competitors including the crewmembers are aware of their responsibilities under this rule.

4.5 [deleted]

5 RULES GOVERNING ORGANIZING AUTHORITIES AND OFFICIALS

The organizing authority, race committee, technical committee, umpires, jury and other race officials shall be governed by the *rules* in the conduct and judging of the event.

6 WORLD SAILING REGULATIONS

6.1 Each competitor, boat owner and *support person* shall comply with the World Sailing Regulations defined as a *rule*. Rule 63.1 does not apply unless *protests* are permitted in the Regulation alleged to have been broken.

6.2 A competitor shall ensure that their crew in a race of the Match, CSS, and Preliminary Regattas, are registered as part of World Sailing's America's Cup Registered Testing Pool.

6.3 The Defender and Challengers shall ensure that the members of their sailing team who may sail for them in a race of the Match, CSS, and Preliminary Regattas, are registered as part of World Sailing's America's Cup Registered Testing Pool promptly after the individual enters into an arrangement with the Defender or Challenger and there is a possibility that the individual may sail for the Defender and Challengers in a race on an AC75 Class Boat. Details of how to register as part of the testing pool will be published when the testing pool is established.

6.4 The individual may only be removed from World Sailing's America's Cup Registered Testing Pool at the conclusion of AC37 or if the Defender or Challenger is certain that the individual will not sail for them in a race of AC37.

6.5 For the purposes of the World Sailing Anti-Doping Code, the racing in an event (as per Protocol Article 5) under these rules is a team sport.

7 LAST POINT OF CERTAINTY

The umpires will assume that the state of the boat, or her relationship to the other boat, has not changed, until they are certain that it has changed.

PART 2

WHEN BOATS MEET

The ***rules*** *of Part 2 apply between* boats *that are sailing in or near the racing area and intend to* ***race****, are* ***racing****, or have been* ***racing****. However, a* boat *not* ***racing*** *shall not be penalized for breaking one of these* ***rules****, except rule 23.1.*

When a boat *sailing under these* ***rules*** *meets a vessel that is not, she shall comply with the International Regulations for Preventing Collisions at Sea (IRPCAS) or government right-of-way rules.*

SECTION A

RIGHT OF WAY

A boat *has right of way when another* boat *is required to* ***keep clear*** *of her. However, some rules in Sections B, C and D limit the actions of a right-of-way* boat.

10 ON OPPOSITE TACKS

When boats are on opposite *tacks*, a *port-tack* boat shall *keep clear* of a *starboard-tack* boat.

11 ON THE SAME TACK, OVERLAPPED

When boats are on the same *tack* and *overlapped*, a *windward* boat shall *keep clear* of a *leeward* boat.

12 ON THE SAME TACK, NOT OVERLAPPED

When boats are on the same *tack* and not *overlapped*, a boat *clear astern* shall *keep clear* of a boat *clear ahead*.

13 [deleted]

SECTION B

GENERAL LIMITATIONS

14 AVOIDING CONTACT

If reasonably possible, a boat shall
(a) avoid contact with another boat,
(b) not cause contact between boats, and
(c) not cause contact between a boat and an object that should be avoided.
However, a right-of-way boat or one sailing within the *room* or *mark-room* to which she is entitled need not act to avoid contact until it is clear that the other boat is not *keeping clear* or giving *room* or *mark-room*.

15 ACQUIRING RIGHT OF WAY

When a boat acquires right of way, she shall initially give the other boat *room* to *keep clear*, unless she acquires right of way because of the other boat's actions.

16 CHANGING COURSE

16.1 When a right-of-way boat changes course, she shall give the other boat *room* to *keep clear*.

16.2 When sailing to a *mark* that is to windward, a *starboard-tack* boat shall not bear away to a course that is below her *proper course* if at that moment the *port-tack* boat that is *keeping clear* by sailing a course to pass to leeward of her has to immediately change course to continue *keeping clear*.

16.3 When sailing to a *mark* that is to leeward, a *starboard-tack* boat shall not luff to a course that is above her *proper course* if at that moment the *port-tack* boat that is *keeping clear* by sailing a course to pass to windward of her has to immediately change course to continue *keeping clear*.

17 [deleted]

SECTION C

AT MARKS AND OBSTRUCTIONS

Rules 18 and 19 do not apply at a starting ***mark*** *surrounded by navigable water or at its anchor line.*

18 MARK-ROOM

18.1 When Rule 18 Applies

(a) Rule 18 applies between boats when they are required to leave a *mark* on the same side and at least one of them is in the zone.

(b) Rule 18 does not apply between boats:

(1) when one boat is approaching a *mark* and one is leaving it;

(2) when the boat entitled to *mark-room* obtained an inside *overlap* and, from the time the *overlap* began, the outside boat is unable to give *mark-room*;

(3) when the boat entitled to *mark-room* leaves the *zone*; or

(4) when the boat entitled to *mark-room* is on the next leg and the *mark* is *clear astern* of her.

18.2 Giving Mark-Room

(a) When rule 18 first applies,

(1) if boats are *overlapped*, the outside boat at that moment shall thereafter give the inside boat *mark-room*.

(2) if boats are not *overlapped*, the boat that has not reached the *zone* shall thereafter give *mark-room*.

(b) If rule 18 no longer applies due to the boat entitled to *mark-room* leaving the *zone*, but is to be applied again, the relationship of the boats considered at the time rule 18 is re-applied.

18.3 [deleted]

18.4 Changing Tack

(a) If *mark-room* for a boat includes a change of *tack*, such tack or gybe shall be done no faster than a tack or gybe to sail her *proper course*.

(b) When an inside *overlapped* right-of-way boat must change *tack* at a *mark* to sail her *proper course*, until she changes *tack* she shall sail no farther from the *mark* than needed to sail that course if this affects the course of another boat before the right-of-way boat changes *tack*. This rule 18.4(b) does not apply at a gate *mark* or a finishing *mark*.

18.5 Sailing Within Mark-Room

When the boat entitled to *mark-room* has sailed farther from the *mark* than needed to sail its *proper course*, it is no longer sailing within the *mark-room* it was entitled to while rule 18 continues to apply.

19 ROOM TO PASS AN OBSTRUCTION

19.1 When Rule 19 Applies

(a) Rule 19 applies between boats when at least one of them is in the zone of an *obstruction*.

(b) Rule 19 does not apply between boats when:

(1) the *obstruction* is also a *mark* the boats are required to leave on the same side;

(2) rule 18 applies between the boats and the obstruction is another boat overlapped with each of them.

(3) the *obstruction* is the *boundary* prior to the starting signal and the boats are passing it on opposite sides; or

(4) rule 20 applies (note rule 20.1(b)(2)).

19.2 Giving Room at an Obstruction

(a) When rule 19 first applies, the right-of-way boat at that time may choose to pass an *obstruction* on either side. Except that, after *starting*, boats shall pass a *boundary* on the side to sail a *proper course*.

(b) When boats are *overlapped*, the outside boat shall give the inside boat *room* between her and the *obstruction*, unless:

(1) she has been unable to do so from the time the *overlap* began;

(2) she is unable to do so because she is giving or taking *mark-room* under rule 18.2(a); or

(3) she is unable to do so because she is taking *room* under rule 20.2.

However, *room* in rule 19.2 does not include *room* to tack unless it is the only option to pass and clear the *obstruction*.

20 ROOM TO PASS A BOUNDARY

20.1 When Rule 20 Applies

(a) Rule 20 applies between boats when at least one of them is in the zone of a *boundary*.

(b) Rule 20 does not apply between boats:

(1) when at least one of them has not started;

(2) when sailing instructions state that rule 19 applies to an identified part of the *boundary*; or

(3) if the boat required to give *room* is unable to do so because she is giving or taking *mark-room* under rule 18.2(a).

20.2 Giving Room at a Boundary

(a) In a match race, when rule 20 first applies, an outside *overlapped* or *clear astern* boat at that moment shall thereafter give an inside or *clear ahead* boat *room* to sail her *proper course*, while that boat is in the *zone* of the *boundary;*

(b) In a fleet race, when rule 20 first applies, an outside *overlapped* or *clear-astern* boat at that moment shall:
   (1) thereafter give an inside or *clear-ahead* boat *room* to sail her *proper course*, while that boat is in the *zone of the boundary;* and
   (2) she shall initially give the other boat *room* to *keep clear* when it is no longer in the *boundary*

(c) When boats are passing a *boundary* on opposite sides, a boat sailing on a leg to a windward *mark* or windward gate shall be considered the inside boat.

SECTION D

OTHER RULES

When rule 22 applies between two boats, Section A rules do not.

21 [deleted]

22 CAPSIZED, ANCHORED OR AGROUND; RESCUING

If possible, a boat shall avoid a boat that is *capsized* or has not regained control after *capsizing*, vessels that are assisting a boat that had *capsized*, a boat that is anchored or aground, or a boat or a vessel that is trying to help a person or vessel in danger.

23 INTERFERING WITH ANOTHER BOAT

23.1 If reasonably possible, a boat not racing shall not interfere with a boat that is racing, its match racing opponent prior to the preparatory signal, or an umpire vessel.

23.2 Except when sailing her *proper course*, a boat shall not interfere with a boat sailing on another leg.

23.3 When boats in different matches meet, any course sailed by either boat shall be consistent with complying with a *rule* or trying to win her own match.

PART 3

CONDUCT OF A RACE

25 SAILING INSTRUCTIONS AND SIGNALS

25.1 The Regatta Director shall publish written sailing instructions for a regatta in accordance with Protocol Article 35.

25.2 The sailing instructions may be changed. Changes to the sailing instructions that bring a scheduled start time for the first race of the day forward will be published before 20:30 on the day before the change takes effect. Other changes to the sailing instructions will be communicated to each boat not less than 5 minutes before the starting signal of the race that is affected via the *RO Comms*.

25.3 The race committee shall schedule races so that each round-robin is completed in order, as soon as possible, based on the available schedule.

26 STARTING RACES

26.1 Races shall be started by using the following signals.

Minutes: seconds before start

3:00 Warning signal
2:10 Preparatory signal;
1:00 End of pre-start entry time
0:00 Starting Signal

26.2 The race committee shall communicate via the *RO Comms* the time of the warning signal for each match.

26.3 In the match racing pairing list, the boat listed on the left or on the top is assigned the port end of the entry line; the other boat is assigned the starboard end of the entry line.

27 OTHER ACTIONS BEFORE THE STARTING SIGNAL

27.1 No later than the warning signal, the race committee shall signal via the *RO Comms* the course to be sailed.

27.2 No later than the warning signal, the race committee may move a starting *mark*.

27.3 Before the starting signal, the race committee may for any reason *postpone* or stop the race via the *RO Comms*.

27.4 Requirements before the start in a match race.

(a) The port entry boat shall

(1) have her *platform border* outside the line that is at a 90° angle to the starting line through the port side starting *mark* at the preparatory signal, and

(2) in the period from the preparatory signal to 1 minute prior to the starting signal, have her *platform border* cross the starting line, the first time from the windward side to the leeward side.

(b) The starboard entry boat shall

(1) have her *platform border* outside the line that is at a 90° angle to the starting line through the starboard side starting *mark* at 10 seconds after the preparatory signal, and

(2) in the period from 10 seconds after the preparatory signal to 1 minute prior to the starting signal, have her *platform border* cross the starting line, the first time from the windward side to the leeward side.

27.5 Boats shall not be under tow between the Warning signal and the Preparatory signal.

28 SAILING THE COURSE

28.1 A boat shall *sail the course*. While doing so, she may leave on either side a *mark* that does not begin, bound or end the leg she is sailing. After *finishing* she need not cross the finishing line completely.

28.2 A boat may correct any errors in *sailing the course*, provided she has not *finished*.

28.3 While *racing*, a boat shall be within the *boundary*.

29 RECALLS

When a boat is *OCS*, it will be promptly identified and notified via the *RO Comms*.

30 [deleted]

31 [deleted]

32 SHORTENING, ABANDONING OR STOPPING RACING

32.1 The race committee may shorten a course by reducing the number of legs to a course no fewer than the *scoring distance*. A shortened course will be signalled via the *RO Comms* and indicate the leg that the shortened course applies to. The boats shall *finish* at a finishing line between the staffs on the gate *marks* that end the leg signalled.

32.2 After the starting signal, the race committee may stop a race for a reason directly affecting the safety or fairness of the competition. The race committee may also stop a race for scheduling reasons. If a match race is stopped under this rule before a boat has *finished*, the race is *abandoned*. This shall be communicated via the *RO Comms*.

32.3 An *abandoned* race may be re-sailed.

32.4 If a boat *starts* and reaches the *zone* of either windward gate *marks* without the need to tack, then the race is stopped and *abandoned*.

33 CHANGING THE NEXT LEG OF THE COURSE

33.1 While boats are *racing* the race committee may change a leg of the course that begins at a rounding *mark* or at a gate by changing the position of the next *mark* (or the finishing line) and signalling all boats before they begin the leg. The next *mark* need not be in position at that time.

33.2 A change of course will be signalled via the *RO Comms* and will include the approximate new position.

33.3 Subsequent legs may be changed without further signalling to maintain the course shape.

34 MARK MISSING

34.1 If a *mark* is missing or out of position while boats are *racing* the race committee shall, if possible, replace it in its correct position or substitute a race committee vessel or inflatable buoy. If a *mark* is substituted, a description of the substitute *mark* will be communicated via the *RO Comms*.

34.2 In the event that the race committee is unable to set a gate, the existing single *mark* shall be rounded to starboard.

35 TIME LIMITS

35.1 The sailing instructions will detail the following time limits:

(a) The leg 1 time limit; and

(b) The race time limit.

35.2 If no boat crosses a line that is from the mark that ends leg 1, on the course axis extending away from the course direction of the next leg, within the leg 1 time limit, the race is stopped and *abandoned*.

35.3 If no boat *finishes* within the race time limit, the race is stopped and if a match race, *abandoned*

35.4 If a boat *sails the course* and *finishes* within the race time limit, the race committee shall stop the race 5 minutes after the first boat has *finished*;

36 RACES TO BE RE-STARTED OR RE-SAILED

If a race is re-started or re-sailed, a breach of a *rule* in the original race, or in any previous restart or re-sail of that race, shall not:

(a) prohibit a boat from competing; or

(b) cause a boat to be penalized except under rule 2, or 69 or under rule 14 when she has caused injury or serious damage.

37 [deleted]

PART 4

OTHER REQUIREMENTS WHEN RACING

Part 4 rules apply only to boats ***racing*** *unless the rule states otherwise.*

SECTION A

GENERAL REQUIREMENTS

40 [deleted]

41 OUTSIDE HELP

A boat shall not receive help from any outside source, except

(a) help for the removal of an injured or ill person. Once a person has been removed from the boat, that person shall not be returned or replaced;

(b) after a collision, help from the crew of the other boat or vessel to get clear;

(c) [deleted];

(d) unsolicited information from a disinterested source that is not received via electronic means, which may be another boat in the same race;

(e) communication via the *RO Comms* with the race committee and umpires and another boat in the same race;

(f) satellite navigation systems used solely to ascertain the boat's position including "aiding" signals such as DGPS (differential GPS), SBAS (space-based augmentation signals), or RTK (real time kinematic) correction data.

42 PROPULSION

A boat shall compete only by using the wind and water to increase, maintain or decrease her speed. Subject to the limits imposed by the AC75 Class Rule, her crew may adjust the trim of the boat including its components and perform other acts of seamanship. This includes repeated trimming or pumping of the sails.

43 EXONERATION

43.1 (a) When as a consequence of breaking a *rule* a boat has compelled another boat to break a *rule*, the other boat is exonerated for her breach.

(b) When a boat is sailing within the *room* or *mark-room* to which she is entitled and, as a consequence of an incident with a boat required to give her that *room* or *mark-room* she breaks a rule of Section A of Part 2, rule 15, or 16, she is exonerated for her breach.

(c) A right-of-way boat or one entitled to *room* or *mark-room* is exonerated for breaking rule 14 if the contact does not cause serious damage, or injury.

43.2 A boat exonerated for breaking a *rule* need not take a penalty and shall not be penalized for breaking that *rule*.

44 PENALTIES GIVEN BY UMPIRES

44.1 After a 'Y flag protest' is communicated to the umpires, they shall decide whether to penalize any boat, or they may act under rule 60.4. They shall communicate via the *RO Comms* one of the following decisions:

(a) 'No penalty.'

(b) The identified boat shall take a penalty by complying with rules 44.2 and 44.3.

(c) The identified boat is disqualified or has retired, and if the race is a Match Race, the match is stopped and awarded to the other boat, unless rule 100.4 applies.

44.2 Penalties

(a) **OCS Penalties**

Penalty for boats that are *OCS*:

(1) while inside the *boundary*, the penalized boat shall act to reduce her VMG / VMC until she is 75 metres behind the other boat or boats that have started without a penalty and, in a fleet race, have crossed the starting line to start no more than five seconds after the starting signal, or

(2) the penalized boat shall *start* as per definition start (a).

A boat that crossed the starting line from the pre-start side to the course side within 3 seconds prior to the starting signal shall take penalty option (1) or (2), otherwise a boat shall take OCS penalty option (2).

(b) **Penalties for breaches of a *rule* in the pre-start, or Part 2 breaches for boats on the same leg of the course or within the *zone* of a *mark***

Penalty for breaches of a *rule* in the pre-start, or Part 2 breaches for boats on the same leg of the course or within the *zone* of a *mark*: after her starting signal and while inside the *boundary*, the penalized boat shall act immediately to reduce her VMG / VMC until she is 75 metres behind the other boat, or in a fleet race, a boat as determined by an umpire.

(c) **Other Penalties after the starting signal**

Penalty for breaches of a *rule* (other than penalties under rule 44.2(a) or 44.2(b)) that is signalled after the starting signal: while inside the *boundary*, the penalized boat shall act immediately to reduce her VMG / VMC until she loses 75 metres compared to a boat (as determined by the Umpires) that has *started* correctly and without a penalty.

44.3 Penalty Limitations

A boat shall complete her penalty within 60 seconds of the signal of the penalty, or within 60 seconds of the starting signal if the penalty was signaled prior to the start. A boat failing to do this will get an additional penalty unless the umpires decide that there are good reasons that prevented the penalty being completed. When a boat has multiple penalties, the time limit for the subsequent penalty will start when the prior penalty is completed.

44.4 Penalty completion

(a) A boat completes her penalty when the umpires determine that a boat has lost the required distance and they have signalled that the penalty is completed via the *RO Comms*;

(b) **[Deleted];**

(c) In a match race, if a boat has a penalty and the other boat is penalized, each penalty shall be cancelled, and this shall be signalled via the *RO Comms*. This rule does not apply to penalties for *OCS*.

(d) **OCS with other penalties**: In a match race, if at least one boat is penalized for *OCS* and the boat(s) penalized for *OCS* crossed the starting line from the pre-start side to the course side within 3 seconds prior to the starting signal: the umpires shall cancel one penalty on the trailing boat and

(1) if the trailing boat still has a penalty, the penalty on the lead boat will be cancelled, leaving the trailing boat the requirement to complete its outstanding penalties; or

(2) if the trailing boat no longer has an outstanding penalty, one penalty on the lead boat shall then be cancelled when both boats are on the same ladder rung of the trailing boat.

(e) When it is clear to the umpires that the penalized boat is reducing her VMG / VMC but the loss of distance is not being incurred as intended, or the situation is not covered in rule 44.2, 44.3, or 44.4(b), the umpires shall make their best effort to calculate what the VMG / VMC reduction should be. When they are satisfied with the loss of distance, the umpires shall signal that the penalty is completed via the *RO Comms*; or

(f) In a match race, if one boat has *finished* and is no longer *racing*, and the other boat has an outstanding penalty, the umpires may cancel the outstanding penalty.

(g) In a fleet race, a boat that *finishes* in accordance with the definition of *finish* (c) shall have the time it crossed the finishing line increased by 20 seconds for each outstanding penalty.

44.5 All Penalties

The following applies to penalties described in rules 44.2 and 44.3:

(a) Distance regarding penalties is measured between the most advanced points of the *platform border* measured along the true wind axis of the non-penalized boat, or as chosen by the umpires.

(b) If a boat has multiple penalties, then

(1) the distance a boat is required to be behind in rule 44.2(a) and 44.2(b), or the distance a boat is required to lose in rule 44.2(c), is multiplied by the number of the penalties given; and

(2) when a boat has both a 44.2(a) or 44.2(b) penalty and a 44.2(c) penalty, the 44.2(a) or 44.2(b) penalty shall be taken prior to the boat taking the 44.2(c) penalty.

(c) **Umpire Errors:**

(1) If the umpires immediately decide the umpire signal communicated via RO Comms is not the intended signal, they shall immediately communicate the correct signal via RO Comms;

(2) If the umpires are certain that a penalty that is not yet completed was an incorrect umpire decision, the penalty shall be removed and signalled as completed via the *RO Comms*.

45 HAULING OUT; MAKING FAST; ANCHORING

A boat shall be afloat and off moorings at her preparatory signal. Thereafter, she shall not be hauled out or made fast except to bail out, reef sails or make repairs. She may anchor or the crew may stand on the bottom. She shall recover the anchor before continuing in the race unless she is unable to do so.

46 PERSON IN CHARGE

A boat shall have on board a person in charge designated by the member or organization that entered the boat. See rule 75.

47 TRASH DISPOSAL

Competitors and *support persons* shall not intentionally put trash in the water. This rule applies at all times while afloat in the *racing* area and on a scheduled race day. The penalty for a breach of this rule may be less than disqualification.

SECTION B

EQUIPMENT-RELATED REQUIREMENTS

48 LIMITATIONS ON EQUIPMENT AND CREW

48.1 A boat shall use only the equipment on board at her preparatory signal.

48.2 A boat shall not permit any person on board to intentionally leave unless ill, injured, or temporarily swimming in order to perform a necessary function. Except after temporarily swimming, a person leaving shall not be accepted back on board nor replaced during the race.

49 [deleted]

50 [deleted]

51 [deleted]

52 [deleted]

53 [deleted]

54 [deleted]

55 [deleted]

56 [deleted]

PART 5

PROTESTS, REDRESS, HEARINGS AND MISCONDUCT

SECTION A

PROTESTS; REDRESS; RULE 69 ACTION

60 RIGHT TO PROTEST OR RULE 69 ACTION

60.1 A boat

(a) may 'Y flag protest' another boat under a rule of Part 2 except rule 14, for an incident in which she was involved;

(b) may 'Red Flag *protest*' another boat for a breach of a *rule*, except for:

(1) rules 1, 14, 27, 28, 42, 44, 47, 87 or a *rule* allowed to be protested under rule 60.1(a);

(2) a Class Rule; and

(3) sailing instructions where race management prohibits boats from protesting that instruction; and

(c) may report to the jury requesting action under rule 60.3(d), or to the Arbitration Panel requesting action under rule 69.2(b).

60.2 The Regatta Director

(a) may *protest* a boat for a breach of a *rule*, but not:

(1) for a rule of Part 2;

(2) for a rule listed in 60.4(a);

(3) for a Class Rule; and

(4) as a result of information arising from an invalid *protest*, or from a report from a competitor other than the representative of the boat herself;

(b) [deleted]; and

(c) may report to the jury requesting action under rule 60.3(d), or to the Arbitration Panel requesting action under rule 69.2(b).

60.3 The jury

(a) may *protest* a boat for a breach of a *rule* when during the hearing of a valid *protest* it learns that the boat, although not a *party* to the hearing, was involved in the incident and may have broken a *rule*;

(b) after receiving a report from the Measurement Committee that a boat has serious damage or injury, and after consulting with the umpires, may disqualify one or both boats for breaking rule 14 without a hearing.

(c) shall consider redress when the Measurement Committee reports that a boat has serious physical damage or injury. This consideration of redress does not require a hearing.
(d) may call a hearing to consider whether a *support person* has broken a *rule*, based on its own observation or information received from any source, including evidence taken during a hearing.
(e) may protest a boat in the Youth or Women's America's Cup regatta for breaking rule 14,

60.4 When the umpires decide that a boat has:
(a) broken rules 27.4, 27.5, 28.3, 42, 44.2, or 47;
(b) gained an advantage by breaking a *rule* after allowing for a penalty;
(c) committed a breach of sportsmanship;
(d) been identified as *OCS*; or
(e) broken rule 41 by receiving physical help;
she shall be penalized under rule 44.1(b) or 44.1(c);
(f) or is *capsized* when *racing*, unless there is an outstanding incident to be decided; or
(g) broken rule 14 and the serious damage or injury has been confirmed by the Measurement Committee; (g) she shall be penalized under rule 44.1(c).

60.5 However, neither a boat nor a committee may *protest* for an alleged breach of rule 69 or a Regulation referred to in rule 6, unless permitted by the Regulation concerned.

60.6 The Arbitration Panel may call a hearing to consider an allegation of a breach of rule 69.1(a) and act under rule 69.2(b).

60.7 After one boat has *started*, if the umpires are satisfied that the other boat will not *finish*, they may signal under rule 44.1(c) that the boat that will not *finish* is disqualified.

60.8 No proceedings of any kind may be taken in relation to any action or non-action by the umpires, except as permitted in rule 62.

61 PROTEST REQUIREMENTS

61.1 Informing the Protestee and Umpires

For 'Y flag protests' a boat shall signal immediately after an incident in which she was involved by pressing the appropriate button on the RMS display. If this signal is not received, boats shall communicate via the *RO Comms*.

61.2 Protest Contents

A *protest* under 60.1(b), 60.2 and 60.3 shall be delivered in writing to the jury (including by email to 'protest@acofficials.org') and be copied to the boat being protested and identify:
(a) the protestor and protestee; and
(b) the incident, including where and when it occurred.

61.3 Protest Time Limit

A *protest* under 60.1(b) shall be lodged no later than sixty (60) minutes after the last race of the day is stopped. Other *protests* shall be lodged within two hours after the receipt of the relevant information. The jury shall extend the time if there is good reason to do so.

62 REDRESS

62.1 Consideration of redress shall be based on a claim or possibility that a boat's score in a race or series has been or may be, through no fault of her own, made significantly worse by:
(a) [deleted]
(b) injury to the crew or serious physical damage to a boat; while she was *racing* because of the action of a boat that was breaking a *rule* of Part 2 and took an appropriate penalty or was penalized; or of a vessel not *racing* that was required to *keep clear* or is determined to be at fault under the *IRPCAS* or a government right-of-way rule;
(c) [deleted]
(d) an action of another boat, or a crew member or *support person* of that boat resulted in a penalty under rule 2 or a penalty or warning under rule 69.2; or
(e) an action by a third party (including a race official) that causes injury to the crew or serious physical damage to a boat while that boat was *racing*.

SECTION B

HEARINGS AND DECISIONS

63 HEARINGS

63.1 Requirement for a Hearing

A boat or person shall not be penalized without a protest hearing, except as provided in rules 44, 60.3(b), 60.3(c), 60.4, 64.3(a), and 69.2(h)(2).

The jury shall hear all *protests* that have been delivered unless the *protest* is withdrawn.

63.2 Type, Time and Place of the Hearing; Time for Parties to Prepare

(a) The jury shall decide if the hearing is an oral hearing or a hearing on papers.

(b) All *parties* to the hearing shall be notified of:

(1) the time and place of the oral hearing; or

(2) the procedures should the hearing be heard on papers.

(c) the *protest* information shall be made available to all *parties*;

(d) the *parties* shall be allowed reasonable time to prepare for the hearing.

63.3 Right to Be Present at an Oral Hearing

(a) The *parties* to the hearing (up to two representatives of each) have the right to be present throughout the hearing of the evidence at an oral hearing (unless such evidence is deemed by the jury to breach design confidentiality). Any witness, other than a member of the jury, shall be excluded except when giving evidence.

(b) If a *party* to the hearing of a *protest* does not come to the hearing, the jury may nevertheless proceed with the hearing. If the *party* was unavoidably absent, the jury may reopen the hearing.

63.4 Conflict of Interest

(a) A jury or Arbitration Panel member shall declare any possible *conflict of interest* as soon as he is aware of it. A *party* to the hearing who believes a member of the jury or Arbitration Panel has a *conflict of interest* shall object as soon as possible. A *conflict of interest* declared by the jury or Arbitration Panel member shall be included in the written information provided under rule 65.2.

(b) A member of the jury or Arbitration Panel with a *conflict of interest* shall not be a member of the committee for a hearing.

63.5 Validity of the Protest

At the beginning of the hearing the jury shall take any evidence it considers necessary to decide whether all requirements for the *protest* have been met. If they have been met, the *protest* is valid and the hearing shall be continued. If not, the committee shall declare the *protest* invalid and close the hearing.

63.6 Taking Evidence and Communicating a Decision

(a) The jury shall take the evidence, including hearsay evidence, of the parties and of their witnesses present at the hearing and other evidence it considers necessary. However, the jury may exclude evidence which it considers is irrelevant or unduly repetitive.

(b) A member of the jury who saw the incident shall, while the parties are present, state that fact and may give evidence.
(c) A *party* present at the hearing may question any person who gives evidence.
(d) The jury shall then give the weight it considers appropriate to the evidence presented, find the facts and base its decision on them.

63.7 [deleted]

63.8 [deleted]

63.9 Hearings under Rule 60.3(d) – Support Persons

If the jury decides to call a hearing under rule 60.3(d), it shall promptly follow the procedures in rules 63.2, 63.3, 63.4 and 63.6, except that the information given to the *parties* shall be details of the alleged breach and a person may be appointed by the jury to present the allegation.

64 DECISIONS

64.1 Standard of Proof, Majority Decisions and Reclassifying Requests

(a) The jury shall make its decision based on a balance of probabilities, unless provided for otherwise in the *rule* alleged to have been broken.
(b) Decisions of the jury shall be by simple majority vote of all members. When there is equal division of votes cast, the chair of the hearing may cast an additional vote.
(c) The jury shall proceed with each case, as a *protest*, request for redress or other type of request, based on the information in the written request or allegation and testimony during the hearing. This permits the type of case to be changed if appropriate.

64.2 Penalties

(a) When the jury decides that a boat that is a *party* to a protest hearing has broken a *rule*, it shall disqualify her unless it decides that the breach has not (or could not reasonably be expected to have) improved the performance of the boat or has not (or could not reasonably be expected to have) had a significant effect on the outcome of a race, in which case it may make another arrangement it decides is equitable which may be to impose no penalty.
(b) However, the jury will not penalize a boat if the Arbitration Panel are dealing with a case regarding the same incident or if the Arbitration Panel has awarded a penalty for a breach of a *rule* regarding the same incident.
(c) In addition to rule 64.2(a), when the jury decide that a boat in the Youth or Women's America's Cup regatta has broken rule 14, it may impose a discretionary points penalty.

64.3 Decisions on Redress

When the jury decides that a boat is entitled to redress under rule 62, it shall consult with the Regatta Director and Measurement Committee and be bound by the opinions of the Measurement Committee regarding times to make repair or replacement. The Jury shall then make as fair an arrangement as possible for all boats affected, whether or not they asked for redress, subject to the redress available to the jury being limited to:

(a) adjusting the score of the race in which the incident being considered occurred. In a Match Race, this is limited to effectively awarding the race to the boat entitled to redress;
(b) granting a delay in the scheduled races involving the boat that are on the same day of the incident being considered;
(c) granting a delay in the scheduled races involving the boat for up to:
  (1) two calendar days following the incident if the incident was in the Round Robin Stage of the Challenger Selection Series; or
  (2) one calendar day following the incident; and
(d) order a re-sail of a race if redress is granted under rule 62;

except that redress cannot delay the schedule for the start of the next stage or the start of the Match, and in a Preliminary Regatta and the Youth or Women's America's Cup regattas, only option (a) is available.

64.4 [deleted]

64.5 Decisions Concerning Support Persons

(a) When the jury decides that a support person who is a *party* to a hearing under rule 60.3(d) or 69 has broken a rule, it may
  (1) issue a warning,
  (2) exclude the person from the event or venue or remove any privileges or benefits, or
  (3) take other action within its jurisdiction as provided by the *rules*.
(b) The jury may also penalize a boat that is a *party* to a hearing under rule 60.3(d) or 69 for the breach of a rule by a support person by changing the boat's score in a single race, up to and including the score for disqualification, when the jury decides that
  (1) the boat may have gained a competitive advantage as the result of the breach by the *support person*, or
  (2) the *support person* committed a further breach after the jury warned the boat in writing, following a previous hearing, that a penalty may be imposed.

65 INFORMING THE PARTIES AND OTHERS

65.1 After making its decision, the jury shall promptly inform the *parties* to the hearing of the facts found, the applicable *rules*, the decision, the reasons for it, and any penalties imposed or redress given.

65.2 A party to the hearing is entitled to receive the above information in writing as soon as reasonably possible.

65.3 Unless there is good reason not to do so, after any hearing, including a hearing under rule 69, the jury may publish the information set out in rule 65.1. The jury may direct that the information is to be confidential to the parties.

66 REOPENING A HEARING

66.1 The jury may reopen a hearing when it decides that it may have made a significant error, or when significant new evidence becomes available within a reasonable time. A *party* to the hearing may not ask for a reopening.

66.2 [deleted]

66.3 [deleted]

67 [deleted]

SECTION C

MISCONDUCT

69 MISCONDUCT

69.1 Obligation not to Commit Misconduct; Resolution

(a) A competitor or *support person* shall not commit an act of misconduct.

(b) Misconduct is:

(1) conduct that is a breach of good manners, a breach of good sportsmanship, or unethical behaviour; or

(2) conduct that may bring, or has brought, the sport into disrepute.

(c) An allegation of a breach of rule 69.1(a) shall be resolved in accordance with the provisions of rule 69. It shall not be grounds for a *protest* and rule 63.1 does not apply.

69.2 Action by the Arbitration Panel acting under rule 69

(a) The Arbitration Panel acting under this rule shall have at least three members.

(b) When the Arbitration Panel, from its own observation or from information received from any source, including evidence taken during a hearing, believes a person may have broken rule 69.1(a), it shall report the matter to the Event Disciplinary Investigating Officer under World Sailing Disciplinary Code 35.4.3 in schedule 3.

(c) [deleted]

(d) If the Event Disciplinary Investigating Officer issues a charge of misconduct, all relevant information the Event Disciplinary Investigation Officer gathers, favourable or unfavourable, shall be disclosed to the Arbitration Panel and to the *parties*.

(e) If the Event Disciplinary Investigating Officer issues a charge of misconduct, the Arbitration Panel shall promptly inform the person of the time and place of the hearing and follow the procedures in rules 63.2, 63.3(a), 63.4, 63.6, 65.1, 65.2, 66, and Appendix N4 except that:
  (1) the 'jury' referenced in rules 63.2, 63.3(a), 63.4 and 63.6 shall be the Arbitration Panel;
  (2) the Event Disciplinary Investigation Officer shall present the allegation; and
  (3) a person against whom an allegation has been made under this rule shall be entitled to have an advisor and a representative with him.

(f) If the person
  (1) provides good reason why he is unable to come to the hearing at the scheduled time, the Arbitration Panel shall reschedule it; or
  (2) does not provide good reason and does not come to the hearing, the Arbitration Panel may conduct it without the person present.

(g) The standard of proof to be applied is the test of the comfortable satisfaction of the Arbitration Panel, bearing in mind the seriousness of the alleged misconduct.

(h) If the allegation or any part of the allegation is upheld, the Arbitration Panel may take one or more of the following actions
  (1) issue a warning;
  (2) take any other action within its jurisdiction (refer Protocol Article 67.3).

(i) A competitor may be penalized under rule 69.2 for the misconduct of a *support person*. However, a penalty may only be imposed on a competitor for the misconduct of a *support person* if
  (1) the competitor may have gained a competitive advantage as a result of the misconduct; or
  (2) the *support person* has committed a further act of misconduct after the competitor has been warned by the Arbitration Panel; or
  (3) the Arbitration Panel decides that such a penalty is necessary to prevent future misconduct of the *support person*.

(j) If the Arbitration Panel

(1) imposes a penalty greater than a disqualification from one race;
(2) excludes the person from the event or venue; or
(3) in any other case if it considers it appropriate,

it shall report its findings, including the facts found, its conclusions and decision to World Sailing in accordance with World Sailing Disciplinary Code 35.4.7 in schedule 3. If the Arbitration Panel has acted under rule 69.2(f)(2), the report shall also include that fact and the reasons for it.

(k) [deleted]

69.3 Action by World Sailing

The disciplinary powers, procedures and responsibilities of World Sailing that apply are specified in the World Sailing Disciplinary Code in schedule 3. World Sailing may impose further penalties, including suspension of eligibility, under that Code.

70 [deleted]

71 [deleted]

PART 6

ENTRY AND QUALIFICATION

75 Competitors shall comply with World Sailing Regulation 19, Eligibility Code.

76 [deleted]

77 [deleted]

78 [deleted]

79 [deleted]

PART 7

RACE ORGANIZATION

84 OFFICIAL NOTICEBOARD

The Official Noticeboard is at the address: http://noticeboard.americascup.com/

85 [deleted]

86 CHANGES TO THE RACING RULES

86.1 A rule (as defined in *rule* (a)) may only be changed with the agreement of COR/D and the approval of World Sailing, except that the Regatta Director may change rule 87.

87 TEAM SUPPORT VESSELS

87.1 A boat
- (a) shall have the primary team support vessel inside the flag area while it is *racing*;
- (b) and its support vessels shall comply with instructions given by the Regatta Director or the Course Marshal in regards to team support vessels;
- (c) Sailing Instructions may change rule 87.1(a)

87.2 Team support vessels:
- (a) shall be clearly identifiable with the boat they support;
- (b) shall have a rescue net able to be fitted on or near the bow for the purpose of crew recovery; and
- (c) that are allowed in the *racing* area under rule 87.3 shall not exceed fifteen meters in length and three meters in height (not including mast / antennae) unless otherwise approved by the Regatta Director.

87.3 The primary team support vessel required to be in the flag area under rule 87.1(a) shall have:
- (a) one person to be the incident co-coordinator;
- (b) one person to be a rescue swimmer;
- (c) one person to support the rescue swimmer;
- (d) one person with appropriate first aid training;
- (e) an AED device (defibrillator);
- (f) a first aid kit that the boat believes is fit for purpose and that includes resuscitation equipment; and
- (g) a spinal board.

No person shall be responsible for more than one role described in rules 87.3(a) to (d).

87.4 Except in the case of an emergency, a team support vessel shall not interfere with boats that are *racing*.

87.5 A boat is responsible for the actions of her support vessel and shall be considered a *party* in any *protest* under this rule 87.

88 [deleted]

89 [deleted]

90 RACE COMMITTEE; SAILING INSTRUCTIONS; SCORING

90.1 [deleted]
90.2 [deleted]
90.3 Scoring
(a) The race committee shall score a race or series as provided in Part 8 and Part 9.
(b) [deleted]
(c) When the race committee determines from its own records or observations that it has scored a boat incorrectly, it shall correct the error and make the corrected scores available to competitors. Only the Jury may take other scoring actions that worsen a boat's score.
(d) The race committee shall implement scoring changes directed by the jury, the Arbitration Panel, or World Sailing as a result of decisions made in accordance with the rules.
(e) Notwithstanding the provisions in rule 90.3(a), (c) and (d), there shall be no changes to race or series scores resulting from action, including the correction or errors, initiated more than 24 hours after;
(1) the *protest* time limit of last race of the series (including a single race series);
(2) being informed of a jury decision after the last race of the series; or
(3) the results of the series are published.

However, in exception, changes to scores shall be made resulting from action under rules regarding Anti-Doping, Betting and Anti-Corruption, or 69, or by a jury acting under a valid hearing.

91 INTERNATIONAL JURY

91.1 There will be an international jury. It shall be composed as required by rule N1 and have the authority and responsibilities stated in rule N2.
91.2 There shall be no appeal from decisions of the international jury constituted in compliance with Appendix N.

92 [deleted]

PART 8

SCORING A MATCH RACING EVENT or STAGE

See rule 90.3

100 SCORING A MATCH RACE

In a match race:

100.1 The winner is the first boat to comply with rule 28.1 or has a race awarded to her under rule 44.1(c), unless she is disqualified or retires. When that boat is disqualified or retires, then the other boat is the winner unless it is disqualified or retires. If both boats are disqualified or retire then both boats will be scored as the loser of the race (both boats scored 0).

100.2 If boats that have complied with rule 28.1 are tied at the finishing line, and neither retires after *finishing* or is disqualified, the race may be re-sailed if the Regatta Director decides that this can be practically completed. If not, each boat will share the points available for that race.

100.3 When only one boat has started and the race is stopped under rule 32.2 due to conditions affecting the safety of the competition, the race shall not be re-sailed, and the boat that has started shall be the winner of the race unless she is disqualified or retires. If neither boat has started within 5 minutes after the starting signal, then the boats will be scored as the loser of the race (both boats scored 0).

100.4 If the umpires penalize a boat for a *capsize* under rule 60.4(f) prior to that boat starting, and the other boat is outside the flag area or is breaking rule 41, the boats will be scored as the loser of the race (both boats scored 0)

101 SCORING A SERIES

101.1 When a boat withdraws from part of a match racing event the scores of all completed races shall stand.

101.2 Scoring the Louis Vuitton Cup Round-Robin Stage

(a) Boats in the Challenger Selection Series Round Robin Stage shall be placed in order of their total scores, highest score ranked first. A round robin will only be scored if races between all the Challengers in that round has been completed.

(b) Ties shall be broken according to rule 102.

101.3 Scoring a Knockout Stage

(a) The Protocol or sailing instructions shall state the minimum number of points required to win a knockout stage between two competitors. The first competitor to achieve the minimum number of points is the winner.

(b) If a boat has not achieved the minimum number of points by the end of the final scheduled day of that series, then the winner shall be the boat with the highest score. However, this rule does not apply to the Match.
(c) Ties shall be broken according to rule 102.

101.4 In a Preliminary Regatta Round-Robin Stage:
(a) Boats shall be placed in order of their total scores, highest score ranked first.
(b) When a round-robin series is not complete;
(1) if each boat in the round robin has been scored in three or more races of a round- robin series by the end of the final scheduled day, the maximum points in the round- robin that are available to all boats is equal to the number of races sailed by the boat having been scored in the fewest number of races (A). The points available for each race win is equal to a fraction determined by dividing (A) by the number of races each Team sailed in (B). These adjusted points are used to score the incomplete round- robin, and
(2) if any boat in the round robin has not been scored in at least three races of a round- robin series, then that round-robin series is excluded from the stage score.
(c) Ties shall be broken according to rule 102.

102 TIES

102.1 Breaking a tie in the Louis Vuitton Cup Round-Robin Stage

In the Challenger Selection Series, ties will only be broken when scoring the Challengers as required by Protocol Article 7.4(a). Ties will only be broken to determine the first and last placed Challenger. References to scores and tie breaking of the Final Preliminary Regatta will only include races between two Challengers (excluding all races between a Challenger and the Defender).

Ties between two or more boats in the Challenger Selection Series round-robin stage shall be broken by the following methods, in order, until all ties are broken:

(a) **Sail Off (where possible).**
(1) When two Challengers are tied, the higher place will be decided in favour of the winner of one race between the tied Challengers.
(2) When three Challengers are tied for first place, the highest place Challenger in the Final Preliminary Regatta progresses to the sail-off second race. If there is no highest place Challenger, the winner of a

draw progresses to the sail-off second race. The other two boats race each other, and the winner progresses to the sail-off second race. The winner of the second race is then first place;

(3) When three Challengers are tied for third place, the lowest place Challenger in the Final Preliminary Regatta progresses to the sail-off second race. If there is no lowest place Challenger, the loser of a draw progresses to the sail-off second race. The other two boats race each other, and the loser progresses to the sail-off second race. The loser of the second race is then last place;

(4) When four Challengers are tied for first place, based on the Final Preliminary Regatta, the highest Challenger races the fourth highest Challenger, and the second highest Challenger races the third highest Challenger. The winner of each race then race each other. The winner of this third race is then first place;

(5) When four Challengers are tied for second place, based on the Final Preliminary Regatta, the highest Challenger races the fourth highest Challenger and the second highest Challenger Races the third highest Challenger. The loser of each race then race each other. The loser of this third race is then last place.

(6) If the second or third race of the sail-off process described in rule 102.1(a)(2) to 102.1(a)(5) is not scored, then the process described in rule 102.3 is used to break the tie in the outstanding races of the sail-off process that was not scored

(b) the Regatta Director shall endeavour to schedule the sail off as required by Protocol 7.3 (d), however if it is not possible to complete the sail off prior to 19:00 on 11 September 2024, then he shall resort to the process described in rule 102.3.

102.2 Breaking a tie in a Knockout Stage (including the Louis Vuitton Cup semi-finals and finals but excluding the Match)

Ties (including 0–0) between competitors in a knockout stage other than the Match shall be broken by the following methods, in order, until the tie is broken. The tie shall be decided in favour of the boat who

(a) wins a one race sail-off if the Regatta Director determines that such a race can be run within the schedule reserved for racing the stage. If there is a tie score before the first race of the final scheduled reserve day, there will be only one race;

(b) has won the most recent match in that knockout stage between the tied competitors;

(c) has the highest place (amongst the Challengers only) in the round-robin stage, applying rule 102.1 if necessary.

102.3 Breaking a tie in a Preliminary Regatta Round-Robin Stage

Ties between two or more competitors in a round-robin stage of a Preliminary Regatta, or as required by rule 102.1(b) shall be broken by the following methods, in order, until all ties are broken. When one or more ties are only partially broken, rules 102.3(a) to 102.3(d) shall be reapplied to them. Ties shall be decided in favour of the boat(s) who

(a) placed in order, has the highest score in the matches between the tied competitors;

(b) when the tie is between two competitors, has won the last match between the two competitors;

(c) has the most points against the boat placed highest in the round-robin stage or, if necessary, second highest, and so on until the tie is broken. When two separate ties have to be resolved but the resolution of each depends upon resolving the other, the following principles shall be used in the rule 102.3c) procedure:

  (1) the higher-place tie shall be resolved before the lower- place tie, and

  (2) all the competitors in the lower-place tie shall be treated as a single competitor for the purposes of rule 102.3(c).

(d) between two competitors, has the overall standing of each competitor in the first two Preliminary Regattas held in Vilanova and Jeddah in 2023, or the winner of a draw if there is no highest place competitor;

(e) when placed in order, has the highest overall standing in the Final Preliminary Regatta; and

(f) is the winner of a draw, using the same principles used to determine a sail off in full.

102.4 There is no tie break in the 37th America's Cup Match.

PART 9

SCORING A FLEET RACING EVENT or STAGE

See rule 90.3

105 SCORING A FLEET RACE

105.1 A race shall be scored if the scoring distance has been reached.

105.2 The points scored for a fleet race are as follows:

Place	1st	2nd	3rd	4th	5th	6th
Points	10	7	5	3	2	1

105.3 A boat's place is determined by its time relative to the other boats in the race. The boat with the shortest time will be placed higher.

105.4 The race committee shall determine the place or scores by applying the following, in order:

(a) each boat that complied with rule 28.1 and not thereafter retiring or being penalized will be placed as per rule 105.3;

(b) each boat that *starts* within 3 minutes of the starting signal, who has not complied with rule 28, and is not *capsized*, retired, or disqualified when the race is stopped, will be placed in order as follows:

(i) boats that have crossed through the gates of more legs when the race is stopped will be placed higher; and

(ii) boats that crossed through the same number of gates to complete the same number of legs in a shorter time will be placed higher.

A boat crosses through the gate when it crosses a line between the gate marks, except if the string representing her track, when drawn taut, subsequently fails to cross that line when the race is stopped. If a boat crossed though their most recent gate with a penalty or was penalized in an incident at that gate, the time they crossed through the gate shall be increased by 20 seconds for each outstanding penalty;

(c) A boat that *starts* within 3 minutes of the starting signal but has not crossed through any gate shall be scored one point;

(d) A boat that *starts* within 3 minutes of the starting signal but is *capsized* when the race is stopped or has retired shall be scored one point; then

(e) A boat that does not *start* within 3 minutes of the starting signal or has been disqualified shall be scored zero points.

105.5 If a boat is disqualified from a race or retires after *finishing*, each boat with a worse finishing place shall be moved up one place.

105.6 If boats are tied at the finishing line the points for the place for which the boats have tied and for the place(s) immediately below shall be added together and divided equally. Boats tied for a race prize shall share it or be given equal prizes.

106 SCORING A FLEET RACING SERIES

106.1 Boats will be ranked in order of their points. The boat with the highest point score will be the winner of the stage and all other boats ranked according to their point score.

107 FLEET RACING SERIES TIES

If there is a tie between two or more boats in a series, the boats shall be ranked in order of their finishing places in the last race both boats were scheduled to compete in. Any remaining ties shall be broken by using the tied boats' finishing places in the next-to-last race and so on until all ties are broken.

APPENDIX N

INTERNATIONAL JURIES

See rule 91.1. This appendix shall not be changed by the notice of race or sailing instructions.

N1 COMPOSITION, APPOINTMENT AND ORGANIZATION

N1.1 An international jury shall be composed of experienced sailors with excellent knowledge of the racing rules and extensive jury experience. It shall be independent of and have no members from the race committee, Rules Committee, or Measurement Committee. The jury shall be appointed by World Sailing.

N1.2 The jury shall consist of a chairman, a vice chairman if desired, and other members for a total of at least five. A majority shall be International Judges.

N1.3 No more than two members (three, in Groups M, N and Q) shall be from the same national authority.

N1.4 (a) The chairman of a jury may appoint one or more panels composed in compliance with rules N1.1, N1.2 and N1.3. This can be done even if the full jury is not composed in compliance with these rules.

(b) The chairman of a jury may appoint panels of at least three members each, of which the majority shall be International Judges. Members of each panel shall be from at least three different national authorities except in Groups M, N and Q, where they shall be from at least two different national authorities. If dissatisfied with a panel's decision, a *party* is entitled to a hearing by a panel composed in compliance with rules N1.1, N1.2 and N1.3, except concerning the facts found, if requested within 5 minutes of receiving a panel's decision.

N1.5 When a full jury, or a panel, has fewer than five members, because of illness or emergency, and no qualified replacements are available, it remains properly constituted if it consists of at least three members and if at least two of them are International Judges. When there are three or four members they shall be from at least three different national authorities except in Groups M, N and Q, where they shall be from at least two different national authorities.
N1.6 When it is considered desirable that some members not participate in discussing and deciding a *protest* or request for redress, and no qualified replacements are available, the jury remains properly constituted if at least three members remain and at least two of them are International Judges.
N1.7 [deleted]
N1.8 [deleted]
N1.9 If the jury or a panel acts while not properly constituted, its decisions may be appealed.

N2 RESPONSIBILITIES

N2.1 An international jury is responsible for hearing and deciding all *protests*, requests for redress and other matters arising under the rules of Part 5. When asked by the organizing authority, the race committee, the Rules Committee, the Measurement Committee, or the Arbitration panel, it shall advise and assist them on any matter directly affecting the fairness of the competition.
N2.2 Deleted
N2.3 The jury shall also decide matters referred to it by the organizing authority, the race committee, the Rules Committee, the Measurement Committee, or the Arbitration Panel.

N3 PROCEDURES

N3.1 Members shall not be regarded as having a significant *conflict of interest* (see rule 63.4) by reason of their nationality, club membership or similar. When otherwise considering a significant *conflict of interest* as required by rule 63.4, considerable weight must be given to the fact that decisions of an international jury cannot be appealed and this may affect the perception of fairness and lower the level of conflict that is significant. In case of doubt, the hearing should proceed as permitted by rule N1.6.
N3.2 If a panel fails to agree on a decision it may adjourn, in which case the chairman shall refer the matter to a properly constituted panel with as many members as possible, which may be the full jury.

N4 MISCONDUCT (Rule 69)

N4.1 The World Sailing Disciplinary Code contains procedures that apply to specific international events with regard to the appointment of a person to conduct any investigation. These procedures override any conflicting provision of this appendix.
N4.2 A person shall be responsible for presenting to the hearing panel any allegations of misconduct under rule 69. This person shall not be a member of the hearing panel but may be a member of the jury. Such a person shall be required to make full disclosure of all material that may come into his possession in the course of his investigation to the person subject to allegations of a breach of rule 69.
N4.3 Prior to a hearing, the hearing panel, to the extent practically possible, shall not act as an investigator of any allegations made under rule 69. However, during the hearing the panel shall be entitled to ask any investigative questions it may see fit.
N4.4 If the panel decides to call a hearing, all material disclosed to the panel in order for them to make that decision must be disclosed to the person subject to the allegations before the hearing begins.

5.2 The AC75 Class Rule (v 2.37 – 12 October 2024)

AC75 CLASS RULE

V2.37

12 October 2024

Contents

1 Introduction
2 Materials
3 Construction methods
4 Commercial products
5 Surface finishes
6 Mass
7 General arrangement
8 Hull geometry
9 Hull structure
10 Foils
11 Foil arms
12 Foil wings
13 Foil flaps and flexures

14 Rudder
15 Mast
16 Sails
17 Mainsail
18 Jib
19 Hydraulics
20 Power sources
21 Control systems
22 Electronic control circuits
23 Instrumentation and logging system
24 Information and display systems
25 Foil cant system
26 Systems communication
27 Media equipment
28 Branding
29 Crew
30 Measurement
31 Yacht configuration
32 Documents
33 Agreement

1 Introduction

1.1 This document defines the rules that govern an **AC75 Class Yacht**, the class of **yacht** chosen to compete in the 37th America's Cup.
1.2 This **AC75 Class Rule** shall be read and interpreted in conjunction with the **AC Technical Regulations**, which together form the **AC75 Class Rules**.
1.3 The **AC75 Class Yacht** is a high-performance monohull intended to:
  (a) promote head-to-head match racing and close competition;
  (b) spearhead the development of sailing through innovative technology, and maintain the America's Cup as the world's premier sailing event;
  (c) ensure the class is relevant to the sport of sailing with connection to the community of sailors;
  (d) be demanding to sail, rewarding the top level of skill for all sailors on the **yacht**;
  (e) provide competitive racing in light and stronger wind conditions; and
  (f) incorporate practical requirements for the launching, retrieval and transportation of the **yacht**.
1.4 The **AC75 Class Yacht** shall be propelled by sails only.
1.5 **Competitors** are ultimately and solely responsible for the safety and structural integrity of the whole (and any part or parts) of their **AC75 Class Yacht**. No

express or implied warranty of safety, stability or structural integrity shall result from compliance with the whole or any part of the **AC75 Class Rules**. Any structural testing required for compliance with the **AC75 Class Rules** does not guarantee safety or structural integrity nor does it relieve the **Competitor** of this responsibility.

2 Materials

2.1 Subject to Rule 2.2, the following components are exempt from the requirements of Rule 2:
  (a) supplied components, such as the **foil arm stocks**, the **FCS** and the **supplied rigging**;
  (b) material specified in the supplied **mast** drawing package;
  (c) ropes and their constituent elements;
  (d) electrical and electronic components, and their enclosures or housings (for the avoidance of doubt this includes Hall effect sensor magnetic shielding materials);
  (e) hydraulic tubing and fittings, except that Rule 2.17 applies;
  (f) carried equipment; and
  (g) safety equipment.

2.2 For the components itemised in Rules 2.1 (d), 2.1 (e), 2.1 (f) and 2.1 (g), the exemption applies only if:
  (a) they have no significant structural contribution;
  (b) each assembly is limited to a maximum density of 11,400 kg/m^3; and
  (c) materials with a density greater than 11,400 kg/m^3 are not used in volumes that have any significant effect on the distribution of mass throughout the **yacht**.

2.3 Material property values detailed herein are to be evaluated at 20°C and 1 atmosphere absolute pressure.

2.4 Materials shall have a maximum density of 11,400 kg/m^3.

2.5 Materials shall have a maximum elastic modulus as detailed below:

Material category	Maximum Modules (GPa)	Certificates Required
Fibre reinforcement in **foils**, **rudders**, **masts** and **battens**	395	Yes
*Fibre reinforcement in thermoplastic components	Unlimited	No
Fibre reinforcement in **commercial pre-consolidated FRP**	Unlimited	No

Material category	Maximum Modules (GPa)	Certificates Required
Commercial hardware	Unlimited	No
Fibre reinforcement in components not listed above	300	Yes
Commercial core material in all components	75	No
Surface treatments	Unlimited	No
Material not listed above	220	No

**As described in Rule 3.3.*

2.6 Fibre modulus in Rule 2.5 is to be measured by one of the following methods, or an equivalent method approved by the **Rules Committee**:
  (a) SACMA-SRM16;
  (b) ASTM D 4018;
  (c) TY-030B;
  (d) JIS R 7601; or
  (e) ISO 10618.

2.7 For the avoidance of doubt, modulus limits on fibre and other materials in Rule 2.5 apply to **FRP** resin additives, such as nanoparticles and microspheres.

2.8 Where certificates are required for a category in Rule 2.5:
  (a) **Competitors** must submit copies of material certificates for each roll of fibre used for that category, where each roll must satisfy the material restrictions herein;
  (b) **Competitors** must supply a declaration that all components of a category only used fibre for which certificates have been supplied. It is not necessary to submit documentation indicating which rolls of material have been used in each individual part; and
  (c) as an exception, material certificates are not required for glass, polyethylene, polyester or polypropylene fibre.

  Further requirements on material certificates may be included in the **Measurement Procedures**.

2.9 The limit on **commercial core** material in Rule 2.5 refers to the maximum solid compressive modulus of elasticity, in any direction, of the constituent material. For example:
  (a) for aluminium honeycomb, the limit applies to the modulus of aluminium, approximately 70 GPa; and
  (b) for a composite **core**, the limit applies to the modulus of the **core** laminate, not the individual fibres or matrix.

2.10 **Core** materials must be **commercial core**. Unexpanded honeycomb may be expanded, and **core** material may be cut and shaped for its intended purpose, but it must not be processed to alter its physical or chemical structure (e.g. it is not permitted to 3D print a **core** material from plastic, since this would be changing the structure of the material). Only the following **core** materials are permitted:

(a) aluminium honeycomb (3000 or 5000 series only, which may be surface treated to prevent corrosion);
(b) meta-aramid (Nomex or equivalent) honeycomb;
(c) para-aramid (N636 or equivalent) honeycomb, except in the **hull shell** that forms the structure of the **hull lower surface**;
(d) timber; or
(e) plastic foam.

2.11 The "Surface treatment" category in Rule 2.5 only applies to material that is:

(a) contained in a surface layer not more than 0.5 mm thick; and
(b) for the purpose of:
  (i) improving resistance to wear, fatigue, or corrosion; and/or
  (ii) fairing or modifying the appearance of a surface.

2.12 The limit on "Material not listed above" in Rule 2.5 applies to all materials that do not fall into the other categories, and refers to the maximum modulus in any direction.

2.13 For all categories in Rule 2.5, **Competitors** must submit a declaration that the material used in all components satisfies Rule 2.

2.14 Metal materials in **foil wings**, **foil flaps** and **rudders** shall not exceed the following values:

Material category	Maximum Yield Strength (MPa)	Maximum Density (kg/m^3)	Evidence Required
Lead alloys with greater than 95% lead content by mass	Unlimited	11400	No
Commercial hardware	Unlimited	11400	No
High strength metals	1500	8000	Yes*
Low strength metals	500	8100	No

Up to 3 kg of high strength metals in each* ***foil* *do not require the provision of evidence, where components wholly manufactured from this material are able to be physically separated from the assembly within which they are housed.*

2.15 For metal materials where evidence is required, this evidence shall report:

(a) yield strength measured by tensile tests:

(i) of a minimum of three witness specimens from the same material batch and subjected to the same heat treatment cycle or other post processing technique;
(ii) performed in accordance with ISO 6892-1 or ASTM E8M by an external testing laboratory accredited by a signatory to the International Laboratories Agreement Cooperation (ILAC) Mutual Recognition Agreement (MRA); and
(iii) with the reported value being the average 0.2% offset yield strength ($R_p0.2$) of the three specimens; and

(b) density measured by:
(i) a manufacturer's technical datasheet showing the composition and nominal density; and
(ii) a mill certificate showing the material meets the composition in the manufacturer's technical datasheet.

2.16 For all categories in Rule 2.14, **Competitors** must submit a declaration that metal materials in **foil wings**, **foil flaps** and **rudders** satisfy Rule 2.14.

2.17 Hydraulic tubing containing more than trace quantities of titanium is prohibited, but this does not preclude the use of titanium in other hydraulic devices or fittings.

2.18 Boron and beryllium are prohibited except:
(a) where used in alloys in concentrations of no more than 0.00042%;
(b) in **commercial hardware**; and
(c) as part of neodymium magnets included in Hall effect sensors and clothing.

2.19 Gases shall have a minimum density of 1.1 kg/m^3, except for nitrogen used within hydraulic systems.

3 Construction methods

3.1 The following components are exempt from the requirements of Rule 3:
(a) supplied components, such as the **foil arms stocks**, the **FCS** and the **supplied rigging**;
(b) ropes and their constituent elements;
(c) **commercial hardware**;
(d) electrical and electronic components, and their enclosures or housings;
(e) hydraulic tubing and fittings;
(f) **carried equipment**; and
(g) safety equipment;

where for components in Rule 3.1 (d), 3.1 (e), 3.1 (f) and 3.1 (g) the exemption applies only if they have no significant structural contribution.

3.2 Applied temperatures and compaction pressures of **FRP** material shall not exceed the following values at any stage during construction, or after construction:

Category	Maximum Temperature (°C)	Maximum Compaction Pressure (bar)
FRP material in **hulls***	135	1.1
Quasi-isotropic FRP plate in **hulls**	135	7.0
FRP material in **sail skins**	Unlimited	Unlimited
Thermoplastic **FRP** material	450	Unlimited
Commercial pre-consolidated FRP	Unlimited	Unlimited
FRP material not listed above	135	7.0

Except thermoplastic **FRP material or **commercial pre-consolidated FRP** in **hulls***

3.3 Thermoplastic **FRP** material in Rule 3.2:
   (a) may be used within any component, including the **hull**;
   (b) shall be restricted to a maximum total mass of 15.0 kg, combining all such material within the **yacht** except that excluded by Rule 3.1; and
   (c) may only be sourced as either:
      (i) constituent material (e.g. pre-preg tape, pre-preg cloth, fibre reinforced additive printing fil- ament); or
      (ii) pre-consolidated solid **FRP** in standard shapes (e.g. plate, bar, rod, tube, but not honeycomb), in which case they must be **commercial pre-consolidated FRP** and the temperature limit applies only after delivery of the component from the manufacturer.

3.4 The maximum pressures in Rule 3.2 refer to the average pressure applied over the surface of a component, or to that part of a component under pressure. Local regions of higher pressure may be applied, for example by hand clamps or mechanical fastenings, provided the average is not exceeded.

3.5 The component of pressure applied by conventional wrapping and winding methods (for construction around a mandrel, or similar) is excluded from the pressure limits given in Rules 3.2.

3.6 Electron beam or other non-thermal radiation cure of **FRP** components is prohibited. This does not prohibit curing **FRP** components by passing electrical current through them to generate heat.

3.7 Construction of a **hull** shall meet the following criteria:

$$k_{LCA} + \sum_{i=1}^{n} a_i (k_{i,PLUG} + k_{i,MOULD}) \geq 2.5$$

where:

*a*i is the proportion of the **hull surface** manufactured by a distinct tooling approach;

n is the total number of distinct tooling approaches required to build the **hull surface**;

$$k_{LCA} = \begin{cases} 1, & \text{if a life-cycle analysis is performed on the \textbf{hull} to the satisfaction of the \textbf{Measurement Committee}} \\ 0, & \text{otherwise} \end{cases}$$

$$k_{PLUG} = \begin{cases} 2, & \text{if a plug is not required} \\ 1, & \text{if at least 80\% of the total mass of the mould plug is constructed of recyclable material (e.g. PET), with that plug being delivered to a recycling plant by 1st January 2024} \\ 1, & \text{if at least 80\% of the total mass of the mould plug is constructed of recycled material} \\ 1, & \text{if at least 80\% of the total mass of the mould plug is constructed of sustainably sourced material (e.g. timber)} \\ 0, & \text{otherwise} \end{cases}$$

$$k_{MOULD} = \begin{cases} 2, & \text{if a mould is not required} \\ 1, & \text{if at least 10\% of the total mass of carbon reinforcement used in the mould is from recycled sources} \\ 1, & \text{if at least 80\% of the fibre reinforcement, by mass, used in the mould is constructed from fibres with low embodied energy (e.g. basalt)} \\ 1, & \text{if at least 80\% of the total mass of the mould is constructed of sustainably sourced material (e.g. timber)} \\ 1, & \text{if at least 50\% of the fibre reinforcement, by mass, used in the mould is natural fibre (e.g. flax)} \\ 0, & \text{otherwise} \end{cases}$$

3.8 The life-cycle analysis in Rule 3.7 shall;
  (a) be submitted as a written report to the **Measurement Committee**;
  (b) follow the guidelines defined by ISO 14040/14044; and
  (c) be a cradle-to-gate life-cycle analysis with at least:
    (i) the carbon footprint represented in kgCO_2e; and
    (ii) the production of solid waste represented in kg,

associated with the construction of the **hull**, including the sourcing of material, in addition to the transport of the **hull** by sea or air to the Match venue but excluding the use and disposal phases.

4 Commercial products

4.1 **Commercial products** shall fall into the following categories:
(a) **commercial core**;
(b) **commercial pre-consolidated FRP**;
(c) **commercial hardware**; and
(d) **commercial paint**.

4.2 Products to be added to the list of approved **commercial products** must:
(a) be readily available for purchase by all **Competitors** at a reasonable market price; and
(b) have a lead time to delivery of no more than twelve months; and
(c) not have been developed directly or indirectly for a **Competitor** or specific group of **Competitors**, unless prior to 31 March 2018.

4.3 The **Rules Committee** shall maintain a list of approved **commercial products** in each category. Such products can be approved and listed en masse, for example by approving an entire catalogue of products from a supplier, providing the details of the specific catalogue (e.g. publication year) are included and a permanent record of that catalogue's contents is available.

4.4 **Commercial products** can be added to the relevant list by **Competitors** submitting a request to the **Rules Committee** at any time prior to 6 months before the first race of the Match. The request must clearly define the **commercial product** and the category for which approval is being requested.

4.5 On receiving a request, the **Rules Committee** shall interpret whether the item is a **commercial product** by following the procedure detailed in the "Interpretation and amendment" section of the **AC Technical Regulations** to determine whether the requested product satisfies Rules 4.2 (a), 4.2 (b) and 4.2 (c). However, they may delay the start of the procedure by up to one month after receiving the request in order to deal with multiple requests in a single batch.

4.6 Once a product has been added to the list of approved **commercial products**, it shall remain there until the end of **AC37** unless it is determined that false or misleading information was provided during the process for a product's approval. In this situation, if one or more **Competitors** has relied on the product's presence on a list of approved **commercial products**, the case may be referred to the Arbitration Panel for resolution.

4.7 **Commercial pre-consolidated FRP**:
(a) is restricted to a maximum combined mass of 150 kg on each **AC75 Class Yacht**;

(b) shall make up no more than 15.0 kg of a **hull**;
(c) shall not be used in a **foil arm fairing**, **foil wing**, **foil flap** or **rudder**; and
(d) shall be sourced as pre-consolidated and cured solid **FRP** material in standard shapes (e.g. plate, bar, rod, tube, but not honeycomb).

4.8 **Commercial hardware**:
(a) is restricted to a maximum combined mass of 150 kg on each **AC75 Class Yacht**;
(b) shall make up no more than 15.0 kg of a **hull**;
(c) shall not be processed to alter its fundamental structure or shape (e.g. machined, re-shaped, melted down or heat-treated), except that pins and fasteners may be trimmed to length; and
(d) may contain **FRP** but must not be entirely made of **FRP**.

4.9 An initial list of **commercial paints** shall include:

Manufacturer	Products
Alexseal	HS Base Coat; HS Clear Coat
Awlgrip	Awlcraft 2000; Topcoats G/H-Line; HDT Clearcoat
Cromax	3050S ChromaClear
GRS Deltron BC	Global Refinish System Deltron Basecoat
MaxNeyer	Matt Semi-Gloss Clear 1-360-0710/ 1-360-0750
Nautix	L2; NX194
Resene	Durepox; Durepox Xtreme Clear; Durepox High Performance Clear
Spies Hecker	Plastic automotive paint; Permasolid HS Automotive Topcoat 27*

**This excludes the Permasolid Texture Component SA 101 and SA 102 that are part of the Spies Hecker Plastic system.*

4.10 Approved **commercial pre-consolidated FRP** and **commercial hardware** shall only be counted in the mass limits of Rules 4.7 and 4.8 where those products do not satisfy the other Rule requirements, such as material and construction limits, at the locations in which they are used.

5 Surface finishes

5.1 Except as permitted in Rules 5.4, 5.5, 5.6 and 5.7, the outermost layer of the **hull**, **foils** (excluding foil systems controlled by Rule 10.3) and **rudder** must be

(a) a **commercial paint** approved by the **Rules Committee** according to Rule 4, who shall only approve paints that are comparable to those on the list provided in Rule 4.9; or

(b) an unpainted steel surface.

5.2 **Competitors** must not alter the chemistry of paints except with products that are a standard part of an approved paint system and used in compliance with the manufacturer's standard guidelines.

5.3 Paints or additives that are designed to reduce surface friction (such as PTFE) shall not be used on the outermost layer of the **hull**, **foils** or **rudder**.

5.4 As an exception to Rule 5.1, occasional regions in the outermost layer of the **hull**, **foils** and **rudder** may be unpainted, providing that:

(a) each region is no more than 0.001 m^2; and

(b) the total area of these regions does not exceed 0.05 m^2 on each **hull**, **foil** or **rudder**.

5.5 Surfaces may be sanded, polished and cleaned, providing that the only substances that remain on those surfaces when the **yacht** is afloat satisfy Rules 5.1 (a), 5.2 and 5.3. Where sanding has unintentionally broken through a permitted surface finish leaving occasional regions of no more than 0.001 m^2 each, these regions are permitted to expose metal, **FRP** or filler as the outermost surface layer of the **hull**, **foils** and **rudder**.

5.6 **Competitors** may apply vinyl or plastic film over the paint for the purpose of branding, providing it complies with Rule 5.8.

5.7 On areas of the **deck**, or on fittings attached to the **deck**, **Competitors** are permitted to apply non-skid products or coatings. The accumulated areas shall not be greater than 20 m^2.

5.8 Devices and finishes whose primary purpose is altering the structure of the boundary layer are prohibited. For the avoidance of doubt:

(a) this prohibition includes, but is not limited to:

(i) electric, magnetic, sonic, thermal and chemical devices;

(ii) patterned or textured finishes, LEBUs; and

(iii) active devices that suck fluid from or blow fluid on to the surface of a component; but

(b) this rule does not prohibit:

(i) surface finishing permitted by Rule 5.5;

(ii) passive macroscopic devices such as slots or slats; or

(iii) passive surface features, such as fences or vortex generators, which extend outside the local boundary layer.

The thickness of the boundary layer δ shall be determined using the formula:

$$\delta = \frac{0.37x}{Re_x^{0.2}}$$

where

x is the local distance from the forward most point of the object;

Re_x is the local Reynolds number (based on *x*); and the following properties and speeds shall be used:

	Velocity (knots)	Density kg/m^3	Dynamic viscosity (Pa.s)
Air	30	1.225	1.789×10^{-5}
Water	30	1025	1.103×10^{-3}

6 Mass

6.1 The table below lists masses and **longitudinal** centres of gravity (LCGs) in the **yacht**-fixed frame (*x*, *y*, *z*). The table is for reference only, and Rule 6.1 does not in itself impose any requirements on the **AC75 Class Yacht**. However, other rules do stipulate requirements by making reference to the data tabulated herein.

Component	Mass (kg)	LCG (m)
Yacht assembly	**6216 – 6256**	**9.029 – 9.384**
Platform	***mP**	***xP**
Hull, rudder, and other parts or components	—	
Port **foil**	*1265 – 1270	
Foil arm fairing/wing/flap/systems	806	
†**Foil arm stock**	464	
Starboard **foil**	*1265 – 1270	
Foil arm fairing/wing/flap/systems	806	
†**Foil arm stock**	464	
†**Foil arm** pins and bearings	64	10.37 – 11.66

Component	Mass (kg)	LCG (m)
†**FCS**	357.8	10.39 – 11.79
Fire safety equipment	7.5	
Platform-weighed **Mast** and **Mainsail** hardware	—	
†**Media equipment**	148.5	10.269
Fire safety equipment	3.75	
Mast (excluding parts weighed with **platform**)	***mMAST**	**xMAST**
Mast tube and attached components, etc.	—	
†**Supplied rigging**	39.5	
†**Media equipment**	27.6	
Mainsail (excluding parts weighed with **platform**)	***mMAIN**	**5.70**
Jib	***53 – 55**	**12.00**
Crew & gear	**716 – 744**	
Crew	*680 – 700	
Crew's **carried equipment**	*32 – 40	
†**Crew supplied media equipment**	4	
Total	**6932 – 7000**	

**Measured, †Supplied equipment*

6.2 **Foils** shall be weighed and their centres of mass, in a plane parallel to **TRP**, shall be determined according to the **Measurement Procedures**. During measurement the **foil flap** angle shall be set to an angle chosen by the **Competitor**. The following restrictions apply:
   (a) Each **foil** must have a mass within the range specified for "Port **foil**" and "Starboard **foil**" in Rule 6.1.
   (b) When **projected** on to a plane parallel to **TRP**, the distance from the **foil cant** axis to the centre of mass of:
      (i) a **foil arm stock** shall be 1.204 m; and
      (ii) a **foil** shall be at least 2.890 m.

6.3 The **platform** mass m, and LCGx, shall be determined in the measurement condition described by Rule 7.7.

6.4 The **mast** mass m_{MAST} and centre of mass (X_{MAST}, Y_{MAST}, Z_{MAST}) shall be

determined in the **mast** measurement condition described by Rule 15.14 where:
(a) centre of mass components in the **mast**-fixed reference frame shall be:
(i) u_{MAST} assumed to equal 0.0 m; and
(ii) v_{MAST} assumed to equal 0.0 m; and
(iii) w_{MAST} as measured; and
(b) converted into a **yacht**-fixed LCG x_{MAST} by assuming a **mast** rake of 5°.

6.5 The **mainsail** mass m_{MAIN} shall be determined in **mainsail** measurement condition as described by Rule 17.22.

6.6 The **Jib** must have a mass within the range specified for "**Jib**" shown in Rule 6.1.

6.7 The **yacht assembly** mass m_Y and longitudinal centre of mass x_Y:
(a) shall be determined by combining the following masses and LCGs:
(i) **platform** mass m_P at LCG x_P;
(ii) **mast** mass m_{MAST} at longitudinal centre of mass x_{MAST};
(iii) **mainsail** mass m_{MAIN} at the LCG specified in Rule 6.1; and
(iv) the **jib** mass taken as the middle of the allowable range specified in Rule 6.1, with an LCG as specified in Rule 6.1; and
(b) must lie within the mass and LCG ranges specified for "**Yacht assembly**" in Rule 6.1.

6.8 Crew must have a mass within the range specified for "Crew" shown in Rule 6.1.

6.9 Crew's **carried equipment**:
(a) must have a mass no greater than the upper end of the range specified for "Crew's **carried equipment**" shown in Rule 6.1; and
(b) may have a mass less than the lower end of the specified range, in which case, ballast shall be added such that the sum of the **carried equipment** mass and the ballast mass lies within the range. Any such ballast:
(i) shall be attached to the top of the **deck** between 6.0 m and 7.0 m forward of **TRP**; and
(ii) shall either be on **LCP**, or be split evenly and located in two parts symmetrically about **LCP**.

6.10 Nothing shall be aboard the **yacht** that is not included in Rule 6.1.

7 General arrangement

7.1 The **AC75 Class Yacht** shall comprise exactly:
(a) one **hull**;
(b) two **foils**;
(c) one **rudder**;
(d) one **mast**, which shall include one set of **supplied rigging**;
(e) one **mainsail**; and
(f) one **jib**.

In addition to those required components listed above, the **AC75 Class Yacht** may also include any other parts or components except where prohibited within the **AC75 Class Rules**.

7.2 Except where otherwise specified, components that are described separately within the **AC75 Class Rules** may be physically constructed as single parts, with virtual splits delineating boundaries across which different rules or declarations may apply.

7.3 No part of the **yacht** except the fairing flaps permitted by Rule 8.21, **foils** and the **rudder** shall lie below the **hull lower surface**.

7.4 No part of the **yacht** except the **mast**, sails, rigging, **foils**, equipment permitted in Rule 27.2 (e) and **media equipment** shall lie more than 1.700 m above **MWP**.

7.5 When **projected** on to **MWP**, no part of the **yacht**, other than the **foils**, **rudder**, **mast**, sails, rigging, **media equipment** and instrumentation permitted by Rule 27, shall lie outside of the area **projected** by the **hull** on to **MWP**.

7.6 The **yacht** shall be capable of being lifted:

(a) by a crane, from one or more primary lifting points located forward of **MRP**, with secondary lines led aft; and

(b) by gantry cranes for measurement, from three or four separate lifting points, where:

(i) lifting points must be arranged symmetrically about **LCP**;

(ii) there must be a lifting point at least 1.5 m either side of **LCP**;

(iii) at least one lifting point must be **longitudinally** separated from two others by at least 8.0 m; and

(iv) each lifting point must attract at least 10% of the weight of the **yacht** in **platform** measurement condition.

7.7 The **platform** measurement condition shall be with:

(a) the **hull** levelled with **MWP** horizontal;

(b) both **foils** canted to;

(i) 7.5° ± 0.5°as shown in Figure 10.2;

(ii) 41.41° ± 0.5° as shown in Figure 10.1; or

(iii) any other angle agreed between the **Competitor** and the **Measurement Committee** provided that the cant angles of both **foils** are the same;

(c) both **foil flaps** set to the centre of their range of motion;

(d) the symmetry plane of the **rudder** aligned to **LCP**;

(e) the **rudder** rake set to the centre of its range of motion;

(f) those components of the **mast** and **mainsail** not included in their respective measurement conditions located on the **deck** in positions representative of their longitudinal centres of mass with the rig stepped and the **mainsail** hoisted; and

(g) other components in their normal sailing positions.

7.8 A **crew zone planform** shall be a rectangle with:
(a) a minimum width of 600 mm;
(b) a minimum length of:
(i) 1400 mm for a recumbent cyclor cockpit;
(ii) 1100 mm for any other **crew zone** that contains a **primary force input device**; or
(iii) 800 mm otherwise;
(c) corners which may be curved with a maximum radius of 300 mm;
where a *recumbent cyclor cockpit* is a **crew zone** that contains a **primary force input device** that will be operated with the saddle or seat bearing point of the crew member less than 400 mm above the centre of rotation of the **primary force input device**.

7.9 Any volume that is designed for a crew member to operate within for a sustained period shall be declared as a **crew zone**, where each **crew zone** shall:
(a) be designed for a single crew member to operate within, in a **normal sailing position**;
(b) shall extend to include the entire volume that any part of the crew member occupies whilst in a **normal sailing position;**
(c) be a volume formed by extruding a **crew zone planform** along an axis orthogonal to **MWP**;
(d) extend in height from **MWP** to 2500 mm above **MWP**;
(e) lie entirely aft of a plane 9.0 m forward of **TRP**; and
(f) not overlap or intersect with another **crew zone.**

7.10 Below its intersection with the **platform upper surface**, each **crew zone** shall be bounded, on or inside its volumetric boundary, by:
(a) an adjacent **crew zone**;
(b) the **perimeter line**; or
(c) a closed physical boundary that shall:
(i) prevent a crew member extending or placing any part of their body into any volume below the **platform upper surface** that is contiguous to the **crew zone**, except those penetrations for the passage of systems, and *limber holes* are permitted, provided that a sphere of 40 mm diameter cannot pass through them; and
(ii) not deflect at any point by more than 10 mm when a sphere of 40 mm diameter is pressed into the boundary with a normal load of 100 N.
where a *limber hole* is a drain hole through a frame or other structure designed to prevent water from accumulating against one side of that structure.

7.11 **Competitors** shall declare a minimum of eight **crew zones** to the **Measurement Committee**, where:
(a) **crew zone** volumes shall be overlayed on the **hull's blueprint**;

(b) a standard poseable mannequin geometry shall be included in each **crew zone**, showing one or more **normal sailing positions** for that **crew zone**;
(c) exactly four **crew zones** shall each contain one **primary force input device**; and
(d) **force input devices**, *seats*, *saddles* and *handlebars* shall be included in the declared geometries at the position of maximum *coverage*. *Seats*, *saddles*, and *handlebars* may be adjusted to accommodate **normal sailing positions** for different crew prior to racing without the requirement of a new geometry declaration.
The standard mannequin can be articulated to represent a reasonable human posture for each normal sailing position. It is contained within the supplied IGES file "AC37 Mannequin.igs" with **SHA**:

528335ced01465dfbc47b4b432dcfd525c63a435f8bceb4d34f85662a89feff-37dd1aa5c68455c09fec92dfcc849cd0e6ffce2a8bdbe9eccd4c4ea178cef1f24

7.12 A **cockpit aperture planform** corresponding to a **crew zone** shall be a rectangle:
(a) with its long side parallel to the long side of the **crew zone planform**;
(b) that lies within, or overlayed with, a **crew zone planform**;
(c) has sides and ends that are offset by no more than 50 mm within the **crew zone planform**;
(d) with corners which may be curved with a maximum radius of 250 mm;
(e) that may be offset by more than 50 mm within the **crew zone planform** at the corners.

7.13 Each **crew zone** shall have a **cockpit aperture** that shall be formed by the intersection of:
(a) **the platform upper surface;**
(b) the extrusion of a **cockpit aperture planform** normal to **MWP**

7.14 No part of the **yacht** except the items listed in Rule 7.16 shall lie within the volume bounded by:
(a) a plane parallel to **MWP** that is 200 mm below the lowest point on the **cockpit aperture**;
(b) a plane parallel to **MWP** that contains the highest point on the **cockpit aperture**; and
(c) the extrusion of the **cockpit aperture** along an axis orthogonal to **MWP**.

7.15 Within Rules 7.16, 7.17 and 7.18, parts of the **yacht** that *move*, are *moved*, or are *movable* are defined to be those parts that have a degree-of-freedom of movement with respect to the part of the **yacht** to which they are attached, where such movement is applicable:
(a) whether the degree-of-freedom of movement is through a kinematic or compliant connection; and

(b) whether the parts *move* as a result of **external forces**, due to the action of the crew or due to the action of another part of the **yacht**.

7.16 Within a **cockpit aperture**, when viewed from above and orthogonal to **MWP** it shall not be possible for any part of a crew member or their clothing to be covered by any part of the **yacht** except:

(a) the **mast**, sails and rigging;

(b) **force input devices** up to a maximum accumulated *coverage* across all **crew zones** of 0.1 m^2 with;

(i) the orientation of **steering wheels** set with the **rudder** parallel to **LCP**;

(ii) any passive input device or wiring that is attached to the rotating part of a **steering wheel** may be considered part of this **force input device** for the purposes of calculating the area in this clause; and

(iii) any other *moveable* components set to the position of maximum *coverage*.

(c) one dedicated *saddle* or *seat* for each **crew zone**, up to a maximum *coverage* of 0.075 m^2 per **crew zone** with the *saddle* or *seat*, where *moveable*, set to the position of maximum *coverage*. A *saddle* or *seat* is a device whose purpose is to sit a specific crew member while racing;

(d) one or two dedicated *handlebars* for each **crew zone**, up to a maximum *coverage* for each *handlebar* of 0.035 m^2 per **crew zone** with the *handlebars*, where *moveable*, set to the position of maximum *coverage*. A *handlebar* is a dedicated device whose purpose is to provide supporting handholds for a specific crew member while racing;

(e) other declared items up to a maximum accumulated *coverage* across all **crew zones** of 0.3 m^2, with any *moveable* components set to the position of maximum *coverage* and the orientation of **steering wheels** set with the **rudder** parallel to **LCP**. These other items may include:

(i) those parts of **force input devices**, *saddles*, *seats* or *handlebars* that exceed their individual *coverage* allowances; and

(ii) items not listed in Rule 7.16 (e) (i); and

(f) all supplied **media equipment** and tactical system equipment

where *coverage* is the area that when viewed from above and **projected** orthogonal to **MWP** is able to cover any part of a crew member or their clothing, and lies within a **cockpit aperture**.

Where more than one category of components within Rules 7.16 (a) – 7.16 (f) has overlapping *coverage*, each component category shall be counted towards its respective *coverage*. However, the *coverage* of components within a single category shall only be counted once at any specific point in the **projection**.

7.17 Apart from permitted movement of **foils, foil arm drums**, **control surfaces** and the flexible covers permit- ted in Rule 7.18 (b):

(a) the only parts of the **yacht** that may *move* are:
   (i) parts *moved* to control movement of a **control surface**, including electrical and hydraulic components attached to **control systems**;
   (ii) hand-held devices whose only purpose is to house **passive input devices** and/or **crew indication devices**;
   (iii) parts *moved* in preparation for, or to organise after controlling a **control surface** (e.g. setting a **jib** car prior to tacking, charging a **hydraulic accumulator** or stowing sheets);
   (iv) within the **FCS**;
   (v) access panels being opened or closed (which must not be into the **hull**);
   (vi) drainage flaps permitted by Rule 8.21;
   (vii) a simple mechanical wind indicator that has no purpose other than indicating the apparent wind direction;
   (viii) mechanical components within electrical systems, such as a cooling fan, a bilge pump, a line or quadrant connecting a string potentiometer to part of a **control system** or **control surface**;
   (ix) seals of penetrations into the **hull**, e.g. a flexible boot, provided such parts *move* only as a result of permitted **control surface** movements and have no purpose other than preventing water ingress;
   (x) zips or similar linear closing devices to close covers permitted by Rule 7.18 (b);
   (xi) slack rigging or hoses;
   (xii) woollies;
   (xiii) parts *moved* solely for safety reasons;
   (xiv) parts *moved* as the result of an unintended breakdown, as determined by the **Measurement Committee**; or
   (xv) liquid flowing in an **LCS**; and

(b) those parts that *move*, are *moved*, or are *movable* shall have no significant effect on:
   (i) aerodynamic loads;
   (ii) hydrodynamic loads;
   (iii) the angular momentum of the **yacht**; or
   (iv) the centre of mass of the **yacht**.

7.18 Components shall not be designed to deform in order to affect the aerodynamic performance of the **yacht**, except for:

(a) **control surfaces**, as a result of:
   (i) external forces;
   (ii) permitted movements of **flight controls**; or
   (iii) permitted movements of **rig controls**; and

(b) flexible covers that fair rebates or penetrations, in the **deck** or in hardware attached to the **deck**, around or through which a **rig** or **rig control system** component (the *component*) *moves*, providing that:
   (i) the deformation is caused by the movement of the *component*;
   (ii) when not deformed, the flexible cover restores the **deck** or hardware towards its fair shape in the absence of the rebate or penetration;
   (iii) the only purpose of the flexible cover is to reduce the aerodynamic drag or maintain attachment of flow in the vicinity of the rebate or penetration; and
   (iv) any change in shape of the covered region, caused by movement of the *component*, is con- fined to a local area around the *component*.

8 Hull geometry

8.1 A **hull's blueprint** shall be an IGES file that represents the geometry that the **hull surface** was designed to. The geometry shall form a single closed volume, and:
   (a) shall include three measurement reference points, located:
      (i) on **MWP** and on **LCP**, at 20.700 m from **TRP**; and
      (ii) on **MWP** and on **TRP**, offset 2.000 m either side of **LCP**;
   (b) penetrations into the closed volume permitted by Rule 8.19 shall be closed with surfaces that connect their edges and are fair with respect to the surrounding **hull surface**;
   (c) conduits through the **hull surface** permitted by Rule 8.18 (a) shall be included in the **blueprint** and their walls shall be deemed to be part of the **deck**; any boundary with the **hull lower surface** shall be where the conduit's exit meets the fair extension of the surrounding **hull lower surface**; and
   (d) internal structure within the closed volume shall not be included, but the positions of bulkheads required to satisfy Rule 8.11 shall be included as separate IGES surfaces.

8.2 Three screws shall be installed on the **hull surface** for the purpose of locating the reference points of Rule 8.1 (a). If a reference point does not lie on the **hull surface**, the screw shall be installed at declared offsets from the reference point, as close as reasonably possible to the reference point, and the exact location of the screw shall be included in the **hull blueprint**.

8.3 When aligned with the reference points of Rule 8.1 (a), the **hull surface** must match its **blueprint** according to a measurement procedure issued by the **Rules Committee**, with tolerances of:
   (a) ±5 mm over the **hull lower surface**; and
   (b) ±10 mm over the **deck**.

8.4 Geometric and flotation requirements pertaining to the **hull surface** within Rule 8 will be measured using the **blueprint** and must be satisfied exactly with no tolerance.

8.5 The aftmost point on the **hull surface** shall lie on **TRP**.

8.6 The **hull lower surface** shall be **symmetric** about **LCP**.

8.7 The forwardmost point on the **hull** shall be no less than 20.600 m and no greater than 20.700 m from **TRP**.

8.8 Any line that connects two points on the **perimeter line projected** on to **MWP** shall lie on or inside that projection of the **perimeter line**.

8.9 The **perimeter line** shall:

(a) lie entirely above **MWP**;

(b) at its greatest distance from **LCP**, lie between 2.400 m and 2.500 m from **LCP**;

(c) at its intersection with a plane 17.000 m forward of **TRP**, lie no more than 1.600 m from **LCP**; and

(d) at its intersection with a plane 19.000 m forward of **TRP**, lie no more than 1.000 m from **LCP**.

8.10 At any **transverse** cross-section through the **hull lower surface**:

(a) no horizontal line shall cut the cross-section more than twice; and

(b) no vertical line shall cut the cross-section more than once below **MWP**.

Parts of a cross-section within cylindrical regions of length 4.000 m and diameter 1.250 m centred on each **foil cant reference point**, and whose axes are aligned with the **foil cant** axes, are excluded from this Rule.

8.11 The **hull surface** shall enclose a volume of at least 60 m^3, which must include:

(a) a watertight bulkhead situated more than 9.000 m forward of **TRP** that forms the aftermost extent of an enclosed watertight volume of at least 35 m^3, where that volume may be subdivided; and

(b) a watertight bulkhead situated between 17.000 m and 19.000 m forward of **TRP**.

For the purposes of this Rule, a bulkhead is considered watertight if it is able to withstand a uniform pressure of 10 kPa from either side, compliance of which shall be demonstrated by analysis. Permissions granted elsewhere in the Rule for penetrations into volumes do not alleviate the requirements for watertight bulkheads to meet this pressure requirement. Penetrations into a watertight bulkhead must not allow water to pass between the volumes the bulkhead separates when a uniform pressure of 10 kPa is applied from either side.

8.12 The **hull surface** shall satisfy flotation Rules 8.13, 8.14 and 8.15 with:

(a) the **yacht assembly's** mass m_Y assumed to be equal to 6200 kg;

(b) the **yacht assembly's** centre of mass (x_Y, y_Y, z_Y) assumed to be equal to (9.350, 0.000, 0.750);

(c) an assumed water density of 1025 kg/m^3;

(d) buoyancy resulting only from the **hull surface** (not the **foils**, **rudder** or other components); and
(e) hydrostatic pressure acting on all parts of the **hull surface** below the flotation water plane, neglecting flooding of:
 (i) volumes that would remain dry assuming that any fairing flaps permitted by Rule 8.21 remain closed; and
 (ii) volumes not included in the **hull surface** such as the **foil** and **rudder wet boxes.**

8.13 When constrained to 0° of heel and floated to equilibrium under the conditions of Rule 8.12, the measurement reference points required by Rule 8.1 (a) shall lie no more than 25.0 mm above or below the flotation waterplane.

8.14 When constrained in heel and left free to float to equilibrium in the other degrees of freedom, the centre of mass of the **yacht assembly** and the centre of buoyancy of the **hull surface**, when both are projected on to the resulting flotation waterplane, must be separated by at least:
(a) 0.050 m at 7° of heel;
(b) 0.300 m at 15° of heel; and
(c) 1.000 m at 35° of heel.

8.15 When constrained to 90° of heel (such that **MWP** is held perpendicular to a flotation waterplane) and left free to float to equilibrium in the other degrees of freedom, under the conditions of Rule 8.12:
(a) the centre of buoyancy of the **hull surface** shall be at least 0.820 m above **MWP**; and
(b) the angle between **LCP** and the flotation waterplane shall be no more than 5°.

8.16 Any distinct retained water volume in a deck recess, cockpit, or other location on the **yacht**, shall be self- draining with the following criteria:
(a) at any water level, a drainage area of at least 0.050 m^2 for every 1.000 m^3 of retained volume shall be present below that level;
(b) the drainage area shall be:
 (i) open to drainage in the absence of a flotation waterplane; and
 (ii) free from obstruction, except for fairing flaps permitted by Rule 8.21;
(c) retained water volumes resulting from a sheet of water of more than 100 mm depth being uniformly deposited over the entire **yacht** need not be considered;
(d) the drainage requirements must be satisfied for the case when **MWP** is horizontal, and for a range of orientations bounded by:
 (i) a rotation of the **yacht** by up to ±10° about a **longitudinal** axis; followed by
 (ii) a rotation of the **yacht** by up to ±2° about a (rotated) **transverse** axis; and
(e) the following regions are exempt from the above requirements:

(i) porous and textured surfaces provided the **Measurement Committee** is satisfied that these are no larger than necessary; and
(ii) a total volume of no more than 3.0 litres comprising incidental features such as hatch gutters and fitting recesses.

The **Measurement Committee** may specify an alternative calculation method or drainage requirement if they believe that the above criteria are insufficient to ensure that the **yacht** is self-draining. For the avoidance of doubt intentional retainment of water is prohibited.

8.17 Two **foil wet boxes** and one **rudder wet box** are permitted within the **hull surface**, where:
(a) each **foil wet box** shall enclose a floodable volume of no more than 300 litres;
(b) the **rudder wet box** shall enclose a floodable volume of no more than 30 litres;
(c) each **wet box** shall be self draining according the criteria in Rules 8.16 (a), 8.16 (b) and 8.16 (d);
(d) volumes of non-porous foam or other material within a **wet box** may be subtracted from the **wet box** volume for the purposes of Rules 8.17 (a), 8.17 (b), 8.17 (c); and
(e) the watertight boundary that separates each **wet box** from the remainder of the enclosed **hull** volume need not satisfy the **hull** structural requirements detailed in Rule 9.2.

8.18 The **hull lower surface** shall form a continuous surface bounded only by the **perimeter line**, with no openings, except for:
(a) the exits of watertight conduits through the **hull** to provide drainage, which shall be:
(i) no larger than required for their permitted purpose; and
(ii) entirely above **MWP**; and
(b) penetrations into the closed volume of the **hull** permitted by Rule 8.19.

8.19 The enclosed volume of the **hull surface**, including the volumes required by Rule 8.11 must be watertight except for penetrations:
(a) into the **foil wet boxes**, providing that the penetrations lie entirely within regions defined by cylinders of length 1.600 m and diameter 1.250 m centred on each **foil cant reference point** and whose axes are aligned with the **foil cant** axes;
(b) into the **rudder wet box**, providing that the penetration lies entirely within 0.200 m of **LCP** and 1.500 m of **TRP**;
(c) on the **deck** and covered by watertight hatches which must not be opened while racing;
(d) for the ejection of water from a bilge pump;

(e) for the passage of systems or rigging, which must be at least 0.500 m above **MWP** and at least 0.200 m above the flotation waterplane in the condition specified by Rule 8.15; or

(f) sealed by means of installed hardware. Openings in installed hardware that would allow passage of water into the watertight volume of the **hull** must be at least 0.500 m above **MWP** and at least 0.200 m above the flotation waterplane in the condition specified by Rule 8.15.

The total cross-sectional area of openings permitted by Rules 8.19 (e) and 8.19 (f) shall be no more than 0.02 m^2, after subtracting the cross-sectional area of rigging or systems passing through.

8.20 A hatch in the **deck** shall provide access to the media hold for installation and servicing of **media equipment**. The hatch shall be no smaller than an ellipse measuring 400 by 600 mm and shall be in a position that enables **media equipment** to be installed in its specified location.

8.21 Fairing flaps on the **hull lower surface**, which are considered open for the purposes of Rule 8.16, are permitted for closing penetrations or conduit exits, provided that they:

(a) are no larger than required to close the drainage area specified by Rule 8.16 (a);

(b) have no purpose other than:

(i) fairing the **hull** surface when water is not draining; and

(ii) preventing reverse flow; and

(c) are incapable of retaining more than 25 L of water, in total, within the **yacht**. As an exception to Rule 8.4, this Rule shall be tested empirically by the **Measurement Committee**, at one or more orientations of the **yacht** not exceeding the range of heel and trim prescribed by Rule 8.16 (d).

9 Hull structure

9.1 The **hull** shall be a **linear component**.

9.2 The **hull shell** is restricted as follows:

(a) The areal density of any part of the **hull shell** shall be at least 2 kg/m^2;

(b) The areal density of any part of any hatch permitted by Rule 8.19 (c) shall be at least 2 kg/m^2; and

(c) Hardware sealed **hull** penetrations permitted by Rule 8.19 (f) shall not be designed to reduce the combined mass of the **hull** and relevant hardware below that which would be achieved in the absence of the penetration.

(Note that this Rule does not imply any stiffness, strength or robustness targets; it exists only to ensure that a **hull shell** is a solid structure and not, for example, a film-covered space frame structure.)

9.3 Any **core** used in the **hull shell** shall have a nominal density greater than or equal to 48 kg/m^3. Up to 10% of the **hull shell**, by area, shall be exempt from this **core** density limit provided:
   (a) the exempt areas are entirely above the **perimeter line**;
   (b) no single exempt area exceeds 5% of the **hull shell**; and
   (c) the exempt areas still satisfy Rule 9.2.

9.4 The **hull** shall be fitted with stanchion sockets for the attachment of lifelines when the **yacht** is ashore. The following requirements apply:
   (a) Sockets shall be located on the edge of the working deck along the full length of the **hull** sides and across the transom, at a maximum spacing of 2.200 m.
   (b) As an exception, sockets are not required in regions where a cockpit wall close to the **perimeter line** forms its own barrier, provided that:
      (i) the **hull surface** extends to at least 600 mm above the cockpit floor;
      (ii) there is no more than 120 mm width of cockpit wall, deck or topside surface, measured from the **perimeter line** to the drop to the cockpit floor;
      (iii) the cockpit is at least 500 mm wide at the required depth, that floor width not to be obscured by **hull surface** or another surface acting as a deck when viewed from above (fittings, pedestals, etc. are permitted to obscure the floor);
      (iv) widths herein are measured parallel to **MWP** and perpendicular to the local **perimeter line**; and
      (v) the first socket beyond the end of the cockpit is a maximum of 300 mm from the last point at which these criteria are met, measured parallel to **MWP** as a girth around the **perimeter line**.
   (c) Sockets shall suit 31.8 mm (1¼") stanchions with a minimum depth of 100 mm.
   (d) Sockets must be capable of resisting a test load, whereby:
      (i) a stiff test stanchion shall be placed in the stanchion socket;
      (ii) a load of 350 N shall be applied to the test stanchion at 600 mm above the top of the stanchion socket, in any direction normal to the stanchion;
      (iii) the load application point must translate by no more than 100 mm; and
      (iv) there must be no damage to the stanchion socket.
   (e) Sockets may be covered or plugged when sailing, providing any such cover or plug can be quickly removed.

10 Foils

10.1 Each **foil** shall comprise only:
  (a) one **foil arm** and one **foil wing**, which shall be connected to each other according to a detail provided within the **foil arm stock** specification.
  (b) one **foil flap**; and
  (c) one or more **foil** systems.

10.2 A **foil** excludes:
  (a) the removable pins and bearings identified in the **foil arm stock** specification referenced in Rule 32.3;
  (b) any **foil arm drum**; and
  (c) any other components inside the **hull surface** that are disconnected from a **foil** when it is removed from the **yacht**.

10.3 **Foil** systems:
  (a) shall only comprise mechanical, electrical and hydraulic components, or optical fibres designed to:
    (i) connect a **foil wing** to a **foil flap** and control its movement;
    (ii) connect segments of a **foil flap**; and/or
    (iii) provide sensor information to the **yacht**;
  (b) must not contribute significantly to the structure or surface area of the **foil wing** or **foil flap**;
  (c) that are above the upper extent of the **foil wing box** when **WSP** is vertical shall be contained entirely within the **foil arm**; and
  (d) that are below the upper extent of the **foil wing box** when **WSP** is vertical:
    (i) shall be contained entirely within the **foil wing box**; and
    (ii) shall have a total combined volume lying outside both the **foil wing hydrodynamic surface** and the **foil flap hydrodynamic surface** that does not exceed 1% of the combined volume enclosed by the **foil wing hydrodynamic surface** and the **foil flap hydrodynamic surface**. This condition shall be satisfied at all **foil flap** angles and twists; and
  (e) shall not themselves produce any hydrodynamic or aerodynamic forces that are significant with respect to the total forces acting on the **yacht**.

10.4 The **foil wing** and **foil flap**, **projected** to **TRP**, must lie entirely within the **foil wing box** in **foil** measurement condition. This Rule shall be satisfied at all **foil flap** rotation angles and twists.

10.5 The entire **foil** must lie between planes 10.000 m and 12.000 m forward of **TRP** when unloaded by **external forces** except gravity and canted to angles of 41.4° and 119.5°. This Rule shall be satisfied at all **foil flap** rotation angles and twists.

10.6 The only **foil arm** movement permitted relative to the **hull** is **cant**, being a rotation about the **foil arm cant** axis, a **longitudinal** axis whose position is defined in Figure 10.2.

10.7 The **foil** shall be capable of reaching **cant** angles of 7.6° and 119.5°.

10.8 For each **foil**, the Wing Symmetry Plane, **WSP**, is identified in Figure 10.1 and is fixed to the **foil wing**, rotating as the **foil arm cants**.

10.9 **Foil** measurement condition shall be with:

(a) the **yacht** levelled in a cradle;

(b) the **foil** unloaded by **external forces**, except gravity;

(c) the **foil wing** correctly mounted on the **foil arm**;

(d) the **foil flap** correctly mounted on the **foil wing**;

(e) the **foil** systems connected to the **foil wing** and **foil flap**; and

(f) the **foil arm** canted such that **WSP** is vertical.

The cant angle in **foil** measurement condition corresponds to a theoretical cant angle of 41.41°. Where a numerical cant angle is given in the Rule, unless specifically referring to an **FCS**-measured cant angle, this cant angle of 41.41° shall be used as a datum for defining other cant angles, with a raising of the **foil** from this position corresponding to an increase in cant.

10.10 **Control surface actuators** are permitted within **foil** systems to rotate **foil flaps** about the axis described in Rule 13.11. Any deformation in the **foil** resulting from this actuation is restricted by Rule 13.14. No other devices are permitted to modify the shape of a **foil**.

10.11 No part of a **foil** except the ODA Lower Belt Assembly and the ODA Head Assembly identified in the **foil arm stock** specification may touch any part of the **yacht** except:

(a) **a foil arm drum;**

(b) hydraulic connections for **foil** systems; and

(c) electrical and optical fibre connections.

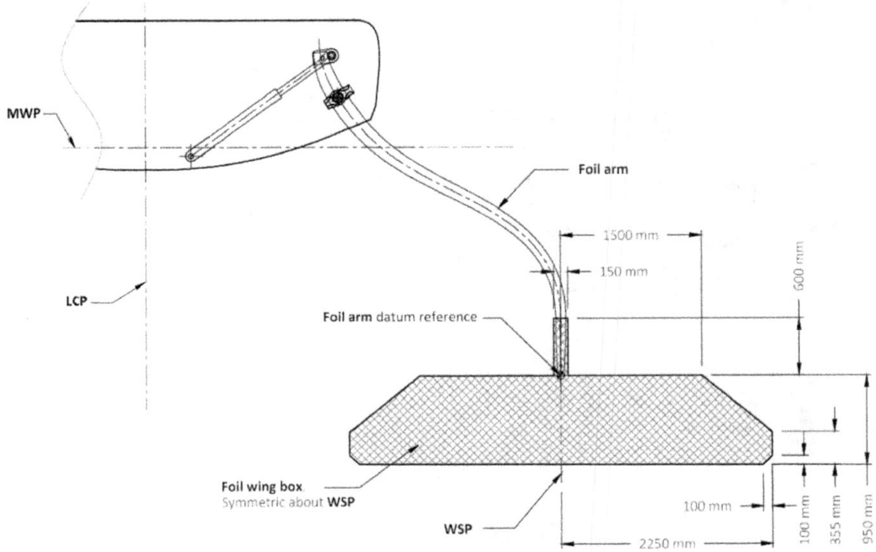

Figure 10.1: The extents of the **foil wing box** are defined by the shaded region in this figure.

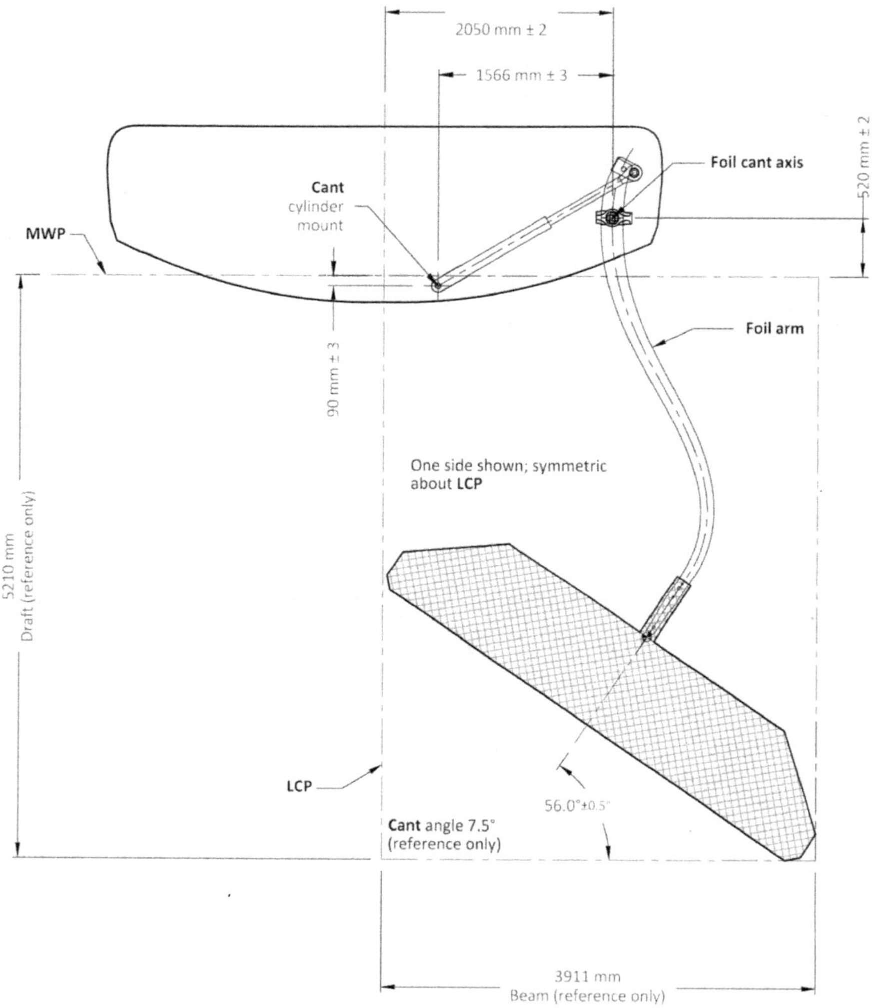

Figure 10.2: **FCS** geometry

11 Foil arms

11.1 Each **foil arm** shall be a **linear component** comprising exactly:
  (a) one **foil arm stock**;
  (b) one **foil arm fairing**; and
  (c) additional material as permitted by the **foil arm stock** specification.

11.2 The **foil arm stock** specification is defined by the document referenced in Rule 32.3.

11.3 The **foil arm stock** must match the **foil arm stock** specification. No modifications are permitted except for:

(a) the surface finish (sanding and painting as permitted in the **foil arm stock** specification);

(b) the installation and repair of optical fibres and fairing over, providing any additional grooves cut for placement of the optical fibres are in the surface of the **foil arm stock** and no wider or deeper than the grooves already provided;

(c) the attachment of permitted **foil arm fairings**, which shall only involve the addition of material bonded to the **foil arm stocks**; no part of the **foil arm stock** may be removed, except for surface preparation prior to bonding and sanding to fair the surface after bonding;

(d) repairs that return the **foil arm stock** to its original state after being damaged in accordance with the **AC Technical Regulations**; and

(e) the addition of material to the **foil arm** leading edge conduit to seal or avoid water retention.

11.4 Except as permitted in Rule 11.3, nothing may be added within a **foil arm stock**, except that **foil** systems may pass through the conduit in the **foil arm** leading edge.

11.5 **Foil arm fairings** are only permitted in the regions indicated in the supplied **foil arm** drawing "ODA Surface Finish Allowance and **Foil Arm Fairing** limitations", and are not permitted in the **foil wing box**.

11.6 In the region indicated in the supplied **foil arm** drawing, the outside surface shape of the **foil arm fairing** must match the shape specified in that drawing within tolerances specified in the **Measurement Procedures**.

11.7 **Foil arm fairings** shall not be capable of transmitting any significant bending, shear or torsional loads between the **foil wing** and the **foil arm**.

11.8 Penetrations into the **foil wet boxes**, as permitted by Rule 8.19 (a), may be closed by a **foil arm drum**, which:

(a) must fit entirely within the cylinder described in Rule 8.19 (a);

(b) must be a **linear component** and, in the absence of **external forces**, must remain undeformed at all **foil cant** angles;

(c) must not translate, and may only rotate about the relevant **foil cant** axis;

(d) may only rotate as a result of **foil cant** rotation; and

(e) may either:

(i) be attached to the **foil arm**, providing it can be disconnected to allow removal of the **foil arm** from the **yacht**; or

(ii) not be attached to the **foil arm** but rotate as a result of contact with the **foil arm**.

12 Foil wings

12.1 A **foil wing** shall be a **linear component**.
12.2 The **blueprint** for a **foil wing** shall be an IGES file that includes:
(a) **the foil wing's hydrodynamic surface;**
(b) surfaces specifying any regions of the **foil wing** classified as **foil flexure**; and
(c) a point that corresponds to the **foil arm** datum reference; and
(d) a line or lines indicating the **foil flap** hinge axes.
These geometries shall represent the geometry that the **foil wing** was designed to.
12.3 A **foil wing** shall match its **blueprint** within tolerances specified in the **Measurement Procedures** with the **foil wing** in an unloaded, undeformed condition, except that if the **foil wing** is measured when hanging or supported by the **foil arm**, an allowance shall be made for deformation due to self-weight.
12.4 A **foil wing** must be **symmetric** about **WSP** in **foil** measurement condition, with a build tolerance of 3.0 mm.
12.5 **Foil wings** shall include at least one cavity of 80 mm in length and 15.6 mm internal diameter that contains an ultrasonic transmitter supplied by Sonotronics Inc., with model number CHP-87-L, or a casing of equivalent size and weight. For the avoidance of doubt, these cavities shall comply with Rule 12.4.

13 Foil flaps and flexures

13.1 A **foil flap** shall comprise one or more *flap segments*, each of which shall be a **linear component**.
13.2 The **blueprint** for a **foil flap** shall be an IGES file representing an assembly that includes:
(a) each *flap segment's* **hydrodynamic surface**, positioned relative to each other as they are assembled into the **foil**, which together form the **foil flap's hydrodynamic surface**;
(b) surfaces specifying any regions of **foil flap** segments classified as **foil flexure**;
(c) surfaces specifying any regions of **foil flap** segments classified as *segment end regions*; and
(d) a line or lines indicating the **foil flap** hinge axes.
These geometries shall represent the geometry that the **foil flap** was designed to.
13.3 A **foil flap** shall match its **blueprint** within tolerances specified in the **Measurement Procedures**. Measurement shall be carried out with the **foil**

flap in an unloaded, undeformed condition, except that if the **foil flap** is measured when hanging or supported by the **foil wing**, an allowance shall be made for deformation due to self-weight.

13.4 *Segment end regions* referred to in Rules 13.2, 13.5 and 13.10 (a) (i) are permitted within cross-sections parallel to **WSP** through a maximum combined total span of 450 mm, where span is measured perpendicular to **WSP**.

13.5 Except within *segment end regions*, at any cross-section parallel to **WSP** there shall be no more than one *flap segment*.

13.6 The following shall be **symmetric** about **WSP** in **foil** measurement condition:

(a) the number and arrangement of **foil flap** segments, where a *flap segment* may cross **WSP** providing it is **symmetric** about **WSP** in **foil** measurement condition;

(b) the **foil flap**, with a build tolerance of 3.0 mm;

(c) the **foil flap** hinge axes, with a build tolerance of 3.0 mm; and

(d) the ranges of rotations and twists that can be achieved.

13.7 A **foil flexure** must be classified as a region of:

(a) a **foil wing**;

(b) a **foil flap**; or

(c) material that is partly **foil wing** and partly **foil flap**, with a virtual split line delineating the boundary.

13.8 Within Rules 13.9 and 13.10 (b) (i):

(a) the stated requirements apply at all cross-sections parallel to **WSP** and all **foil flap** rotation angles;

(b) the *chord length* at a given cross-section and a given **foil flap** rotation angle is the linear distance, measured perpendicular to **TRP**, between the foremost point and the aft most point in the cross-section;

(c) the *chord length* of a **foil flexure** means the total *chord length* measured from the foremost point of any **foil flexure** to the aft most point of any **foil flexure** in that cross-section;

(d) the following shall be neglected when determining *chord length*:

(i) the **foil arm** and any **foil** system;

(ii) any part of the **foil wing** that is aft of the aft most point of the **foil flap** in any cross-section; and

(iii) hinges or other parts of a **foil flap** or **foil wing** which occur at occasional cross-sections for connection between the **foil wing** and **foil flap**.

13.9 The *chord length* of a **foil flap** shall be no more than 50% of the *chord length* of the **foil**.

13.10 At any cross-section parallel to **WSP**:

(a) within *segment end regions*:

(i) the *chord length* of a **foil flexure** shall be no more than 50% of the *chord length* of the **foil**;

(b) elsewhere:

(i) the *chord length* of a **foil flexure** shall be no more than 20% of the *chord length* of the **foil**; and

(ii) a **foil flexure** shall not extend to the aft most point of the cross-section.

13.11 At any cross-section parallel to **WSP**, the only permitted movement of a **foil flap** relative to a **foil wing**, except for deformation restricted by Rule 13.14, is a rotation about a hinge axis that:

(a) must be designed to be stationary with respect to the **foil wing** at that section;

(b) may have some movement resulting from play in a mechanical bearing, provided that play is not designed to produce a non-stationary hinge axis; and

(c) need not lie inside the cross-section of the **foil wing** or **foil flap**, but must be at a finite distance from the **foil**.

13.12 Every tangent to a hinge axis shall subtend an angle of at least 45° to **WSP**.

13.13 At any cross-section parallel to **WSP**, a **foil flap** shall not rotate about the hinge axis by more than ±45 ° from a central position.

13.14 The cross-sectional shapes of the **foil wing** and **foil flap** shall lie within ±2.0 mm of their **blueprint's** local cross-section, except over the surface of any **foil flexure**, to be satisfied:

(a) at any cross-section through a **foil** perpendicular to the local **foil flap** hinge axis;

(b) for all **foil flap** rotation angles and twists; and

(c) in the absence of **external forces** except gravity.

13.15 In the absence of **external forces**, a **foil flexure** shall only deform as the result of differential rotation between those parts of:

(a) a **foil wing** and a **foil flap**; or

(b) different **foil flap** segments,

that are not classified as **foil flexure**. A **foil flexure** may touch or come into contact with a **foil** system, provided that contact does not significantly affect the external surface shape of the **foil flexure**.

14 Rudder

14.1 A **rudder** shall be a single **linear component**.

14.2 For the purpose of the component limits in the **AC Technical Regulations**:

(a) any material attached to the **rudder** below the **hull lower surface** must be declared as part of the rudder;

(b) any part that does not make up the **linear component** of the **rudder** shall not be part of the **rudder**; and

(c) any removable part of the **rudder linear component** that is entirely above the **hull lower surface** can optionally be declared as part of the **rudder**, but if it is declared as part of the **rudder** in the Version A declaration, it will always be controlled by the component limits in the **AC Technical Regulations**.

14.3 The **blueprint** of a **rudder** shall be an IGES file that includes:

(a) the **rudder's hydrodynamic surface**; and

(b) a point entity indicating the position of the lower **bearing centre**.

These geometries shall represent the geometry that the **rudder** was designed to.

A change in the position of the lower **bearing centre** does not in itself constitute a change according to the component limits in the **AC Technical Regulations**, but since it is defined in the **blueprint**, it does invalidate a Measurement Certificate.

14.4 A **rudder** shall match its **blueprint** within tolerances specified in the **Measurement Procedures**. Measurement shall be carried out with the **rudder** in an unloaded, undeformed condition, except for self-weight if the **rudder** is measured when hanging or supported in the **hull**.

14.5 The **wetted** part of the **rudder** must be **symmetric** about the **rudder** centre plane when unloaded by **external forces** except gravity, with a build tolerance of 3.0 mm.

14.6 With the **rudder** centre plane aligned with **LCP**, and unloaded by **external forces** except gravity, and at all rake angles that can be achieved, no **wetted** part of the **rudder** shall extend:

(a) aft of **TRP**; or

(b) forward of a **transverse** plane 1.500 m forward of **TRP**.

14.7 At all yaw and rake angles that can be achieved, and unloaded by **external forces** except gravity, no **wetted** part of the **rudder** shall extend further outboard than planes offset from **LCP** by 1.500 m both to port and to starboard.

14.8 With the **rudder** centre plane aligned with **LCP**, there must be an achievable rake angle at which the lowest 0.500 m of the **rudder**, when **projected** to **MWP**, has an area of at least 0.300 m^2.

14.9 Only the following **rudder** movements are permitted relative to the AC75 **yacht**:

(a) yaw, being a rotation about an axis joining the lower and upper **bearing centres**; and

(b) rake, being a rotation about a **transverse** axis through the lower **bearing centre**.

14.10 When unloaded by **external forces** except gravity, the **rudder** must not touch any part of the **yacht** except:

(a) a lower bearing, whose **bearing centre** must be a fixed point that lies within 3 mm of **LCP**;

(b) an upper bearing, whose **bearing centre** can move, but must always lie within 3 mm of **LCP**;

(c) optical fibre and electrical connections for instrumentation within an **ILS**;

(d) a device whose only purpose is to react yaw moment and control yaw angle, connected to the **steering control system**; and

(e) the **hull lower surface** within 0.500 m of any yaw axis as defined in Rule 14.9 (a).

14.11 The lower and upper **bearing centres** must be vertically separated by at least 600 mm.

14.12 No device shall be used to induce deformation in the **rudder**; any deformation may only be the result of **external forces** and reactions by components permitted in Rule 14.10.

15 Mast

15.1 A **mast** specification will be issued according to Rule 32.3 which will include details of:

(a) **the mast surface specification;**

(b) the minimum required **mast tube** laminate and construction details;

(c) the **supplied rigging**;

(d) **mast** fittings and spreaders, some of which may be specified as supplied components which must be sourced from a nominated supplier;

(e) the rig plan, including required chainplate and **MRP** positions on the **hull**;

(f) the supplied **mainsail** buoyancy system; and

(g) legacy **mast tube** modification procedures.

The word *specification* within Rule 15 refers to the parts of this **mast** specification.

15.2 Except where otherwise indicated within the **AC75 Class Rules**, all components of the **mast** listed in Rule 15.1 must match the specification. The **mast tube** can be either:

(a) a new **mast tube** built according to the specification; or

(b) a legacy **mast tube** modified according to the legacy **mast tube** modification procedures detailed in the specification.

15.3 The **blueprint** of a **mast tube** shall be a zip file of two-dimensional drawings in PDF format that include:

(a) complete laminate drawings of the **mast tube**; and

(b) details of any changes from a previous version of the **mast tube**;

15.4 With the **mast** unloaded and supported horizontally in two cradles, with the aft face upwards, positioned 3.0 m and 20.9 m above the ball:

(a) the external surface of the **mast tube** shall match the **mast surface specification** to within ±3 mm for any cross-section orthogonal to the aft face of the **mast surface specification**; and

(b) the aft face of the **mast tube** shall be straight within ±10 mm along the length of the **mast tube**.

15.5 As exceptions to Rule 15.4:

(a) rebates for the attachment of components are permitted providing such rebates are filled to match the **mast surface specification** within the tolerance required by Rule 15.4 (a); and

(b) additional holes with a maximum diameter of 21 mm are permitted in the **mast tube**, including through bulkheads, for fasteners used to attach fittings. Such holes must not reduce the stiffness or strength of the **mast tube** and **Competitors** may be required by the **Measurement Committee** to provide documentation supporting this.

(c) openings or covers over openings in legacy **mast tubes** for legacy one-design fittings that are no longer in the **mast surface specification.**

15.6 The *specification* prescribes the minimum required laminate for the **mast tube**, which may be reinforced by:

(a) using laminates comprising greater fibre weight, resin content, number of layers, **core** density, and/or **core** thickness than provided in the *specification*;

(b) adding laminate external to the **mast surface specification**, providing it remains within the tolerances given in Rule 15.4.

The outer layer of the **mast tube** laminate from the *specification* shall not be sanded other than for local repairs and reinforcements performed after the **mast tube** has been cured, but may be painted or covered in branding material such as vinyl.

15.7 Laminates are not required to meet the *specification* within 300 mm of the intersection between the aft face of the **mast tube** and the **mast upper plane.**

15.8 Openings in the aft face of the **mast tube**, in addition to those in the **mast surface specification**, are permitted to provide access to permitted systems, and to allow passage of **rig control systems** and instrumentation cables. Such additional openings shall be no larger than required, and shall have:

(a) a maximum dimension of 150 mm;

(b) a maximum area of 0.018 m^2;

(c) a minimum distance of 250 mm between the boundaries of any two openings; and

(d) a maximum combined total area of 0.1 m^2.

Any fastener holes in the aft face used for the attachment of fittings as permitted in Rule 15.5 (b) do not count as openings in this Rule.

15.9 The **mast** shall be positioned and tensioned on the **hull** in a **dock tune** prescribed by the rig plan specification. Neither the **mast**, nor the positions of **MRP** and the **hull** chainplates shall be adjusted relative to the **hull** except for:

(a) rotation of the **mast** about **MRP** by the action of a device, or devices, attached to the **mast** within the **mast lower zone**;

(b) movement of **rig control systems** within the **mast lower zone** for the purpose of controlling the mainsail;

(c) incidental movement of fairings or **mast** components in the **mast lower zone** due to contact with the crew, **hull**, deck gear, rigging or other items attached to the **hull**; and

(d) movement of the **mast** due to adjustment of permitted **rig control systems**.

15.10 The **supplied rigging** shall not be modified except for:

(a) the addition of one fairing or vibration mitigation device per **supplied rigging** element, which when installed shall fit within a cylinder of 100 mm diameter and 600 mm length;

(b) maintenance permitted in the manual provided by the **supplied rigging** manufacturer; and

(c) other repairs approved by the **supplied rigging** manufacturer.

15.11 No components of the **mast**, other than rigging and components of the specification are permitted to extend more than:

(a) 7800 mm aft of the aft face of the **mast surface specification** or 20 mm forward of the leading edge of the **mast surface specification**, within the **mast lower zone**;

(b) 30 mm aft of the aft face of the **mast surface specification**, between the **mast lower zone** and a plane 300 mm below the **mast upper plane**;

(c) 3 mm outside of the **mast surface specification**, forward of the aft face of the **mast surface specification** between the **mast lower zone** and a plane 300 mm below the **mast upper plane**;

(d) 100 mm aft of the aft face of the **mast surface specification** within 300 mm of the **mast upper plane**; or

(e) 20 mm outside of the **mast surface specification**, forward of the aft face of the **mast surface specification**, within 300 mm of the **mast upper plane**.

These restrictions will be measured at the local height in the **yacht**-fixed reference frame with an assumed **mast** rake of 5°. If components of the **mast** extend below the **mast surface specification** then for the purpose of this measurement the **mast surface specification** will be extended to the local height of the measurement.

15.12 As an exception to Rule 15.11, up to two rigid or flexible handles are permitted to be attached to the **mast** or to the **mainsail** within the **mast lower zone**, provided their only purpose is to provide handholds for the crew.

15.13 No part of the **mast** shall extend beyond, or be capable of extending beyond, the **mast upper plane** except for **media equipment**.

15.14 The **mast** in **mast** measurement condition shall:

(a) be capable of being weighed by horizontal suspension from two points at least 20.0 m apart;

(b) have the **supplied rigging** positioned loosely, with lower end fittings within 100 mm of **MRP**;

(c) include all halyards positioned as they would be with all sails hoisted; and

(d) include all components that are attached to the **mast** when it is arranged in **dock tune** and remain on the **yacht** whilst racing. Other components of the **mast** shall be included in the **platform** measurement condition.

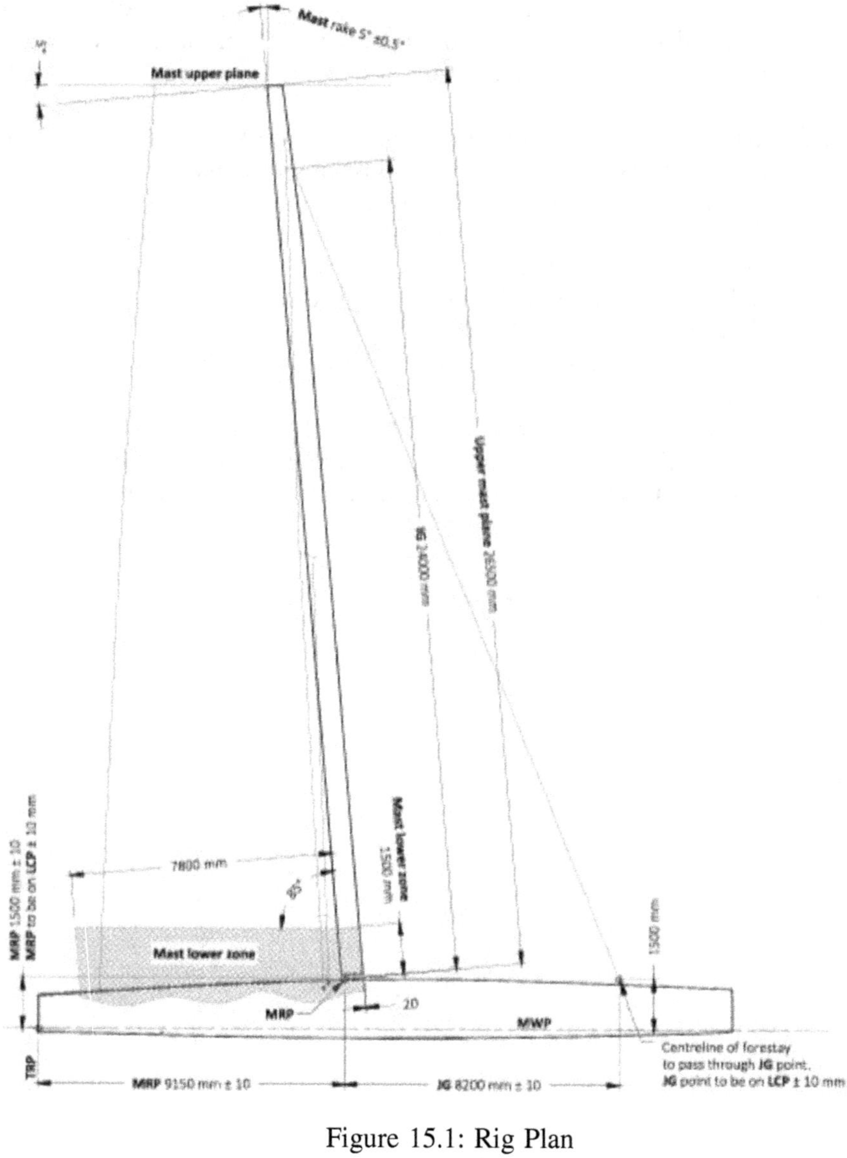

Figure 15.1: Rig Plan

16 Sails

16.1 The **blueprint** of a **sail skin** shall be a two-dimensional drawing in PDF format that includes:

(a) dimensions for all sail measurements that are restricted by the **AC75 Class Rule**;
(b) details of any area changes with respect to the previous version of the **sail skin**;
(c) the area of the **sail skin** that remains unmodified from the declared Version A, expressed on the drawing shown by annotated lines/hatching/shading, etc. and as a numerical value in square metres; and
(d) the total area of sail skin bounded by the luff, head, leech and foot.

16.2 Shore based sail measurements are to be carried out with **battens** installed under minimal compressive load.

16.3 Openings through **sail skins** are prohibited whilst racing. This rule does not prohibit access panels that are fully covered and closed whilst racing. Penetrations may exist that are either small such as those created by stitching, or filled such as penetrations used for attaching **sail hardware**. Control lines shall not pass from one side of a **sail skin** to the other.

16.4 Stiff **sail skin** reinforcements are permitted within 1.0 m of **head points**, **peak points**, **clew points**, **tack points** and anywhere within the **mast lower zone**. Elsewhere, **sail skins** shall be capable of being folded without clearly visible structural failure.

16.5 **Battens**:
(a) shall pass through a 75 mm diameter circle;
(b) shall be single-piece components without hinges or other mechanisms;
(c) shall, when unloaded and without **external forces**, have a straight central axis to a tolerance of 5 mm over any 1000 mm length and 25 mm over their entire length;
(d) shall not be inflatable; and
(e) shall be located inside a sail pocket not exceeding 260 mm in internal width measured normal to the lengthwise axis of the **batten.**

Battens of the **Mainsail** that are located entirely within the **mast lower zone** are not restricted by this rule.

16.6 When measured on a flat surface, the **leech** of a **sail skin** can deviate in angle by no more than 10° through any distance along the **leech** from 200 mm below to 200 mm above any **batten** or associated **sail hardware.**

16.7 The 25%, 50% and 75% **sail skin** girths are taken from the 25%, 50% and 75% **leech points** to the nearest point on the **luff** as illustrated in Figures 18.1 and 17.2. If hollows exist in the **leech** between **battens** adjacent to a girth measurement point then the girth shall be taken beyond the **leech** to a straight line that bridges the **leech** between these **battens**.

17 Mainsail

17.1 A **mainsail** must comprise exactly two **sail skins**. Other components that may make up a **mainsail** are limited to:
(a) **battens;**
(b) connections between **sail skins** and **battens** as permitted in Rule 17.19;
(c) **sail hardware;**
(d) **leech**, **head** and **foot** lines no greater than 6 mm in diameter, and no more than one line at any point along a **sail skin** edge;
(e) **rig control systems** as described in Rule 17.20;
(f) fairings as permitted in Rule 17.16;
(g) up to two safety handles as permitted by Rule 15.12;
(h) a supplied **mainsail** buoyancy system as prescribed in Rule 17.21;
(i) components of an **ECC**;
(j) components of **CIS**; and
(k) **woollies.**

17.2 When determining a specific **mainsail** measurement length or girth, the greatest value from both **sail skins** shall be taken.

17.3 When calculating a **mainsail** girth, the offset between the local **luff** of a **sail skin** and the aft face of the **mast surface specification** shall be added to the girth measurement.

17.4 The **luff** of any **skin** of a **mainsail** shall not be forward of the aft face of the **mast surface specification** at any point.

17.5 **Mainsail** girths shall be limited as follows:

		Minimum	Maximum
GF	**Foot girth** (m)	7.000	7.400
G25	25% girth (m)	6.000	6.600
G50	50% girth (m)	5.000	5.800
G75	75% girth (m)	3.600	4.700
GH	**Head girth** (m)	2.000	3.400

17.6 **Mainsails** shall comply with:

$$130.0 < \frac{26.5}{12} \times (G_F + 4G_{25} + 2G_{50} + 4G_{75} + G_H) < 145.0$$

For the avoidance of doubt, this formula is a girth restriction only and shall not be used as a measurement of sail area.

17.7 Angles relative to a straight line from the **head point** to the **peak point**, illustrated in Figure 17.1, are limited by:

(a) $90° \leq \alpha_P \leq 115°$ for all lines that pass through any two points, at least 100 mm apart, that lie on the **leech** between 300 mm and 800 mm from the **peak point**; and

(b) $\alpha_H \leq 95°$ for all lines that pass through any two points, at least 100 mm apart, that lie on the **luff** between 500 mm and 1500 mm from the **head point**.

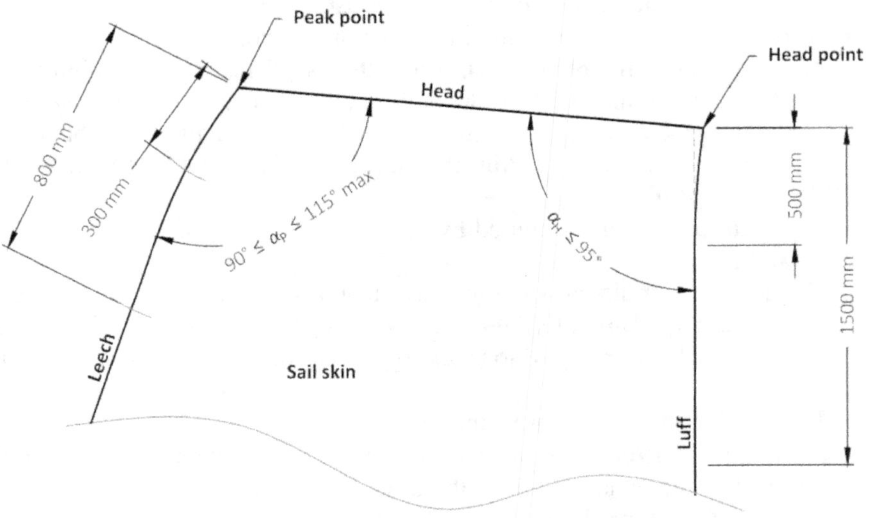

Figure 17.1: Example measurement of α_P and α_H

17.8 The **head points** of both **skins** of a **mainsail** shall be below the **mast upper plane**.

17.9 No part of a **skin** of a **mainsail** may extend more than 10 mm above a straight line from the **peak point** to the **head point**.

17.10 The **mast lower zone** shall be identified on each **sail skin** with the **mainsail** in its highest possible position with the yacht at rest.

17.11 No part of the **mainsail** is permitted to extend more than 7800 mm aft of the local **mast surface specification**. This restriction will be applied at the local height in the **yacht**-fixed reference frame with an assumed **mast** rake of 5°. If the **mainsail** extends below the **mast surface specification** then the **mast surface specification** will be extended to the local height of the measurement.

17.12 Each **skin** of the **mainsail** shall have at least one continuous attachment to the **mast tube** from 1.5 m above **MRP** to 0.5 m below the **head point**. This attachment shall not have any gaps or overlaps that would allow a line to pass through.

17.13 With the exception hardware within the **mast lower zone**, the largest dimension of any **sail hardware** for a **mainsail** shall not exceed 650 mm.

17.14 After sailing, with the **mast** still stepped in the **yacht**, the **mainsail** shall be lowered completely below the top of the **mast lower zone** without assistance from anyone who is completely above that zone. As an exception, crew may go aloft to resolve occasional, unforeseen issues.

17.15 The **mainsail** shall be capable of being removed from the **mast**, with the **mast** stepped, without damage to either the **mast** or **mainsail**.

17.16 **Mainsail** fairings are permitted only for the purposes of:

(a) fairing **rig control systems**, where they shall lie entirely within the **mast lower zone**, may be flexible, and may be attached to the **sail skins**; and

(b) sealing the area between **sail skins**, where they shall be flexible and shall only attached to each **skin**, that attachment lying entirely within 100 mm of the **head**.

Mainsail fairings permitted by this shall not be considered to be part of a **sail skin**.

17.17 The **mast** and **mainsail** shall not have features such as flaps, excess **sail skin** material, or **rig control system** fairings designed to cover or fair the crew in their normal sailing positions except occasionally when the **mainsail** is well-eased.

17.18 Each **sail skin** of a **mainsail** may have:

(a) up to 10 **battens** that run from within 100 mm of the **luff** to within 100 mm of the **leech** and are above the **mast lower zone**;

(b) up to 6 **battens** shorter than 1.0 m that have one end terminating within 50 mm of the **leech** and are above the **mast lower zone**; and

(c) any number of **battens** that lie entirely within the **mast lower zone**.

17.19 With the exception of fairings permitted by Rule 17.16 (b), connections between **skins** of a **mainsail** or between **battens** of a **mainsail** above the **mast lower zone** may only:

(a) be entirely within 400 mm of the **luff** or the **leech** of a **sail skin**;

(b) span no more than 150 mm vertically with the **mainsail** in an unloaded state; and

(c) be no closer than 2.0 m for any **leech** connection permitted by Rule 17.19 (a).

Within the **mast lower zone** there is are no restrictions on connections between **sail skins** or **battens**.

17.20 **Rig control systems** may not be attached to or bear upon the **mainsail** above the **mast lower zone** identified on each **sail skin** in Rule 17.10, except:

(a) the **mast tube** through means permitted in Rule 15.9; and

(b) **leech** lines within 50 mm of the **leech** of a **mainsail skin** provided their purchase systems or other controls are entirely within the region identified in Rule 17.10.

17.21 A supplied **mainsail** buoyancy system, as defined in the **mast** specification in in Rule 15.1, shall be attached to the starboard **sail skin** of the **mainsail** so that the position markers of the supplied **mainsail** buoyancy system remain within 100 mm of the **head** of the starboard **sail skin**. **Competitors** shall adhere to any inflation regulations provided in the **mast** specification.

17.22 The **mainsail** in **mainsail** measurement condition shall include all components of the **mainsail** that are attached to the **mainsail** before it is hoisted. Components of the **mainsail** that are attached to the **mainsail** during or after the hoist shall be included in the **platform** measurement condition.

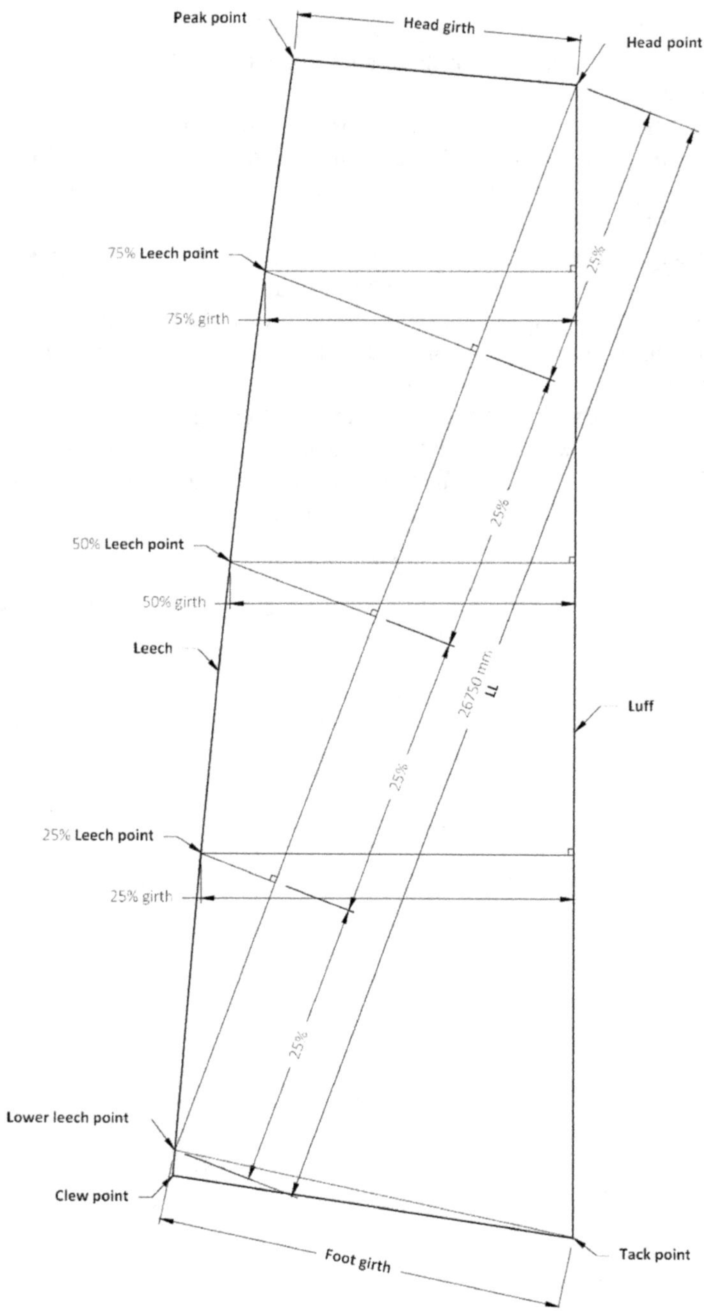

Figure 17.2: **Mainsail** Measurement

18 Jib

18.1 The components that may make up a **jib** are limited to:
  (a) exactly one **sail skin**;
  (b) up to 8 **battens**, which can terminate on any sail edge, and shall not be adjusted while the **jib** is hoisted;
  (c) **sail hardware;**
  (d) **luff** attachment devices permitted in Rule 18.6;
  (e) **head pennants;**
  (f) **luff**, **leech**, **head** and **foot** lines no greater than 6 mm in diameter and their associated purchase systems.
  (g) ballast, that serves no purpose other than increasing sail weight, located within 1.0 m of the **tack point**.
  (h) components of an **ECC**; and
  (i) **woollies.**

18.2 The largest dimension of any **sail hardware** for a **jib** shall not exceed 350 mm.

18.3 **Jibs** shall be hoisted and lowered without assistance from crew aloft. As an exception, crew may go aloft to resolve occasional, unforeseen issues.

18.4 The **head** of any **jib** shall be below **IG**.

18.5 **Jibs**, when hoisted, shall be connected to the forestay by hanks or luff pockets or a combination of both.

18.6 Hanks for connecting the **jib** to the forestay shall:
  (a) extend no more than 75 mm forward of the **luff**, measured perpendicular to the **luff**;
  (b) be no more than 100 mm in length, measured parallel to the **luff**; and
  (c) be no closer than 200 mm to each other, except within 1.000 m of the **head point** or **tack point**.

18.7 Other than within 100 mm of **supplied rigging** fittings, **luff** pockets of **jibs** shall be:
  (a) capable of being folded flat along the leading edge without sustaining damage; and
  (b) no more than 150 mm wide, when measured internally with the pocket closed, perpendicular to the luff.

  Luff pockets of **jibs** may extend up to 300 mm above the **head point** and such extensions will not be included in the evaluation of the **head**.

18.8 No component of the yacht shall be attached to, or bear upon a **jib** except:
  (a) sheets, or purchase systems of sheets, attached to a single piece of **sail hardware** within 400 mm of the **clew point**;
  (b) a halyard in 1:1 configuration attached:
    (i) within 400 mm of the **head point** of the **jib**; or

(ii) to the upper end of a **head pennant**, the lower end of that **head pennant** being attached within 400 mm of the **head point** of the **jib**;

(c) a cunningham system near the **tack point**;
(d) the forestay;
(e) electrical wiring for the sole purpose of making connections to **ECC** components;
(f) **luff**, **leech**, **head** and **foot** lines; and
(g) the **deck**, which may be attached to the **jib** within 300 mm of the intersection of the **deck** and the forestay, and bear upon it elsewhere.

18.9 Maximum **jib** measurements shall be:

	Jibs with **LL** ≤ 18.0 m	**Jibs** with **LL** > 18.0m
LP	7.050 m	7.050 m
50% girth	0.59**LP**	(0.869-0.0155**LL**)**LP**
75% girth	0.40**LP**	(0.859-0.0255**LL**)**LP**
Head girth	0.17**LP**	(0.699-0.0294**LL**)**LP**

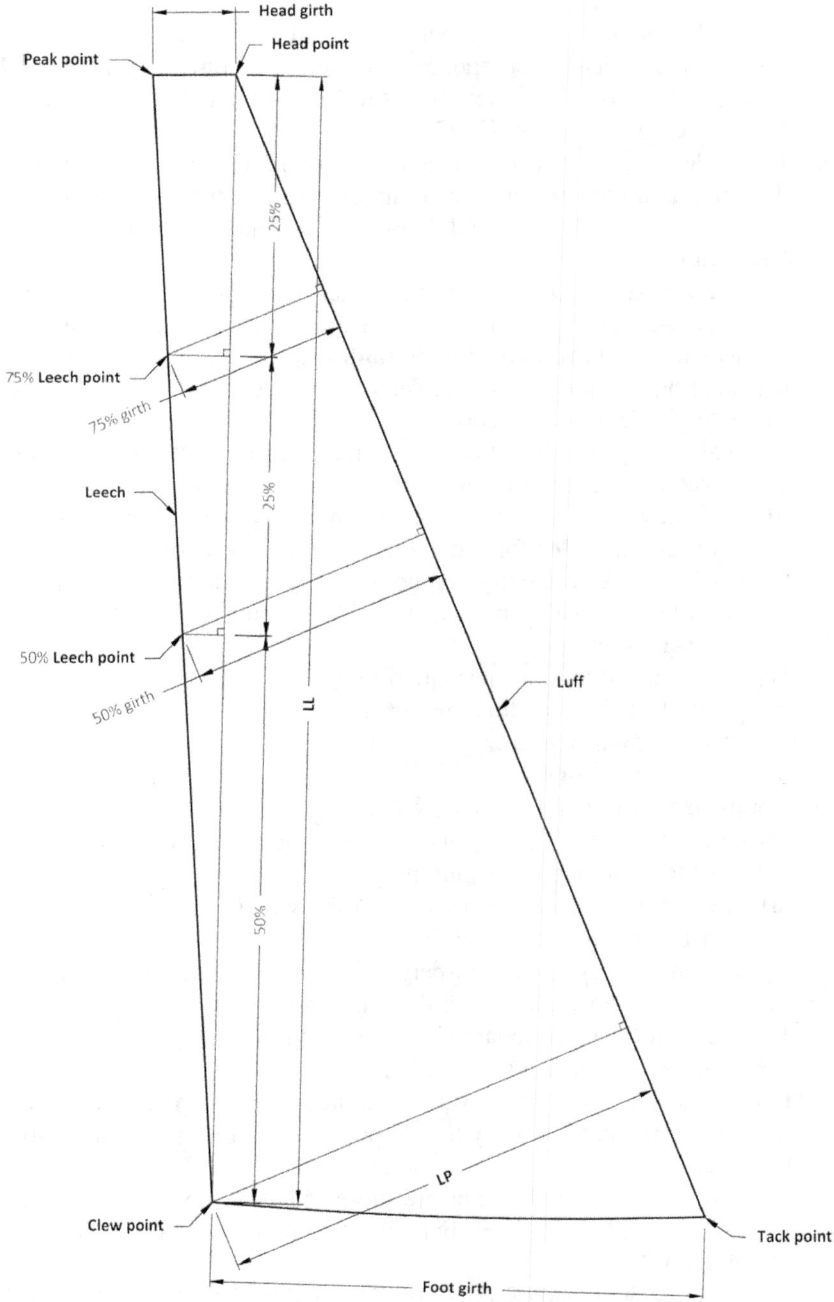

Figure 18.1: **Jib** Measurement

19 Hydraulics

19.1 Rule 19 applies to all components except the **FCS**.

19.2 Hydraulic circuits and components are permitted only as part of an **HCC** or an **LCS**. If a hydraulic system fulfils functions of an **HCC** as well as an **LCS**, it shall be considered an **HCC**.

19.3 Hydraulic circuits and components are permitted only for the purpose of adjusting **control surfaces** with **control surface actuators**, for managing the flow of hydraulic fluid to and from these actuators or as part of an **LCS**.

19.4 Hydraulic actuators:

(a) Shall have exactly two **nodes**, except in the case of a conventional double-ended ram (one with a piston rod on either side of the piston) which shall have two or three **nodes**;

(b) shall have **nodes** whose movement relative to each other is confined to a single degree-of-freedom;

(c) shall always produce the same force or torque between its **nodes** when subjected to a given combination of hydraulic pressures;

(d) shall always exhibit the same extension velocity or rotational velocity between its **nodes** for a given combination of hydraulic flows; and

(e) may be **mechanically** supported through additional contact points providing no additional functionality is gained in terms of controlling **control surfaces**.

19.5 **Hydraulic actuators** are permitted only as:

(a) parts of **control surface actuators**;

(b) **transmission actuators; and**

(c) **master actuators.**

19.6 Components in an **HCC** or an **LCS** must be sized appropriately for their permitted use. It is prohibited to use additional, oversized or highly-deformable components or plumbing:

(a) to control the mass distribution on the **yacht**;

(b) to act as a **yacht state** sensor;

(c) to store energy (except in permitted **hydraulic accumulators**); or

(d) for any purpose other than that permitted by Rule 19.3.

Oil reservoirs shall be no larger than required for supplying permitted **HCCs**, including appropriate reserve volumes.

19.7 Pumps used to convert power transmitted through **primary force input devices** by the crew into hydraulic power within an **HCC** are restricted as follows:

(a) The only permitted pumps are those radial piston pumps of type R and RG supplied by HAWE Hydraulik SE listed in the catalogues identified by HAWE as:

(i) "D 6010 – 09-2021 – 1.3", printed on 15th November 2021; and

(ii) "D 6010 D - 02-2021-1.0", printed on 17th February 2021.

(b) Pumps must be selected from the listed catalogue options, in terms of "Basic type", "Delivery flow coding", "Versions", "Seals" and "Supplement". Specifically, the "Delivery flow coding" must be selected from the tables in Section 2.2 of either catalogue, and may not be a "further combination" indicated in the catalogue as "available on request". No customised variations can be ordered, and each pump must be a standard order pump identified by the catalogue codes detailed in Section 2 of the catalogues.

(c) Pumps may not be modified from their as-supplied condition, except:

(i) for maintenance and replacement of parts with identical spares in order to return a pump to its original condition; and

(ii) to reconfigure a pump from one catalogue configuration to another catalogue configuration, which must exactly match a configuration permitted by Rule 19.7 (b).

(d) **Competitors** must declare to the **Measurement Committee** the catalogue code of each pump they have installed on the **yacht**.

This Rule does not prohibit the use of **hydraulic intensifiers** downstream of the standard pumps.

19.8 The pump drive ratio, being the ratio of the rotational velocity at the input to a pump, divided by the rotational velocity at which the crew provides power into a **primary force input device**, shall be fixed for each **primary force input device** to pump connection, and shall not be adjusted whilst racing.

19.9 Any rotational velocity ratio other than 1:1, at any point in a drivetrain between a **primary force input device** and a pump permitted by Rule 19.6 shall be fixed whilst racing, and shall only be realised by:

(a) a chain, such as a bicycle chain, transmitting torque between two sprockets of different diameters; and/or

(b) gearboxes permitted by Rule 19.12.

For the avoidance of doubt, single-input single-output driveshaft connections such as a 90° bevel boxes are unrestricted, provided the input shaft rotational velocity is equal to the output shaft rotational velocity.

19.10 Any drivetrain connection between a **primary force input device** and a pump permitted by Rule 19.7 shall be permanently connected; that is, it shall not be clutched in and out. That is, turning a specific **primary force input device** shall always have the effect of turning the same pump or pumps, and always with the same rotational velocity ratio to the **primary force input device**.

19.11 As an exception to Rules 19.8, 19.9 and 19.10, one ratchet mechanism per **primary force input device** is permitted, providing its only purpose is to restrict torque to being transferred in a downstream direction only from a **primary force input device** to a driveshaft. Such a ratchet mechanism:

(a) shall not be controlled or adjusted when racing;
(b) shall only have the effect of disengaging the **primary force input device** from all downstream drive- shafts and pumps together; and
(c) shall function such that if the driveshaft connected to the **primary force input device** is turning more quickly than the **primary force input device**, no significant torque is transmitted from the **primary force input device** to any systems.

If a ratchet mechanism is used, the **primary force input device** shall only be capable of transmitting torque when turned in one direction, that direction remaining fixed whilst racing.

19.12 Gearboxes used within a drivetrain described by Rule 19.9 to effect a rotational velocity and torque ratio are restricted as follows:
(a) The only permitted gearboxes are the planetary gearboxes of type AE and AER, including the AES and AERS variants, supplied by APEX Dynamics, Inc and listed in the catalogues identified by APEX as:
(i) "APEX-2022-11-AEAER SERIES-1.0-TWN" printed in November 2022; and
(ii) "APEX AER STAINLESS" publication number SS-030418.
(b) Gearboxes must be selected from one of the listed catalogue options, in terms of "Gearbox Size" and "Ratio". No customised variations can be ordered.
(c) Gearboxes may not be modified from their as-supplied condition, except for maintenance and re- placement of parts with identical spares in order to return a gearbox to its original condition.
(d) **Competitors** must declare to the **Measurement Committee** the catalogue code of each gearbox they have installed on the **yacht**.

19.13 Where one or more **primary force input devices** (upstream) are **mechanically** connected through a drivetrain to more than one pumps (downstream) permitted by Rule 19.6, a split in the torque from any up- stream driveshaft to turn two or more downstream driveshafts shall only be realised by:
(a) one or more chains, such as bicycle chains, transmitting torque from a sprocket on the upstream driveshaft to a sprocket on the downstream driveshaft; and/or
(b) a direct in-line shaft coupling between an upstream driveshaft and a pump, naturally limited to two such pumps per upstream driveshaft arranged with one at either end.

19.14 Hydraulic pumps and hydraulic motors that have a continuously variable displacement are prohibited except within the **flight power pack**.

19.15 **Valves** within a **control surface actuator** need not be physically mounted on the **hydraulic actuator**, but for each **control surface actuator** a single closed boundary on a hydraulic circuit diagram representative of the **yacht's HCCs** shall:

(a) enclose all parts of an **HCC** that are part of that **control surface actuator**; and
(b) exclude all other hydraulic lines or components of the **yacht**.

Any parts of an **HCC** that are part of a **control surface actuator** shall not be part of any other **control surface actuator**.

19.16 The **flight HCC** shall have the circuit layout indicated in figure 19.1, with no additional branches or lines, where:

(a) the **flight HCC** shall be entirely self-contained and disconnected from any other **HCC**;
(b) there shall be a single **flight power pack** which shall provide only a single pressure supply port;
(c) the box labelled "PRV" indicates that a pressure relief valve is required downstream of the **flight power pack**;
(d) the pressure supply line shall then branch to supply the three **appendages**;
(e) the three boxes labelled "**Valves**" indicate that **valves** are permitted to control flow out of the **flight power pack** or to each **appendage**. Any combination of **valves** not elsewhere prohibited are per- mitted within these boxes;
(f) the high pressure circuit shall then branch to supply each **control surface actuator** (labelled "CSA") driving each **flight control**;
(g) a check valve to prevent reverse flow shall be present immediately upstream of each **control surface actuator**;
(h) any combination of **transmission actuators** not elsewhere prohibited are permitted within each control surface actuator;
(i) the dashed lines indicate that each **foil flap control system** may contain one or more **control surface actuators**;
(j) each **control surface actuator** and any pressure relief valves shall return oil to a common **low pressure circuit**;
(k) outside of the **flight power pack**, the boxes labelled "**Valves**" and the **control surface actuators**, there shall be no hydraulic components other than those indicated and inline passive devices such as filters, radiators, lines and connectors.

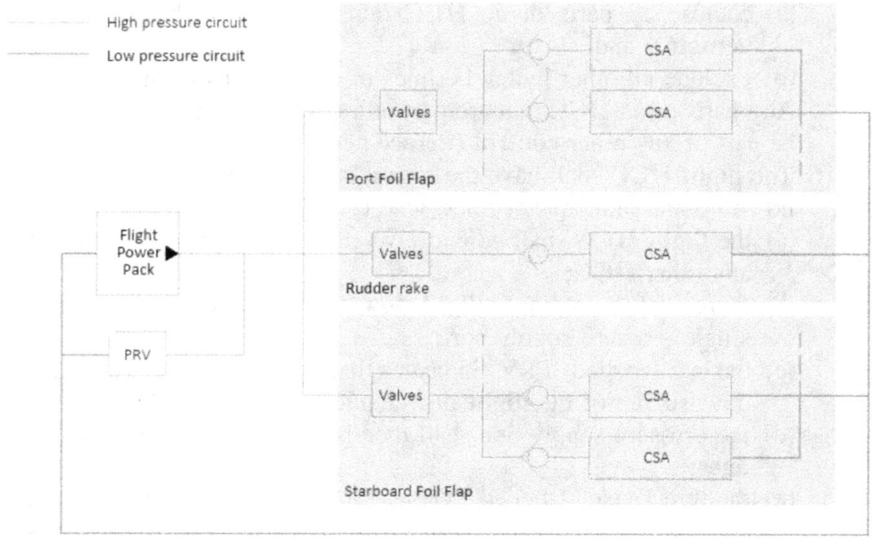

Figure 19.1: **Flight HCC**

19.17 Within the **flight HCC**, **hydraulic intensifiers** and **master actuators** are only permitted within the **flight power pack**.

19.18 Standard pressure relief valves shall:

(a) be manufactured by HYDAC with a model code of the form "DB4E-01X-xxxPyyy" or "DB4E-01X-xxxVyyy" where:

(i) "xxx" indicates the upper extent of the valve's pressure range;

(ii) "yyy" indicates the factory-preset opening pressure; and

(iii) if the "DB4E-01X-xxxVyyy" model is used, the lock nut shall be drilled through adjacent faces to enable a lock wire and lead seal to be installed.

(b) be set to open at a maximum pressure of 600 bar;

(c) be present in any circuit downstream of:

(i) pumps powered by **primary force input devices**;

(ii) the **flight power pack**;

(iii) any **hydraulic accumulator** permitted by Rule 19.20 (a);

(iv) any **hydraulic actuator** chamber from which oil can be **recovered**;

(v) any **master actuator**; and

(vi) any **hydraulic intensifiers** that are capable of increasing pressure (i.e. pressure intensifiers).

For each device (i) to (vi) above, the pressure relief valve shall be located at any point within that part of a circuit downstream of the device that is always subject to the output pressure of the device; that is, before any other valves or restrictions; and

(d) vent to a **low-pressure circuit**.

This Rule is a minimum requirement for pressure relief valves, and does not prohibit the use of additional pressure relief valves, nor the use of pressure relief valves of a different type elsewhere within an **HCC**.

19.19 **Hydraulic actuators** and **hydraulic intensifiers** are permitted to incorporate a gas spring return providing:

(a) any gas volumes:

(i) shall contain a constant mass of gas, except for unintended leakage;

(ii) may be physically separate from the **hydraulic actuators** and **hydraulic intensifiers** they operate on;

(iii) may be shared between **hydraulic actuators** and **hydraulic intensifiers**; and

(iv) are subject to Rule 19.6;

(b) any **hydraulic actuator** or **hydraulic intensifier** that:

(i) is capable of draining oil that can be **recovered**; or

(ii) contains gas which, when expanding, can do work on a **control surface**;

shall have a pressure relief valve on the gas volume set to open at a maximum pressure of 30 bar, which shall be manufactured by R. Conrader Company with model number SRV250; and

(c) the total swept volume of gas within **hydraulic actuators** and **hydraulic intensifiers** that satisfy Rule 19.19 (b), combining all such devices, does not exceed 6 litres.

19.20 Energy may only be stored within **HCCs**:

(a) by one supplied high-pressure **hydraulic accumulator** per **yacht** with a maximum capacity (gas plus hydraulic fluid) of 2.0 litres, the specification of which is given by Rule 19.21;

(b) by one or more high-pressure **hydraulic accumulators** in the **flight HCC**;

(c) by gas in low-pressure **hydraulic accumulators** with a maximum gas pressure of 6 bar;

(d) by gas in **hydraulic actuators** and **hydraulic intensifiers** as permitted by 19.19; and

(e) as elastic energy resulting from the compression of hydraulic fluid, any entrained air and the expansion of plumbing, subject to Rule 19.6.

19.21 The high-pressure **hydraulic accumulator** permitted by Rule 19.20 (a) may be either:

(a) a **hydraulic accumulator** supplied by Cariboni S.r.l. with one of the following Cariboni part numbers:

(i) ACC A 2 29898;
(ii) ACC A 2 29905 (includes stroke sensor and gas valve);
(iii) ACC A 2 29909 (includes gas valve);
(iv) ACC A 2 30156; or

(b) one of the above models of Cariboni **hydraulic accumulator** modified as follows:
(i) the inside of the cylinder barrel may have a coating applied;
(ii) the piston seals and wear bands may be replaced with alternative seal and wear band designs; and
(iii) the piston may be modified by Cariboni, or replaced by Cariboni with a similar piston, to accept alternative piston seals and wear bands, providing that any modified design shall be approved by the **Measurement Committee** who shall verify that the modification is to permit seal and wear band changes only, and does not affect the **hydraulic accumulator** volume.

COR/D will publish any recommended modifications if and when they become available.

20 Power sources

20.1 Power that does work on a **control surface** to adjust its shape, position or orientation can only be supplied:
(a) through **control systems** as permitted by Rules 20.2 and 20.3;
(b) by **external forces** acting on that **control surface**; or
(c) by the release of stored energy permitted by Rule 20.4.

20.2 The **flight HCC** shall only be powered by batteries via a single **flight power pack**. The **flight power pack** shall only supply power to components within the **flight HCC**.

20.3 The **Steering control system** and **rig control systems** may be powered by the crew, via **force input devices**.

20.4 The only forms of energy storage and release to move a **control surface** permitted under Rule 20.1 (c) are:
(a) the storage of elastic energy within the structure and rigging of the **yacht** and its:
(i) uncontrolled release as the structure and rigging returns towards its natural condition; or
(ii) controlled release and recovery via an **HCC**, where not elsewhere prohibited;
(b) the storage of a maximum of 50 J of elastic energy per system of springs or lines, and its controlled or uncontrolled release, where a system is a single spring or line, or a collection thereof that perform a specific function within a **rig control system**; and

(c) the storage of energy permitted by Rule 19.20, and its release into another part of an **HCC**.

20.5 The use of flywheels or gyroscopes to store energy or mechanically provide stabilising forces to the **yacht** is prohibited. Any rotating mass on the **yacht** shall be no larger than required for its permitted purpose.

20.6 Pneumatic components shall not be used in **control systems**, except that gas may be used within an **HCC** where permitted by Rules 19.20 (c) and 19.19.

20.7 All electrical systems must be powered by supplies operating at no more than 60 V.

20.8 Batteries or regulated power supplies:

(a) are permitted to be shared between **ECCs**, the **ILS**, the **CIS**, the competitor network (as drawn in Figure 26.1) and any **CCTV systems**, provided that where these systems are required to be **isolated**, the **isolated** wiring begins at the first junction point beyond these supplies;

(b) will be supplied with the **FCS** and the **Media System**, which may be separate supplies or a combined supply providing power to both systems; and

(c) that are provided with the **FCS** or the **Media System** may be shared with the systems listed in Rule 20.8 (a) if permitted by the **FCS** and **Media System** specifications respectively.

21 Control systems

21.1 **Control surfaces** shall only be controlled by:

(a) direct contact of the crew on a **control surface**; or

(b) the crew using one or more **control systems**.

21.2 **Flight controls** shall only be controlled by a **flight control system** where:

(a) **transmission actuators** are only permitted within the **flight control system**

(i) as part of the **flight power pack**; and

(ii) as permitted by Rules 19.16 (e) and 19.16 (h);

(b) a **rudder** or **foil flap** shall have as many **flight controls** as it has separately controlled **control sur- face actuators**, where a **control surface actuator** is separately controlled if, from a hardware and wiring perspective (i.e. irrespective of software), it is possible to control it independently from other **control surface actuators**;

(c) control signals sent to a specific **control surface actuator** within the **flight control system** shall be derived only:

(i) from the **internal state** of that **control surface actuator**; and

(ii) as permitted by Rule 21.2 (e);

(d) control signals sent to the **flight power pack** shall be derived only:

(i) from the **internal state** of the **flight power pack**; and

(ii) as permitted by Rule 21.2 (e);

(e) control signals sent to **control surface actuators** within the **flight control system** and the **flight power pack** are further permitted to be derived from:

(i) the **steering wheel** rotation angle about its rotation axis, providing that the **steering wheel** angle is not modulated by the **steering control system** or **rig control systems** to transmit information to the **flight control system** that is unrelated to the steering function of the **rudder**;

(ii) status flags supplied by the **FCS** to the **ECC**;

(iii) signals supplied by the crew via **passive input devices**; and

(iv) the **internal state** of any **ECC** that controls the **flight control system**. and

(f) it is prohibited to:

(i) adjust any **flight control** by any means other than through **control surface actuators**; or

(ii) connect different **flight controls** together with **control systems** to achieve feedback between different **flight controls**.

21.3 The **steering control** shall only be controlled by the **steering control system** where:

(a) **steering wheels** shall be connected to the **steering control** such that, except for elasticity and play in the connection, there shall be an immutable relationship between each **steering wheel** angle and the **steering control**. This connection shall be either:

(i) a **mechanical** connection; or

(ii) a hydraulic master-slave connection utilising one or more **master actuators mechanically** connected to the **steering wheels**;

(b) **steering wheels** shall only be adjusted by:

(i) the crew; and

(ii) the **steering control system**, including **external forces** acting on the **rudder** transmitted to the **steering control system**; (ii) and

(c) any **passive input devices** whose purpose is to modulate the **steering control** shall operate only in a discrete and occasional sense; that is, to adjust a setting. This does not prohibit continuous or proportional **passive input devices** being used to modulate the **rig control system** which may share the same **HCC** as the **steering control system**, providing such inputs do not provide a practical means by which the crew can control the **steering control**.

21.4 Adjustment of the **rig** shall only be controlled by a **rig control system** where:

(a) each **rig control** shall be declared by a **Competitor** to the **Measurement Committee**, and must satisfy the definition of a **rig control**; not every **rig** degree-of-freedom must be declared as a **rig control**, but the rules that refer to **rig controls** apply to all those **rig controls** that are declared;

(b) **rig controls** are restricted to:
  (i) **mast** rotation permitted by Rule 15.9 (a);
  (ii) degrees-of-freedom of **control systems** that are only attached to or only bear upon the **main-sail** within the **mast lower zone**;
  (iii) **mainsail leech** line adjustment;
  (iv) **jib** sheet degrees-of-freedom, including car position;
  (v) **jib** cunningham extension and retraction; and
  (vi) **jib leech** line adjustment; and

(c) each **control surface actuator** used within a **rig control system**:
  (i) shall be assigned, by declaration, to a single **rig control**;
  (ii) shall have the primary function of adjusting the declared **rig control**; and
  (iii) may influence other **rig controls.**

21.5 Control signals sent to **transmission actuators** within the **steering control system** and **rig control system** shall be derived only from:

(a) **passive input devices**, subject to Rule 21.3 (c);
(b) the orientation and angular velocity of, and the load applied to **primary force input devices** (which shall not use the wireless power meters required by Rule 21.13 (d));
(c) the **steering control** degree-of-freedom;
(d) torque about the **rudder** yaw axis between the **rudder** and the **steering control system**;
(e) **steering wheel** rotation angle or torque about its rotation axis;
(f) the position, deflection or orientation degree-of-freedom declared as a **rig control** that has at least one **control surface actuator** assigned to it, according to Rule 21.4 (c), such as traveller or **jib** car position;
(g) **mast** rotation, whether or not it is declared as a **rig control**;
(h) loads applied by **rig control systems** to the **rig**, or to devices functioning as a **rig control**, such as **jib** sheet or car loads; and
(i) **the internal state of control surface actuators, transmission actuators, hydraulic intensifiers and master actuators within the steering control system and rig control systems;**
(j) status and diagnostic messages transmitted from the **FCS** to the **ECC**; and
(k) pressures or temperatures within **HCCs** that form part of the **steering control system** or **rig control systems;**
(l) fluid levels or piston positions within **hydraulic accumulators** within **HCCs** that form part of the steering control system or rig control systems; and
(m) the **internal state** of an **ECC** that controls the **steering control system** or **rig control systems.**

21.6 Control signals sent to the **FCS** to adjust **foil cant** shall be derived only from:

(a) **passive input devices;**
(b) status and diagnostic messages transmitted from the **FCS** to the **ECC**; and
(c) the **internal state** of an **ECC** that manages the relevant **passive input devices** and communication with the **FCS**.

21.7 **Control surface actuators** shall be designed and used only for transmitting load to or from **control surfaces** to control their position, orientation or deformation. It is prohibited for **control surface actuators** to be installed if their primary purpose is to provide declared degrees-of-freedom which are measured rather than controlled.

21.8 A **control surface actuator** is restricted as follows:
(a) The **control surface actuator** shall control either a single **flight control**, a single **steering control** or a single **rig control**.
(b) The **control surface actuator** shall have at least one **point of action** on a **control surface**, the other(s) shall lie:
 (i) on a part or parts of the **yacht** that the **control surface** is permitted to move or deform about; or
 (ii) anywhere else on the same **control surface**.
(c) The force or torque generated or reacted between parts of the **control surface actuator** shall only be reacted or generated **mechanically** between **point(s) of action** on the **control surface** and the other **point(s) of action**.
(d) The translation or rotation generated or experienced between parts of the **control surface actuator**, through the **mechanical** connection, shall result in, or be the result of, translation, rotation or deformation of the **control surface**.
For the avoidance of doubt, if two or more **control surface actuators** act upon the same **control surface**, as long as each individual **control surface actuator** meets the class rules, the combined actions of multiple actuators by superposition may result in different, or no movement of the **control surface**.
(e) The **mechanical** connection may at times be slack such that force, torque, translation or rotation may not always be coupled, providing it sometimes satisfies, or could satisfy, conditions 21.8 (c) and 21.8 (d).
(f) The **mechanical** connections between the **control surface actuator** and its **points of action** may be distributed contacts or connections, subject to Rule 21.8 (a).

21.9 **Transmission actuators** within a **control surface actuator** are only permitted as:
(a) **valves**, subject to Rule 19.15; and

(b) **stops and locks**, whose only function shall be to restrict or stop movement between two parts of the **hydraulic actuator**, or between the **hydraulic actuator nodes**.

21.10 None of a **master actuator's nodes** shall lie on a **control surface** or on a part of a **control system** that transmits load to, or is subject to load from a **control surface**.

21.11 **Passive input devices** are restricted as follows:

(a) The electrical control signal produced by a **passive input device** shall relate only to a crew member's manual input. Neither the device nor the signal produced by it shall be significantly affected by the **yacht state**, except for unintended manual input caused, for example, by a crew member falling on to a button.

(b) No part of a **control system** shall:

(i) modify the limits of travel or operation of a **passive input device**;

(ii) physically aid a crew member to operate a **passive input device**; nor

(iii) control or provide any feedback to a **passive input device**.

21.12 Only the following **force input devices** are permitted:

(a) **primary force input devices**, restricted to a maximum of four such devices that each allow a single crew member to provide power;

(b) **steering wheels**, which;

(i) need not be circular, but must rotate to control **rudder** yaw angle; and

(ii) must have a perimeter that lies entirely outside a circle of diameter 0.450 m centred on the axis of rotation;

and

(c) **force input devices** permanently connected to a single **rig control** that:

(i) operate on that **rig control mechanically**; and

(ii) are only operated by a single crew member at once.

21.13 Primary force input devices shall:

(a) comprise handles or pedals connected to crank arms;

(b) be turned by crew such that those parts of a crew's body that deliver power to a **primary force input device** shall move in a circular motion transmitting power into the handles or pedals;

(c) not provide any means of crew inputting power other than that described by Rule 21.13 (b);

(d) incorporate a power meter on at least one of every pair of crank arms, pedals or handles that shall:

(i) use an ANT+ protocol for transmitting power data;

(ii) be suitably waterproofed;

(iii) provide accurate power data to the satisfaction of the **Measurement Committee** and **AC Media**;

(iv) shall measure all the power that the crew input to **primary force input devices**, except that if only measuring power input by one arm or one leg, it may be assumed that power input by the other arm or leg is identical; and

(v) be paired with the **Media System** to the satisfaction of **AC Media**.

21.14 Rules 21.2, 21.3, 21.5, 21.6, 22.2 and 22.3 may be satisfied by a combination of the hardware and software used within a **control system**.

22 Electronic control circuits

22.1 Sensors within, or inputs to an **ECC** shall measure only:

(a) those properties that are permitted by Rules 21.2 (c), 21.2 (d), 21.5 and 21.6 to be inputs to the **FCS**, **flight control system**, **steering control system** and **rig control systems**;

(b) the **internal state** of an **ECC**;

(c) the status of a float switch within a bilge pump;

(d) the ambient outside air temperature; or

(e) the air temperature, airborne particle density, or gas concentration within the **hull**.

22.2 Proxy measurements can be used to estimate any measurement permitted by Rule 22.1, providing those proxies do not supply any additional useful information. For example:

(a) a linear displacement may be a proxy for a permitted angular rotation measurement;

(b) a **foil flap** angle may be a proxy for the extension that forms part of the **internal state** of a **hydraulic actuator**, and need not be sensed directly at the **nodes** of the corresponding actuator providing it does not supply additional useful information;

(c) a pressure sensor at the outlet of a **flight power pack** may be a proxy for the pressure at the inlet of a **control surface actuator**, providing:

(i) there are no valves, restrictions or other means of changing the pressure, except normal pipe losses, between the two locations of the **flight HCC**; and

(ii) no additional useful information is gained by using a sensor located there rather than at the **control surface actuator** itself;

and

(d) the **steering control** may be a proxy for **steering wheel** angle, providing it does not supply information that is more useful than the **steering wheel** angle; but

(e) the measurement of a **foil flap** angle, remote from the **point of action** of a **control surface actuator**, used to estimate the twist induced by hydrodynamic load is not a proxy for actuator extension; and

(f) sail twist is not a proxy for **mainsail** sheet load or extension.

22.3 Multiple direct and proxy measurements can be used to estimate any measurement permitted by Rule 22.1, provided that:

(a) any additional measurements are used for redundancy only;

(b) the multiple measurements are processed to provide a single estimate of a measurement permitted by Rule 22.1 before being used in a **control system**; and

(c) the combination of measurements provides no useful information to the crew or to a **control system** beyond:

(i) that which would be supplied by an accurate and reliable measurement permitted by Rule 22.1; and

(ii) an indication of a sensor failure.

22.4 Time, as supplied by the **Media System**, or as an internal clock within the **ECC**, may be used within all **control systems** within an **ECC**, whether or not it is explicitly permitted in any Rules that govern particular **control systems**.

22.5 **ECCs** shall not contain sensors that measure the state of the **FCS**.

22.6 Only the following **electric actuators** are permitted within an **ECC**:

(a) **transmission actuators;**

(b) motors of the **flight power pack**;

(c) cooling devices and bilge pumps inside the **hull surface**, providing they have no significant effect on the aerodynamic or hydrodynamic performance of the **yacht**; and

(d) devices within electronic circuits that affect only the circuits themselves, and have no other influence on a **control system** or the **yacht state**, such as CPU cooling fans and relays.

22.7 Except as permitted in Rules 22.6, an **ECC** must be incapable of having any significant effect on the **yacht state**.

22.8 An **ECC** shall:

(a) be **hardwired**; and

(b) have wiring that is **isolated** from other devices and systems, except for:

(i) connections shown in Figure 26.1; and

(ii) connections from common power supplies permitted by Rule 20.8 (a).

23 Instrumentation and logging system

23.1 The **ILS** shall:

(a) be **hardwired**;

(b) have wiring that is **isolated** from other devices and systems, except for:

(i) connections shown in Figure 26.1; and

(ii) connections from common power supplies permitted by Rule 20.8 (a);

(c) not be capable of having any significant effect on the **yacht state**; and
(d) not include any **crew indication devices** or devices which otherwise provide information to crew.

23.2 Only the following sensors within, or inputs to an **ILS** are permitted:
(a) strain and load sensors, subject to Rule 23.3;
(b) sensors that measure the **internal state** of the **ILS**;
(c) an input from the **Media System** as detailed in Rule 26.6; and
(d) sensors that measure the air temperature, airborne particle density, or gas concentration within the hull.

23.3 Strain and load sensors within the **ILS**:
(a) shall only be capable of directly measuring strain or load:
(i) at the sensor location; and
(ii) transmitted through the primary load paths of the **hull**, **appendages** and **mast**, and not for example within a pressure sensor;
(b) may include temperature sensors for thermal compensation;
(c) shall not be located on, nor measure strains within sails or **battens**;
(d) shall provide no **yacht state** information other than:
(i) load, strain, and quantities derived from those measurements; and
(ii) temperature where needed for compensation.

23.4 It is prohibited to measure the flying shapes of the sails or the deformed shape of the **mast**, except with strain gauges that lie entirely within the **mast tube**.

24 Information and display systems

24.1 The **CIS**:
(a) shall be incapable of measuring any part of the **yacht state**;
(b) shall not be capable of having any significant effect on the **yacht state**; and
(c) may use short range wireless communication in **crew indication devices** and associated interface hardware (e.g. access points) for communication onboard the **yacht**, but must be configured to use only information available within the **CIS** permitted by Rule 26.8.

24.2 A crew indication device:
(a) must only provide visual and/or audio feedback to the crew; tactile or other non-audio-visual feed- back is not permitted;
(b) must be incapable of measuring any part of the **yacht state**; and
(c) must be incapable of significantly affecting the **yacht state**.

24.3 Only the following sensors are permitted within a **CIS** or **crew indication device**:
(a) the state of user input controls on **passive input devices**;
(b) those sensors required to perform its permitted function, such as an ambient light sensor;

(c) WiFi and Bluetooth transceivers, where permitted within the **CIS**;
(d) sensors that measure the **internal state** of the **CIS**; and
(e) sensors that measure the air temperature, airborne particle density, or gas concentration within the hull.

24.4 As an exception to Rules 24.2 (b) and 24.3, a **crew indication device** in the **CIS** containing sensors such as accelerometers or solid-state gyroscopes shall be considered incapable of measuring any part of the **yacht state** if those sensors are disabled and access to them is locked by Samsung Knox management software. This will require that:
(a) the **crew indication device** is a Samsung device running Android version 10 or later;
(b) the device is set to be in "Developer mode";
(c) the "Sensors Off" option in the "Quick Settings Developer Tiles" is set to be on;
(d) in the presence of a member of the **Measurement Committee**:
(i) the device's sensors are disabled by clicking the "Sensor off" button in the expanded status bar;
(ii) a profile from Samsung Knox Manager is applied that disables GPS, Bluetooth, Camera, External SD Card, Settings and Expand Status Bar;
and
(e) the **Competitor** provides the **Measurement Committee** with access to the Samsung Knox administration account so they can audit the device profiles.

24.5 Stand-alone **CCTV systems** are permitted providing that:
(a) they comprise one or more cameras, one or more displays, cabling, and optionally **passive input devices**, power supplies, splitters, switchers, digitisation, recording devices including standard compression;
(b) they are **hardwired**;
(c) cameras are installed either:
(i) in a **foil**; or
(ii) entirely below 1.700 m above **MWP**;
(d) neither the camera nor any hardware or software stabilises the image, whether mechanically or digitally, such that any image shown on a screen moves according to the part of the **yacht** to which the respective camera is attached;
(e) multiple camera images may be displayed on a single screen, with each camera image occupying a distinct part of the screen; screens may switch between showing images from different cameras, either by manual selection or on a predefined low-frequency sequence; however, images from multiple cameras may not be overlaid on each other, nor switched at a frequency greater than 0.5Hz;

(f) they do not display (or communicate in another manner) any **yacht state** information beyond that which could be seen by the naked eye; this does not preclude digitisation or global contrast enhancement of the video stream, but does prohibit the addition of overlays, edge detection, object recognition, the display of motion estimates of regions in the image, etc.; and

(g) except for cameras' image sensors, such systems shall be incapable of measuring any part of the **yacht state**; and

(h) they shall not be capable of having any significant effect on the **yacht state**.

25 Foil cant system

25.1 Details of the **FCS**, the system to control the **cant** rotation of the **foils**, are specified by the document referenced in Rule 32.3. When racing, the **FCS** must be configured as required by the specification.

25.2 The **FCS** shall be installed in the **yacht** with the **cant** cylinder mounts and **foil cant** axes located as shown in Figure 10.2.

25.3 **Fire safety equipment** of a total mass indicated in the row below "**FCS**" in the mass table of Rule 6.1 shall be installed, and shall have an LCG that lies within 0.5 m of the LCG of the supplied **FCS** batteries.

25.4 **Foil cant** shall only be physically controlled using the **FCS**.

25.5 The **FCS** will provide, using specified protocols:

(a) a port for communication with the **ECC**, where the **FCS** will:

(i) receive commands from the **ECC**;

(ii) transmit status and diagnostic messages to the **ECC**, including a status flag to indicate when a **foil** is in a fully raised position (within a tolerance detailed by the specification);

and

(b) a port for transmitting data to the **Media System**, where:

(i) the **Media System** will provide non-delayed channels to the **CIS** providing **foil** cant cylinder pressures, which will only be transmitted when the cant of both **foils** is no more than 90° as measured by the **FCS**; and

(ii) the **Media System** will provide all supplied **FCS** channels to the **ILS** for logging and re- transmission to the **CIS** according to Rule 26.8 (d).

For the avoidance of doubt, the **FCS** will not transmit ram extension, ram pressure or **cant** angle to the **ECC**.

25.6 **COR/D** might specify system updates which must be installed by all **Competitors**, these updates being frozen according to Rule 32.3. Any further system updates after the time of freezing can only be specified by unanimous agreement of all **Competitors**.

26 Systems communication

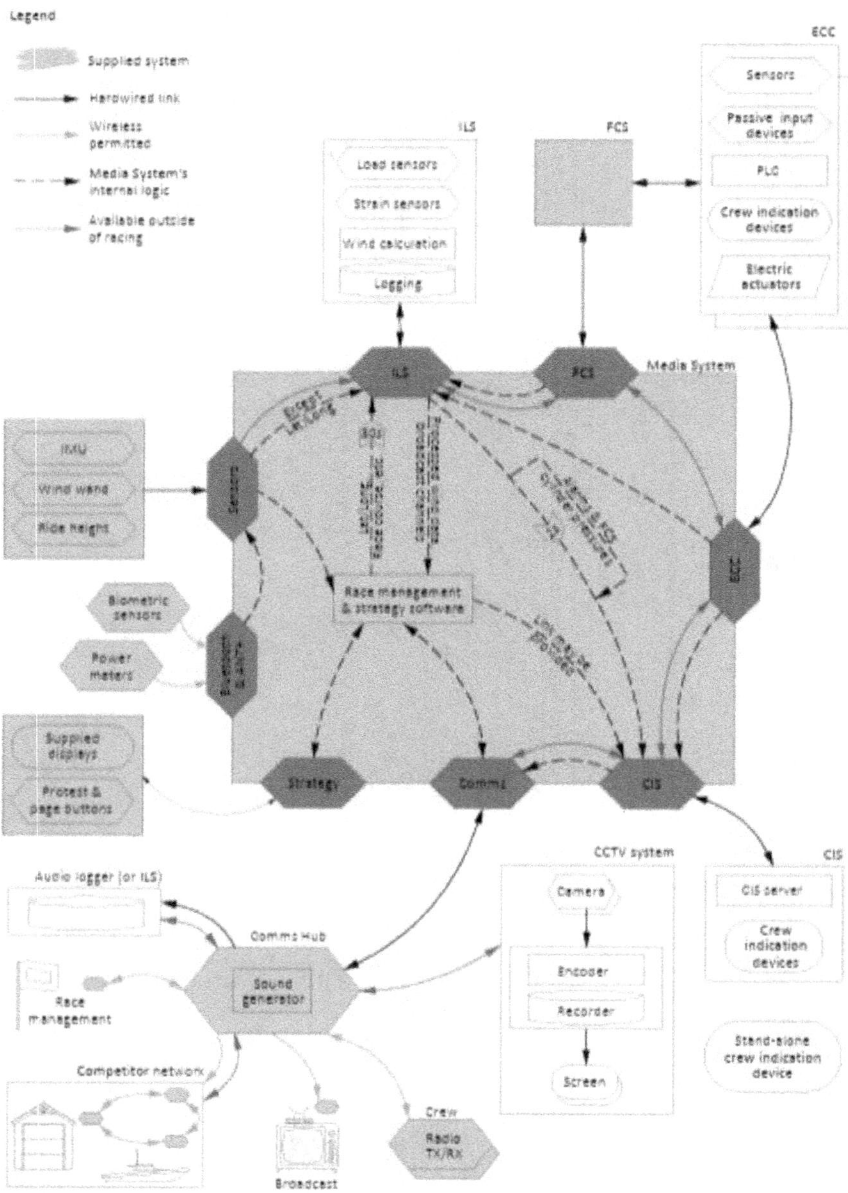

Figure 26.1: Permitted communication between electronic systems

26.1 Electric or electronic components or circuits are permitted only as:
(a) part of an **ECC**, **ILS**, **CIS**, **FCS** or **CCTV system**;
(b) shared power supplies permitted by Rule 20.8 (a);
(c) stand-alone **crew indication devices**, such as wristwatches, that are incapable of measuring or receiving any part of the **yacht state**;
(d) devices for data and audio communication with **Competitors'** chase boats and shore bases, only as shown in Figure 26.1 and subject to Rule 26.12;
(e) supplied and required by **AC Media** or the **Measurement Committee**, including permitted devices connected to these supplied components;
(f) ultrasonic transmitters in **foil wings** and **rudders**; and
(g) components used when not racing, that when racing have been disconnected from all circuits and power sources to the satisfaction of the **Measurement Committee**, and when disconnected are incapable of providing any useful electrical or electronic function.

26.2 No information exchange between any electrical systems is permitted except as shown via specified communication arrows in Figure 26.1, where:
(a) data transmission must be strictly one-way where indicated by directional arrows, although two- way protocols (e.g. acknowledge and retry) are permitted provided that no two-way information is exchanged other than that required to manage the communication channel;
(b) a supplied **Media System** will provide communication between systems as shown by the "**Media System's** internal logic", where the specific implementation of this information exchange will be further detailed in the **Media System** specification referenced in Rule 32.3; and
(c) the dark hexagonal ports drawn on the boundaries of the **Media System** represent communication nodes, where any information shown flowing in is permitted to be re-transmitted out, where indicated by directional arrows.

26.3 Communication between any systems on the **yacht** permitted by Rule 26.2 must be **hardwired** except where wireless communication is expressly permitted by arrows marked "wireless permitted" in Figure 26.1.

26.4 **ECC** hardware, **ILS** hardware and any **CCTV system** hardware shall be incapable of communication by any means other than **hardwired** information transfer.

26.5 The combination of the **ECC**, **ILS**, and **CIS** shall provide a data stream to the **Media System**, which:
(a) shall include data channels specified by:
(i) **AC Media** for broadcast, such as, but not limited to: true wind speed, true wind angle and true wind direction, **hydraulic accumulator** pressure and **rudder** angle; and

(ii) the **Measurement Committee** for verification of compliance with the **AC75 Class Rules**, such as, but not limited to: **control surface** positions and crew inputs to **passive input devices**;

(b) shall be:

(i) the most accurate data available;

(ii) measured using **Competitor**-supplied sensors, unless the **media equipment** specification or the **Measurement Committee** specifies supplied sensors for certain measurements or permits certain channels to be estimated rather than measured; and

(iii) at the specified frequency;

(c) shall use a protocol to be specified in accordance with Rule 32.3; and

(d) may include alarm event messages generated by the **ILS**, which may only contain:

(i) an alarm category ID code, being an integer between 1 and 10; and

(ii) a single floating point number representing the magnitude of an alarm value.

26.6 The **Media System** will transmit to the **ILS**:

(a) non-delayed data from the **FCS**;

(b) a non-delayed data stream supplied by any connected **ECC**;

(c) the following non-delayed data channels from any supplied fibre-optic gyro IMUs, wind wands and ride-height sensors:

(i) velocity components in a ground-fixed frame;

(ii) acceleration components in a yacht-fixed frame;

(iii) rotation rates in a yacht-fixed frame;

(iv) heading, heel, trim and their derivatives;

(v) IMU diagnostic or status information;

(vi) raw wind wand data;

(vii) ride-height sensor data;

(viii) altitude above water (if an altitude estimate is implemented within the **Media System**); and

(ix) a timestamp;

(d) non-delayed **primary force input device** power meter data received over ANT+ as required by Rule 21.13 (d);

(e) a non-delayed estimate of tidal current velocity and direction; and

(f) the following channels delayed by approximately 30 s, transmitted with original timestamps so that the data can be re-synchronised for logging:

(i) latitude and longitude;

(ii) race course information, which might include start time, boundary lines, mark positions, and penalties; and

(iii) tactical race information such as time-to-kill and time-to-boundary.

26.7 It is prohibited for any non-supplied system to estimate the latitude, longitude or position of the **yacht** on the race course, whether absolute or relative to marks or lines of the course, using integration of data provided in Rule 26.6 (c) or otherwise.

26.8 The **Media System** will transmit to the **CIS**:

(a) a non-delayed data stream supplied by any connected **ECC**;

(b) non-delayed alarm event messages supplied by the **ILS**, which:

(i) once dispatched for a particular category ID, will not be dispatched again for the same cate- gory ID for 10 s; and

(ii) will be limited when racing to a maximum total number of alarms of 20 per race;

(c) non-delayed **FCS** cant cylinder pressures, subject to Rule 25.5 (b) (i); and

(d) the data stream supplied by the **ILS**, delayed by approximately 2.0 s;

26.9 The **Media System** will include a tactical pre-start and race boundary application developed by **AC Media** in conjunction with **COR/D**. The system will include screens to display tactical information to the crew, and the option for some audio cues to be transmitted to crew radios. A *Tactical Software Specification* will be provided according to Rule 32.3, and the application shall include:

(a) a capability to read **Competitor**-supplied performance polar data from the **ILS**, so that a **Competitor** can tune pre-start timing predictions to their **yacht**;

(b) time-to-start information;

(c) predictions of time-to-kill to the start line;

(d) time-to-boundary predictions;

(e) lay-lines information; and

(f) other tactical information.

It is prohibited to provide any other pre-start or tactical race information to the crew, or to process or modify the **Media System** supplied pre-start or tactical information.

26.10 The *Tactical Software Specification* might include:

(a) the provision of a small subset of non-delayed tactical race data to the **CIS**, such as time-to-start, time-to-kill, time-to-boundary and heading, for display on **Competitors'** screens; or

(b) the option of supplied tactical race data screens to display **Competitor**-generated data channels.

26.11 The **Media System** will transmit the time of day to all connected systems, from an NTP server synchronised by GNSS; for clarity, this is not shown in Figure 26.1.

26.12 Figure 26.1 shows a supplied *Comms Hub*, a communications system providing audio and data communication between the **Media System**, the crew, **Competitors'** chase boats and shore bases, race management, and broadcast, where:

(a) the scope of this system is subject to amendment and will be further detailed according to Rule 32.3;
(b) where elements of the system are supplied, they will be the only communication systems permitted for the functions they fulfil;
(c) if elements of the system (other than broadcast and race management) are not supplied, this Rule will be updated to allow **Competitors** to implement their own systems with similar capabilities; and
(d) if the supplied system does not provide audio and data communication off the **yacht** to **Competitors'** chase boats, communication antennae for this purpose may be installed on the **aft media post** in the regions detailed by Rule 27.5, subject to the approval of the **Measurement Committee**.

26.13 When not racing, the **Media System** will open communications ports between the **ECC**, **ILS**, **CIS** and the *Comms Hub*, and provide a test mode for **Competitors** to test the race configuration. The **Media System** will broadcast a flag to connected systems to indicate whether or not it is in race mode.

26.14 In the event of electrical or radio interference between a **Competitor's** systems and **media equipment**, **Competitors** will work with **AC Media** to find a practical solution, to the satisfaction of the **Measurement Committee**.

27 Media equipment

27.1 The Rules in this section define the most significant design constraints imposed in order to accommodate the **media equipment**. Additional requirements shall be detailed by the **media equipment** specification documentation referenced by Rule 32.3.

27.2 **Media equipment** includes, but is not limited to:
(a) **a Media System;**
(b) a Comms Hub, subject to Rule 26.12;
(c) a **media bowsprit**, including:
  (i) a wind wand, B&G model WS310 or similar;
  (ii) a ride-height sensor; and
  (iii) possibly radiators for cooling the **FCS** and **Media System**;
(d) an IMU fixed to the **hull**, and possibly a second IMU near the masthead;
(e) an **aft media post**;
(f) masthead unit, including:
  (i) antennae; and
  (ii) possibly a wind wand, B&G model WS310 or similar if supplied;
(g) cameras and microphones;
(h) brackets or other mounting devices;

(i) cabling; and
(j) cable management hardware.

27.3 The areas shown in Figures 27.1, 27.2 and 27.3 shall be reserved for the **media equipment**. Additional reserved areas for cameras, microphones, sensors, processors, cabling and batteries shall be detailed in the **media equipment** specification.

27.4 The reserved area for the internal **media equipment** hold, shown in Figure 27.1, shall have an additional clearance volume around the hold which is defined by:
(a) a extrusion in the x direction of the forward face of the cuboid by 700 mm; and
(b) an extrusion of 375 mm of the planes parallel with **LCP** away from **LCP**.
This additional volume may be shared with **Competitor** equipment subject to the approval of the **Measurement Committee** and **AC Media**.

27.5 As an exception to Rule 27.3, **AC Media** shall permit **Competitors** to install communications antennae within the aft-most reserved area shown in Figure 27.1 on the **aft media post** as further detailed in Figure 27.4.

27.6 The **media equipment** specification:
(a) will identify a region close to the centre of the **yacht** within which the supplied IMU must be mounted; and
(b) may provide an option to lease the supplied IMU in advance of the **Media System** being installed.

27.7 The **hull** shall be fitted with interfaces specified by the **media equipment** specification documentation for the attachment of the:
(a) **Media System** and associated **media equipment**;
(b) **aft media post**, mounting details given in Figure 27.4; and
(c) **media bowsprit.**

27.8 The mounting surfaces for the **aft media post** and **media bowsprit** shall be submitted to the **Measurement Committee** for approval. Mounting details for the **aft media post** are shown in Figure 27.4.

27.9 **media equipment** shall be installed by **AC Media**.

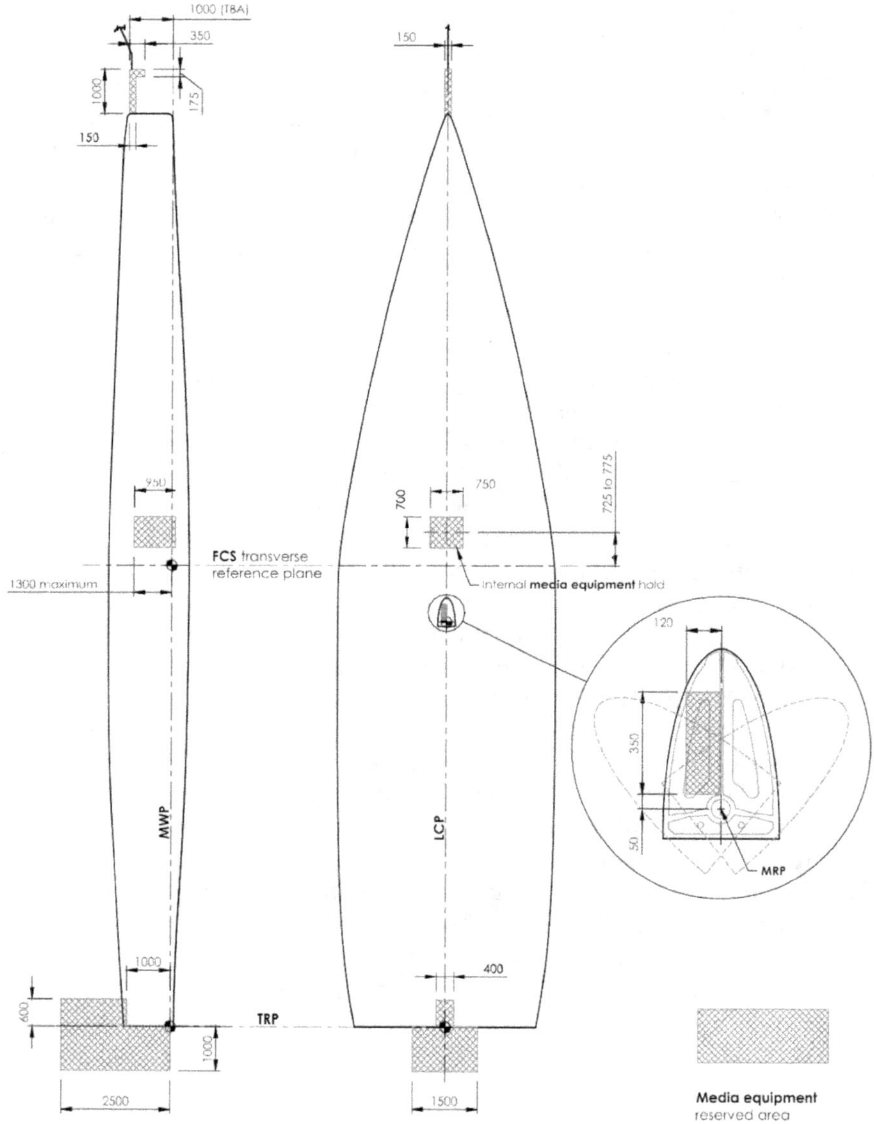

Figure 27.1: Reserved areas for **media equipment**

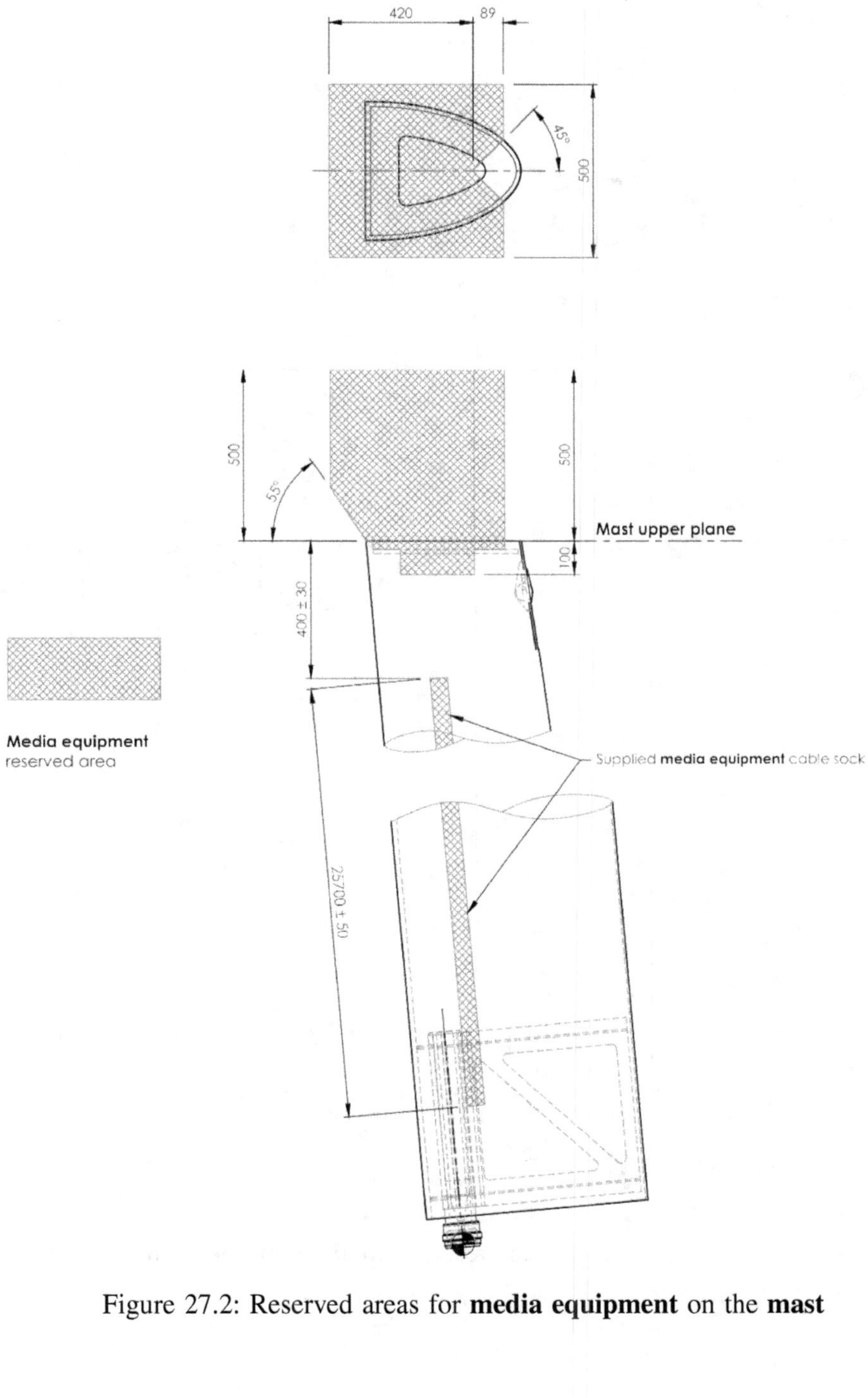

Figure 27.2: Reserved areas for **media equipment** on the **mast**

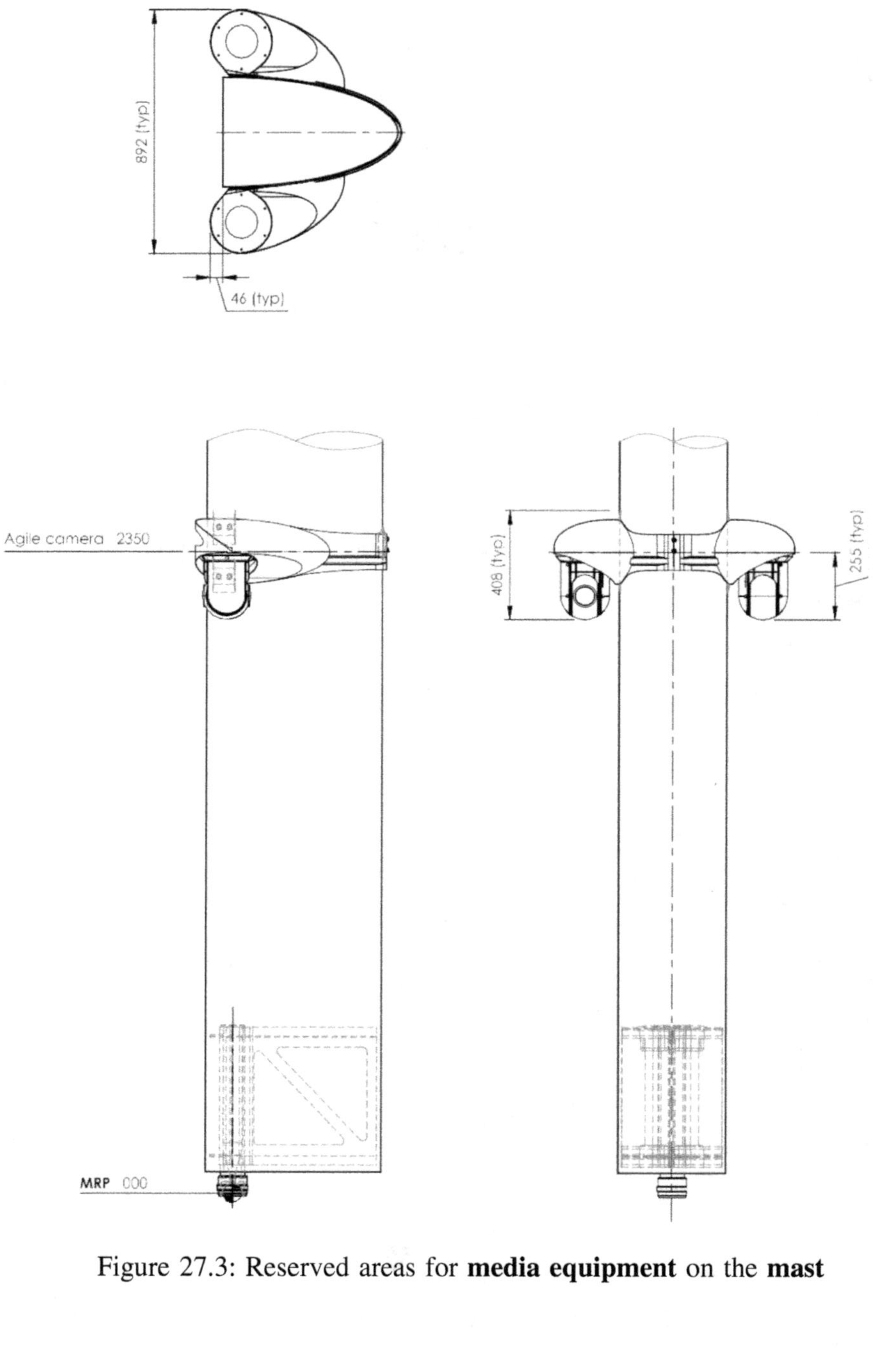

Figure 27.3: Reserved areas for **media equipment** on the **mast**

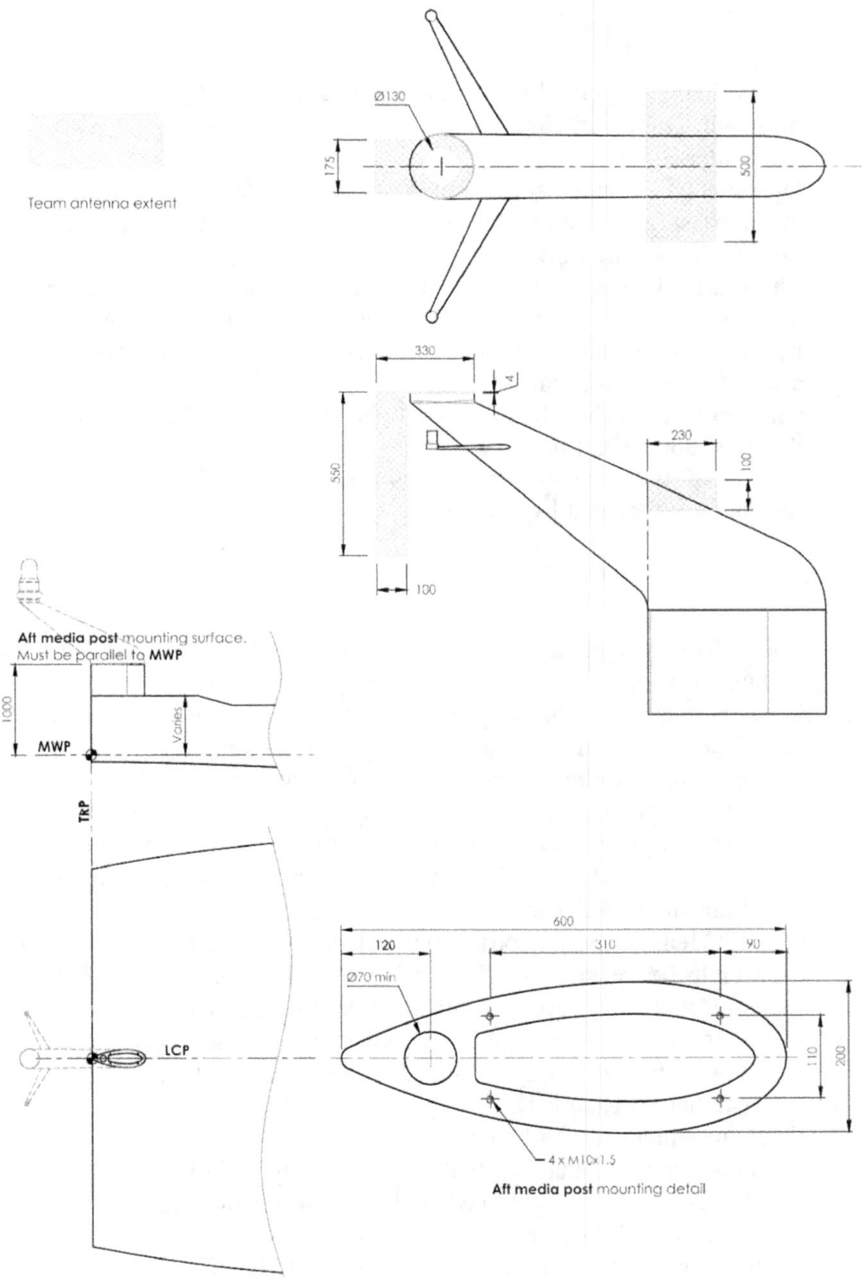

Figure 27.4: **Aft media post** mounting details and areas reserved for team antenna

28 Branding

28.1 Areas shall be reserved for **event** branding and country flags on the **jib** and **mainsail**. No advertising, other signage or graphics shall be affixed within these areas.

28.2 On the outward facing sides of both **mainsail skins**, an area shall be reserved encompassing the area within 6600 mm of the **mast upper plane** within the extents of the **sail skin**.

28.3 The **mainsail event** branding shall not restrict sail girth measurements. If **event** branding does not fit on a particular sail then the **Competitor** shall notify the organising authority who will mandate an alternative branding arrangement for the sail.

28.4 On both sides of the **jib**, an area defined by a radius of 2800 mm centred on the **tack point** shall be reserved.

28.5 Details of the content for the reserved areas shall be provided in the document referenced by Rule 32.3.

29 Crew

29.1 There shall be eight crew members, unless reduced by accident, who shall all be human beings.

29.2 Crew members shall be weighed at crew weighs organised by the **Measurement Committee** in accordance with the **Measurement Procedures**, where:

(a) crew shall be dressed only in light underwear;

(b) crew weighs shall take place two days prior to the first race of each **AC75 event stage**, except that if any racing is scheduled during the two days prior to that **AC75 event stage**, no new crew weigh for that **AC75 event stage** shall take place;

(c) the **Measurement Committee** will use the weights recorded at crew weighs for verification of compliance until the next crew weigh, at which point those recorded weights shall be updated; and

(d) when racing, the total of the recorded crew weights corresponding to the crew members on the **yacht** for that race shall be within the range specified in Rule 6.1.

29.3 Each crew member shall wear:

(a) a buoyancy aid that meets the flotation standard of ISO 12402-5 or ISO 12402-6 (CE 50 Newtons) and that is capable of being removed or deflated in the water within five seconds;

(b) a helmet to a minimum standard of CE EN 1077, CE EN 966, ASTM 2040, or Snell S-98 and with at least 300 cm^2 of the exterior surface brightly coloured. **Competitors** shall satisfy the **Measurement Committee** that the brightly coloured region can be seen from above the water with the crew lying face down or face up in the water;

(c) a blade with a length between 50 mm and 150 mm;

(d) at least one personal air supply containing compressed air equivalent to at least 40 litres uncompressed volume each, which does not require the use of hands when in use;

(e) a pocket for carrying **crew supplied media equipment** with minimum dimensions 80 mm x 200 mm x 30 mm; and

(f) **crew supplied media equipment**, which shall be worn in a manner directed by **AC Media** to the satisfaction of the **Measurement Committee**.

29.4 The following items shall be secured and distributed on the **yacht** at locations that would be easily accessible in the event of a capsize:

(a) at least four blades, each with a length between 50 mm and 150 mm; and

(b) at least four personal air supplies containing compressed air equivalent to at least 40 litres uncompressed volume each, which do not require the use of hands when in use.

29.5 The total mass of **carried equipment** worn or carried by each crew member shall be:

(a) a minimum of 2.5 kg at the start of a race, but may be reduced during a race due to consumption of food or drink;

(b) a maximum, when dry, that is dependent on expected air temperature as follows;

(i) 6.5 kg if under 18°C;

(ii) 5.5 kg if 18-23°C; or

(iii) 5.0 kg if over 23°C.

Following the Notice of Race for an **event** being published, the **Measurement Committee** shall specify which of these limits apply to an **AC75 event stage** based on the published monthly average temperature for the first day of racing in that **AC75 event stage**; and

(c) no more than 3.0 kg in excess of the dry maximum when soaked and allowed to drain for 1 minute according to the **Measurement Procedures**.

29.6 Any **crew supplied media equipment** or **carried equipment** brought aboard by a crew member must be worn, attached to, or carried by that crew member at all times when racing. This does not prohibit items of **carried equipment** also being attached to the **yacht**.

29.7 **Carried equipment** shall not be designed to retain water for the purpose of increasing mass.

29.8 **Carried equipment** shall:

(a) not be designed to provide aerodynamic fairing of any part of the **yacht** or crew; and
(b) not exhibit any geometric features that extend its shape beyond that which is necessary for any permitted function.

29.9 Crew shall not enter the watertight volume of the **hull**.

29.10 In any normal sailing condition whilst foiling, no part of the crew shall be between the **skins** of the **mainsail**, or a region between the vertical extension down from the **foot** of each **mainsail skin**, other than:
(a) briefly, to cross the **yacht**;
(b) to resolve unforeseen issues; or
(c) by accident.

29.11 Crew shall remain entirely aft of a plane 9.0 m forward of **TRP**, except that:
(a) Crew may go forward of 9.0 m briefly to cross the **yacht**, to resolve unforeseen issues, or if this happens by accident.
(b) Any crew that go forward of a plane 11.0 m forward of **TRP** may only do so as permitted by Rule 29.11 (a), and unless they are forward by accident:
(i) must be tethered to either **hull** or a fitting attached to the **hull** which can withstand the same load as the tether; where
(ii) tethers shall comprise a harness and safety line that complies with ISO 12401, the safety line being no longer than 2 m; and
(iii) such fittings and tethers are not required by **Competitors** who elect to never go forward of the 11.0 m plane while racing.
(c) Crew shall remain forward for no longer than required to resolve any issue.
(d) For a crew member to be forward of 9.0 m or 11.0 m by accident, they must find themselves there as a result of falling or stumbling. If not tethered to the **yacht**, they must not resolve any issue on the **yacht** whilst forward of 11.0 m.

29.12 If requested by the **Measurement Committee** for verifying compliance with Rules 29.11 (a) and 29.11 (b) whilst racing, lines parallel to **TRP**, at least 50 mm wide and of a colour contrasting to the **deck** shall be marked across the **deck** such that their aft edges are no more than:
(a) 9.00 m forward of **TRP**; and
(b) 11.00 m forward of **TRP**.

29.13 In any normal sailing condition whilst foiling, each crew member shall operate approximately in a declared **normal sailing position**, except:
(a) briefly, to cross the **yacht**;
(b) to resolve unforeseen issues; or
(c) if they move or are caused to move by accident.

29.14 **Competitors** shall demonstrate to the satisfaction of the **Measurement Committee** that each crew member can move from their **normal sailing**

position to a position completely outside the **perimeter line** of the yacht within 5 seconds:

(a) with all other crew members remaining in their **crew zone**; and

(b) with all crew members moving to a position outside the **perimeter line** of the **yacht** at the same time.

29.15 **Competitors** shall demonstrate to the satisfaction of the **Measurement Committee** that two crew members (the *rescuers*) can aid any unconscious crew member in a **normal sailing position** (the *casualty*), where:

(a) the following tests shall be completed, each within 15 seconds:

(i) moving the *casualty* to a position completely outside the **perimeter line** of the **yacht**;

(ii) supplying emergency air and disconnecting any devices that strap, clip, or otherwise connect the *casualty* to the **yacht**; and

(iii) disconnecting any devices that strap, clip, or otherwise connect the *casualty* to the **yacht**, without movement of their neck or spine;

(b) the starting point for the *rescuers* shall be the **platform upper surface** of the **yacht** close to the *casualty* but completely outside the **crew zone**;

(c) the **Competitor** shall select the *rescuers*; and

(d) the *casualty* shall be a manikin, which:

(i) shall be supplied by Ruth Lee Ltd, with the model code "RLN100RBR", described as a "100kg Duty Range Manikin with facemask and soft feet";

(ii) shall be strapped, clipped or otherwise connected to the **yacht** as the crew member would be in their **normal sailing position**; and

(iii) shall be wearing the **carried equipment** normally worn by the equivalent crew member.

(e) Handles, straps or other lifting arrangements on the *casualty* may not be used in the tests prescribed by Rule 29.15. Handles, straps or other lifting arrangements on the **carried equipment** worn by the *casualty* may be used, provided it is the same **carried equipment** normally worn by the crew while racing.

29.16 Each test prescribed by Rules 29.14 and 29.15 shall be satisfied:

(a) with the **yacht**, without sails, moored alongside a pontoon with approximately zero heel angle. A second pontoon may be used on the opposite side of the **yacht**;

(b) with any devices to strap, clip, or otherwise connect a crew member to the **yacht** in their **crew zone** engaged at the start of the test;

(c) without the removal or movement of any part of the **yacht**, except parts that strap, clip or otherwise connect a crew member to the **yacht**, or parts of mechanisms used to effect a release of those connections; and

(d) for any possible orientations of **force input devices** required by the **Measurement Committee**, thereby simulating a situation where such force input devices cannot be moved or rotated.

30 Measurement

30.1 The **Measurement Procedures** shall be issued according to Rule 32.2.

30.2 The **Measurement Procedures** will specify measurement tolerances for quantities restricted or required by the **AC75 Class Rules**, which shall relate to the accuracy of the measurement equipment. In some cases, **Competitors** may be required to meet a **Measurement Committee's** measurement exactly; in others, a measurement that falls within the equipment's measurement tolerance may be sufficient. For example:

(a) when first weighing a **platform** for an **AC75 event stage** the **Measurement Committee** may require the **platform** to be ballasted to meet its required mass exactly, as measured by their equipment; but

(b) on subsequent re-measurement, if no changes have been made by the **Competitor**, the **Measurement Committee** may require only that the **platform** matches its previously weighed mass within the tolerance of the measurement equipment.

30.3 **Competitors** shall permit the **Measurement Committee** to take samples of material from components of the **yacht** to ensure compliance with Rule 2.

30.4 **Competitors** shall permit the **Measurement Committee** to take samples of paint or vinyl from components of the **yacht** to ensure compliance with Rule 5.

30.5 **Competitors** shall assist the **Measurement Committee** in understanding the function and operation of mechanical, hydraulic and electrical systems onboard the **yacht**.

30.6 Compliance with **control system** rules may be determined by a combination of hardware inspection, code inspection, interviews and affidavits.

30.7 On request, **Competitors** shall provide the **Measurement Committee** with source code and compiled executables of any software installed on the **yacht** that the **Competitor** has access to, and shall assist them in the understanding of such code. However, **Competitors** shall not be restricted by the **Measurement Procedures** to using hardware or software that is easy to inspect: where full code inspection is impractical, some aspects of software compliance shall rely solely on interviews and affidavits.

30.8 The **Measurement Committee** shall issue a measurement certificate for a **yacht** when they have:

(a) concluded that she complies with the **AC75 Class Rules**;

(b) received completed declarations and affidavits as required by the **AC75 Class Rules** and as addition- ally required by the **Measurement Committee** or the **Rules Committee** at their discretion.
(c) received all documentation as required by the **AC75 Class Rules** and by other notices published by the **Measurement Committee** or the **Rules Committee**, and confirmed that the documentation is satisfactory; and
(d) received the **yacht** configuration declaration required by Rule 31.2.

30.9 Once a measurement certificate has been issued, some changes to the **yacht** shall be permitted without requiring re-measurement. The scope of these permitted changes shall be detailed in the **Measurement Procedures** and shall include changes such as:
(a) routine maintenance on mechanical, hydraulic and electrical systems;
(b) changes to sensor calibrations; and
(c) changes to **ILS** and **CIS** software.

The **Measurement Committee** may further agree specifics of what can and cannot be changed without re-measurement with individual **Competitors**, based on the system design of their **yacht**. For example, classes of **ECC** settings that are incapable of affecting measurement compliance, such as soft pressure- relief valve setting and calibration of **passive input devices**, may be permitted changes. However, if there is any doubt, a **Competitor** is obliged to inform the **Measurement Committee** of any changes that have been made.

30.10 Aside from changes permitted without re-measurement, the configuration of a **yacht** with respect to other design details not recorded on her measurement certificate may be changed providing the **Measurement Committee** is able to verify compliance of those changes with respect to the **AC75 Class Rules** prior to racing. The **Measurement Procedures** shall include details of time scales required for re-measurement, which shall vary according to the part of the **yacht** being changed and checked, but will include provisions such as:
(a) verification of a **yacht assembly** mass and **longitudinal** centre of mass, which is likely to be checked the morning of a race; and
(b) a deadline prior to a race for the measurement of any **mainsails** or **jibs**, or any permitted modifications of sails, with a permission that a **Competitor** may select which pre-measured sail configurations to use for a race at any time up to the warning signal of that race.

A **Competitor** shall ensure that the **Measurement Committee** is available and has sufficient time to re-measure their **yacht** before making any such change.

31 Yacht configuration

31.1 The *declaration deadline* for an **AC75 event stage** shall be 120 hours before the scheduled start of the first race of that **AC75 event stage**.

31.2 Prior to the *declaration deadline*, **Competitors** shall declare confidentially to the **Measurement Committee**:

(a) the **yacht** configuration to be sailed in; and

(b) a component *substitution schedule*; for the **AC75 event stage**.

31.3 The declared **yacht** configuration must include:

(a) the declared component ID, version and **blueprint SHAs** of the:

(i) hull;

(ii) **foil arm stocks**, **foil wings**, and **foil flaps**;

(iii) rudder;

(b) the declared component ID and version of the **mast tube**; and

(c) IGES files and corresponding **SHAs** of the port and starboard **linear components** that each combine a **foil arm stock**, **foil arm fairing** and **foil wing**.

31.4 The *substitution schedule* details the order of replacement components to be substituted in the event of loss or damage to a declared component, part of a component, or an associated system. A **Competitor's** *substitution schedule* shall remain confidential between that **Competitor** and the **Measurement Committee**. The *substitution schedule* may specify that:

(a) damage to some sub-components of a **foil** may necessitate replacement of the other components of a **foil**, but damage to one **foil** shall not correspond to replacement of the other **foil**;

(b) damage to a **foil** system may necessitate replacement of a **foil**, or parts of that **foil**;

(c) damage to parts of a **mast** may necessitate replacement of a **mast tube**; and

(d) damage to specific parts of a component may necessitate changing to a different version of the same component, for example:

(i) a declared **yacht** configuration specifies **rudder** 2 version C;

(ii) the *substitution schedule* states that if **rudder** 2 version C is damaged only in the area of the "elevator" (which is defined by a drawing supplied by the **Competitor**), the component is to be replaced by **rudder** 2 version B;

(iii) the *substitution schedule* states that if **rudder** 2 version C is damaged elsewhere, the component is to be replaced by **rudder** 1 version D;

(iv) regardless of where the damage occurs, **rudder** 2 version C shall be reinstated on the **yacht** if and when it is repaired.

31.5 A **yacht's** measurement certificate shall be the form provided in Figure 31.1 with all fields completed. The information on a measurement certificate shall correspond to the declared **yacht** configuration.

31.6 Once a measurement certificate has been issued to a **Competitor** for the **AC75 event stage**, it shall not be amended or replaced at any time after that **AC75 event stage's** declaration deadline, unless:

(a) a component listed on the certificate is damaged or lost and the conditions in Rule 31.7 are met;

(b) a **Competitor** is permitted to change a component according to Rule 31.8; or

(c) the original certificate is withdrawn and is subsequently re-instated according to procedures in the "Non-compliance with the Class Rules" section of the **AC Technical Regulations**.

31.7 In the event of damage or loss to a component listed on the measurement certificate, a new measurement certificate shall only be issued subject to the following conditions:

(a) the **Measurement Committee** must be completely satisfied that the damage or loss was unintentional, and that a repair in accordance with the **AC Technical Regulations** is not possible in time for the **Competitor's** next race. The **Measurement Committee** may request sailing data, video, inspection of components, interviews with or affidavits from team members to confirm this;

(b) if the **Measurement Committee** permits a component to be replaced, it shall only be replaced with the next component identified on the *substitution schedule*;

(c) if a damaged component is replaced, and that component can be repaired, but not in time for the next race, the **Competitor** shall submit to the **Measurement Committee** an estimated repair schedule and must repair the component as quickly as possible. As soon as the component is repaired, it must be reinstalled, and the original measurement certificate shall be reinstated.

31.8 With reference to Rule 31.7, if:

(a) the damage occurs in an **AC75 event stage** in which the *damaged* ***Competitor*** is racing only one other **Competitor** (not, for example, a fleet race or round-robin stage);

(b) the **Measurement Committee** permits the *damaged* **Competitor** to replace a damaged component and issues a new measurement certificate; and

(c) the damage is not ruled, by the Umpires or **Jury**, to have been caused through the fault of the other **Competitor**; then

the other **Competitor** competing in the **AC75 event stage** shall also be entitled, if they choose, to change the corresponding component to the next component identified on its *substitution schedule*, and a new measurement certificate shall be issued.

In this event, when the *damaged* ***Competitor*** reinstates that repaired component, the **Measurement Committee** shall inform the other **Competitor**, who can then choose whether to reinstate its original component. This choice to reinstate a component, or not, shall only be available at the time that, and if the **Competitor** chooses to re-instate, they shall be required to make the change at the next available opportunity, taking into account the racing schedule and the time required to make the change.

31.9 If a **yacht's** measurement certificate is withdrawn according to Rule 6.1 of the **AC Technical Regulations**, and the **Measurement Committee** determines that a declared component that has previously been measured as Rule-compliant is no longer Rule-compliant, the **Regatta Director** in consultation with the **Measurement Committee** may permit a **Competitor** to:

(a) declare a new **yacht** configuration that specifies a different component;

(b) declare a new version of that component, and declare a new **yacht** configuration that specifies that new component version; or

(c) declare a new **yacht** configuration that specifies a different, previously declared version of that component;

providing that the change to the **yacht** configuration is the minimum change required to allow the **yacht** to become Rule-compliant, subject to Rule 31.10.

31.10 The decision as to which of the options within Rule 31.9 is permitted shall be taken by the **Regatta Director** in consultation with the **Measurement Committee** and the affected **Competitor**. The option chosen shall be the one which, out of those that are achievable within a practical time-frame, will make the least difference to the performance of the **yacht**. For example:

(a) if a change can be made to modify a declared component to a new configuration, and that change will have less performance impact (positive or negative) than changing to a different component or previous version of a component, that option shall be chosen; but

(b) if the component cannot be readily made Rule-compliant, the component shall be changed to a different component.

31.11 With reference to Rule 31.9, the **Regatta Director** may also permit one option as a temporary solution (e.g. switch of a component to another component), to be followed by another option (e.g. modification of the original component) when there has been sufficient time for that option to be implemented. Such a permission shall only be granted if the **Regatta Director** is satisfied that the **Competitor** can gain no advantage by means of using the temporary option over their original configuration.

31.12 Where a **Competitor** is permitted to declare a new **yacht** configuration according to Rule 31.9, the **Regatta Director** in consultation with the

Measurement Committee may also permit changes to be made to the component substitution schedule, providing:

(a) they relate only to the changes in the declared **yacht** configuration; and

(b) any change to the component substitution schedule is the minimum change required to be compatible with the change to the declared **yacht** configuration.

31.13 When racing, the configuration of a **yacht** must match the configuration recorded in her measurement certificate, except:

(a) for a change in measurement **yacht assembly longitudinal** centre of mass xY, of up to ±25 mm from the recorded value.

(b) where a specific exemption is granted according to procedures within the **AC Technical Regulations** relating to damage to the **yacht**.

37th America's Cup

AC75 CLASS MEASUREMENT CERTIFICATE

Competitor

Certificate
Certificate number
Supersedes number
Date

Mass
Yacht assembly mass — kg
Longitudinal centre — m

Hull

Mast

Rudder

Port foil
Foil arm stock
Foil wing
Foil flap
Linear component

Starboard foil
Foil arm stock
Foil wing
Foil flap
Linear component

Measurers
Measured and found to comply with the AC75 Class Rule:

Figure 31.1: Measurement certificate

32 Documents

32.1 The following documents shall be available to all **Competitors** on the **Official Noticeboard** or other locations advised by the **Rules Committee**:
(a) the list of approved **commercial products**;
(b) the **Measurement Procedures**; and
(c) the specifications listed in Rule 32.3.

32.2 The **Measurement Committee**, in consultation with the **Rules Committee**:
(a) will issue the **Measurement Procedures** on or before 01/03/2023;
(b) may issue parts of those procedures relevant to construction or component logging in advance of the full document; and
(c) may amend the **Measurement Procedures** at any time, subject to Rule 32.4.

32.3 **COR/D** will issue the following specifications on or before the dates specified, and may amend them at any time subject to Rule 32.4:

Date	Rule	Item
01/07/2022	15.1	**Mast**
01/07/2022	10	**Foil arm stock**
01/10/2022	19.20 (a)	High-pressure **hydraulic accumulator**
01/10/2022	19.7 (a)	Manual hydraulic pump
01/03/2023	25.1	**FCS**
01/03/2023	27	**Media equipment**
01/03/2023	26	**Media System**
01/03/2023	26.9	Tactical software
01/03/2023	28	**Event** branding

32.4 Amendment of the **Measurement Procedures** or any of the specifications listed in Rule 32.3 shall require consultation with all **Competitors** and the approval of the **Rules Committee**. The **Rules Committee** shall approve changes that are beneficial to:
(a) the operational requirements of an **event**;
(b) media coverage of an **event**;
(c) the fairness of an **event**, including the ability of the **Measurement Committee** to perform their duty;
(d) the functionality, reliability or safety of a supplied system; or
(e) the availability of supplied components;
providing that they are satisfied that all **Competitors** have been consulted, and that the impact of the proposed changes on all **Competitors** is

commensurate with the need for the change, taking account of the state of each **Competitor's** design, construction, training and race programmes.

33 Agreement

33.1 **COR/D** agreed to the publication of version 1.0 of these **AC75 Class Rule** on the 17th day of March 2022.

33.2 This version of the **AC75 Class Rule** shall replace the previous version and be in force when stamped by the **Rules Committee**. The replacement of the previous version with this version is an amendment according to Rule TR-7.1 (a).

5.3 AC40 Class Rule (v 1.5 – 17 October 2023)

AC40 CLASS RULE

v1.5

17 October 2023

Contents

1 Introduction
2 General arrangement
3 Mass
4 Supplied components and repairs
5 Surface finishes and branding
6 Rig, sails and rigging
7 Control system and electronics
8 Media equipment
9 Crew
10 Measurement
11 Permitted modifications

12 In class modifications
13 Interpretation and amendment
14 Documents
15 Definitions
16 Publication

1 Introduction

1.1 This document defines the rules that govern an **AC40 Class Yacht**.
1.2 Where words or phrases are printed in bold type, their meaning is defined in Rule 15 of this **AC40 Class Rule**. Where words or phrases are printed in italic type, their meaning has a local definition that only applies within that section of this **AC40 Class Rule**. These terms may be used in modified grammatical forms, in which case any modification to the term relates to a corresponding modification of the definition.
1.3 An **AC40 Class Yacht** shall comply with the **AC40 Class Rule** when racing, and at other times as required by the **AC40 Class Rule**.
1.4 This **AC40 Class Rule** is a closed rule: anything not specifically permitted is prohibited.
1.5 An **AC40 Class Yacht** must match the **AC40 Specification** when racing.
1.6 **Teams** are ultimately and solely responsible for inspecting their **AC40 Class Yachts**. No express or implied warranty of safety shall result from compliance with the whole or any part of the **AC40 Class Rule**.

2 General arrangement

2.1 Most components of an **AC40 Class Yacht** are supplied by licensed manufacturers nominated by the **Class Authority**.

2.2 An **AC40 Class Yacht** has the following supplied components:

Component	Supplier
one **hull**	McConaghy Boats
two **foils**	McConaghy Boats
one **rudder**	McConaghy Boats
one **mast**	Southern Spars
one set of standing rigging	Southern Spars
one **jib** with hardware	North Sails
one **mainsail** with hardware	North Sails
one **mainsail** buoyancy system	Yotti New Zealand
control and instrumentation systems	McConaghy Boats
media equipment	as required for a regatta
other supplied components	McConaghy Boats

2.3 In addition to the above supplied components, an **AC40 Class Yacht** shall have:
 (a) running rigging, detailed in the **AC40 Specification**;
 (b) safety equipment, detailed in Rule 2.6;
 (c) optional branding, permitted by Section 5;
 (d) optional **woollies**, permitted by Rule 6.11;
 (e) optional chafe protection tape on hoses and lines;
 (f) optional modifications and additions permitted by Section 11;
 (g) optional halyard tails; and
 (h) optional VHF radios.

2.4 Nothing shall be onboard an **AC40 Class Yacht** except:
 (a) the components listed in Rules 2.2 and 2.3;
 (b) any crew ballast required by Rule 3.6; and
 (c) crew, their **carried equipment** and any **crew supplied media equipment**, detailed in Section 9.

2.5 Components must be assembled and installed to form an **AC40 Class Yacht** in accordance with the **AC40 Specification**.

2.6 **Teams** shall secure and distribute the following safety equipment on their **AC40 Class Yacht** at locations that would be easily accessible in the event of a capsize:
 (a) at least two blades with lengths of no more than 150 mm; and
 (b) at least four personal air supplies containing compressed air equivalent to at least 40 litres uncompressed volume each, which do not require the use

of hands when in use, unless these are brought on as **carried equipment**, permitted by Rule 9.4.

These items are included in the **platform** mass during measurement.

2.7 Inspection hatch and access covers shall be securely fastened to prevent water ingress to the **hull**.

2.8 Drainage fairing flaps shall be closed, except that when there is water in the cockpits, the drainage fairing flaps shall be opened as soon as practical to drain that water, and thereafter closed.

3 Mass

3.1 The table below lists component masses and centres of gravity (CG). Except for the **mast**, the CG is the distance forward of the transom datum; for the **mast**, it is the distance along the **mast** above the **mast** rotation point.

The masses below include allowances for paint and vinyl finishes permitted by Rule 5.9.

Component	Mass (kg)	CG (m)
Yacht assembly	**2118-2126**	**5.64**
Platform	***1832**	***5.79**
Hull and other parts or components	—	
Rudder	*38	
Port **foil**	*361	
Foil arm	143.5	
Foil wing/flap/systems	217.5	
Starboard **foil**	*361	
Foil arm	143.5	
Foil wing/flap/systems	217.5	
Platform-weighed **Mast** and **Mainsail** hardware	—	
†**Media equipment**	—	
Mast (excluding parts weighed with **platform**)	***160**	***7.85**
Mast tube and attached components, etc.	133	
Standing rigging	24	
Strops, running rigging, etc.	—	
†**Media equipment**	—	
Mainsail (excluding parts weighed with **platform**)	***109**	
Jib	***17-25**	
Crew, **carried equipment** & **crew supplied media equipment**	***360**	
Total	**2478-2486**	

**Measured, †Regatta dependant*

3.2 Where component masses and centres of gravity in Rule 3.1 are marked with an asterisk, the components shall meet the specifications within the tolerances specified in the **Measurement Procedures**.

3.3 The **platform** and **mast** shall be weighed in their respective measurement conditions specified by the **Measurement Procedures**, whereby:

(a) the **platform** mass and centre of gravity in Rule 3.1 are intended to represent the mass and longitudinal centre of gravity of the heaviest **AC40 Class Yacht**;

(b) the **mast** mass and centre of gravity in Rule 3.1 are intended to represent the mass and *vertical* centre of gravity of the heaviest **mast**;

(c) the **AC40 Measurement Committee** shall calculate the mass required as ballast, to the nearest 1.0 kg, to add to any **platform** or **mast** to bring it to the specified mass. Any such ballast must be attached as specified in the **Measurement Procedures** to match the respective centres of gravity; and

(d) if an **AC40 Class Yacht** is damaged during a regatta and the repair results in an estimated addition of over 2.0 kg then the **AC40 Class Yacht** may be weighed and the ballast adjusted to account for the change in mass and centre of gravity of this **AC40 Class Yacht**.

3.4 In the event of manufacturing differences that place a component outside of the allowed tolerance, the mass table may be updated.

3.5 The combined mass of crew, **carried equipment** and **crew supplied media equipment**, must not exceed the value specified in Rule 3.1.

3.6 After crew weigh in, ballast in the form of bags of lead shot shall be added up to the value for "Crew, **carried equipment** & **crew supplied media equipment**" specified in Rule 3.1. This will be attached to the seat plinths of each crew member. Ballast will be distributed between bags to achieve a centre of gravity position of crew and ballast combined, when the crew are sitting in their respective seats, that is as close as possible to the equivalent of four crew members each of 90 kg (including carried/supplied equipment) sitting in the seats.

3.7 Ballast or other equipment shall not be moved for the purpose of changing trim or stability.

3.8 Nothing shall be aboard the **AC40 Class Yacht** that is not included in Rule 3.1, where components listed in Rule 2.3 that have been added to the **yacht** shall be included in the **platform**, **mast** or sail weights as appropriate.

3.9 When racing, the mass of the **AC40 Class Yacht** excluding crew, **carried equipment**, **crew supplied media equipment** and the **rig** shall not be less than, or more than 5.0 kg greater than its mass in **platform** measurement condition.

3.10 Variations to the mass table may be published for a particular regatta by the **AC40 Measurement Committee** to allow for different **media equipment** weights, crew requirements or other factors.

4 Supplied components and repairs

4.1 **AC40 Class Yacht** components must match the **AC40 Specification** and be in the same condition and configuration as they were received from the manufacturer, except where modifications or repairs are expressly permitted or required by the **AC40 Class Rule**.

4.2 The supplied components listed in Rule 2.2:

(a) shall be marked by the relevant manufacturer indicating that they have been built to the **AC40 Specification**. Specifically:

(i) the **hull**, **foil arms**, **foil wings**, **rudder**, and **mast** shall have an alloy identification tag glued on and laminated over;
(ii) the sails shall have a North Sails order entry number on them; and
(iii) elevators shall have an identification number written inside the **rudder** foot rebate;

(b) may have branding added as permitted by Rule 5;
(c) may be repaired as permitted by Rule 4.4;
(d) may be replaced as permitted by Rules 4.6, 4.7 and 4.8; and
(e) may not be modified except where explicitly permitted by the **AC40 Class Rule**.

4.3 If an **AC40 Class Yacht** component has been modified beyond the limitations permitted by this **AC40 Class Rule** then it shall be reverted to its original configuration prior to the measurement period for a regatta. **Teams** that have modified a component such that it cannot be restored to the original configuration shall purchase and install a replacement component.

4.4 Repairs can be *major* or *minor*, where:

(a) *major* repairs include anything that restores the structural load path of any damaged component; and
(b) *minor* repairs are repairs that are not *major* repairs, such as:
(i) surface finish repairs, including those permitted by Rule 5;
(ii) other maintenance where the shape, range, mass and function of the repaired component is not significantly changed; and
(iii) local surface patching and application of chafe protection on the surfaces of sails.

Procedures relating to *major* repairs need to be specified by the relevant manufacturer and approved by the **AC40 Measurement Committee**. *Minor* repairs may be carried out without the need for specification or prior approval.

4.5 Repairs permitted by Rule 4.4 shall restore components to their original condition, except where the resultant changes:

(a) are as small as reasonably possible considering the time until the next race;
(b) provide no significant performance or weight advantage;
(c) if *major*, are approved in writing by the **AC40 Measurement Committee** in consultation with the **Class Authority**; and
(d) if *minor*, are approved by the **AC40 Measurement Committee** during measurement.

4.6 Except as permitted by Rules 4.7 and 4.8, **AC40 Class Yacht** components may only be replaced with identical spares:

(a) supplied directly from the component manufacturer where those components are listed in the document referenced by Rule 14.2 (d); or
(b) supplied by the official AC40 suppliers listed in Rule 2.2;

4.7 **AC40 Class Yacht** components whose geometries are included within the "3D Printed Parts" folder referenced by Rule 14.2 are permitted to be replaced with 3D printed components sourced or manufactured directly by **Teams**, providing they are built to the following specification:
   (a) Material: Nylon 12 / Nylon PA12
   (b) Process: MJF, SLS or other process that produces similar quality
   (c) Supplier: Any; www.weerg.com is recommended.

4.8 **AC40 Class Yacht** components or systems may, as a temporary measure for racing, be modified or replaced with non-identical spares, where:
   (a) they are damaged or malfunctioning and cannot be satisfactorily repaired according to Rule 4.4 or replaced according to Rule 4.6, prior to the next race;
   (b) the replacement or modified components or systems provide no significant performance or weight advantage; and
   (c) the replacement or modified components or systems are approved by the **AC40 Measurement Committee** in consultation with the **Class Authority**.

4.9 Any permitted replacement, modification or repair shall not allow for additional water retention by the AC40 Class Yacht.

5 Surface finishes and branding

5.1 All component surfaces shall retain their original finishes, except:
   (a) for *minor* repairs, described by Rule 4.4, to surfaces that remain out of the water in foiling and displacement sailing modes;
   (b) where otherwise permitted.

5.2 Surfaces may be sanded, polished and cleaned, providing that:
   (a) the shape of the surface remains within tolerances specified in the **Measurement Procedures**;
   (b) the surface material is not fundamentally changed (e.g. from paint to a bare finish), except where otherwise permitted; and
   (c) no substances remain on the surfaces when the **AC40 Class Yacht** is afloat, other than:
      (i) the component's original surface finish; or
      (ii) a finish explicitly permitted by the **AC40 Class Rule**.

5.3 **Foil arm drums** may be faired to the **hull surface**, but the **hull surface** shall not be otherwise modified.

5.4 **Foil wing** actuator access hatches and lever access hatches may be:
   (a) potted to align them with the shape of the **foil wing** upstand; and
   (b) faired around the perimeter line and over fasteners.

5.5 Minor paint touch-ups are permitted, and must be applied using an approved paint specified in Rule 5.6.

5.6 Approved commercial paints are:

Manufacturer	Products
Alexseal	HS Base Coat; HS Clear Coat
Awlgrip	Awlcraft 2000; Topcoats G/H-Line; HDT Clearcoat
Cromax	3050S ChromaClear; Centari 600 Basecoat
GRS Deltron BC	Global Refinish System Deltron Basecoat
MaxMeyer	Matt Semi-Gloss Clear 1-360-0710/ 1-360-0750
Nautix	L2; NX194
Resene	Durepox; Durepox Extreme Clear; Durepox High Performance Clear
Spies Hecker	480 Hi Tec; 8650; Plastic automotive paint; Permasolid HS Automotive Topcoat 27*

**This excludes the Permasolid Texture Component SA 101 and SA 102 that are part of the Spies Hecker Plastic system.*

5.7 Non-skid products or coatings may be applied on areas of the **deck** where crew operate when racing or preparing to race.

5.8 Surface areas of the **hull** and sails may be reserved for regatta branding, as notified by the event authority.

5.9 Outside of any regatta reserved areas, the following **AC40 Class Yacht** components may have ink, paint or plastic film applied, subject to the 'Permitted finish' below, providing it is not used for the purpose of altering the structure of the boundary layer. Any applied finish shall have a mass that falls within the limits below:

Component	Permitted finish	Mass limit
hull	plastic film	5 kg
mast	plastic film	2 kg
foil arms	plastic film	250 g (per **foil arm**)
foil wings	Resene Durepox (black)	entire **foil wing** surface
mainsail	ink, paint* or plastic film	2.5 kg (per **sail skin**)
jib	ink, paint* or plastic film	3 kg
rudder	paint*	500 g

**must be an approved commercial paint specified in Rule 5.6.*

5.10 **Teams** shall permit the **AC40 Measurement Committee** to take samples of paint or plastic film from components of the **yacht** to ensure compliance with Rule 5.9.

5.11 **Yacht hulls** are supplied white for heat rejection. It is the responsibility of the **Team** to ensure any permitted additions do not adversely affect the thermal integrity of their **yacht hull**.

6 Rig, sails and rigging

6.1 **Teams** shall prepare and install running rigging according to the **AC40 Specification**, including the Running Rigging Cut-sheet referred to by Rule 14.2 (c). No other running rigging, such as bungee cords, is permitted on the **yacht**.

6.2 Where given in the **AC40 Specification**, running rigging line lengths shall fall within the indicated tolerances, and shall be inspected by the **AC40 Measurement Committee**. In particular, it is prohibited to adjust the length or configuration of lines to affect the range of motion of control systems such as the **mast** rotation.

6.3 All running rigging shall remain fully led according to the **AC40 Specification** when racing.

6.4 The **mast** and standing rigging shall be positioned and tensioned on the **hull** according to the dock tune procedure prescribed by the **AC40 Specification**, and shall not be adjusted except as permitted by Rule 6.10.

6.5 One **jib** and one **mainsail** shall be hoisted and configured as described in the **AC40 Specification.**

6.6 The sailing instructions for a particular regatta may indicate that the choice of **jib** for each race will be specified by the Principal Race Officer, to be determined by the expected wind speed range; otherwise, any **jib** may be hoisted.

6.7 The supplied **mainsail** buoyancy system must be positioned and inflated according to the **AC40 Specification**.

6.8 The gantline may be moused using a 2 mm mouse line provided it can be retrieved without crew going aloft.

6.9 The winches used for hoisting the sails shall be removed from the **yacht** for racing.

6.10 When racing, the only permitted adjustments of the **mast**, rigging and sails are:

(a) by the following hydraulic rig control systems controlled from the cockpit:

(i) **mast** rotation system;

(ii) traveller;

(iii) mainsheet;

(iv) **mainsail** cunningham;

(v) **mainsail** clew adjuster;

(vi) **jib** cunningham;
(vii) **jib** inhaul; and
(viii) **jib** sheet;

(b) manual adjustment of leech and foot lines;
(c) manual backwinding of the **jib**; and
(d) incidental movement due to contact with the crew, **hull**, deck gear, rigging or other items attached to the **hull**.

6.11 Any number of **woolies** may be added to a **jib** or **mainsail** outside of areas designated for regatta branding.

6.12 Running rigging may be replaced during a regatta with the approval of the **AC40 Measurement Committee**.

7 Control system and electronics

7.1 **AC40 Class Yachts** are supplied with:

(a) a hydraulic system that includes:
(i) rig control systems listed in Rule 6.10;
(ii) a foil cant system that controls the cant rotation of **foils**; and
(iii) a flight control system that controls **foil** flap angles and **rudder** rake;

(b) a PLC;
(c) an inertial navigation system;
(d) a ride height sensor;
(e) an autopilot system;
(f) a wind wand;
(g) an instrumentation and logging system; and
(h) information and display systems.

7.2 Hydraulics may be maintained but shall not be modified. Hydraulic oil shall only be replaced with mineral hydraulic oil with classification HLP32 or HVLP32.

7.3 Pressure relief valves shall not be adjusted.

7.4 The latest official versions of the supplied software, as advised by the **Class Authority**, shall be installed on:

(a) the PLC;
(b) the batteries; and
(c) the display screens.

7.5 The inertial navigation system shall be calibrated such that the **yacht**, when levelled to the satisfaction of the **AC40 Measurement Committee**, reads zero trim and zero heel. The calibration shall not be adjusted after measurement.

7.6 The ride height sensor shall measure ride-height correctly to the satisfaction of the **AC40 Measurement Committee**.

7.7 Crew members shall not carry electric or electronic components except:

(a) standalone devices, such as basic wristwatches, that are incapable of measuring or receiving any information on the position, orientation, velocity or state of the **AC40 Class Yacht**; and

(b) spare display screens permitted by Rule 9.5.

7.8 Control circuits, electronics and software shall not be modified.

8 Media equipment

8.1 The media equipment supplied for a regatta shall be the same for all **yachts**.

8.2 Media equipment shall be installed by the **Regatta Authority** and may not be removed without their permission.

8.3 The **crew supplied media equipment** shall be the same for all crews competing in the same race and shall be worn in a manner directed by the **Regatta Authority** to the satisfaction of the **AC40 Measurement Committee** unless otherwise notified in the Notice of Race. The **Regatta Authority** shall indicate the periods in which media equipment must be worn and switched on.

8.4 The **Class Authority** will publish details of an *official onboard communication system*, which shall be the only communication system permitted to be used on the **yacht** when racing unless otherwise notified by the **Regatta Authority**.

8.5 **Teams** that install the *official onboard communication system* themselves shall do so according to the **A40 Specification**, and may then use the system when racing. Otherwise, the **Regatta Authority** will require **Teams** to remove any other communications systems and will install the *official onboard communication system* for racing.

9 Crew

9.1 There shall be four crew members, unless reduced by accident, who shall all be human beings.

9.2 The Notice of Race of a regatta may provide restrictions on the crew such as gender or age.

9.3 Each crew member shall wear:

(a) a buoyancy aid that meets the flotation standard of ISO 12402-5 or ISO 12402-6 (CE 50 Newtons) and that is capable of being removed or deflated in the water within five seconds;

(b) a helmet to a minimum standard of CE EN 1077, CE EN 966, ASTM 2040, or Snell S-98 and with at least 300 cm^2 of the exterior surface brightly coloured. **Teams** shall satisfy the **AC40 Measurement Committee** that the brightly coloured region can be seen from above the water with the crew lying face down or face up in the water;

(c) a blade with a length of no more than 150 mm;

(d) a pocket for carrying **crew supplied media equipment** with minimum dimensions 80 mm x 200 mm x 30 mm; and
(e) **crew supplied media equipment** as required by Rule 8.3.

9.4 Each crew member may wear one or more personal air supplies containing compressed air equivalent to at least 40 litres uncompressed volume each, which does not require the use of hands when in use. If these are not worn, they are required to installed in the **yacht** as prescribed by Rule 2.6.

9.5 Each crew member may carry one spare display screen, providing:
(a) it is of the same specification as the supplied display screens, and has the same software installed;
(b) it has been measured and approved by the **AC40 Measurement Committee**;
(c) it is at all times carried by the crew member, in a pocket or similar, such that the screen is not visible to any crew members, unless there is a failure of another onboard screen;
(d) it shall not be used to provide information to any crew members that would not have clear visibility of that same information from their normal sailing positions.

9.6 The total mass of **carried equipment** worn or carried by each crew member shall be:
(a) a maximum, when dry, that is dependent on expected air temperature as follows;
(i) 6.5 kg if under 18°C;
(ii) 5.5 kg if 18-23°C; or
(iii) 5.0 kg if over 23°C;
The **AC40 Measurement Committee** shall specify which of these limits apply to an AC40 regatta based on the published monthly average temperature for the first day of racing in that AC40 regatta; and
(b) no more than 3.0 kg in excess of the dry maximum when soaked and allowed to drain for 1 minute according to procedures issued by the **AC40 Measurement Committee.**

9.7 Any **crew supplied media equipment** or **carried equipment** brought aboard by a crew member must be worn, attached to, or carried by that crew member at all times when racing, except that a carried spare display screen may be mounted on the **yacht** in the event of a failure of another display screen.

9.8 Crew members shall be weighed at crew weighs organised by the **AC40 Measurement Committee**, where:
(a) crew shall be dressed in full gear with all **carried equipment** including **crew supplied media equipment**;
(b) crew weighs shall take place at times published by the **AC40 Measurement Committee**; and

(c) the **AC40 Measurement Committee** will use the weights recorded at crew weighs to determine the required ballast. Recorded weights will be updated at each subsequent crew weigh and the required ballast redetermined accordingly.

9.9 Clothing and equipment shall not be designed to retain water for the purpose of increasing mass.

9.10 Crew shall not promote the ingress of water into the volume of the **hull**, for instance by capsizing. In the event of a capsize, the volume of the **hull** shall be checked to ensure it is empty of water before the start of the next race.

9.11 While the **yacht** is foiling, crew shall remain in the cockpit and entirely inside the **perimeter line** of the **yacht**, unless by accident. If the crew intentionally leave the cockpit:

(a) the **yacht** must be in displacement mode;
(b) they shall attempt to return to the cockpit prior to the **yacht** taking off;
(c) they must not contact the **foils**; and
(d) they shall not enter the watertight volume of the **hull**.

10 Measurement

10.1 The **Measurement Procedures** shall be issued according to Rule 14.1.

10.2 The **AC40 Measurement Committee** may place seals on equipment or otherwise mark equipment as part of the measurement process.

10.3 The **AC40 Measurement Committee** shall issue a measurement certificate for a **yacht** when they have:

(a) concluded that she complies with the **AC40 Class Rule** and the **AC40 Specification**;
(b) received completed declarations and affidavits as required by the **AC40 Class Rule** and as additionally required by the **AC40 Measurement Committee** at their discretion; and
(c) received all documentation as required by the **AC40 Class Rule** and by other notices published by the **AC40 Measurement Committee**, and confirmed that the documentation is satisfactory.

10.4 Once a measurement certificate has been issued, some changes to the **yacht** shall be permitted without requiring re-measurement. The scope of these permitted changes shall be detailed in the **Measurement Procedures** and shall include changes such as routine maintenance on mechanical, hydraulic and electrical systems.

10.5 Compliance with control system and electronics rules may be determined by a combination of hardware inspection, software inspection, interviews and affidavits.

10.6 A **yacht's** measurement certificate may be withdrawn by the **AC40 Measurement Committee** at any time if they suspect she no longer complies with the **AC40 Class Rule** or the **AC40 Specification.**

10.7 If a **yacht** is unintentionally damaged and cannot be repaired in time for her next race, the **AC40 Measurement Committee** in consultation with the **Regatta Authority** may permit a measurement certificate to be issued or retained despite her no longer complying with the **AC40 Specification**, provided they are satisfied that no performance advantage could be gained.

AC40 Class Yacht

AC40 CLASS MEASUREMENT CERTIFICATE

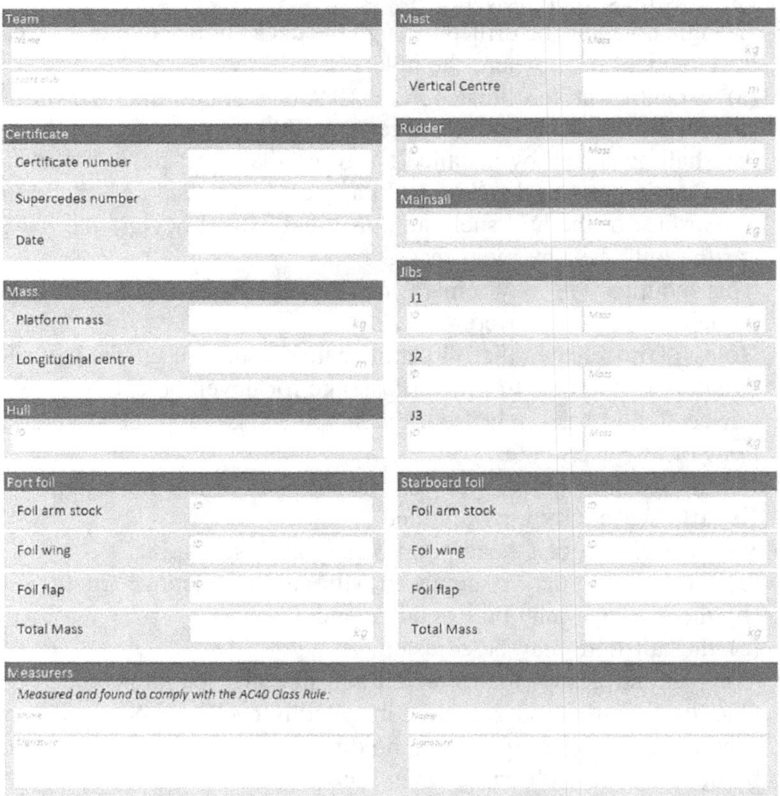
Team
Name
Yacht club
Certificate
Certificate number
Supercedes number
Date
Mass
Platform mass kg
Longitudinal centre m
Hull
ID
Port foil
Foil arm stock ID
Foil wing ID
Foil flap ID
Total Mass kg
Mast
ID Mass kg
Vertical Centre m
Rudder
ID Mass kg
Mainsail
ID Mass kg
Jibs
J1
ID Mass kg
J2
ID Mass kg
J3
ID Mass kg
Starboard foil
Foil arm stock ID
Foil wing ID
Foil flap ID
Total Mass kg
Measurers
Measured and found to comply with the AC40 Class Rule:
Name
Signature
Name
Signature

Figure 10.1: AC40 Measurement certificate

11 Permitted modifications

11.1 Crew seats may be replaced with alternative seats of the same mass with the approval of the **AC40 Measurement Committee**.

11.2 Two holes may be drilled through the **hull lower surface** for the installation of cameras (for development use), where the holes:
(a) are centred at coordinates *xyz* = (7.054 m, ±0.356 m, -0.180 m);
(b) shall be circular and no larger than 40 mm diameter; and
(c) shall be sealed by installed hardware that must remain watertight under a static pressure head of 70 kPa, must be bonded only to the inside surface of the hull shell, and must not extend beyond the fair surface of the hull shell.

This modification may remain in the **yacht** when racing, but any installed cameras must be removed.

11.3 A single hole may be drilled through the **deck** for installation of a camera (for development use), where the hole:
(a) is centred at coordinates *xyz* = (8.950 m, 0.000 m, 1.018 m);
(b) shall be circular and no larger than 70 mm diameter; and
(c) shall be sealed by installed hardware that must remain watertight under a static pressure head of 10 kPa, must be bonded or bolted to the inside surface of the hull shell, and must not extend beyond the fair surface of the hull shell by more than 3 mm.

This modification may remain in the **yacht** when racing, but any installed camera must be removed.

11.4 Holes of no greater than 40 mm diameter may be drilled in the internal structure of the **hull** to provide passage for development systems; however, advice should be sought from the supplier regarding the structural implications of any such holes.

11.5 Modifications required for the installation of media equipment by the **Regatta Authority** are permitted.

11.6 Within 800 mm of a head point of any **mainsail skin**:
(a) the luff tape may be replaced with an equivalent product;
(b) the luff tape may be extended; and
(c) the luff flare may be adjusted.

11.7 Vinyl sail stripes on the **mainsail** and **jibs** may be removed.

11.8 One drink bottle holder may be installed in each cockpit, which may not be used for any other purpose than holding a crew member's drink bottle. Drink bottles shall not be carried when racing.

11.9 Additional minor modifications listed in the document referenced by Rule 14.2 (f) are permitted.

11.10 Any modifications not specifically listed here, in the document referenced by Rule 14.2 (f), or elsewhere in the **AC40 Class Rule** are prohibited when racing.

12 In class modifications

12.1 This section describes changes that are permitted to made by Competitors in the 37th America's Cup to **AC40 Class Yacht** components for development and testing purposes.

12.2 The changes described in Rules 12.5 and 12.7 are not permitted when racing.

12.3 Components originally built for an **AC40 Class Yacht** can exist in the following states:

(a) *Rule compliant*, whereby a component satisfies all the relevant rules of the **AC40 Class Rule.** Only *rule compliant* components may be installed for racing. Any component that is *rule compliant* is necessarily also an **in class** component;

(b) **In class**, whereby a component qualifies for specific conditions set out in the AC Technical Regulations 'Component limits and modifications' section. An **in class** component may have been modified from its *rule compliant* condition to a limited extent, within the constraints set out in this Section;

(c) *Out of class*, whereby a component has been modified beyond the extents permitted by this Section. Such a component is not, in that state, an **AC40 Class Yacht** component.

12.4 An **in class** component of an **AC40 Class Yacht** is a **hull surface**, **foil arm**, **foil wing**, **foil flap**, **rudder**, **mast tube** or **sail skin** that has been supplied as an **AC40 Class Yacht** component and has not been modified from its supplied condition beyond the limits set out in Rules 12.5, 12.6 and 12.7.

12.5 For an **AC40 Class Yacht** supplied **hull** to remain **in class** there shall be:

(a) no modifications to the **hull lower surface** except those permitted elsewhere in the **AC40 Class Rule**; and

(b) no modifications to the **deck**, except:

(i) those permitted elsewhere in the **AC40 Class Rule**;

(ii) modifications in the vicinity of the cockpits;

(iii) modifications around the **jib** track and mainsheet traveller areas for the purpose of changing sheeting arrangements; or

(iv) other minor modifications to the **deck**.

Any such **deck** modifications shall not significantly alter the global aerodynamic shape of the **deck**.

12.6 For the following supplied **AC40 Class Yacht** components to remain **in class**, they shall not be modified except as permitted elsewhere in the **AC40 Class Rule**:

(a) **foil wings**, **foil flaps**, **foil arm stocks**, their systems, actuators and sensors;
(b) **rudders**; and
(c) **mast tubes.**

The extent of a **foil arm stock**, being part of a **foil arm**, is indicated in a supplied drawing which forms the **foil arm stock** specification.

12.7 For supplied **AC40 Class Yacht jib** and **mainsail** skins to remain **in class**, they shall not be modified except as permitted elsewhere in the **AC40 Class Rule**, and:

(a) in the first sailing periods after launch, the **Class Authority** iterated through minor details of the **mainsail** and **jib** and these modifications were restricted to:
   (i) minor changes to geometry such as repositioning of the clew; and
   (ii) local reinforcements to address issues such as chafe and minor structural issues that do not affect the flying shape of the sail; and;
(b) in order that other **Teams** are not disadvantaged by having access to fewer sail developments, they may choose to sail with their **jib** and **mainsail** skins in any of the configurations tested by the **Class Authority**, with those sails remaining **in class**.

The **Class Authority** will publish all configurations used in the process of determining the final configuration.

12.8 Except within the **foils**, modifications to **AC40 Class Yacht** mechanical, hydraulic and electrical systems do not prevent **AC40 Class Yacht** components from remaining **in class**.

12.9 A yacht comprising some original or modified **AC40 Class Yacht** components is classified as an **AC40 Class Yacht**, but not necessarily one that is *rule compliant*, so long as its **hull** remains **in class**. If such a yacht is modified so that the **hull** is no longer **in class**, the yacht is no longer classified as an **AC40 Class Yacht**.

13 Interpretation and amendment

13.1 The **Class Authority** may from time to time issue updates to the **AC40 Specification**, which shall require **Teams** to modify their **yachts** in accordance with the updated **AC40 Specification**. These updates shall be published as optional, recommended or mandatory; if mandatory, a time by which the updates must be applied shall be indicated.

13.2 **Teams** may request clarification from the **Class Authority** on any aspect of the **AC40 Specification**.

13.3 The **AC40 Class Rule** may be amended by the **Class Authority** at any time.

13.4 A **Team** may submit a Rule Enquiry regarding the **AC40 Class Rule** to the **Class Authority** in the form of:
  (a) an interpretation request;
  (b) an amendment proposal; or
  (c) a combination of the above.

13.5 A request submitted according to Rule 13.4 shall be a Microsoft Word document or compatible format, so that it can be edited easily.

13.6 The Class Authority shall respond with an interpretation or amendment which shall be circulated to all **Teams**.

13.7 Advice or opinions given on the meaning of a Rule are not binding except through a circulated interpretation.

14 Documents

14.1 The **AC40 Measurement Committee**, in consultation with the **Class Authority** will issue the **Measurement Procedures** at least two months prior to the first **AC40 Class Yacht** regatta, and may amend them at any time.

14.2 The **Class Authority** has issued the following documents:
  (a) AC40 User Manual;
  (b) AC40 Commissioning Manual;
  (c) Running Rigging Cut-sheet;
  (d) AC40 Direct Purchase Parts List, itemising commercial components that may be replaced according to Rule 4.6 (a);
  (e) 3D Printed Part geometries in STP format, within the folder "AC40/Rig & Sails/3D Printed Parts"; and
  (f) AC40 Permitted Minor Modifications List, itemising minor modifications permitted by Rule 11.9.

14.3 The **Class Authority** has issued the following drawings:

Drawing	File path
Rudder interface	AC40/Appendages
Foil arm interface	AC40/Appendages
Electronics hardware schematics	AC40/Electrical
Exterior hull and deck geometry	AC40/Hull/031 400_AC40 Hull.igs
Hydraulics circuit diagram	AC40/Hydraulics/514 00 400C_AC40 overview circuit.pdf
Rig plan & loading	AC40/Rig & Sails/031 400 001A_Rig Plan.pdf
Mast and sail interface	AC40/Rig & Sails/North Sails data
Mast specification	AC40/Rig & Sails/

14.4 The documents and drawings listed in Rules 14.2 and 14.3 form part, but not all, of the **AC40 Specification**. These drawings are available in a folder labelled 'AC40' whose location shall be notified by the **Class Authority**.

14.5 The **Class Authority** may amend the documents and drawings listed in Rules 14.2 and 14.3, and will notify all **Teams** of any such amendment.

15 Definitions

15.1 **AC40 Class Rule**

The rule governing the yachts to be used in the first and second Preliminary Regattas of the 37th America's Cup, the associated Youth and Women's America's Cups, and any other AC40 series racing, including all amendments to, interpretations of and rulings relating to that rule.

15.2 **AC40 Class Yacht**

A yacht that complies with or could comply with the **AC40 Class Rule**.

15.3 **AC40 Measurement Committee**

A Committee responsible for ensuring an **AC40 Class Yacht** satisfies the **AC40 Class Rule**.

15.4 **AC40 Specification**

The collection of published information that defines the components that comprise an **AC40 Class Yacht** and their arrangement with respect to each other, including information embodied in the design of supplied components. The **AC40 Specification** in its entirety does not exist in a fully documented form, but combines information from the user manuals, the supplied components them- selves, the software supplied and installed, and general sailing knowledge. For example, the **AC40 Specification** shall include:

(a) the arrangement of cockpit controls installed in the **yacht** as supplied, whether or not these details exist in a published drawing; and
(b) the fact a halyard is led up the mast and over the mainsail halyard sheave, whether or not that information is stated explicitly in any published document.

15.5 **Carried equipment**

Clothing, safety equipment, other equipment, food and drink carried aboard by the crew, excluding **crew supplied media equipment.**

15.6 **Class Authority**

The organisation responsible for the management of the AC40 Class, currently AC37 Event Limited.

15.7 **Crew supplied media equipment**

Equipment supplied by the **Regatta Authority** to be worn or carried by the crew.

15.8 **Deck**

That part of the **hull surface** that is not the **hull lower surface**.

15.9 **Foil**

An appendage that can provide hydrodynamic side force and vertical lift.

15.10 **Foil arm**

A component of a **foil** that connects the foil cant system to the **foil wing**.

15.11 **Foil arm drum**

A fairing to close a penetration in the **hull** that allows rotation of a **foil** about the **foil arm** rotation axis.

15.12 **Foil arm stock**

A supplied component forming the structural spar of a **foil arm** combined with a leading edge. The items included in the foil arm stock are defined in the **Foil arm stock** specification.

15.13 **Foil flap**

A component of a **foil** that can be adjusted relative to a **foil wing** by a **foil** system.

15.14 **Foil wing**

A component of a **foil** that, together with a **foil flap**, typically generates most of the hydrodynamic vertical lift of the **foil**.

15.15 **Hull**

The main body of the **AC40 Class Yacht**, including the bottom, sides, transom, **deck**, cockpit and internal structure but not the **mast**, rigging, sails, **foils**, **rudder** or fittings.

15.16 **Hull lower surface**

The lower part of a **hull surface** that is divided by the **perimeter line**, extending downwards from the **perimeter line**.

15.17 **Hull surface**

The external surface of a **hull** divided into the **deck** and **hull lower surface** by the **perimeter line**.

15.18 **In class**

The status of a supplied component that has not been modified outside the scope of any modifications explicitly permitted by the **AC40 Class Rule**.

15.19 **Jib**

A sail set forward of the **mast** hoisted on the forestay.

15.20 **Mainsail**

The combination of sail skins and associated components that are hoisted on the **mast**.

15.21 **Mast**

An assembly comprising the **mast tube** with any attached components and rigging that is not hoisted with the **mainsail** or **jib**. It includes **mainsail** support structures and control systems such as booms that are not part of the **mainsail** as well as the rigging, halyards, spreaders, fittings, luff tracks, fairings, instrument displays, instrument sensors, cameras, cables, **media equipment**, flotation systems and hydraulic rams that remain as part of the rig whilst sailing. Sheets shall be considered as part of the **mast** if they cannot be easily disconnected from **mast** structures and control systems.

15.22 **Mast tube**

The principal spar of the **AC40 Class Yacht**, including the components listed in the **mast tube** BOM of the **mast** specification as well as any components or structure which alter the global stiffness of the **mast**. The **mast tube** excludes any other attached components such as luff tracks, **mainsail** support structures and control systems as well as taping or local reinforcements for the connection of such components.

15.23 **Measurement Procedures**

A document detailing the procedures for the measurement of an **AC40 Class Yacht**, including measurement tolerances, written by the **AC40 Measurement Committee** and approved and published by the **Class Authority**.

15.24 **Media Equipment**

Media hardware supplied by the **Regatta Authority**.

15.25 **MWP**

Measurement waterline plane.

15.26 **Perimeter line**

The line on the **hull surface** that forms the perimeter of the **hull surface** when projected on to **MWP**. Where there are multiple coincident points on the perimeter of the projected **hull surface**, the **perimeter line** shall pass through the highest point of each set of coincident points. The projected shape of the **hull surface** is the shape of a shadow it casts on **MWP** from a parallel light source acting normal to **MWP**.

15.27 **Platform**

The **hull**, **foils**, **rudder** and other systems, hardware, fittings, rigging and supplied equipment that is weighed with those components.

15.28 **Regatta Authority**

The body responsible for managing an AC40 regatta, currently AC37 Event Limited (ACE).

15.29 **Rig**

The combination of the **mast**, **mainsail** and **jib**.

15.30 **Rudder**

An appendage positioned on the centreline of the **hull** which is rotated to affect yaw and trim.

15.31 **Sail skin**, also **skin**

A thin and predominantly flexible membrane of a **jib** or **mainsail. Sail skins** include stickers, branding, batten pockets, luff pockets, attachment devices such as bolt ropes and zips as well as any reinforcements such as edge tapes or corner patches.

15.32 **Team**

A participant in an **AC40 Class Yacht** regatta, whether an America's Cup Competitor, youth team, women's team or team unrelated to the America's Cup.

15.33 **TRP**

Transom reference plane.

15.34 **Woolly**

A piece of wool or light fabric used only for flow visualisation.

15.35 **Yacht**

An AC40 Class Yacht.

16 Publication

16.1 When signed below on behalf the **Class Authority**, this version of the **AC40 Class Rule** shall be in effect and shall supersede all previous versions.

AC40 Class Authority	
Name: Daniel Bernasconi	Signature
Date: 2023-10-17	

5.4 AC Technical Regulations (v 1.27 – 8 September 2024)

AC TECHNICAL REGULATIONS

V1.27

8 September 2024

Contents

1 Introduction
2 Language

3 Reference frames and units
4 Component limits and modifications
5 Measurement
6 Non-compliance with the Class Rules
7 Interpretation and amendment
8 Meteorological and oceanographic data
9 Shrouding
10 Reconnaissance
11 Definitions
12 Agreement

1 Introduction

1.1 This document, the **AC Technical Regulations**, defines rules that govern **yachts** sailed by **Competitors** in the 37th America's Cup. It also includes rules relating to shrouding, **Competitors'** chase boats, weather collection and reconnaissance.

1.2 The **AC Technical Regulations** shall be read and interpreted in conjunction with the **AC75 Class Rule** and AC40 Class Rule.

1.3 Rules that classify or provide interpretation within the **AC Technical Regulations**, for instance the "Language", "Reference frames and units" and "Definitions" sections, apply to all documents that comprise the **Class Rules**.

1.4 The **AC75 Class Rule**, the **AC40 Class Rule** and the **AC Technical Regulations** shall be in force from their first publication in non-draft form (without the word 'Draft' on the cover), and **Competitors** shall comply with them until the completion of the final race of the 37th America's Cup.

1.5 The **AC75 Class Rule**, the **AC40 Class Rule** and the **AC Technical Regulations** include:

(a) rules that govern an **AC75 Class Yacht** and an **AC40 Class Yacht**, including how they are constructed and how they are raced, which shall apply during measurement and when racing, unless stated otherwise; and

(b) rules that govern:

(i) procedures of measurement, declaration, interpretation, amendment;

(ii) limits on quantities, manufacture, modification and testing of components;

(iii) weather collection, shrouding, reconnaissance; and

(iv) other matters that are not separately addressed in the **Protocol**; which shall apply at all times unless stated otherwise.

The applicable time-period over which a Rule is in force shall be indicated by the context, but if there is any doubt, shall apply at all times.

2 Language

2.1 The official language of the **Class Rules** is English.
2.2 Within the **Class Rules**, the word "Rule" is a reference to a rule of the **Class Rules**, and unless specified otherwise is a reference to a rule within the same document.
2.3 Where words or phrases are printed in bold type their meaning is defined in Rule 11 of the **AC Technical Regulations**. Bold terms may be be used in modified grammatical forms, in which case any modification to the term relates to a corresponding modification to the definition.
2.4 In some document viewers, the definition of terms in bold may be seen as a tooltip. Although these tooltips are intended to provide the correct and full definitions, they should not be relied upon; the text printed in Rule 11 of the **AC Technical Regulations** is the only authoritative source.
2.5 Where words or phrases are printed in italic type their meaning has a local definition that only applies within that section of the **Class Rules.**
2.6 The interpretation of words not defined in bold shall be made with reference to The Oxford English Dictionary, as it exists online at www.oed.com (or such later official website of the Oxford English Dictionary). In interpretation, the **Rules Committee** shall determine the most appropriate definition of a word within the Oxford English Dictionary, or if no appropriate definition is found, from another authoritative source.
2.7 The words "can" and "may" are permissive, but the permission is restricted when followed by the words "not", "only" or similar. The words "will", "must", and "shall" are mandatory.
2.8 The word "or" is used as an "inclusive or", meaning the same as "and/or", except where it is clearly an "exclusive or" from the grammar or context, such as when:
(a) it is preceded by the word "either"; or
(b) the options separated by the "or" are logically exclusive.
2.9 Where the word "significant" is used, it means "non-negligible", or "sufficiently great or important to be consequential or influential". As an exception, the phrase "significant figure" has its usual mathematical meaning.
2.10 The phrase "for the avoidance of doubt" indicates that the subject that follows is already controlled by a more general Rule, but the specific Rule is included to remove any potential uncertainty in interpretation.

3 Reference frames and units

3.1 The Measurement Waterline Plane, **MWP**, is defined as the horizontal reference plane of the **yacht**.

3.2 The Longitudinal Centre Plane, **LCP**, is defined as a vertical reference plane, orthogonal to **MWP**.
3.3 The Transom Reference Plane, **TRP**, is defined as the vertical reference plane orthogonal to **MWP** and **LCP**.
3.4 The reference planes **MWP**, **LCP** and **TRP** are fixed to the **yacht**, translating and rotating as the **yacht** moves in space.
3.5 Except where otherwise specified, terms such as "above", "below", "up", "down", "forward" and "aft" refer to directions or relative positions aligned to the *xyz*-axes in the **yacht**-fixed reference frame, where:
   (a) the origin is at the intersection of **TRP**, **LCP** and **MWP**;
   (b) *x* is the **longitudinal** axis, positive forward;
   (c) *y* is the **transverse** axis, positive to port;
   (d) *z* is the vertical axis, positive up.
3.6 The **mast** and **mainsail** shall be measured in a **mast**-fixed reference frame, where:
   (a) the origin is at **MRP**;
   (b) *u* is an axis perpendicular to the shear web of the **mast tube**, positive towards the front of the **yacht**;
   (c) *v* is an axis perpendicular to *u* and *w*, positive towards port; and
   (d) *w* is an axis parallel to the intersection of the shear web of the **mast tube** with the **mast centre plane**, positive up.
3.7 The following tolerances shall be applied to all dimensions specified in the **Class Rules**:
   (a) where a measurement is required to be a specific value:
      (i) where decimal places for a unit are given, the measurement shall be accurate to the least significant figure indicated. For example, if a Rule states that a length must be 5.0 m, that length must be at least 4.95 m and less than 5.05 m;
      (ii) where decimal places for a unit are not given, the measurement shall be accurate to within 1% of the figure indicated. For example, if a Rule states that a component must weigh 1000 kg, that component must weigh between 990 kg and 1010 kg inclusive; and
   (b) where a measurement is required to be "at least", "at most", "no less than", "no greater than", "a minimum", "a maximum", "between", "within a range", or other similar wording, no tolerance beyond that limit or outside that range is permitted, but the permitted measurement is inclusive of the limit value. For example, if a Rule states that a length must be no more than 5 m, that length must be no more than 5.000000 m.
3.8 Pressures in the **Class Rules** refer to gauge pressures unless otherwise specified.

4 Component limits and modifications

4.1 Key components of **AC75 Class Yachts** and **LEQ12 yachts** are restricted in quantity and degree of modification. Any listed component that serves or partly serves the purpose of a listed component shall be counted, where:

(a) a component **launched** on an **AC75 Class Yacht** or a **surrogate yacht** shall be treated as an **AC75 Class Yacht** component; and

(b) a component **launched** on an **LEQ12 yacht** shall be treated as an **LEQ12 yacht** component.

4.2 As an exception to Rule 4.1, **in class AC40 Class Yacht** supplied components are not counted in the quantity limits imposed by these Rules if they are installed on an **in class AC40 Class Yacht hull**. However, if:

(a) an **AC40 Class Yacht** supplied component is modified such that it is no longer **in class**; or

(b) installed on any **yacht** except an **in class AC40 Class Yacht hull**; and **launched**, it is then treated as a new **LEQ12 yacht** component.

4.3 For an **AC75 Class Yacht**, the components in the table below are restricted in quantity and degree of modification.

Component	Legacy quantity	Legacy immutable portion	New quantity	New immutable portion	Total quantity
Hull surfaces	1	87.5% area*	1	87.5% area	2
Foil arm stocks	4	See Rule 4.13	4	100% mass	4
Foil wings	2	100% mass	3†	80% mass	5
Foil flaps	2	100% mass	5‡	80% mass	7
Rudders	2	80% mass	2	80% mass	4
Mast tubes	1	See Rule 4.14	2	80% mass	3
Mainsail skins	8	85% area	12	85% area	20
Jib skins	10	85% area	15	85% area	25

* See Rule 4.9. †See Rule 4.10. ‡See Rule 4.11.

4.4 For an **LEQ12 yacht**, all components **launched** after 17th March 2021 shall be counted in the applicable limits. The components in the table below are restricted in quantity and degree of modification.

Component	New quantity	New immutable portion
Hull surfaces	1	87.5% area
Foil arm stocks	2	80% mass
Foil wings	4	80% mass
Foil flaps	4	80% mass
Rudders	1	80% mass
Mast tubes	1	80% mass
Mainsail skins	10	85% area
Jib skins	13	85% area

4.5 The values in the column "Legacy quantity" of Rule 4.3 are the maximum number of legacy components that a **Competitor** may **launch**. A legacy component:

(a) is a component that was declared by a Competitor of **AC36**, which need not be the same **Competitor** that is using it as a legacy component in **AC37**;

(b) in the case of a **foil flap**, is a pair of **AC36** foil flaps, since they were defined as separate items for each side of a **foil wing** in **AC36**;

(c) must have a *Version A* for **AC37** that exactly matches a configuration in which that component was declared to the **Measurement Committee** during **AC36**, where:

(i) such configuration need not be the configuration in which that component was first **launched** during **AC36**, nor the final configuration of that component in **AC36**;

(ii) such configuration need not have been **launched** during **AC36** providing it was declared to the **Measurement Committee** according to the component declaration procedures of **AC36**; and

(iii) the **Competitor launching** a legacy component in **AC37** must provide a declaration to the **Measurement Committee** that the declared configuration matches a declared **AC36** configuration. That declaration must include the date that the specific configuration was declared during **AC36**, and the relevant documentation such as IGES files or drawings supplied to the **AC36** Measurement Committee at that time. If the component has transferred ownership, this declaration must be supported by the **AC36** Competitor that originally declared the com- ponent; and

(d) once declared in **AC37** in accordance with Rule 4.25, is treated in the same way as a new **AC37** component in terms of change and repair allowances described in this Rule subject to the "Legacy immutable portions" tabulated in Rule 4.3.

4.6 The values in the column "New quantity" of Rules 4.3 and 4.4 are the maximum number of new components that a **Competitor** may **launch**. A new component need not be newly built; it could be a modified or unmodified component that was previously declared in **AC36** or **AC37** if that component cannot be declared as a legacy component, or if a **Competitor** chooses not to declare it as a legacy component.

4.7 The values in the column "Total quantity" of Rule 4.3 are the maximum number of components, whether new or legacy, that a **Competitor** may **launch**.

4.8 The quantities tabulated in Rules 4.3 and 4.4 are limits applying per **Competitor**, not per **yacht**.

4.9 The **hull lower surface** of a legacy **hull** cannot be modified; changes to the **hull surface** of a legacy **hull** shall be confined to the **deck**.

4.10 The second and third new **AC75 Class Yacht foil wings** declared by a **Competitor** must have an identical *Version A* design to their first declared new **AC75 Class Yacht foil wing**. Those second and third new **foil wings** must also retain the same immutable portion as the first declared new **foil wing** throughout **AC37**.

4.11 The five new **AC75 Class Yacht foil flaps** shall have between them a maximum of two distinct *Version A* designs, and the new **foil flaps** corresponding each of those two *Version A* designs shall retain the same immutable portions as the first declared of each design throughout **AC37**.

4.12 An **AC75 Class Yacht's foil arm stock** is supplied either with a separate leading edge, or with the leading edge already bonded to the structural spar of the **foil arm stock**. Whether combined or separated, a **Competitor** may **launch** no more leading edges and no more structural spars of the **foil arm stock** than the quantity shown in Table 4.3. However, leading edges up to the permitted quantity may be added to, removed from and swapped between the structural spars of **foil arm stocks**, providing the leading edges and structural spars are weighed, ballasted, numbered and tracked accordingly either by the manufacturer, or subsequently by the **Measurement Committee**.

4.13 The **AC37** *Version A* of a legacy **foil arm stock** shall match the **AC36 foil arm stock** specification. The only modifications that may be made to a legacy **foil arm stock** are to:

(a) update it to match the **AC37 foil arm stock** specification detailed in the "Foil arms" section of the **AC75 Class Rule**; or

(b) to return it to match the **AC36 foil arm stock** specification.

4.14 **AC75** legacy **mast tubes** shall only be modified from their **AC37** *Version A* of the component:
  (a) within the **mast lower zone**; and
  (b) where permitted by drawing "031 AC37 610_Legacy Mast Mod. - Shear Web & Inner Skin Removal" of the AC75 **mast** specification:
    (i) for changes specified as the legacy **mast tube** modification procedure; or
    (ii) for other changes within "Region[s] of permitted change" indicated in the drawing.

4.15 An **AC75** legacy **mast tube** that has been modified according to the legacy **mast** modification drawing of the **mast** specification can be re-declared as a *grandfathered* **mast tube**, where:
  (a) the **mast tube** from which a *grandfathered* **mast tube** is derived must satisfy the requirements of a legacy component prescribed by Rule 4.5, but if it has not been **launched** as a legacy component it shall not count against the "Legacy quantity" limits;
  (b) *Version A* of a *grandfathered* **mast tube** shall be identical to a version of the corresponding legacy **mast tube** that conforms to the legacy **mast** modification drawing of the **mast** specification;
  (c) *Version A* of a *grandfathered* **mast tube** can be a hypothetical configuration permitted by Rule 4.23;
  (d) any region of a *grandfathered* **mast tube** that remains unmodified from its *Version A* must match the specification of a **mast tube** required by the version 1.28 of the **AC75 Class Rule**, except where changes are required by the legacy **mast** modification drawing;
  (e) any region of a *grandfathered* **mast tube** that is modified from its *Version A* shall meet the specifications required for a new **mast** by **AC75 Class Rule** section 15, including the minimum laminate requirements;
  (f) except for the above requirements and permissions, a *grandfathered* **mast tube** shall be deemed to be a new **mast tube** and shall:
    (i) be assigned a new ID, distinct from its **AC36** ID;
    (ii) count against the "New quantity" limit; and
    (iii) be subject to the "New immutable portion" limit tabulated in Rule 4.3; and
  (g) both legacy **mast tubes** and *grandfathered* **mast tubes** are eligible for inclusion in an **AC75 Class Yacht** Measurement Certificate.

4.16 **New Competitors** may substitute up to 4 legacy **mainsail skins** and 5 legacy **jib skins** for equivalent replicas of legacy **sail skins**, provided that:
  (a) the **New Competitor** owns a legacy **hull** with **AC36** sail number 1, 2, 3 or 4 (the *paired **hull***);
  (b) each new replica **sail skin** has an identical blank design to a version of a **sail skin** that was:

(i) **launched** by a **Competitor** of **AC36**; and
(ii) first hoisted on a **mast** stepped on the *paired* ***hull***;
(c) each replica **skin** is only ever hoisted on a **mast** stepped on the *paired* ***hull.***

4.17 The following new **AC75 Class Yacht** components may not be installed on a legacy **AC75 Class Yacht hull**:
(a) **foil wings**;
(b) **foil flaps**;
(c) **rudders**;
(d) **mainsail skins**; and
(e) **jib skins.**

4.18 A component shall be counted in the applicable limits regardless of whether that component satisfies the specific Rules controlling its parameters in the **Class Rules**. In the event that a test component cannot readily be identified as a specific component type, a classification of type and quantity shall be determined by the **Rules Committee** by following the interpretation process detailed in Rule 7.5, where:
(a) components shall be classified according to resemblance in form or function to **AC75 Class Yacht** components, whatever their scale;
(b) test components shall be counted even if they only resemble one aspect of an **AC75 Class Yacht** component, without matching the overall functionality; and
(c) in an extreme case, a single test component may be ruled as comprising multiple declared com- ponents if it is effectively serving the purpose of multiple components, depending on its method of installation in a **yacht**. For example, a double-ended **rudder** that could be installed either way up, with only one half of the component tested at a time, could be ruled as two declared **rudders**. However, a conventional **rudder** that could be installed at different extensions, or an asymmetric **foil wing** with different design concepts on either side of its connection to a **foil arm** shall be treated as a single component.

4.19 **Competitors** must track listed components and versions of those components in a spreadsheet with the following columns:
(a) ID: a number indicating the identity of a physical component;
(b) Version: a letter (or letters) indicating the version letter the component;
(c) SHA: the **SHA** of the component's **blueprint**;
(d) Mass: the mass of the component, for components whose change percentage is controlled by mass;
(e) Area: the controlled surface area of the component, for components whose change percentage is controlled by area;
(f) Comment: text briefly describing the component or type of modification.

Each row shall represent a version of a specific component. The rows shall be grouped by the component ID, where the first row for each component must be the declared *Version A* of that component.

4.20 The ID for a new **AC75 Class Yacht** component shall be distinct from any ID of the same **AC75 Class Yacht** component type **launched** by the same **Competitor** in **AC36**, such that any component from either **AC36** or **AC37** can be uniquely identified by the combination of the **Competitor** that launched it and the com- ponent's ID.

4.21 A new **AC75 Class Yacht hull's** ID or *hull number* shall be allocated by the **Measurement Committee** when it is **launched. Competitors** shall inform the **Measurement Committee** when this occurs, and *hull numbers* will be allocated sequentially, starting with 9, except that culturally objectionable numbers may be skipped at the discretion of the **Measurement Committee.**

4.22 *Hull numbers* for **AC40 Class Yachts** shall be allocated sequentially by the manufacturer, starting at 1.

4.23 *Version A* of a component is the version from which changes to that component are compared and measured. It may be the configuration in which the component was **launched**, or some other hypothetical configuration.

4.24 *Version A* of new **AC75 Class Yacht** components must comply with the relevant rules for that component type.

4.25 Except when restoring a component to a previously declared version, a new version of a component must be declared:

(a) for components whose change percentage is controlled by mass, whenever any change is made to that component, even if there are no changes to its **blueprint**; and

(b) for components whose change percentage is controlled by area, whenever that component changes with respect to its **blueprint**.

4.26 **Competitors** may declare components and component versions by emailing an updated copy of the Rule 4.19 spreadsheet to the **Measurement Committee**. If a component or version of a component has not previously been declared, it must be declared within 48 hours of the component being **launched**.

4.27 For components whose change percentage is controlled by mass, the mass for the first **launched** version of a component must be determined by weighing that component. For other versions, a calculated mass can be declared based on the changes made to a **launched** component, or on a hypothetical configuration, but the **Measurement Committee** may require a component to be weighed at any time.

4.28 The material substance of the portion of the component indicated in Rule 4.3 and 4.4 must remain immutable through the life of the component, whereby:

(a) at least the indicated percentage of the mass or surface area of every version of the component must remain unmodified from *version A* of the component;

(b) a common portion of at least the indicated percentage of the mass or surface area of *version A* of the component must remain unmodified and must match all declared versions of the component; and

(c) if *Version A* does not represent a physical version of a component, the immutable portion of the component must be referenced to material that would be present if the component was modified to *Version A*.

4.29 For **hulls**, **foil wings**, **foil flaps**, **rudders** and **mast tubes**:

(a) the immutable portion of the component may comprise several disjoint regions divided by modified material, but those separate regions must remain in an identical position and orientation with respect to each other through the life of the component;

(b) the **blueprint** of all versions of the component except *Version A* must include a surface entity or entities that enclose (for mass) or overlay (for surface area) regions that satisfy Rules 4.28 (a) and 4.28 (b); and

(c) all **blueprints** for a component must be aligned with respect to these surface entities such that they overlay exactly across all versions.

4.30 For **sail skins**:

(a) the immutable portion of the component may comprise several disjoint regions divided by modified material, and these regions are not required to be in the same position or orientation with respect to each other through the life of the component;

(b) addition or removal of branding or stickers shall not count as modified area provided the structure of the **sail skin** is not significantly altered;

(c) addition of material for repairs or local reinforcement shall not count as modified area provided the original **sail skin** remains; and

(d) replacement of **sail skin** components such as edge tapes, chafe patches, batten pockets, batten end patches, webbings and associated block patching for maintenance will not be counted as modified **sail skin** area.

4.31 Where the **sail skin** of an **LEQ12 yacht** has been accidentally damaged significantly beyond normal wear and tear, and beyond reasonable repair as demonstrated by a **Competitor** to the satisfaction of the **Measurement Committee**, the **Measurement Committee** may give permission for substitution of damaged or absent **sail skin** material, or replacement of the whole **sail skin** provided that:

(a) the **sail skin** has been hoisted on 15 or fewer sailing days;

(b) the replacement material is built only once the **sail skin** has been taken out of service, and that **sail skin** is not installed with the **yacht** afloat again until that repair or replacement is complete;

(c) the replacement material is identical to the material of the **sail skin** that was damaged, where:

(i) the same blank as the damaged **sail skin** shall be provided by the **sail skin** manufacturer; and

(ii) the same re-cuts shall be applied to match the declared version of the damaged **sail skin**;

(d) the **Competitor** informs the **Measurement Committee** when ordering the replacement material and when the repair is complete, and provides the **Measurement Committee** with documentation they require; and

(e) any immutable area that has been declared for the damaged version of the **sail skin** shall remain applicable to the repaired or replaced **sail skin**.

4.32 Changes permitted by Rules 4.30 (c), 4.30 (d) and 4.31 must be no larger than required to address the areas that require repair, reinforcement or maintenance and shall not modify the global behaviour of the original sail.

4.33 As an exception to Rule 4.28, material within a component that has been:

(a) replaced with identical or equivalent material as part of a repair permitted by Rule 4.34;

(b) temporarily repaired according to Rule 4.35; or

(c) modified locally in way of a fitting, or to open, close or change penetrations permitted by the "Hull geometry" section of the **AC75 Class Rule**;

qualifies as an unmodified region.

4.34 It is permitted to repair or replace a new or legacy **hull surface**, **foil arm stock**, **foil wing**, **foil flap**, **rudder** or **mast tube** to restore it to an **AC37** declared configuration, where:

(a) the material substance need not be the same material as in the declared component, providing that except where modification is permitted, surface geometry is identical and the material specification is equivalent to the satisfaction of the **Measurement Committee**; for example:

(i) dry fibre may be substituted for an equivalent pre-preg fibre;

(ii) two plies of 150 g/m^2 may be substituted for one ply of 300 g/m^2; or

(iii) fibre may be substituted for fibre of a different modulus, provided that there is no significant change in the component's stiffness or behaviour under load;

(b) any construction forming part of the repair or replacement is built or prepared only once that com- ponent has been taken out of service, and that component is not installed with the **yacht** afloat again until that repair is complete;

(c) the restriction in Rule 4.34 (b) does not apply to the construction of:

(i) flat monolithic plate which has a uniform construction across the plate;

(ii) flat sandwich panel which has a uniform construction across the panel;

(iii) round tubes of uniform construction and cross-sectional shape;

(iv) parts that do not comprise any of a component's immutable portion when installed;

(v) **commercial products**; or

(vi) commercially available products such as screws or bolts, if approved by the **Measurement Committee.**

but does apply to any incorporation of those components within a repair;

(d) in the case of a repair requiring replacement of more than 1 kg of material, a **Competitor** must inform the **Measurement Committee** when commencing the repair or replacement, and must provide the **Measurement Committee** with documentation they require; and

(e) a **Competitor** alone shall decide whether to repair or replace a component, and no evidence of damage is required.

4.35 If a **hull**, **foil arm stock**, **foil wing**, **foil flap**, **rudder** or **mast tube** is unintentionally damaged and a repair or replacement in accordance with Rule 4.34 cannot be completed in time for the **Competitor's** next race, the **Measurement Committee** may permit a temporary repair using alternative materials and construction methods, providing that:

(a) the repair is no larger than required;
(b) the repaired component is no lighter than prior to the damage;
(c) the repaired component provides no performance advantage over a repair satisfying Rule 4.34;
(d) the outside shape of the repaired component is as close as possible to its shape prior to the damage;
(e) after the repair, the **yacht** still satisfies the **Class Rules**; and
(f) the temporary repair is replaced by a repair in accordance with Rule 4.34 as soon as possible.

5 Measurement

5.1 The **Measurement Committee** may place measurement marks or seals on **yacht** components during construction or upon their completion. These marks or seals may include, but are not limited to, reference screws, punch marks, measurers' signatures, cable ties and stickers, on components or component tooling. **Competitors** shall permit inspections, allow such marks to be placed, and shall not move, remove or alter any such marks or seals without the express consent of the **Measurement Committee.**

5.2 **Competitors** shall permit the **Measurement Committee** to:

(a) interview team members; and
(b) require team members to complete affidavits,

relating to questions from the **Measurement Committee** on design, construction or use of components on the **yacht**.

5.3 Except where specified, it is not the responsibility of a **Competitor** to provide categorical proof of compliance with the **Class Rules**. Where proof by inspection or measurement is impractical, the **Measurement Committee** shall rely on interviews, affidavits and reference documentation. However, it always remains the responsibility of a **Competitor** to ensure that their **yacht** complies with the **Class Rules**, including in areas that cannot be easily measured.

5.4 Leading up to **events**, the **Measurement Committee** will publish dates of measurement periods, during which **Competitors** may present their **yachts** for measurement. The **Measurement Committee** will inspect the **yachts** for compliance with the **Class Rules**, and **Competitors** shall provide whatever assistance is reasonably requested by the **Measurement Committee** to facilitate this process.

5.5 The **Measurement Committee** shall use its own equipment for measuring a **Competitor's yacht**, except that a **Competitor's** equipment may be used at the discretion of the **Measurement Committee** if it is calibrated against the **Measurement Committee's** equipment and sealed to their satisfaction.

5.6 When weighing components of a **yacht**, **Competitors** shall be permitted to dry any water on the surface of those components and replace wet rigging with equivalent dry rigging. The **Measurement Committee** shall make reasonable allowances for wet sail weights.

5.7 Where specific tolerances for component measurement are not given in the **Class Rules**, the **Measurement Committee** may make an allowance for unintended distortion of a component during manufacture when checking the shape of such a component against its **blueprint**.

5.8 The **Measurement Committee** shall, at times they choose during **AC37**, make spot checks of compliance with component declarations by requiring a **Competitor** to declare to them what component versions they sailed with on their last sailing day. The **Measurement Committee** may also request, and **Competitors** shall supply, **blueprints** corresponding to those component versions and declared **SHAs**.

5.9 Except as otherwise specified, **Competitors** are not required to routinely supply construction drawings of declared components. However, if the **Measurement Committee** have any doubt as to the compliance of a component they may request such drawings, which shall then be supplied by the **Competitor**.

5.10 **Competitors** shall inform the **Measurement Committee** immediately if they make any changes or repairs to the **yacht** that could affect her measurement certificate or her compliance with the **Class Rules**.

5.11 The **Measurement Committee** reserve the right to re-measure or inspect any aspect of a **yacht** at any time, before or after sailing, and may publish procedures for regular measurement inspections.

5.12 When a measurement period is open:

(a) if the **Measurement Committee** believes there is ambiguity as to whether an element of a **Competitor's yacht** satisfies the **Class Rules**, they shall seek the advice of the **Rules Committee**. If the ambiguity remains, the **Rules Committee** shall rule confidentially on the compliance or otherwise of the **yacht**, based on the information presented to them by the **Measurement Committee**, after which a measurement certificate may be issued or withheld;

(b) if the **Rules Committee** becomes aware of an element of a **Competitor's yacht** that may not satisfy the **Class Rules**, they shall ask the **Measurement Committee** to inspect the element and report to them. The **Rules Committee** shall then rule confidentially on the compliance or otherwise of the **yacht**, after which a measurement certificate may be withdrawn or withheld;

(c) decisions on the compliance of a **yacht** made by the **Measurement Committee** and/or the **Rules Committee** may subsequently be changed by the **Measurement Committee** or the **Rules Commit- tee** if new information comes to light, or if they believe the original decision was made in error. Only an interpretation or an amendment to the Rule providing clarification shall provide a **Competitor** with a guarantee of continuing compliance of an ambiguous design element; and

(d) if a measurement certificate is withheld from a **Competitor**, the **Measurement Committee** shall explain in full the reasons why the **yacht** does not comply with the **Class Rules**, including the detail of decisions made or advice given by the **Rules Committee**.

5.13 During training or racing, **Competitors** shall permit the **Measurement Committee** to install small video cameras onboard their **yachts** to assist the **Measurement Committee** in determining compliance, where:

(a) the mass of these cameras shall not be included in the measurement mass of the **yacht**;

(b) the **Measurement Committee** shall where possible locate the cameras in locations that minimise any increase in aerodynamic drag, providing they are still able to capture the details required; and

(c) **Competitors** shall not adjust nor deliberately obstruct the view from these cameras.

6 Non-compliance with the Class Rules

6.1 After a measurement certificate has been issued for an **event** or **AC75 event stage**, if the **Measurement Committee**:

(a) determines that it has issued a measurement certificate in error, and that a **yacht** is non-compliant with the **Class Rules**;

(b) determines that a new interpretation issued by the **Rules Committee** renders a **yacht** non-compliant with the **Class Rules**;

(c) determines that a **yacht** is non-compliant with the **Class Rules** as a result of a query of compliance by a **Competitor** detailed by Rule 6.7; or

(d) is informed by the **Rules Committee** that a **yacht** is non-compliant with the **Class Rules** following the process described by Rule 5.12 (b);

they shall notify the **Regatta Director**, notify all **Competitors** and follow the process detailed in Rule 6.2. No penalty shall be applied relating to races sailed when non-compliant unless a condition within Rule 6.3 is also found to apply.

6.2 If a **Competitor's yacht** is found to be non-compliant with the **Class Rules** according to Rule 6.1, a determination of the **Competitor's** ability to rectify the non-compliance in time for the next race shall be made by the **Regatta Director** in consultation with the **Measurement Committee**, and:

(a) if they find that the **Competitor** is able to rectify the non-compliance, and the **yacht** can be re- inspected before the next race, the **Measurement Committee** shall withdraw the **yacht's** measurement certificate immediately;

(b) otherwise, the **Regatta Director** may grant a grace period which shall end no later than:

(i) the end of the following day, if the **yacht** has a race on the following day that is scheduled to start within 24 hours of the current time; otherwise

(ii) the end of the current day;

the current time being the time at which the **Measurement Committee** notifies the **Regatta Director** and all **Competitors** of the non-compliance. The **Measurement Committee** shall withdraw the **yacht's** measurement certificate at the expiry of any grace period.

6.3 After a measurement certificate has been issued for an **event** or **AC75 event stage**, if the **Measurement Committee** determines that:

(a) a **yacht** has been modified without the approval of the **Measurement Committee** and:

(i) may no longer be compliant with the **Class Rules**; or

(ii) no longer matches the configuration specified in her measurement certificate; or

(b) a **Competitor** has made a false declaration;

they shall withdraw the **yacht's** measurement certificate and follow the process detailed in Rule 6.4.

6.4 If a **yacht's** measurement certificate has been withdrawn according to Rule 6.3, and the **yacht** has raced in a non-compliant configuration, the **Measurement Committee** shall notify the **Jury**, the **Regatta Director** and all **Competitors** with details of:

(a) the non-compliance;

(b) any races the **yacht** may have raced in whilst non-compliant; and

(c) the **Measurement Committee's** assessment of any potential performance implications of the non- compliance.

6.5 On receiving notification from the **Measurement Committee** according to Rule 6.4, the **Regatta Director** shall review the non-compliance, requesting further investigation if necessary. As a result, if the **Regatta Director** determines that the non-compliance is:

(a) unintentional, and unlikely to have impacted the outcome of a race, the **Jury**, in consultation with the **Regatta Director** may impose a fine on the **Competitor**;

(b) intentional, or could have impacted the outcome of a race, the **Jury**, in consultation with the **Regatta Director** may disqualify the **yacht** from:

(i) the last race in which the **yacht** competed if the **yacht** competed in only one race while non-compliant; or

(ii) the last two races in which the **yacht** competed whilst non-compliant.

6.6 A **Competitor** whose measurement certificate has been withdrawn must rectify the non-compliance, present their **yacht** for re-measurement and receive a new measurement certificate prior to being eligible for any further racing in the current **event** or **AC75 event stage**.

6.7 During an **event**, a **Competitor** may query the compliance of another **Competitor's yacht** by sending an email to the **Measurement Committee** that details the potential areas of non-compliance. The **Measurement Committee** shall investigate and:

(a) if the **Measurement Committee** finds that the **yacht** complies with the **Class Rules**, they shall notify the **Regatta Director** and all **Competitors** with details of the investigation and an explanation as to why they are satisfied that the **yacht** continues to comply; or

(b) if the **Measurement Committee** finds that the **yacht** does not comply with the **Class Rules**, they shall proceed according to Rule 6.1.

6.8 The total number of measurement compliance queries that may be made by each **Competitor** shall be limited as follows:

(a) two queries in each Preliminary Regatta;

(b) three queries in the America's Cup Challenger Selection Series; and

(c) two queries in the America's Cup Match.

Any measurement compliance queries that result in the **Measurement Committee** determining that the **yacht** in question is non-compliant with the **Class Rules** shall be excluded from these limits.

6.9 If a **yacht** is unintentionally damaged whilst racing to the extent that she is no longer compliant with the **Class Rules**, or no longer matches the configuration specified in her measurement certificate, the **Measurement Committee** shall notify the **Regatta Director** with details of:

(a) the non-compliance;

(b) any races the **yacht** may have raced in whilst non-compliant; and

(c) the potential performance implications of the non-compliance.

If the **Regatta Director** in consultation with the **Measurement Committee** determine that the non- compliance is unlikely to have increased the performance of the **yacht**, no penalty shall be applied relating to races already sailed; otherwise, the **Regatta Director** shall inform the **Jury** who in consultation with the **Regatta Director** may impose a penalty at their discretion.

6.10 After a **yacht** has been damaged as described by Rule 6.9, if:

(a) it is not possible for repairs to be made to restore the **yacht** to a compliant condition in time for her next race (after accounting for any changes permitted by a substitution schedule); and

(b) the **Measurement Committee** determines that any damage or subsequent temporary repair could not positively impact the performance of the **yacht**;

the **yacht** may be granted an exemption to the specific **Class Rules** or parts of her measurement certificate that she cannot comply with, and permitted to race.

6.11 The decision to grant an exemption described in Rule 6.10 shall be made by:

(a) the **Regatta Director** in consultation with the **Measurement Committee**, for any races that are scheduled on the same sailing day in which the damage occurred; and

(b) the **Jury**, in consultation with the **Regatta Director** and the **Measurement Committee**, for any races on subsequent sailing days. In this case, prior to making their decision, the **Jury**:

(i) may decide to provide details of the damage, repair and substitution options to other **Competitors** affected by their decision so that those **Competitors** have an opportunity to provide relevant technical feedback; and

(ii) must be entirely satisfied that Rules 6.10 (a) and 6.10 (b) apply; prior to granting such an exemption.

In any case in which an exemption is granted, the **yacht** shall be restored to a compliant condition as soon as possible.

7 Interpretation and amendment

7.1 The **AC75 Class Rule** may be amended:

(a) at any time by unanimous consent of **Competitors**, either:

(i) via the mechanism described in Rules 7.5; or

(ii) by another process;

(b) at any time by the **Rules Committee**, with the agreement of **COR/D** and the **Regatta Director** (if they have been appointed), for changes relating to:

(i) supplied or specified components;

(ii) the supplied ultrasonic transmitter specified in the "Foil Wings" section of the **AC75 Class Rule**;

(iii) standard pressure relief valves and the supplied high-pressure **hydraulic accumulator** specified in the "Hydraulics" section of the **AC75 Class Rule**;
(iv) the use of Samsung Knox management software specified in the "Crew information system" section of the **AC75 Class Rule**;
(v) the permission or requirement for additional **hull** penetrations, ducts, fans, radiators or other components for cooling the internal **hull** volume and enclosed systems;
(vi) safety;
(vii) **media equipment** specifications; or
(viii) **event** branding,

including their impact on masses and centres of mass controlled by **AC75 Class Rule**. In making any such amendments, the **Rules Committee** shall consider the impact of their proposed changes on all **Competitors**, taking account of the state of their design and construction programmes, so that any burden imposed is commensurate with the need for amendment.

(c) by **COR/D** alone for the items listed in Rule 7.1 (b) if the **Rules Committee** has not yet been appointed.

7.2 The **AC40 Class Rule** may be amended at any time by the **Defender**.

7.3 The **AC Technical Regulations** may be amended:
(a) according to the same conditions that apply to the **AC75 Class Rule** in Rule 7.1;
(b) for Rule 4, "Component limits and modifications", by **COR/D** at any time; and
(c) for Rule 10, "Reconnaissance", by **COR/D** at any time.

7.4 If the date for the first race of the 37th America's Cup Match is announced to be at any time before 1st January 2024 or after 1st September 2024, any dates within the **AC75 Class Rule** and **AC Technical Regulations** may be amended by **COR/D** during the 10 **working days** following such an announcement. This Rule applies to both an original announcement of the date, and to any subsequent announcement of a change in date.

7.5 A **Competitor** may submit a Rule Enquiry regarding the **AC75 Class Rule** or **AC Technical Regulations** to the **Rules Committee** in the form of:
(a) an interpretation request;
(b) an amendment proposal, with or without additional commentary;
(c) two or more alternative proposals for an amendment; or
(d) a combination of the above.

7.6 Requests submitted according to Rule 7.5:
(a) shall be a Microsoft Word document or compatible format, so that it can be edited easily;
(b) may include references to relevant paragraph numbers within the **Class Rules**, indicated as "75-X.X", "40-X.X" or "TR-X.X", but should not

include formal excerpts of those Rules except where used directly in the context of the question;

(c) shall be in a form that can be directly and immediately forwarded to all **Competitors** without the need for further editing; and

(d) shall be submitted by email to the **Rules Committee** or if advised, to a specific Rule Enquiry email address.

A mechanism may be implemented whereby these requests are forwarded automatically to **Competitors** as soon as they are received; otherwise, the **Rules Committee** shall forward them as soon as possible. In either case, the email subject line of the forwarded request shall include a sequential Rule Enquiry number.

7.7 The **Rules Committee** can also initiate a Rule Enquiry, providing that it does not reveal a design characteristic that might not have been considered by all **Competitors**.

7.8 When the **Rules Committee** receives a Rule Enquiry:

(a) The **Rules Committee** shall immediately publish the Enquiry, if not automatically distributed.

(b) By 8pm of the 4th **working day**, considering the day that the Rule Enquiry is published as the first **working day**, **Competitors** may reply to the **Rules Committee** to:

(i) consent to a draft amendment;

(ii) supply comments on the interpretation and/or amendment proposal; or

(iii) propose an alternative amendment wording.

(c) Within 4 **working days** of the feedback from **Competitors** being due:

(i) *If* there is sufficient consent to implement a proposed amendment according to the conditions of Rules 7.1, 7.2 and 7.3, *then* the **Rules Committee** shall amend the relevant documents of the **Class Rules**, publish the new version, and mark the Rule Enquiry as closed.

(ii) *Else if* the **Rules Committee** consider that there is the possibility that the issue can be re- solved by an amendment, *then* they shall propose or revise a draft amendment, this option being preferred to an interpretation.

(iii) *Else if* there was no interpretation question as part of Rule Enquiry, the **Rules Committee** shall mark the Rule Enquiry as closed, there being no agreement on a proposed amendment.

(iv) *Else if* at least one interpretation draft has previously been circulated and the **Rules Committee**, having reviewed all feedback, is satisfied that the interpretation cannot be improved *then* they shall publish the previously circulated interpretation draft as a final interpretation and mark the Rule Enquiry as closed.

(v) *Else* the **Rules Committee** shall propose or revise a draft interpretation response, subject to Rule 7.9.

(d) If not closed, the process shall then return to step 7.8 (b).

7.9 At the step described by Rule 7.8 (c) (v), if the **Rules Committee**, after considering the feedback from **Competitors**, determine an interpretation request included in the Rule Enquiry to be unreasonably long, or to cover an unreasonably large number or matrix of possible scenarios, they may withdraw the request and request the original **Competitor** to re-submit the Rule Enquiry with an interpretation request that limits the scope of the question to those elements which better clarify ambiguity in the **Class Rules**.

7.10 The Rule Enquiry, all **Competitor** responses, and all draft and final responses by the **Rules Committee** shall be published by the **Rules Committee** to the Official Noticeboard (as defined in the **protocol**). **Competitor** responses will not be published until either all responses have been received or the deadline detailed by Rule 7.8 (b) has passed, whichever is earlier. The Rule Enquiry and responses from the **Rules Committee** shall be published as soon as they are issued.

7.11 Rule Enquiries and response documents from **Competitors** shall be published in the form in which they are received without any additional information indicating who they are from. **Competitors** may anonymise their submission.

7.12 The **Rules Committee** may, at their discretion, shorten any of the times allowed in Rule 7.8, particularly leading up to **events**.

7.13 With the agreement of the **Competitor** seeking the amendment or interpretation, the **Rules Committee** may lengthen any of the times allowed in Rule 7.8.

7.14 Interpretations shall be based on the following principles:

(a) interpretations shall consider only the words in the **Class Rules**, not their possible intent;

(b) where wording is ambiguous, the most reasonable and natural interpretation of the written words within the context of any other relevant **Class Rules** shall be taken;

(c) if a part of the **Class Rules**, or the understanding of it created by the application of clause 7.14 (b), is found to directly contradict another part, a part that refers to more detail shall take precedence over a part that is more general; and

(d) finally, if there remains ambiguity or contradiction as to whether a particular feature is permitted, and that ambiguity or contradiction cannot be resolved by application of the above clauses, an interpretation shall be permissive.

7.15 Draft responses from the **Rules Committee** shall not constitute a ruling of any form. Whilst **Competitors** may comment on these drafts, they are inadmissible as evidence of any interpretation of the **Class Rules** unless published as final.

7.16 The **Rules Committee** may seek the advice of independent experts, including members of the **Measurement Committee**, when considering an interpretation.

7.17 **Competitors** shall not conduct any private correspondence with the **Rules Committee** regarding any Rule, interpretation or amendment. Correspondence shall only be in the form described by Rule 7.5, or within a group forum which all **Competitors** are invited to attend.

7.18 Advice or opinions on the meaning of a Rule, from a member of the **Measurement Committee** or **Rules Committee**, are not binding except through an interpretation.

7.19 Once an interpretation has been issued as final, it cannot be modified without the explicit agreement of all **Competitors**.

7.20 Interpretations that relate specifically to wording within the **Class Rules** that has since been amended no longer apply.

7.21 Separately to the interpretation and amendment process described in the above rules, **Competitors** may request clarification of the construction or operational requirements of specified or supplied components including **foil arm stocks**, **mast tube** specifications, **supplied rigging** and the **FCS**. Requests for clarification should be made to the **Rules Committee** who, after consultation with the designers of those parts, will issue a clarification notice to all **Competitors**.

8 Meteorological and oceanographic data

8.1 After the announcement of the **Match venue**, **Competitors** shall only collect weather, wind, sea state or sea current instrument data relevant to the **Match venue**:

(a) from devices that measure weather, wind, sea state or sea current within 100 mm of a sensor mounted on any of a **Competitor's** *eligible* **yachts**;

(b) from a chase boat that is *supporting* one of that **Competitor's** *eligible* **yachts**, limited to two chase boats per **yacht**, which must be the primary chase boats for that **yacht**; and

(c) as permitted by the **Protocol**.

8.2 With reference to Rule 8.1, **Competitor's yachts** are *eligible* provided that:

(a) **Competitors** shall be limited to a maximum of two *eligible* **yachts** per day; and

(b) during an **event**, whenever any of a **Competitor's yachts** are within their *racing period*, the only *eligible* **yachts** for that **Competitor** shall be those **yachts** that are currently within their *racing period*, where a *racing period* for a **yacht** is the period that:

(i) begins 45 minutes before the warning signal of that **yacht's** race; and

(ii) ends at the completion of that race.

8.3 A *supporting* chase boat is defined as follows:

(a) On any sailing day, during the time that a **Competitor's yacht** is away from the dock, a *supporting* chase boat must spend at least 80% of that time:

(i) following, towing or alongside their **yacht**;

(ii) setting marks for their **yacht**;

(iii) waiting or manoeuvring on a course on which their **yacht** is sailing;

(iv) travelling directly between the **Competitor's** shore base and their **yacht**; or

(v) at a **Competitor's** shore base.

(b) When a **Competitor's yacht** is not sailing, a *supporting* chase boat shall only:

(i) travel directly to and from the **Competitor's** shore base for the purpose of refuelling or maintenance; or

(ii) remain at a **Competitor's** shore base.

8.4 When at the **Match venue**, after it has been announced, wind measuring devices shall only be installed on **Competitors'** chase boats if:

(a) they are *supporting* their **yacht**;

(b) the wind measuring devices are covered rendering them inoperable; or

(c) the **Regatta Director** has given permission for their use.

9 Shrouding

9.1 No component or part of the **yacht** shall be covered for the purpose of hiding it from reconnaissance once it has been **launched**, or when it is about to be **launched** (i.e. prepared for being lifted into the water), unless:

(a) it is not being used for sailing operations on that day; or

(b) the item providing cover (the 'cover') is a part of the **yacht** that satisfies the **AC75 Class Rules**, and remains in the same position whilst sailing.

9.2 Any temporary cover used for physical or sun protection during sailing operations shall be immediately removed at the request of reconnaissance teams. The **Measurement Committee** may remove the right of a **Competitor** to use any such covers if they believe the covers are being used to hinder the role of reconnaissance units.

10 Reconnaissance

10.1 Applicability

(a) This section sets out the regulations governing a Joint **Competitor** Reconnaissance Programme and other **Competitor** reconnaissance activity.

(b) The Joint Reconnaissance Programme shall be in place from the first official publication of these **AC Technical Regulations**.

(c) For each **Competitor** the Joint Reconnaissance Programme shall end:

(i) two months before the first race of the *Final Preliminary Regatta* for any **yacht** sailed by that **Competitor** in the **Match venue**; after which there will be no **Recon Unit** appointed to follow that **Competitor's yachts** in the **Match venue**; or

(ii) one week before the first race of the *Match* for any **yacht** sailed by a **Competitor** anywhere other than the **Match venue**, after which there will be no **Recon Unit** appointed to follow that **Competitor's yachts**.

(d) At the following times and places:

(i) the venue of each of the first and second *Initial Preliminary Regattas*, during the time period starting at 08:00 seven days before the programmed start of the first race and ending at 23:59 on the day of the final race (in the local time zone of the regatta); and

(ii) any venue designated by the **Regatta Director** for *Official Training* or *Official Practice*, on the days that are designated as *Official Training* days or *Official Practice* days the restrictions and requirements of Rule 10.13 do not apply, and any sailing by a **Competitor** in an **in class AC40 Class Yacht** is not required to be notified, observed or declared as a **Sailing Session**.

(e) At times and places other than those exempted by Rule 10.1 (d), any *operation* by a **Competitor** in an **in class AC40 Class Yacht** shall be notified as required by Rule 10.6. If the **Recon Administrator** determines that the deployment of the **Recon Unit** is not required, Rules 10.5 (a), 10.7, 10.9 and 10.12 (a) (ii) shall not apply.

(f) An **in class AC40 Class Yacht** is one whose components restricted by Rule 4.4 are all **in class**.

(g) Within Section 10, when italicised:

(i) *operate* or *operation* means to launch, sail, tow, move, test, measure, assemble, modify, disassemble or similar.

(ii) *component* means a **hull**, **foil arm stock**, **foil wing**, **foil flap**, **rudder**, **mast tube**, **mainsail skin**, **jib skin** or significant part thereof.

(iii) *Initial Preliminary Regatta, Final Preliminary Regatta, Official Training* and *Official Practice* are defined by the **Protocol**.

(h) Once the Joint **Competitor** Reconnaissance Programme has ended according to Rule 10.1 (c), Rule 10.15 shall apply.

10.2 **RMP**

(a) Within two weeks of their entry into the 37th America's Cup being accepted, or within one week of the first official publication of these **AC**

Technical Regulations, whichever is later, each **Competitor** shall appoint a team member as their recon representative and notify the **Recon Administrator** of this person. This person shall be a member of all **RMPs** that the **Competitor** is a part of.

(b) Any change in a **Competitor's RMP** representative shall be notified to the **Recon Administrator**.

(c) The **Recon Administrator** may convene and manage meetings of **RMPs**, but shall not be entitled to vote.

(d) Decisions within **RMPs** shall be made by a majority vote. In the event of a tie, a casting vote shall be given to:

(i) the **Defender**, for the **RMP** that follows the **Challenger of Record**; and

(ii) the **Challenger of Record**, for all other **RMPs**.

(e) Any **Competitor** currently in default of its obligation under Article 20 of the Protocol shall be ineligible to participate in an **RMP**.

10.3 **Recon Unit** appointment

(a) One **Recon Unit** shall be appointed to follow each **Competitor**, that appointment to occur during the two months before a **Competitor's** first **Sailing Session** (see Rule 10.6).

(b) Each **Recon Unit** will comprise two people, of which at least one shall hold any licence required to operate the recon vessel in the operating country.

(c) It is envisaged that **Recon Unit** personnel shall have expertise in sailing and the America's Cup environment, and that at least one member of the team shall have experience in media content generation. However, the decision on personnel will be solely the responsibility of the relevant **RMP**.

(d) An **RMP** may ask an **Observed Competitor** for a recommendation of suitable local personnel but shall not be obliged to follow that recommendation.

(e) Compensation for each **Recon Unit** will be the same for all contracted **Recon Units**, as outlined in Part 12 of these Conditions; other contractual terms will also be identical except as otherwise required by applicable laws. Initial discussions with prospective **Recon Unit** personnel shall be between those prospective personnel and the respective **RMP**. When an agreement is reached, the **RMP** shall inform the **Recon Administrator** of their chosen personnel, who will then confirm the appointment with the recon personnel and make arrangements for payment of their compensation. The **Recon Administrator** shall not refuse any appointment unless a person is not legally permitted to work in the given role, or is determined by the Arbitration Panel to be unsuitable for the role following an application by the **Observed Competitor** or the **Recon Administrator**.

(f) A **Recon Unit** shall be engaged from one week before the first **Sailing Session** until the termination of the joint reconnaissance programme.

(g) A **Recon Unit** shall travel with their **Observed Competitor** to any location where they are sailing, including the **Match venue**, except that they shall only travel to the venue of an *Initial Preliminary Regatta* if the **Observed Competitor** is sailing at that venue:

(i) outside of the period during which sailing in an **in class AC40 Class Yacht** is not required to be notified, observed or declared as a **Sailing Session** by Rule 10.1 (d); or

(ii) any **yacht** other than an **in class AC40 Class Yacht**,

where the italicised terms are defined by the **Protocol**. Travel and accommodation costs for each **Recon Unit** shall be dealt with in accordance with Part 12 of these Conditions.

(h) Alternatively, an **RMP** may elect to switch their **Recon Unit** personnel to local personnel at each venue at which their **Observed Competitor** is sailing.

10.4 **Recon Unit** replacement

(a) An **RMP** may elect to replace a **Recon Unit** at any time, subject to any notice period or other restriction contained in their contract or applicable law. Such notice period is anticipated to be one month but may vary according to applicable law.

(b) In the event that a **Recon Unit** is to be replaced, the **RMP** shall inform the **Recon Administrator**, who shall make the necessary contractual arrangements.

(c) An **RMP** shall be required to replace a **Recon Unit** if that **Recon Unit** is no longer able to work in the country that their **Observed Competitor** is sailing.

10.5 Recon vessels

(a) During any **Sailing Session**, an **Observed Competitor** must make a recon vessel available to their **Recon Unit**, which shall:

(i) be at least 9 m long, of a form equivalent to a Protector rib;

(ii) have a top speed in flat water of at least 45kts;

(iii) provide a windscreen and covered area for at least two people;

(iv) be in good working order;

(v) be otherwise suitable as a working recon vessel;

(vi) be moored at or within five minutes' walk of that **Observed Competitor's** base, and accessible to the **Recon Unit**;

(vii) be available for use by the **Recon Unit** at least one day before any **Sailing Session**, and always remain available for that **Sailing Session**.

(b) In the event that there is a disagreement between the **Observed Competitor** and the **Recon Administrator** as to the validity of the licence held by the **Recon Unit** driver, or the legality or capability of the **Recon Unit** driver to operate the recon vessel, the **Observed Competitor** shall provide a suit- ably qualified driver to drive the recon vessel, who shall operate under the direct instruction of the appointed **Recon Unit**.

(c) With the agreement of the **Recon Administrator** in consultation with the respective **Recon Unit**, an **Observed Competitor** may provide a recon vessel whose specifications fall slightly below those required by Rule 10.5 (a). However, if this recon vessel proves unfit for purpose as determined by the **Recon Administrator** and the **Recon Unit**, the **Observed Competitor** shall be required to replace the recon vessel with a vessel that meets the requirements of Rule 10.5 (a) within a time frame determined by the **Recon Administrator**.

(d) An **Observed Competitor** shall make best endeavours to ensure the provided recon vessel is al- ways in service. If the provided vessel is at any time inoperable or out of service, and a suitable replacement boat is not available, the **Recon Unit** shall be entitled to observe from the **Observed Competitor's** primary chase boat.

(e) An **Observed Competitor** shall either ensure the recon vessel boat is fuelled for a day, or provide the **Recon Unit** with a fuel card or other payment method for purchasing fuel.

(f) Subject to the relevant **Recon Unit's** operational requirements, an **Observed Competitor** may on occasion place team members, VIPs or media on the provided recon vessel, to accompany the **Recon Unit**, but the boat shall be skippered by the **Recon Unit** who shall make all decisions about the boat's location and schedule. If additional personnel on recon vessels are found to hinder the operational duties of the **Recon Units**, the combination of all **RMPs** can elect to suspend this right.

(g) Unless agreed otherwise between the **Recon Unit** and the **Observed Competitor**, a **Recon Unit** shall only use the recon vessel for reconnaissance of an **Observed Competitor** whilst sailing, before sailing, or after sailing, or to re-fuel the vessel, etc.

10.6 Notification

(a) An **Observed Competitor** shall notify their **RMP** and the **Recon Administrator** a minimum of two months prior to their first roll out of a new **yacht** into *public view* at any *sailing venue*, in preparation for their first **Sailing Session**, where:

(i) *public view* means a location from where there is a line of sight to any part of the **yacht** from a viewing point that is readily and easily accessible to the general public, accessible by foot or by boat (using a sightline 2 m above mean sea level for any boat), and within 200 m of the location of the mast base of the **yacht**; and

(ii) a *sailing venue* is a location where a **Competitor** will launch a **yacht** and the zone within a radius of 10 km around that location.

(b) An **Observed Competitor** shall notify their **RMP** and the **Recon Administrator** a minimum of two months before sailing at a new location (i.e. a location at which the **Observed Competitor** has previously never sailed any **Yacht**).

(c) It is strictly prohibited for a **Competitor** to sail or tow a **yacht** at any location without having notified their **RMP** and the **Recon Administrator** as required above.

(d) Once a **Recon Unit** is appointed, the **Recon Administrator** shall put them in contact with their **Ob- served Competitor**, who shall arrange access and notification.

(e) An **Observed Competitor** must provide 24 hours' notice to their **Recon Unit**, **RMP** and the **Recon Administrator** of their intent to *operate* on a **yacht** or any of its *components* in *public view* at a *sailing venue* for any reason.

(f) The **Competitor** should notify the **Recon Unit** again, as soon as possible, if that **yacht** or *component's operation* notified according to Rule 10.6 (e) is cancelled. They shall keep the **Recon Unit** informed of planned *operation* times.

(g) If the **Competitor** intends to leave a **yacht** or a **yacht** *component* in *public view* for an extended period without conducting an *operation*, they must notify their **Recon Unit** and the **Recon Administrator**. The **Recon Administrator** will determine which days are appropriate for the **Recon Unit** to be deployed and notify the **RMP** of their decision.

(h) If the **yacht** notified according to Rule 10.6 is an **in class AC40 Class Yacht**, this shall be declared to the **Competitor**'s **Recon Unit** and the **Recon Administrator**. The **Recon Administrator** will determine which days are appropriate for the **Recon Unit** to be deployed and notify the **RMP** of their decision.

(i) A **Competitor** must notify a **Recon Unit** of planned **Sailing Sessions**, days off and extended non- sailing periods as soon as they are known and notify them again as soon as possible if those plans change. The notice period for any such notification of a **Sailing Session** shall not be less than the gap between consecutive **Sailing Sessions**.

(j) Each time a **Competitor** sends an updated component schedule to the **Measurement Committee**, a copy shall also be sent to their **RMP**, **Recon Unit** and **AC Media**. This component shall indicate component IDs and versions but need not include any descriptions.

(k) Notification shall be by text or email.

10.7 Access

(a) On any day which shall be notified according to Rule 10.6 (e), if an **Observed Competitor** intends to launch, sail or tow any of their **yachts**, they shall provide their **Recon Unit** access to the forecourt on which they roll-out, or from which they launch their **yachts** in a location that provides an unobstructed view of the **yacht** (except where obstructed by the **yacht's** cradle, etc). Such location shall be no more than 25m from the location of the mast base of the **yacht** when preparing to launch, or when in *public view* for any reason if not preparing to launch.

(b) A **Competitor** shall provide access to the edge of a wharf overlooking the **yacht** when at the dock, or to the dock itself, at a location that provides an unobstructed view of the **yacht** and is no further than 25m from the mast base of the **yacht.**

(c) **Recon Units** must abide by the health and safety regulations of the **Observed Competitor**, and may be required to move from the nominated locations during crane operations, etc. However, the **Observed Competitor** shall not impose health and safety regulations on their **Recon Unit** that are above and beyond those of the **Observed Competitor's** own team members, and shall provide the **Recon Unit** with the appropriate health and safety training if necessary for them to observe a **yacht** launch.

(d) Following a sailing day, a **Competitor** shall provide access to one sailor who sailed on the **yacht** that day, or a designer who was on the water, for an interview lasting no more than 3 minutes, within 15 minutes of docking. This interview shall be with a:

(i) helmsperson at least 25% of the occasions;

(ii) foil or aero trimmer, or grinder, on at least 25% of the occasions;

(iii) a designer on at least 25% of the occasions.

(e) On request, a **Competitor** shall provide access to a suitable member of their technical team to pro- vide commentary or explanation on an aspect of another **Competitor's yacht**, a recent interpretation draft, **Class Rules** amendment, or similar.

(f) **Competitors** shall not be obstructive in answering interview questions, and whilst they are permitted to withhold confidential information, shall provide an informative report on the sailing day.

10.8 Recon equipment

(a) **AC Media**, in conjunction with the **Recon Administrator**, shall provide to each **Recon Unit** a standard set of recon equipment including cameras, video cameras, gimbals, a hand-held anemometer, laptops and software.

(b) **Recon Units** shall not use any photo or video equipment for recon except that standard equipment provided, and/or their own personal mobile phones.

10.9 **Recon Unit** duties

Prior to and during any **Sailing Session** at a *sailing venue*, a **Recon Unit** shall:

(a) Take photos and video of a **Competitor's yacht** on each

   (i) roll-out into *public view*, whether launching or not;

   (ii) launch and lift-out, whether sailing or not;

   (iii) sailing session.

(b) Follow a sailing day on the water, record the amount of sailing time vs. stoppage and towing time, sails used, approximate wind speeds and sea-state, approximate boat speeds and sailing angles, significant events, crew changes, etc.

(c) Interview a team member following a day's sailing, asking about what was learnt, how the day went, and for feedback on any new *components*, design features or events observed whilst sailing.

(d) Within six hours of the end of a sailing day, upload all photos and videos recorded to the **Recon File Store**. In exceptional circumstances, a **Competitor** may request to the **Regatta Director** that the publication of footage to the **Recon File Store** is delayed. Such a request shall only be granted by the **Regatta Director** if:

   (i) a **Competitor's yacht** reveals new branding that is commercially sensitive, in which case the footage shall be made available in the usual time-frame to **Competitors** only, but its wider publication shall be delayed. Such an embargo shall be granted to each **Competitor** no more than twice during any rolling twelve month period; or

   (ii) one of more of a **Competitor's** crew members have been seriously injured.

   The length of any publication delay granted to a **Competitor** shall be decided by the **Regatta Director**, who shall balance the **Competitor's** request with the requirements of **AC Media**.

(e) As soon as possible, compile and collate images, videos and daily summaries for distribution to **Competitors** and **AC Media**. These summaries shall include observations and comments on photos and videos, in addition to some statistics, and shall be uploaded to the **Recon File Store**. The format of the reports may be specified by **AC Media**.

(f) A **Competitor** from a **Recon Unit's RMP** may propose specific areas of interest to focus on, but any information captured by the **Recon Unit** shall be shared equally with all **Competitors** via the **Recon File Store**. A **Recon Unit** shall not provide any photos, video or other data to any **Competitor** except via the **Recon File Store**, but this does not prohibit verbal discussions between a **Competitor** and a **Recon Unit**.

(g) On request from **AC Media**, a **Recon Unit** shall interview a member of their **Observed Competitor's** technical team on specific technical questions, and upload that interview to the **Recon File Store**.

(h) Take photos and video of a **Competitor's yacht** when in *public view* or when it is not in an enclosed structure, such as during roll-out, lifting or afloat, whether or not it is a sailing day.

10.10 On-water management

(a) When a **Competitor's yacht** is away from the dock and either stationary or on a side-tow, a recon vessel shall remain at least 75 m from the **yacht**.

(b) When a **Competitor's yacht** is on a bow tow, a recon vessel shall remain at least 100 m from the **yacht** and aft of her beam.

(c) When a **Competitor's** yacht is sailing, a recon vessel shall make best endeavours to remain at least 100 m from the **yacht** and aft of a crosswind line passing through the bow of the yacht, except as permitted by Rule 10.10 (d).

(d) As an alternative requirement to Rule 10.10 (c), when a **Competitor's yacht** is sailing around a race- course with racing buoys or marks placed by a **Competitor** or the **Regatta Director**, a recon vessel may be positioned:

(i) outside a circle of radius 100 m centred on each racecourse buoy or mark; and

(ii) 100 m beyond laylines to any racing buoy or mark, thereby being off the racecourse, with laylines estimated by assuming a tacking or gybing angle of 120 degrees, using the current wind direction.

10.11 **AC Media**

(a) **AC Media** shall employ a dedicated technical writer with sailing and America's Cup expertise to edit and supplement recon data with technical commentary sourced from:

(i) Analysis of information provided by **Recon Units**

(ii) New *component* declarations; and

(iii) Interpretation and amendment analysis.

(b) **AC Media** shall publish edited information supplied by **Recon Units** on a technical area of the Official America's Cup Website and the Official America's Cup Social Media Channels. This will include feature stories, interviews, photos, videos and sailing statistics.

(c) Stories and interviews provided by **Recon Units** shall be credited on the website with the names of the **Recon Unit** personnel, which is intended to encourage good quality commentary and content from those teams.

10.12 Costs

(a) The compensation for each member of a **Recon Unit** shall be a:

(i) monthly retainer to be agreed by **COR/D**;

(ii) an additional contracted rate to be agreed by **COR/D** for any day that falls within a **Sailing Session.**

These costs shall be borne by the **Observed Competitor**. The **Recon Administrator** will calculate and invoice each **Observed Competitor** for the relevant **Recon Unit** costs on a monthly basis.

(b) It is expected that **Recon Unit** members will, in general, already be based in the location where the **Observed Competitor** will be sailing. As such, when operating at the home base of the **Observed Competitor**, no additional expenses shall be payable to a **Recon Unit**. However, an **RMP** may choose to make their own arrangements to provide accommodation and travel expenses for their chosen **Recon Unit** if necessary, those costs to be shared equally between the **Competitors** of that **RMP**.

(c) An **Observed Competitor** shall be responsible for providing travel and accommodation for their **Re- con Unit**, for any venue at which they sail away from their home base except the **Match venue**. Such travel and accommodation shall be of a standard equivalent to that provided to that **Competitor's** own team members.

(d) The **Recon Administrator** shall arrange travel and accommodation for **Recon Units** at the **Match venue**, these costs to be shared by all **Competitors.**

10.13 Restrictions

(a) Within Rule 10.13:

(i) a *supporting* chase boat is as defined in Rule 8.3;

(ii) a *VIP boat* is a vessel as defined in Rule 10.13 (b);

(iii) a *delivery boat* is any vessel operated by a **Competitor** that is, at a particular time, neither a *supporting* chase boat nor a *VIP boat*. For example, she may be a chase boat being used to check weather conditions when not sailing, or a chase boat on a delivery trip.

(iv) a *venuė authorised* for a given **Competitor** is either the **Match venue**, the venue of an *Initial Preliminary Regatta* (as defined in the **Protocol**), or a venue at which that **Competitor's yacht** is currently sailing.

(b) For a vessel to be a *VIP boat*:

(i) the only purpose of the vessel when used as a *VIP boat* shall be for a **Competitor** to host VIPs such as sponsors, officials, or dignitaries at a *venue authorised* for that **Competitor**;

(ii) no team members of a **Competitor** shall be onboard except those essential to the hosting of the VIPs. In general, this means that no sailing team, design team, shore crew, meteorologists or coaches shall be onboard, except in the case where such a person holds a dual role in a team, for example, a member of senior management that is also in the sailing team;

(iii) a **Competitor** shall notify the **Recon Administrator** of the vessel's identity, its purpose in relation to the **Competitor**, and the names and roles of any of that **Competitor's** team members who may be onboard with specific duties to host VIPs; and

(iv) the **Recon Administrator** shall approve a vessel as a *VIP boat* and the list of team members that may be onboard when they are satisfied it meets the requirements in this Rule. They shall then notify all **Competitors** with the details required by Rule 10.13 (b) (iii).

(c) A **Competitor's** boat (any vessel operated by a **Competitor** other than a **yacht**) may at different times be only one of:

(i) a *supporting* chase boat;

(ii) a *VIP boat*; or

(iii) a *delivery boat.*

A vessel may switch between these three classifications at any time whilst at a dock, providing that she always meets the requirements of her current classification. In the event that a vessel is classified as a *supporting* chase boat for only part of a sailing day, the requirements of Rule 8.3 (a) shall apply only for that proportion of the day.

(d) A given **Competitor** shall not go on the water at any venue at which another **Competitor's yacht** is sailing unless it is also a *venue authorised* for that given **Competitor**.

(e) **Competitors** are prohibited from carrying out their own reconnaissance on other **Competitors**, and shall not go on the water at any time for the purpose of observing another **Competitor's yacht**.

(f) Taking photos or videos of another **Competitor's yacht** is prohibited, except that at a *venue authorised* for a given **Competitor**:

(i) another **Competitor's yacht** is permitted to appear occasionally in the background of videos taken from onboard the given **Competitor's yacht**; and

(ii) casual photos (but not videos) taken by a **Competitor's** team members on a mobile phone from shore are permitted.

(g) It is prohibited to make any electronic position, speed or course measurements of the performance of another **Competitor's yacht**.

(h) **Competitors** shall not obstruct **Recon Units** from performing their roles efficiently, and shall be always courteous and considerate to their assigned **Recon Unit**.

(i) At any *venue authorised* for more than one **Competitor**, the following rules shall apply to all of a **Competitor's** boats, and those onboard them. A tick indicates that a permission or requirement applies, a cross indicates that it does not apply, and symbols in parentheses refer to details in the text.

		Supporting Chase Boat	*VIP Boat*	*Delivery Boat*
(i)	A flag of the indicated colour, at least 300 mm square, must be flown from a high point on the vessel that is clearly visible to other vessels. (✓) Not required if the vessel is always a *VIP boat*.	✓	(✓)	✓
(ii)	Authorisation is required from the **Recon Administrator** to hold this boat classification.	✗	✓	✗
(iii)	Wind gear is permitted subject to Rule 8. (✗) Any wind gear must be covered. (✓) Only if the vessel is a sailing vessel and the **Competitor** signs a declaration to the **Recon Administrator's** satisfaction that the wind data is not available to the **Competitor**; otherwise it must be covered.	✓	(✓)	(✗)
(iv)	A **Competitor's** boat may follow another **Competitor's yacht**. (✓) Only if the vessel is also following their own **yacht**.	(✓)	(✓)	✗
(v)	A **Competitor's** boat may hold position on a course area, or traverse a course area, where another **Competitor** is training. (✓) Only if that **Competitor's yacht** is also on that course area.	(✓)	✓	✗
(vi)	A **Competitor's** boat is permitted within 250 m of another **Competitor's yacht** whilst: • assisting in an emergency; • at her own dock; or • transiting through a narrow channel without stopping to make observations, providing the purpose of the trip is not reconnaissance.	✓	✓	✓
(vii)	A **Competitor's** boat is otherwise permitted within 250 m of another **Competitor's yacht**. (✓) Only if operating according to Rule 10.13 (i) (iv) or 10.13 (i) (v).	(✓)	(✓)	✗
(viii)	A **Competitor's** team members are permitted onboard. (✗) Only if authorised by the **Recon Administrator** for hosting VIPs.	✓	(✗)	✓
(ix)	**Competitors** are permitted to capture photos and videos of other **Competitors**.	✗	✗	✗
(x)	Guests are permitted to capture photos and videos of other **Competitors** on handheld mobile phones only, with no external stabilisation, providing that footage is not taken for the benefit of the **Competitor**.	✗	✓	✗

10.14 Remedies

(a) A **Competitor** that fails to:

(i) notify a **Recon Unit** of an intended outing;

(ii) provide a suitable recon vessel or access to their primary chase boat;

(iii) provide a driver that operates according to Rule 10.5 (b); or

(iv) provide other access as required herein;

shall be referred to the **Regatta Director** and is subject to a fine of NZ$10,000 for the first offence, NZ$20,000 for the second offence, and so on for each subsequent offence.

(b) If the breach in Rule 10.14 (a) is considered to be deliberate by the relevant **RMP**, in consultation with their **Recon Unit**, the matter shall be referred initially to **Regatta Director** and ultimately to the Arbitration Panel who shall determine additional remedies (including points penalties).

(c) If a **Competitor** fails to give the required notification for a **Recon Unit** to witness the launch of a new *component* or *component* version, as declared to the **Measurement Committee**, in addition to the fine listed above, that **Competitor** shall be obliged to immediately make that *component* available for viewing to the **Recon Unit**, whether on the **yacht** or otherwise.

(d) Any other breach of these conditions shall also be referred to the **Regatta Director** in the first instance, and ultimately to the Arbitration Panel for remedy.

10.15 After the Joint Reconnaissance Programme

(a) Once the Joint Reconnaissance Programme has ended for a **Competitor**, other **Competitors** may observe that **Competitor** onshore and on the water subject only to:

(i) the restrictions of the **Protocol**, other than paragraph 41.2 (a); and

(ii) the remaining clauses within Rule 10.15.

(b) Except where safety protocols issued by the **Regatta Director** (in accordance with **Protocol** Article 41.3 (b)) governing the operation of support boats within a *racing area* (as defined by the **Protocol**) are in force, any vessel being operated by a **Competitor** in proximity of another **Competitor's yacht** shall comply with the restrictions for a recon vessel in Rule 10.10, in addition to complying with **Protocol** Article 41.3 (a).

(c) It is prohibited for a **Competitor** to detect the position, speed, course or other position-related information of another **Competitor's yacht** using radar, laser range-finding, optical tracking or other method that can report equivalent performance data.

(d) When an observed **Competitor's yacht** is *under way*, it is prohibited for an observing **Competitor** to take photos or video of the that **yacht** unless:
   (i) they are captured by handheld cameras onboard a chase boat or media boat that is also *under way*, and which has an LOA of less than 16m;
   (ii) they are captured by handheld cameras from ashore; or
   (iii) the observed **Competitor's yacht** inadvertently and occasionally appears in the background of photos or video taken from cameras installed on a **yacht** or chase boat.

(e) Within this Rule, a vessel that is *under way* is one which is afloat and not:
   (i) anchored;
   (ii) tied to a dock or other vessel;
   (iii) held on station by an automated system; or
   (iv) otherwise held in position except by manual control of the driver.

11 Definitions

11.1 **AC Media**

As defined in the **Protocol**.

11.2 **AC Technical Regulations**

The technical regulations governing the yachts, including **AC75 Class Yachts** and **LEQ12 yachts**, used by any **Competitor** in addition to any rules specific to the class of yacht. This included all amendments to, interpretations of and rulings regarding such technical regulations.

11.3 **AC36**

The 36th America's Cup, and the time period spanning from the completion of the final race of the 35th America's Cup to the completion of the final race of the 36th America's Cup.

11.4 **AC37**

The 37th America's Cup, and the time period spanning from the completion of the final race of the 36th America's Cup to the completion of the final race of the 37th America's Cup.

11.5 **AC40 Class Rule**

The rule governing the yachts to be used in the first and second America's Cup Preliminary Regattas, the Youth America's Cup and the Women's America's Cup and/or in any other regattas sailed in AC40

Yachts (if any), including all amendments to, interpretations of and rulings regarding such class rule.

11.6 **AC40 Class Rules**

The combination of the **AC40 Class Rule** and the **AC Technical Regulations**.

11.7 **AC40 Class Yacht**

A yacht that complies with or could comply with the **AC40 Class Rule**.

11.8 **AC75 Class Rule**

The rule which, together with the **AC Technical Regulations** governs the yachts to be used in the Final Preliminary Regatta, America's Cup Challenger Selection Series and the Match, including all amendments to, interpretations of and rulings regarding such class rule.

11.9 **AC75 Class Rules**

The combination of the **AC75 Class Rule** and the **AC Technical Regulations**.

11.10 **AC75 Class Yacht**

A yacht that complies with or could comply with the **AC75 Class Rules**.

11.11 **AC75 event stage**

One of:
(a) an entire Preliminary Regatta, if raced in **AC75 Class Yachts**;
(b) a Round Robin stage of the Challenger Selection Series;
(c) the Semi-Finals stage of the Challenger Selection Series;
(d) the Finals stage of the Challenger Selection Series; or
(e) the entire Match,
where those regattas or parts of regattas listed above are detailed in the **Protocol**.

11.12 **Aft Media Post**

A post attached near the transom of the **hull** which forms part of the **media equipment**.

11.13 **Appendage**

A **foil** or a **rudder**.

11.14 **Batten**

A beam used to locally stiffen a sail.

11.15 **Bearing centre**

The centre of rotation of a bearing.

11.16 **Blueprint**

An IGES file, drawing or other document or collection thereof that provides information about the design and/or construction of a version of a component. Specific requirements for **blueprints** for each component type are provided in the relevant sections of the **AC75 Class Rule**, these specific requirements taking precedence over this general definition.

11.17 **Cant**

Rotation of a **foil** about the **foil arm** rotation axis.

11.18 **Carried equipment**

Clothing, safety equipment, other equipment, food and drink carried aboard by the crew, excluding crew supplied media equipment.

11.19 **CCTV system**

Closed-circuit television system: a **hardwired** camera and display system.

11.20 **Challenger of Record**

As defined in the **Protocol**.

11.21 **CIS**

Crew information system: an electronic system connected to the **Media System** to display the raw or processed **Competitor** data output from the **Media System** to the crew, and to provide voice communication between the crew.

11.22 **Class Rules**

The combination of:
(a) **the AC Technical Regulations;**
(b) the **AC75 Class Rule**; and
(c) the **AC40 Class Rule**.
Where the term is used in relation to an **AC75 Class Yacht** or an **AC40 Class Yacht**, it refers to the **AC Technical Regulations** in combination with either the **AC75 Class Rule** or the **AC40 Class Rule** respectively.

11.23 **Clew point**

The intersection or projected intersection of the **leech** and **foot** of a **sail skin**. The **leech** or **foot** will be projected tangentially from the point where the **leech** or **foot** curvature reduces below a radius of 1.0 m when approaching the intersection.

11.24 **Clutch or shifter**

A **transmission actuator** that adjusts the transmission of mechanical power to or within a **control system**.

11.25 **Cockpit aperture**

A closed line bounding the upper extent of a cockpit.

11.26 **Commercial core**

The **core** category of a **commercial product**.

11.27 **Commercial hardware**

The hardware category of a **commercial product**.

11.28 **Commercial paint**

The paint category of a **commercial product**.

11.29 **Commercial pre-consolidated FRP**

The pre-consolidated **FRP** category of a **commercial product**.

11.30 **Commercial product**

A classification of products controlled by the "Commercial products" section of the **AC75 Class Rule**.

11.31 **Competitor**

As defined in the **Protocol**. Where the term **Competitor** is used in the context of interpretations or amendments, it refers only to those **Competitors** that are still competing and who are not in default of their payment obligations required by the **Protocol** and **Class Rules**.

11.32 **Control surface**

One of the following:
(a) a **foil flap**;
(b) a **rudder**; or
(c) a **rig**.
Where position, orientation, movement or control of a **control surface** is mentioned herein, that position, orientation, movement or control is

implied to be relative to the **yacht**, except that for a **foil flap**, it is relative to the **foil wing** to which it is attached.

11.33 **Control surface actuator**

A single **hydraulic actuator** together with any rods, struts, cables, sheets, turning blocks etc. used to connect it **mechanically** to a single **control surface**, optionally including any number of **transmission actuators** used to adjust that **control surface**, as declared by the **Competitor**.

11.34 **Control system**

A system used for the adjustment of **control surfaces**, including all mechanical, hydraulic and electrical components involved in supplying or transmitting power or information used for such adjustment.

11.35 **COR/D**

The **Challenger of Record** and the **Defender** jointly.

11.36 **Core**

Material that is bonded between two structural **FRP** skins in a sandwich construction, primarily to transfer shear. **Core** includes any material that is bonded to both skins, such as a corrugated laminate between two skins, but excludes:
(a) solid laminate or metal used within edge, taper or local reinforcement details; and
(b) adhesives and resins used to bond skins and core, or to fill honeycomb cells.

11.37 **Crew indication device**

Any device that:
(a) contains an electronic system, or is connected directly or indirectly to an electronic system;
(b) displays or plays audibly information that it has received or generated internally;
(c) is worn or installed on the **yacht**;
(d) can be seen or heard by the crew, directly or indirectly; and
(e) may process data internally, such as a display, LED or speaker.

11.38 **Crew supplied media equipment**

Equipment supplied by **AC Media**, the **Regatta Director** or any other organising authority to be worn or carried by the crew.

11.39 **Crew zone**

A volume designed for a crew member to operate within.

11.40 **Deck**

That part of the **hull surface** that is not the **hull lower surface**.

11.41 **Defender**

As defined in the **Protocol**.

11.42 **Dock tune**

The state of the rig as it is positioned on the **hull** before and after sailing with no sails hoisted.

11.43 **ECC**

Electrical control circuit: an electrical and/or electronic circuit within a **control system** and/or for sending commands to an **FCS**.

11.44 **Electric actuator**

An electric linear or rotary motor, or functionally equivalent device, that converts electric power into force and translation, and/or torque and rotation.

11.45 **Event**

Any regatta that forms part of the 37th America's Cup.

11.46 **External forces**

Forces applied from outside the **yacht** to the **yacht**, such as fluid pressure, fluid dynamic friction and gravity.

11.47 **FCS**

Foil cant system: a supplied system for controlling the rotation of the **foils** about the **foil arm cant** axes.

11.48 **Fire safety equipment**

Equipment such as heat-resistant boxes, floodable baths, panels, hoses, smoke detectors, or extinguishers which has no purpose other than reducing the risk or impact of a fire within a specified or supplied battery; or, equivalent ballast such as sand bags and tie-downs, which has no purpose other than equalising mass of the aforementioned equipment.

11.49 **Flight control**

A degree-of-freedom of motion, or deformation, being:

(a) the rotation or twist of a cross-section parallel to **WSP** of a **foil flap** about a hinge axis; or

(b) the rotation of the **rudder** about its rake axis,

where each **flight control** shall relate to a single **control surface actuator**.

11.50 **Flight control system**

The **control system** used to control all **flight controls**.

11.51 **Flight HCC**

The **HCC** that forms part of the **flight control system**.

11.52 **Flight power pack**

A combination of one or more electric motors driving one or more hydraulic pumps, used to power the **flight HCC**. Low-pressure reservoirs, **hydraulic accumulators**, **transmission actuators**, filters, radiators, lines and connectors may also be included in the **flight power pack**.

11.53 **Foil**

An appendage that can provide hydrodynamic side force and vertical lift.

11.54 **Foil arm**

A component of a **foil** that connects the **FCS** to the **foil wing.**

11.55 **Foil arm drum**

A fairing to close a penetration in the **hull** that allows **cant** rotation of a **foil arm**.

11.56 **Foil arm fairing**

Those parts of a **foil arm** that are not part of the **foil arm stock**. Although a **foil arm fairing** may be referred to in the singular, it can comprise several unconnected parts, each attached to a different region of the **foil arm**.

11.57 **Foil arm stock**

A component forming the structural spar of a **foil arm** combined with a leading edge. For an **AC75 Class Yacht** and an **in class AC40 Class**

Yacht, the **foil arm stock** shall be a supplied component with included items defined in the relevant **Foil arm stock** specifications.

11.58 **Foil cant reference point**

The point at the intersection of the **foil cant** axis and the **FCS transverse** reference plane, as defined in the one-design **FCS** specification.

11.59 **Foil flap**

A component of a **foil** that can be adjusted relative to a **foil wing** by a **foil** system.

11.60 **Foil flexure**

A region of a **foil wing** and/or **foil flap** that is declared by the **Competitor** as flexible.

11.61 **Foil wing**

A component of a **foil** that, together with a **foil flap**, typically generates most of the hydrodynamic vertical lift of the **foil**.

11.62 **Foil wing box**

A 2D region with extents defined in the "Foils" section of the **AC75 Class Rule**.

11.63 **Foot**

The bottom edge of a **sail skin**.

11.64 **Foot girth**

The distance from the **tack point** to the **clew point** for a **jib sail skin** or **tack point** to the **lower leech point** for a **mainsail sail skin**.

11.65 **Force input device**

A device that is moved by one or more crew members to provide control and/or power input, and whose movement, resistance to movement or response can, where expressly permitted within the **AC75 Class Rules**, be affected by certain parts of the **yacht state**. Examples are:
(a) a sheet or winch connected to a sail;
(b) a **steering wheel** connected through cables to a **rudder**.

11.66 **Force input device, primary**

A **force input device** that allows crew to provide power to mechanical drive trains and **HCCs**, comprising only that part of the system which is directly turned by the crew, excluding any gearing or ratio changes.

11.67 **FRP**

Fiber-reinforced polymer matrix composite.

11.68 **Hardwired**

Physically connected by electrical wires, including localised electro-magnetic or optical coupling be- tween system components (e.g. galvanic isolation of protocol bus, optical isolation of IO device) provided information exchange is confined to the wiring circuit.

11.69 **HCC**

Hydraulic control circuit.

11.70 **Head**

The top edge of a **sail skin**.

11.71 **Head girth**

The distance from the **head** point to the **peak point** of a **sail skin**.

11.72 **Head pennant**

A nominally round piece of rigging used as an extension of a halyard to accommodate a sail with reduced **luff** length.

11.73 **Head point**

The intersection or projected intersection of the **luff** and **head** of a **sail skin**. The **luff** or **head** will be projected tangentially from the point where the **luff** or **head** curvature reduces below a radius of 1.0 m when approaching the intersection.

11.74 **Hull**

The main body of the **yacht**, including the bottom, sides, transom, **deck**, cockpit and internal structure but not the **mast**, rigging, sails, **appendages** or fittings.

11.75 **Hull lower surface**

The lower part of a **hull surface** that is divided by the **perimeter line**, extending downwards from the **perimeter line**.

11.76 **Hull shell**

The monolithic or sandwich panel construction that forms the structure of the **hull surface**, excluding:
(a) internal structure and local reinforcements such as bulkheads, ring frames, longitudinal beams, stringers and taping details; and
(b) surface finishes such as paint and vinyl.

11.77 **Hull surface**

The external surface of a **hull**, where:
(a) fittings such as pedestals, helm wheels and deck gear shall be excluded; and
(b) local details may be excluded, provided they have no significant aerodynamic, hydrodynamic or hydrostatic effect. Examples of such details that may be excluded are:
  (i) local reinforcements for deck hardware;
  (ii) recesses for winches; and
  (iii) local foot rests.
The **hull surface** is divided into the **deck** and **hull lower surface** by the **perimeter line**.

11.78 **Hydraulic accumulator**

A pressure storage reservoir in which hydraulic oil can be held under pressure applied by a spring, a raised weight, the hydrostatic head of the fluid itself, or compressed gas. A **hydraulic accumulator** is not a **hydraulic actuator** providing it cannot do work, or have work done on it, via its **mechanical** connection to or contact with the **yacht**.

11.79 **Hydraulic actuator**

A hydraulic device such as a ram or motor that converts:
(a) hydraulic pressure into force or torque, and flow into translation or rotation; or
(b) force or torque into hydraulic pressure, and translation or rotation into flow.

11.80 **Hydraulic actuator node**, also **node**

A **hydraulic actuator** interface that may comprise distributed contacts or connections and forms part of the primary load path that transmits load to or from the **hydraulic actuator**.

11.81 **Hydraulic intensifier**

A pressure or flow intensifier, being a device whose sole function is to modify the pressure and flow rate within an **HCC** by converting:

high flow and low pressure into lower flow and higher pressure; or low flow and high pressure into higher flow and lower pressure.

11.82 **Hydrodynamic surface**

The external surface of a **foil wing**, **foil flap**, **foil flap** segment or **rudder** as declared by a **Competitor**, where:

(a) the surface shall form one or more closed volumes;
(b) **foil** systems shall be excluded; and
(c) local details and openings may be excluded, provided they have no significant aerodynamic or hydrodynamic effect.

11.83 **IG**

The intersection of the centre line of the forestay with the leading edge of the **mast**, as shown in the ″Mast″ section of the **C75 Class Rule**.

11.84 **ILS**

Instrumentation and logging system: an electronic instrumentation circuit including devices such as sensors, processing units and logging systems.

11.85 **In class**

The status of a supplied component that has not been modified outside the scope of any modifications explicitly permitted by the **Class Rules**.

11.86 **Internal state**

The specific condition of a device, comprising:

(a) **for a hydraulic actuator, hydraulic accumulator, hydraulic intensifier, control surface actuator, transmission actuator or flight power pack:**
  (i) the extension, rotation, velocity or angular velocity of one part of the device with respect to another part of the device;
  (ii) the hydraulic pressure within any part of the device, including the inlet and outlet;
  (iii) the force or torque between two parts of the device that extend or rotate with respect to each other;
  (iv) the temperature within any part of the device;
  (v) the electrical voltage across or current through any part of the device; and
  (vi) the above properties of any **transmission actuators** within the device;
(b) for an **ECC**, **ILS** or **CIS**:
  (i) the voltage, current or temperature within that system; and

(ii) the voltage, current, temperature, state-of-charge or similar information from electrical power supplies that power that system or electrical devices controlled by that system;

providing that if any **yacht state** information is present in any of the above data for an **ECC**, **ILS** or **CIS**, that data shall be excluded from the **internal state**.

11.87 **Isolated**

Electrically insulated so as to prevent the passage of electricity, and physically separated so that isolation is apparent by inspection. **Isolated** cabling may be bundled together, so long as individual cables within a bundle can be followed, but cables from two **isolated** systems must not share common connectors.

11.88 **JG**

The distance between **MRP** and the intersection of the forestay and a plane 1.500 m above **MWP** with the rig at dock tune as shown in the ″Mast″ section of the **AC75 Class Rule**.

11.89 **Jib**

A sail set forward of the **mast** hoisted on the forestay.

11.90 **Jury**

As defined in the **Protocol**.

11.91 **Launched**

(a) First installed on an **AC75 Class Yacht** with that yacht afloat where the term appears in relation to an **AC75 Class Yacht**.
(b) First installed on an **AC40 Class Yacht** with that yacht afloat where the term appears in relation to an **AC40 Class Yacht**.
(c) First installed after 1 March 2021 on a **LEQ12 yacht** with that yacht afloat where the term appears in relation to a **LEQ12 yacht**.

11.92 **LCP**

Longitudinal centre plane.

11.93 **LCS**

Liquid Cooling System is a hydraulic system with the sole purpose to cool components, systems or fluid within the **yacht** by the movement of a fluid, and has no effect on the **yacht state** other than that resulting from the transfer of heat, does not provide feedback to other systems on the yacht and can not do any work.

11.94 **Leech**

The aft edge of a **sail skin**.

11.95 **Leech points**

For any **sail skin** a **leech point** is the intersection of the **leech** and a line perpendicular to the line from the **lower leech point** to the **head point** taken at the corresponding percentage of **LL** from the **lower leech point**. **Leech points** are illustrated in the "Jib" and "Mainsail" sections of the **AC75 Class Rule**.

11.96 **LEQ12 yacht**

Any sailing yacht (or platform towed to simulate a sailing yacht) including an **AC40 Class Yacht**, that exceeds 6 m LOA, is less than or equal to 12 m LOA (including all fittings when sailing such as rudder struts and bowsprits, but excluding instrumentation and structure required only to support that instrumentation) and that is capable of producing meaningful design or performance information for use either directly or indirectly in the design, construction or sailing of an **AC75 Class Yacht**, excluding yachts of classes existing on 17th March 2021, providing they are used only with their standard equipment for participation in and preparation for their in-class racing.

11.97 **Linear component**

A component of the **yacht**:
(a) that has no moving parts or mechanisms;
(b) for which any two points on or within it must either always be in contact, or never be in contact;
(c) whose overall deformation at any point, in response to normal sailing loads, is approximately linear; and
(d) that always returns to the same state in the absence of applied load.

A **linear component** may be constructed from multiple parts and fastened together **mechanically** or with an interference fit, or contain voids in materials such as wood or foam which may open or close under normal sailing loads. Such connections and materials are exempt from Rule 11.97 (b) provided that the components, connections or materials are not engineered to provide deliberately non-linear characteristics through internal contact mechanisms.

11.98 **LL**

The distance from the **head point** to the **clew point** for a **jib sail skin** or the lower **leech point** for a mainsail sail skin.

11.99 **Longitudinal**

Orthogonal to **TRP**.

11.100 **Low-pressure circuit**

Hydraulic circuits within an **HCC** that:
(a) supply oil from reservoirs and return oil to reservoirs;
(b) operate at no more than 6 bar when the oil is in any static equilibrium condition; and
(c) are incapable of delivering oil to a **hydraulic actuator**, **hydraulic accumulator** or **hydraulic intensifier** at more than 6 bar.

11.101 **Lower leech point**

For any **sail skin** of the **mainsail** the **lower leech point** is the intersection of a 26.750 m radius circle centred at the **head point** and the **leech** or the projection of the **leech**. For any **jib** the **lower leech point** is at the **clew point**.

11.102 **LP**

The distance, measured perpendicular to the **luff**, from the **luff** to the **clew point** of a **sail skin**.

11.103 **Luff**

The forward edge of a **sail skin**.

11.104 **Mainsail**

The combination of **sail skins** and associated components that are hoisted on the **mast**.

11.105 **Mast**

An assembly comprising the **mast tube** with any attached components and rigging that is not hoisted with the **mainsail** or **jib**. It includes **mainsail** support structures and **control systems** such as booms that are not part of the **mainsail** as well as the **supplied rigging**, rigging, halyards, spreaders, fit- tings, luff tracks, fairings, instrument displays, instrument sensors, cameras, cables, **media equipment**, flotation systems and hydraulic rams that remain as part of the rig whilst sailing. Sheets shall be considered as part of the **mast** if they cannot be easily disconnected from **mast** structures and **control systems**.

11.106 **Mast centre plane**

The plane perpendicular to the aft face of the **mast surface specification** and coincident to the lengthwise centre line of the aft face of the **mast surface specification**.

11.107 **Mast lower zone**

The lower **mast** zone as shown in the "Mast" section of the **AC75 Class Rule**.

11.108 **Mast surface specification**

The external surface of the **mast tube** as given in the **mast** specification.

11.109 **Mast tube**

The principal spar of the **yacht**. For the **AC75 Class Yacht** this includes the one design laminate provided in the **mast** specification as well as any team designed reinforcements permitted by the **AC75 Class Rules**. The **mast tube** excludes any attached components such as luff tracks, **mainsail** support structures and **control systems** as well as taping or local reinforcements for the connection of such components.

11.110 **Mast upper plane**

The plane oriented at 95° to the aft face of the **mast surface specification** at w=26.5 m in **mast**-fixed reference frame, as shown in the "Mast" section of the **AC75 Class Rule**.

11.111 **Master actuator**

A **hydraulic actuator** whose sole function is to convert force or torque into hydraulic pressure, and translation or rotation into flow, that pressure and flow being delivered to a **control surface actuator**.

11.112 **Match venue**

As defined in the **Protocol**.

11.113 **Measurement Committee**

A committee responsible for ensuring a **yacht** satisfies the **Class Rules**.

11.114 **Measurement Procedures**

A document detailing the procedures for the measurement of a **yacht**, including measurement tolerances, written by the **Measurement Committee** and approved and published by the **Rules Committee**.

11.115 **Mechanically**

Only through contact of components, without the use of hydraulic, pneumatic, magnetic or electrical components.

11.116 **Media Bowsprit**

A bowsprit which forms part of the **media equipment**.

11.117 **Media Equipment**

The hardware supplied by **AC Media**, including the **Media System**.

11.118 **Media System**

A supplied system for managing the flow of data, audio and video around the **yacht** and off the **yacht** for broadcast.

11.119 **MRP**

Mast rotation point. The point about which the mast base rotates relative to the **hull**.

11.120 **MWP**

Measurement waterline plane.

11.121 **New Competitor**

As defined in the **Protocol**.

11.122 **Normal sailing position**

A declared position that indicates where a crew member normally operates.

11.123 **Observed Competitor**

The **Competitor** that a specific **Recon Unit** is engaged in providing reconnaissance on.

11.124 **Official noticeboard**

As defined in the **Protocol**.

11.125 **Passive input device**

A device that is moved by a crew member to produce an electrical control signal, such as a button, joystick, slider or touch screen.

11.126 **Peak point**

The intersection or projected intersection of the **leech** and **head** of a **sail skin**. The **leech** or **head** will be projected tangentially from the point where the **leech** or **head** curvature reduces below a radius of 1.0 m when approaching the intersection.

11.127 Perimeter line

The line on the **hull surface** that forms the perimeter of the **hull surface** when **projected** on to **MWP**. Where there are multiple coincident points on the perimeter of the **projected hull surface**, the **perimeter line** shall pass through the highest point of each set of coincident points.

11.128 **Planform**

A geometry when **projected** to **MWP**.

11.129 **Platform**

The **hull**, **foils**, **rudder** and other systems, hardware, fittings, rigging and supplied equipment that is weighed with those components.

11.130 **Platform upper surface**

The upper surface of the **platform**, being the surface of the **platform** that is visible when viewed from above and orthogonal to **MWP**.

11.131 **Point of action**

A point on the **yacht** or **control surface** to which a **control surface actuator** is **mechanically** connected or contacts which transmits the load to or from the **control surface actuator**.

11.132 **Primary force input device**

See Force input device, primary.

11.133 **Projected**

The **projected** shape of a part is the shape of a shadow cast by that part on the specified plane from a parallel light source acting normal to that plane.

11.134 **Protocol**

The Protocol governing the 37th America's Cup made between the Royal New Zealand Yacht Squadron and Royal Yacht Squadron Limited.

11.135 **Quasi-isotropic FRP plate**

Flat, monolithic, in-plane quasi-isotropic **FRP** plate of uniform thickness, that is of dimensions no larger than 600 mm x 1200 mm x 50 mm at the time compaction pressure greater than 1.1 bar is applied.

11.136 **Recon Administrator**

A Regatta Official such as the Regatta Director, their assistant, or other appointed person who man- ages contractual matters for the Joint Recon Programme. Until such time that the **Recon Administrator** is appointed, their role will be undertaken by a representative from **COR/D**.

11.137 **Recon file store**

An online file storage resource, with upload access to a specific folder provided to each **Recon Unit** and download access to all folders provided to all **Competitors**.

11.138 **Recon Unit**

A team of two people engaged to provide reconnaissance and media on a specific **Competitor**.

11.139 **Recover**

To drain oil from a **hydraulic actuator** chamber to:
(a) another **hydraulic actuator** chamber (whether or not of the same **hydraulic actuator**); or
(b) a high-pressure **hydraulic accumulator**; without first passing to a **low-pressure circuit**.

11.140 **Regatta Director**

As defined in the **Protocol**.

11.141 **Rig**

The combination of the **mast, mainsail** and **jib**.

11.142 **Rig control**

A degree-of-freedom of motion, or deformation, of:
(a) the **rig**; or
(b) a device, such as a **jib** car, that is **mechanically** connected to the **rig**. In this case, the **mechanical** connection may at times be slack, such as when there is a slack sheet between a **jib** car and the **jib**.

11.143 **Rig control system**

A **control system** used to control a **rig control**.

11.144 **RMP, Recon Management Panel**

For a specific **Observed Competitor**, the **RMP** is a panel comprising one team member from each **Competitor** except the **Observed**

Competitor, responsible for determining the personnel in a specific **Recon Unit**.

11.145 **Rudder**

An appendage positioned on the centreline of the **hull** which is rotated to affect yaw and trim.

11.146 **Rules Committee**

A committee responsible for administering **Class Rules** enquiries, ruling on interpretations of the **Class Rules**, publishing and amending official documents as specified in the **Class Rules** and other responsibilities as detailed in the **Class Rules**.

11.147 **Sail hardware**

Components of a sail for the purpose of attachment or applying pre-tension of sail controls and **battens**. If two or more components are rigidly connected together then they will be considered as a single piece of **sail hardware**.

11.148 **Sail skin**, also **skin**

A thin and predominantly flexible membrane of a **jib** or **mainsail**. **Sail skins** include stickers, branding, **batten** pockets, **luff** pockets, attachment devices such as bolt ropes and zips as well as any reinforcements such as edge tapes or corner patches.

11.149 **Sailing session**

For a specific **Observed Competitor**, a **sailing session** is any period during which the **Observed Competitor** will be sailing a **yacht** at any location. Any periods of less than 3 days between sailing days do not constitute a break in a **sailing session**. For example, if sailing on days 1-3, 6-10 and 12-13, but then not again until day 17, the **sailing session** begins on day 1 and ends on day 13.

11.150 **SHA**

An SHA-512 of a component's **blueprint**, generated according to the Secure Hash Standard (SHS) (FIPS PUB 180-4) issued by the National Institute of Standards and Technology. This shall be generated using a tool such as the Windows software "Hash Tool" by DigitalVolcano Software.

11.151 **Steering control**

A degree-of-freedom of motion, being the rotation of the **rudder** about its yaw axis, excluding any incidental yaw change resulting from **rudder** rake change;

11.152 **Steering control system**

The **control system** used to control the **steering control**.

11.153 **Steering wheel**

A wheel used by the crew to steer the **yacht**.

11.154 **Stop or lock**, also **stop and lock**

A **transmission actuator** that **mechanically** limits or locks the extension or orientation of:
(a) **a hydraulic actuator;**
(b) a **control surface**; or
(c) part of a **control system**.

11.155 **Strop**

A length of rope with its two ends spliced together forming a continuous ring or band.

11.156 **Supplied rigging**

The supplied forestay, V1 cap shrouds and D1 lower shrouds.

11.157 **Surrogate yacht**

As defined in the **Protocol**.

11.158 **Symmetric**

A component that is required to be **symmetric** must be designed to be exactly symmetric, and the built shape must lie within the specified tolerance of the designed shape everywhere on its surface. Such a component must also be designed to be almost exactly symmetric in its structure, where any structural asymmetry can only result from details such as:
(a) asymmetries at the individual ply level (e.g. lap joints or staggers), provided the overall laminate has symmetric structural behaviour;
(b) fastenings across the symmetry plane; and
(c) right-handed screw threads;
which are not designed to induce asymmetric structural behaviour.

11.159 **Tack point**

The intersection or projected intersection of the **luff** and **foot** of a **sail skin**. The **luff** or **foot** will be projected tangentially from the point where the **luff** or **foot** curvature reduces below a radius of 1.0 m when approaching the intersection.

11.160 **Transmission actuator**

A mechanical assembly including a part or parts that move, when electrically or hydraulically energised, or de-energised and possibly driven by a spring return, being a:

(a) **valve**;
(b) **stop or lock**; or
(c) **clutch or shifter.**

Power supplied to a **transmission actuator** can do no work on a **control surface**, or on oil or gas within an **HCC**, except for incidental work such as the displacement of oil by the plunger in a **valve**, or a component of force applied by a chamfered lock pin that engages on a ram, providing such work is insignificant in the context of overall power supplied to a **control surface**.

11.161 **Transverse**

Orthogonal to **LCP**.

11.162 **TRP**

Transom reference plane.

11.163 **Valve**

A **transmission actuator** that controls the flow of oil within an **HCC**, such as a check valve, pressure relief valve, or electrically powered control valve.

11.164 **Wet box**

A volume within the **hull surface** that is separated from the remainder of the enclosed volume of the **hull** by a watertight boundary, and shares a penetration with the **hull surface**.

11.165 **Wetted**

The **wetted** part of a component is that part of a component that extends or can extend outside of the **hull surface** below the **perimeter line**.

11.166 **Woolly**

A piece of wool or light fabric used only for flow visualisation.

11.167 **Working day**

A period of 24 hours excluding:
(a) Sundays;
(b) Saturdays prior to 3 months before the first race of the America's Cup Match;
(c) 15/4/2022 to 18/4/2022;
(d) 25/12/2022 to 3/1/2023;
(e) 7/4/2023 to 10/4/2023;
(f) 25/12/2023 to 2/1/2024; and

where the above are defined using the current time zone in Spain, being either Central European Time (CET, UTC+1) or Central European Summer Time (CEST, UTC+2). For example a working day beginning on Friday 8th July 2022 at 09:00 CEST ends on Monday 11th July 2022 at 09:00 CEST.

11.168 **WSP**

Wing symmetry plane.

11.169 **Yacht**

a) An **AC75 Class Yacht** where the term appears in the **AC75 Class Rule**.
b) An **AC40 Class Yacht** where the term appears in the **AC40 Class Rule**.
c) **An AC75 Class Yacht or a LEQ12 yacht where the term appears in the AC Technical Regulations.**

11.170 **Yacht assembly**

The combination of the **platform**, the **mast**, the **mainsail** and the **jib**.

11.171 **Yacht state**

The specific condition of the **yacht**, comprising any of the following:
(a) the position and orientation of any part of the **yacht** with respect to an earth-fixed datum;
(b) the position and orientation of any part of the **yacht** with respect to the body of water on which she is sailing;
(c) the position and orientation of any **control surface** with respect to the **yacht**;
(d) the position and orientation of a **foil** with respect to the **yacht**;
(e) the shape of any **control surface** or **foil**;
(f) the position and orientation of any **force input device** or part thereof, with respect to the yacht;
(g) the stress, strain, tension and force in any part of the **yacht**, except in **passive input devices**;
(h) other force-related quantities in any part of the **yacht**;

(i) the volume, velocity, flow rate or pressure of fluid within, or acting on, any part of the **yacht**;
(j) all absolute measures of the above and quantities measured relative to each other;
(k) all time derivatives of the above;
(l) all proxies of the above;
(m) all quantities derived from any of the above; and
(n) all quantities from which the above can be derived or approximated.

12 Agreement

12.1 **COR/D** agreed to the publication of version 1.0 of these **AC Technical Regulations** on the 17th day of March 2022.
12.2 This version of the **AC Technical Regulations** shall replace the previous version and be in force when stamped by the **Rules Committee**. The replacement of the previous version with this version is an amendment according to Rule TR-7.1 (a).

5.5 Race Conditions – 37th America's Cup Challenger Selection Series ("Louis Vuitton Cup Conditions")

RACE CONDITIONS

37TH AMERICA'S CUP CHALLENGER SELECTION SERIES

LOUIS VUITTON CUP

These Conditions have been agreed under Article 34.2 of the Protocol Governing the 37th America's Cup (**Protocol**) by the Royal New Zealand Yacht Squadron as the Defender of the America's Cup (**RNZYS**) and the Royal Yacht Squadron as the Challenger of Record (**COR**). They shall govern the Challenger Selection Series for the 37th America's Cup (**Louis Vuitton Cup**).

The words defined in the Protocol, the AC75 Class Rule and the AC Technical Regulations shall have the same meaning in these Louis Vuitton Cup Conditions.

A reference to time means Central European Summer Time (**CEST**).

1. ORGANIZING AUTHORITY

1.1 The America's Cup Event Authority, AC37 Event Limited, is the Organizing Authority (**OA**) of the Louis Vuitton Cup.

2. RULES

2.1 The conduct of the Louis Vuitton Cup will be governed by the documents listed in Article 33.1 of the Protocol having the precedence stipulated Article 33.2, including the World Sailing Racing Rules of Sailing America's Cup Edition, referred to in Article 33.1(d) as the Racing Rules (**RRSAC**).

2.2 The Sailing Instructions for the Louis Vuitton Cup will be issued in accordance with the requirements of Article 35(a) of the Protocol.

3. ELIGIBILITY

3.1 The Protocol, along with the AC75 Class Rule and the AC37 Technical Regulations, define the eligibility of Competitors, Yachts and Crew.

3.2 Article 30 of the Protocol establishes the requirement of Nationality for all Crew racing in the Louis Vuitton Cup and the Match. Competitors shall declare the nationality of each eligible crew member on a date and in a manner to be determined by COR/D and detailed in a Notice to Competitors to be issued on or before 1 March 2024.

4. RACE AREA

4.1 The Racing Area for the Louis Vuitton Cup is detailed in Event Authority Notice to Competitors No 1 dated 30 November 2022.

5. FORMAT AND SCHEDULE

5.1 In accordance with Article 7 of the Protocol, the Format of the Louis Vuitton Cup shall comprise:
   a. a Round Robin stage in accordance with Article 7.3, consisting of a Double Round Robin where each Competitor will race each of the other Competitors twice;
   b. a Semi-Final stage in accordance with Article 7.4; and
   c. a Final stage in accordance with Article 7.5.

5.2 The racing schedule for the Louis Vuitton Cup is as prescribed in the attached Schedule 1 entitled AC37 Barcelona Racing Schedule.

5.3 If required to ensure the completion of the number of scheduled races in a particular stage, or to ensure a knockout stage does not finish earlier than intended, the racing schedule (including the number of races to be raced each day) may be altered by the Regatta Director in consultation with COR/D and ACE. If, during any stage, there is a forecast of adverse wind and/or sea conditions for a particular race day received in advance of that race day and there is a reserve day with suitable conditions available prior to the scheduled race day, then the Regatta Director may elect to utilise that reserve day for racing in consultation with COR/D and ACE. In such a circumstance the Regatta Director shall give the Competitors notice of his intention to potentially utilise such a reserve day not less than 24 hours prior to the day.

5.4 It is the intention of the OA that the Final stage is not to be completed prior to 2 October 2024 and the Regatta Director shall be cognisant of this when deciding whether to utilise a Reserve Day for racing during this stage.

5.5 The designated Reserve Day on 30 September 2024 during the Final stage shall only be used if racing is at that time at least two races behind schedule, unless otherwise agreed by COR/D and the Regatta Director.

6. MEASUREMENT AND INSPECTION

6.1 Measurement will be undertaken by the Measurement Committee in accordance with the requirements of the Protocol, the AC 75 Class Rule, the AC Technical Regulations and the current published Measurement Procedures.

7. COURSE

7.1 The Course Configuration for the Louis Vuitton Cup is specified in Article 37.2 of the Protocol with further Course details to be provided in the Sailing Instructions in accordance with Article 37.1(b) of the Protocol.

8. WIND LIMITS

8.1 Wind Limits for the Louis Vuitton Cup are as specified in Article 36 of the Protocol.

9. WARNING SIGNAL

9.1 Unless otherwise agreed by COR/D in consultation with the Regatta Director, the scheduled time of the Warning Signal for the first race on each Race Day shall not be before 1400 hours.
9.2 Unless otherwise prescribed, the intention of the Regatta Director will be to sail four races per day during the Double Round Robin and Semifinal stages and two races per day the Final Stage.

10. TIME LIMITS

10.1 The time limits as agreed by COR/D will be prescribed in the Louis Vuitton Cup Sailing Instructions.

11. UMPIRES & INTERNATIONAL JURY

11.1 The Umpires and an International Jury consisting of the appointed Umpires will be appointed in accordance with the requirements of the Protocol and the RRSAC.

12. COMMUNICATIONS

12.1 The following supplied equipment shall be carried aboard whilst racing:
a. Media equipment and a Media System as required by Class Rule 8.
b. If required to do so by the Regatta Director, each yacht (and its primary support boat), shall carry a two-way Safety Radio.

13. LIABILITY & INSURANCE

13.1 Attention is drawn to the RRSAC Fundamental Rule 3 - Decision to Race:

"The responsibility for a boat's decision to participate in a race or to continue racing is hers alone".

13.2 All Competitors and their personnel taking part in the Louis Vuitton Cup do so at their own risk.

14. ANTI-DOPING

14.1 Competitors shall comply with the World Sailing Anti-Doping Code for the 37th America's Cup.

15. SPORTS BETTING

15.1 Attention is drawn to Article 39 of the Protocol prohibiting sports betting on the part of Competitors, their team members and all Officials.

16. AMENDMENTS

16.1 These Louis Vuitton Cup Conditions may only be amended with the agreement of the COR and RNZYS.

Dated this 19th day of January 2024

Issued by the Royal New Zealand Yacht Squadron and the Royal Yacht Squadron under

Article 34.2 of the Protocol Governing the 37th America's Cup.

SCHEDULE 1

AC37 2024 BARCELONA RACING SCHEDULE

20-Aug-24	T	Practice									
21-Aug-24	W	Official Practice	FINAL PRE-LIM (Single RR + MR Final)				*(Pairings are indicative only.)*				
22-Aug-24	T	Racing Final Prel	2 vs 1	3 vs 6	4 vs 5	3 vs 4					
23-Aug-24	F	Racing Final Prel	6 vs 1	2 vs 5	6 vs 4	2 vs 3					
24-Aug-24	S	Racing Final Prel	1 vs 5	4 vs 1	5 vs 3	6 vs 2	Configuration declaration for the RR's				
25-Aug-24	S	Racing Final Prel	5 vs 6	1 vs 3	4 vs 2	MR Final					
26-Aug-24	M	Measurement									
27-Aug-24	T	Measurement									
28-Aug-24	W	Measurement	ROUND ROBINS (x6 Teams)				*(Pairings are indicative only.)*				
29-Aug-24	T	Racing RR1	5v4	3v1	6v2	5v3					
30-Aug-24	F	Racing RR1	2v4	1v6	3v2	4v6					
31-Aug-24	S	Racing RR1	1v5	6v3	5v2	4v1					
1-Sep-24	S	Racing RR1&2	6v5	4v3	2v1	4v5					
2-Sep-24	M	Reserve									
3-Sep-24	T	Racing RR2	1v3	2v6	3v5	4v2					
4-Sep-24	W	Racing RR2	6v1	2v3	6v4	5v1					
5-Sep-24	T	Reserve									
6-Sep-24	F	Reserve									
7-Sep-24	S	Racing RR2	3v6	2v5	1v4						
8-Sep-24	S	Racing RR2	5v6	3v4	1v2						
9-Sep-24	M	Reserve	Configuration declaration for the Semis				YOUTH REGATTA				
10-Sep-24	T	Reserve					Training & Briefing				
11-Sep-24	W	Reserve					Training				
12-Sep-24	T	Measurement					Practice Day				
13-Sep-24	F	Measurement	LVC SEMIS (First to win x5)				Practice Day				
14-Sep-24	S	Racing SF	R1	R1	R2	R2	Training				
15-Sep-24	S	Racing SF	R3	R3	R4	R4	Training				
16-Sep-24	M	Racing SF	R5	R5	R6	R6	Maintenance				
17-Sep-24	T	Reserve					R1	R2	R3	R4	Group 1
18-Sep-24	W	Racing SF	R7	R7	R8	R8	R1	R2	R3	R4	Group 2
19-Sep-24	T	Racing SF	R9	R9			Reserve				
20-Sep-24	F	Reserve					R5	R6	R7	R8	Group 1
21-Sep-24	S	Reserve	Configuration declaration for the Finals				R5	R6	R7	R8	Group 2
22-Sep-24	S	Reserve					R1	R2	R3	R4	Final x6 Teams
23-Sep-24	M	Reserve					Reserve				
24-Sep-24	T	Measurement									
25-Sep-24	W	Measurement	LVC FINALS (First to win x7)								
26-Sep-24	T	Racing LVC Final	R1	R2			MR FINAL				
27-Sep-24	F	Reserve					WOMENS REGATTA				
28-Sep-24	S	Racing LVC Final	R3	R4			Training & Briefing				
29-Sep-24	S	Racing LVC Final	R5	R6			Training				
30-Sep-24	M	Reserve					Practice Day				
1-Oct-24	T	Racing LVC Final	R7	R8			Training				
2-Oct-24	W	Racing LVC Final	R9	R10			Practice Day				
3-Oct-24	T	Reserve					Training				
4-Oct-24	F	Racing LVC Final	R11	R12			Maintenance				
5-Oct-24	S	Racing LVC Final	R13				R1	R2	R3	R4	Group 1
6-Oct-24	S	Reserve					R1	R2	R3	R4	Group 2
7-Oct-24	M	Reserve	Configuration declaration for the Match								
8-Oct-24	T	Measurement					R5	R6	R7	R8	Group 1
9-Oct-24	W	Measurement					R5	R6	R7	R8	Group 2
10-Oct-24	T	Measurement					Reserve				
11-Oct-24	F	Measurement	MATCH (First to win x7)				R1	R2	R3	R4	Final x6 Teams
12-Oct-24	S	Match	R1	R2							
13-Oct-24	S	Match	R3	R4			MR FINAL				
14-Oct-24	M	Reserve									
15-Oct-24	T	Reserve									
16-Oct-24	W	Match	R5	R6							
17-Oct-24	T	Reserve									
18-Oct-24	F	Match	R7	R8							
19-Oct-24	S	Match	R9	R10							
20-Oct-24	S	Match	R11	R12							
21-Oct-24	M	Match	R13								
22-Oct-24	T	Reserve									
23-Oct-24	W	Reserve									
24-Oct-24	T	Reserve									
25-Oct-24	F	Reserve									
26-Oct-24	S	Reserve									
27-Oct-24	S	Reserve									

5.6 Match Conditions – 37th America's Cup Match – Barcelona, Spain ("Match Conditions")

MATCH CONDITIONS

37TH AMERICA'S CUP MATCH

Barcelona, Spain

These Conditions (**Match Conditions**) have been agreed under Article 34.1 of the Protocol Governing the 37th America's Cup (**Protocol**) by the Royal New Zealand Yacht Squadron Incorporated as the Defender of the America's Cup ("**RNZYS**") and the Royal Yacht Squadron Limited as the Challenger of Record (**COR**), acting together as COR/D.

These Match Conditions will govern the 37th America's Cup Match (**Match**).

The words defined in the Protocol, the AC75 Class Rule and the AC Technical Regulations shall have the same meaning in these Match Conditions.

A reference to time means Central European Summer Time (**CEST**).

1. ORGANIZING AUTHORITY

1.1 The America's Cup Event Authority, AC37 Event Limited, is the Organizing Authority (**OA**) of the Match.

2. RULES

2.1 The conduct of the Match will be governed by the documents listed in Article 33.1 of the Protocol having the priority stipulated Article 33.2, including the World Sailing Racing Rules of Sailing America's Cup Edition (referred to in Article 33.1(d) as the **Racing Rules**).

2.2 The Sailing Instructions for the Match will be issued in accordance with the requirements of Article 35 of the Protocol.

3. ELIGIBILITY

3.1 The Protocol along with the AC75 Class Rule and the AC37 Technical Regulations define the eligibility of Yachts and Crew.

4. RACE AREA

4.1 The Racing Area for the Match is detailed in Schedule 2 of the Event Authority Notice to Competitors No 1, dated 30 November 2022.

5. SCHEDULE

5.1 The dates and schedule for the Match is detailed in Schedule 1 of the Event Authority Notice to Competitors No 1, dated 30 November 2022.

6. MEASUREMENT AND INSPECTION

6.1 Measurement will be undertaken by the Measurement Committee in accordance with the requirements of the Protocol, the AC 75 Class Rule and the AC37 Technical Regulations.

7. YACHT CONFIGURATION

7.1 The Yacht configuration requirements are detailed in Rule 31 of the AC75 Class Rule, the Match is an event stage for the purposes of this rule.

8. COURSE

8.1 The Course Configuration for the Match is specified in Article 37.2 of the Protocol.

9. WIND LIMITS

9.1 Wind Limits for the Match are specified in Article 36 of the Protocol.

10. WARNING SIGNAL

10.1 Unless otherwise agreed by COR/D in consultation with the Regatta Director, the scheduled time of the Warning Signal for the first race on each Race Day shall not be before 1400 hours.

10.2 Unless otherwise prescribed, the intention of the OA will be to sail two races per Race Day except as follows:
- (a) One race on Wednesday 16 October 2024, being also the day of the final of the AC Women's Regatta.
- (b) Up to two races on the Spare Race Day, Friday 18 October 2024.

11. TIME LIMITS

11.1 The time limits as agreed by COR/D will be prescribed in the Sailing Instructions for the Match.

12. INTERNATIONAL JURY

12.1 An International Jury will be appointed in accordance with the requirements of the Protocol and the Racing Rules.

13. COMMUNICATIONS

13.1 The following supplied equipment shall be carried aboard whilst racing:
- (a) Media equipment and a Media System as detailed in the AC75 Class Rule.
- (b) Each yacht (and its primary support boat), shall carry a two-way Safety Radio, if required to do so by the Regatta Director, who shall issue such radios.

14. LIABILITY & INSURANCE

14.1 All Competitors and their personnel taking part in the Match do so at their own risk.

15. ANTI-DOPING

15.1 Competitors shall comply with the Anti-Doping Code for the 37th America's Cup to be incorporated in the Racing Rules.

16. SPORTS BETTING

16.1 Attention is drawn to Article 39 of the Protocol prohibiting sports betting on the part of Competitors, their Team Members and all event officials engaged by or on behalf of ACE.

21. AMENDMENTS

21.1 These Match Conditions may only be amended with the agreement of COR/D.

5.7 Sailing Instructions for the Louis Vuitton Cup Challenger Selection Series Including Amendment 8

SAILING INSTRUCTIONS for the

Louis Vuitton Cup Challenger Selection Series

Including amendment 8

1. DOUBLE ROUND ROBIN SCHEDULING

Attachment A contains the schedule of the matches that make up the Double Round Robin stage. This attachment will be changed as required and published showing the date when changed.

2. COMMUNICATIONS

2.1 A Boat and all its support vessels shall monitor the Chase-boat channel when in the Flag Area.

2.2 When instructed by the Regatta Director at approximately 5 minutes prior to the Warning signal, the boat scheduled for the next race and its primary support vessel shall then monitor the Race Channel for race management communications until the race is stopped.

2.3 A Boat is prohibited from protesting a breach of this SI 2.

3. TIME LIMITS

3.1 The Leg 1 time limit will be 12 minutes (refer RRSAC 35.1(a)).

3.2 The 'time limit' for a race will be 45 minutes (refer RRSAC 35.1(b)).

4. CREW LIST

4.1 Competitors shall lodge their intended crew list onto the web based spreadsheet by 12:00 each race day. Details of the spreadsheet have been provided to teams. Changes to the list can be made up until the Warning signal. The Regatta Director will share the crew list with others for rule and media purposes. A yacht is prohibited from protesting a breach of this SI 4.

5. COURSES

5.1 **Course number: 4**

Start - W Gate - L Gate – W Gate - Finish

Course number: 6
Start - W Gate - L Gate - W Gate - L Gate - W Gate – Finish
Course number: 8
Start - W Gate - L Gate - W Gate - L Gate - W Gate – L Gate - W Gate – Finish

6. MARKS

6.1 The marks are branded autonomous buoys that are approximately 3.0m x 3.5m with a signal mast.
6.2 The starting line will be between the signal masts on the marks used in the starting area.
6.3 The finishing line will be between the signal masts on the marks used in the finishing area.

7. DELAY OF START TIME

7.1 A boat has one delay card in each stage of the Louis Vuitton Cup Challenger Selection Series that may be used to delay the starting time of that boat's next scheduled start by 15 minutes. A boat wishing to use their delay card shall inform the Regatta Director prior to the Warning signal. The Regatta Director will then delay the start time of that race by at least 15 minutes.
7.2 The boat receives their delay card back if, following the delay pursuant to SI 7.1, the boat requests the delay card back within the protest time limit and the Regatta Director is satisfied that:
(a) the boat could not interface with the RMS data; or
(b) the Programmable Logic Controller (PLC) for the FCS had an error that rendered the FCS inoperable, which could be verified by inspection of the relevant log files;
without fault from the boat.

5.8 Sailing Instructions for the 37th America's Cup Match Including Amendment 1

SAILING INSTRUCTIONS for the

37th America's Cup Match

Including amendment 1

1. COMMUNICATIONS

1.1 A Boat and its primary support vessels shall monitor the Race Channel when in the Flag Area.
1.2 All of the boat's support vessels shall monitor the Chase-boat channel when in the Flag Area.
1.3 A Boat is prohibited from protesting a breach of this SI 1.

2. TIME LIMITS

2.1 The Leg 1 time limit will be 12 minutes (refer RRSAC 35.1(a)).
2.2 The 'time limit' for a race will be 45 minutes (refer RRSAC 35.1(b)).

3. CREW LIST

3.1 Competitors shall lodge their intended crew list onto the web based spreadsheet by 12:00 each race day. Details of the spreadsheet have been provided to teams. Changes to the list can be made up until the Warning signal. The Regatta Director will share the crew list with others for rule and media purposes. A yacht is prohibited from protesting a breach of this SI 3.
3.2 .

4. COURSES

4.1 **Course number: 4**

Start - W Gate - L Gate – W Gate - Finish
Course number: 6
Start - W Gate - L Gate - W Gate - L Gate - W Gate – Finish
Course number: 8
Start - W Gate - L Gate - W Gate - L Gate - W Gate – L Gate - W Gate – Finish

5. MARKS

5.1 The marks are branded autonomous buoys that are approximately 3.0m x 3.5m with a signal mast.
5.2 The starting line will be between the signal masts on the marks used in the starting area.
5.3 The finishing line will be between the signal masts on the marks used in the finishing area.

6. DELAY OF START TIME

6.1 A boat has one delay card for the 37th America's Cup Match that may be used to delay the starting time of that boat's next scheduled start by 15 minutes. A boat wishing to use their delay card shall inform the Regatta Director prior to the Warning signal. The Regatta Director will then delay the start time of that race by at least 15 minutes.
6.2 The boat receives their delay card back the next day if, following the delay pursuant to SI 6.1, the boat requests the delay card back within the protest time limit and the Regatta Director is satisfied that:
   (a) the boat could not interface with the RMS data; or
   (b) the Programmable Logic Controller (PLC) for the FCS had an error that rendered the FCS inoperable, which could be verified by inspection of the relevant log files;

   without fault from the boat

5.9 Documents Governing the Youth and Women's America's Cup

5.9.1 YOUTH AND WOMEN'S AC AGREEMENT (NOTICE OF RECE – VERSION 15) FOR THE 2024 YOUTH AMERICA'S CUP AND THE WOMEN'S AMERICA'S CUP

Youth and Women's AC Agreement (Notice of Race – version 15)

for the 2024

Youth America's Cup and the **Women's America's Cup**

The Youth America's Cup and the Women's America's Cup are for teams representing the Yacht Clubs of the 37th America's Cup Teams ('AC Team') as well as invited teams representing Yacht Clubs from countries not represented in the 37th America's Cup ('Invited Team')

1. ORGANISING AUTHORITY

1.1. The Organizing Authority is America's Cup Event Limited ('ACE') including any affiliate or subsidiary entity which is authorized to undertake activity on its behalf.

2. RULES

2.1. The Youth and Women's AC Regattas shall be governed by the rules as defined in The Racing Rules of Sailing, America's Cup Edition, except as amended in the Sailing Instructions ('SI').

2.2. The Youth AC Regatta and the Women's AC Regatta are each separate events that share the common rules set out in Notice of Race ('NoR') 2.1. A team in one event is considered separate to a team in the other event and separate to a Competitor in the 37th America's Cup, even if both teams share common crew, management, club representation and branding.

2.3. ACE will publish a Safety Protocol that forms part of this Notice of Race ('NoR') by 2 April 2024. This will apply for the scheduled racing and training in AC40 yachts as detailed in NoR 7.

2.4. ACE will publish sailing instructions ('SI') for the Youth America's Cup and the Women's America's Cup by 17 August 2024. Included in the SI will be the provision for the Regatta Director to stop a boat from starting or continuing to race if they believe there is an unacceptable risk of serious damage or injury to any boat or people.

2.5. Each team shall follow all instructions and directions from the representatives of ACE or Race Officials. This will include instructions and directions from an ACE appointed shore team regarding the yachts and assist this shore team in the set-up, maintenance, launch and haul-out of the yacht(s).
2.6. Times referred to in the rules shall be the local time in Barcelona, Spain.
2.7. The rules, including schedule, may be modified and/or amended by ACE at any time.

3. COMMUNICATION

3.1. Notices will be posted on the online official noticeboard which is a subpage on ac37noticeboard.acofficials.org.
3.2. A WhatsApp group may be formed for official communication between the Race Officials / Organisers and teams when at the venue. Details of any such group will be communicated to teams when this applies.

4. VENUE AND RACING AREA

4.1. The Youth and Women's AC Regattas shall be held in the waters off Barcelona, Spain.
4.2. The onshore operations will be located at the Port Olímpic, Barcelona.

5. YACHTS

5.1. The Youth and Women's AC Regattas shall be raced in foiling AC40 yachts, except that the yachts are not subject to compliance with the AC40 Class Rule. The AC40 is a yacht with four crew who sit in pods on each side of the hull. The crew does not move around the boat so it is expected that two of the crew will share the helm duties (alternating depending on the tack of the yacht) the boat and the other two crew will control the sails. All controls are powered controls.
5.2. Yachts will be provided and will be configured by ACE to be of equal performance. Teams will not change the configuration of a yacht in any way without the specific approval of ACE.
5.3. Yachts will be shared between teams. To the extent reasonably practicable, an AC Team will sail on the yacht belonging to its associated Competitor in the 37th America's Cup.
5.4. Teams shall not be entitled to seek redress against any actual or perceived discrepancy between the yachts provided. This may change RRSAC 62.1(a).

6. RACING FORMAT

6.1. Teams will be divided into two groups of six by ACE and race a qualifying series of up to eight fleet races. If reasonably practicable, AC Teams will all be in one group.

6.2. The top three teams from each group that ACE determines remain available to compete, will progress to a final series of up to four fleet races. Scores from the qualifying series will not count in the final series.

6.3. The top two teams from the final series that ACE determines remain available to compete, will race one match race to determine the winner. If this race cannot be scored, the winner will be the team scheduled to be in the match race who is ranked highest in the Final Series, applying RRSAC 107 if necessary.

7. SCHEDULE

7.1. The Youth AC Regatta is scheduled to be:

Date (in 2024)	**Schedule**
Tue 10 September	Event Briefing for Teams Practice for Invited Teams (time period to be confirmed)
Wed 11 September	Practice for Invited Teams (time period to be confirmed)
Thu 12 September	Practice for Invited Teams (time period to be confirmed)
Fri 13 September	Practice for AC Teams (time period to be confirmed)
Sat 14 September	Practice for Invited Teams in morning
Sun 15 September	Practice for AC Teams in morning
Mon 16 September	Practice for all teams
Tue 17 September	Qualifying Series – Group A - 2 x races
Wed 18 September	Qualifying Series – Group A - 2 x races
Thu 19 September	No Racing
Fri 20 September	Qualifying Series – Group B - 1 x races
Sat 21 September	Qualifying Series
Sun 22 September	No Racing
Mon 23 September	Qualifying Series

Date (in 2024)	**Schedule**
Tue 24 September	Qualifying Series and/or Final Series
Wed 25 September	Final Series – Spare
Thu 26 September	Single Match Race to determine winner
Fri 27 September	Match Race - Spare

7.2. The Women's AC Regatta is scheduled to be:

Date (in 2024)	**Schedule**
Fri 27 September	Event Briefing for Teams
Sat 28 September	Practice for Invited Teams in morning
Sun 29 September	Practice for Invited Teams in morning
Mon 30 September	Practice for Invited Teams (time period to be confirmed)
Tue 01 October	Practice for AC Teams in morning
Wed 02 October	Practice for Invited Teams in morning
Thu 03 October	Practice for AC Teams (time period to be confirmed)
Fri 04 October	No Practice (boat maintenance)
Sat 05 October	Qualifying Series
Sun 06 October	Qualifying Series
Mon 07 October	No Racing
Tue 08 October	Qualifying Series
Wed 09 October	No Racing
Thu 10 October	Qualifying Series
Fri 11 October	Qualifying Series and Final Series
Sat 12 October	Final Series – Spare
Sun 13 October	Single Match Race to determine winner
Mon 14 October	Match Race – Spare
Tue 15 October	Match Race – Spare

7.3. The window for racing on a race day is scheduled to be between 14:00 and 16:00.

7.4. The Group or Groups who will race, and any change to the window for racing, will be published by 20:30 the day before it applies.

8. ELIGIBILITY

8.1. **AC Team**: Each Competitor in the 37th America's Cup shall arrange for a team to be entered in each of the Youth America's Cup and the Women's America's Cup, representing the country of the Competitor's yacht club.

8.2. Prospective teams from countries represented by a Competitor in the 37th America's Cup are advised to contact that Competitor for information as to the selection process for who will represent that Competitor's yacht club.

8.3. **Invited Team**: In addition to the AC Teams, ACE intends to invite teams representing yacht clubs from countries other than countries represented by a Competitor in the 37th America's Cup. ACE intends to accept up to seven entries from Invited Teams in each of the Youth and Women's AC Regattas.

8.4. If an Invited Team withdraws or becomes ineligible, ACE may accept another entry.

8.5. ACE will only accept one entry per country in the Youth America's Cup or the Women's America's Cup.

8.6. An invited team may represent more than one yacht club if all the yacht clubs represented by the team are from the same country,

9. ENTRY PROCESS

9.1. **AC Teams:** The Yacht Club of the AC Team, or their duly authorised representative, shall complete the Initial Information document found in NoR Appendix A.

9.2. **Invited Team - Expression of Interest**: Yacht Clubs from countries not represented by an AC Team may lodge their expression of interest for an invitation to enter a team in:

(a) the Youth America's Cup;
(b) the Women's America's Cup; or
(c) both the Youth America's and the Women's America's Cup.

Yacht clubs lodge their expressions of interest to be an invited team by:

(1) completing the Initial Information document found in NoR Appendix A; and
(2) paying the Application Fee detailed in NoR 10.1.

ACE will only review any such expression of interest when the fee has been received by ACE.

9.3. The entry process schedule is as follows:

Date	Action
Tue 1 November 2022	Lodgement period for Initial Information Document opens
Tue 31 January 2023	AC Team Initial Information Document shall be received by ACE.
Wed 1 February 2023	ACE may start to issue invitations and accept entries (NoR 9.6(b))
Fri 30 June 2023	Lodgement period for Initial Information Document closes
Wed 1 May 2024	Entry List published by this date

9.4. ACE will liaise with teams as part of the process of determine which yacht clubs will be invited to enter one or both regattas.
ACE will be seeking plans and/or details as to the skills and experience that the prospective team possess to be able to fund, prepare, and race AC40 yachts in a high level of competition.

9.5. If requested by ACE, AC Teams shall provide plans and/or details as to the skills and experience of the prospective team to be able to fund, prepare, and race AC40 yachts in a high level of competition.

9.6. **Invitation to Enter**:

(a) All AC Teams will be issued invitations to enter by ACE and shall complete the entry requirements.

(b) Following consideration by ACE, yacht clubs that have expressed an interest to receive an invite may be invited by ACE to enter a team.

9.7. ACE's determination on who to invite and to accept shall be final and shall not be subject to review or redress. This may change RRSAC 62.1(a).

9.8. **Entry**: A team has entered the regatta after it has accepted the invitation from ACE to enter, paid the required entry fee to ACE in accordance with the terms detailed by ACE, and complies with any other requirements detailed in the invitation.

9.9. ACE may extend the entry process for any reason or close the lodgement of expressions of interest earlier if ACE has accepted the intended number of entries.

9.10. If a team fails to pay the fees as detailed in NoR 10.2, 10.3, 10.4, or the damage deposit / damage bond detailed in NoR 11, then ACE may reject an entry (included previously accepted entries) prior to the first race and may not refund the application fee or the entry fee.

10. FEES

10.1. An application fee of €5,000.00 shall be paid to ACE from yacht clubs that submit an expression of interest to receive an invitation to compete in either or both regattas. A yacht club expressing an interest to compete in both the Youth and Women's AC regatta only must pay the one application fee. This fee will be refunded to applicants who are not invited to either regatta, or who choose not to enter either regatta.

10.2. An entry fee shall be paid to ACE by each invited team to enter each of the Youth AC Regatta and the Women's AC Regatta. The entry fee is:

Entry Type	Entry Fee
AC Teams in both the Youth and Women's AC Regattas	€0.00
A Yacht Club whose Invited Team is participating in one of Youth or Women's AC Regattas.	€45,000.00
A Yacht Club whose Invited Teams are participating in both the Youth and Women's AC Regattas.	€67,500.00

10.3. An Insurance contribution fee shall be paid to ACE by 1 May 2024. This fee is:

Entry Type	Insurance Contribution
AC Teams in both the Youth and Women's AC Regattas	€24,000.00
A Yacht Club whose Invited Team is participating in one of Youth or Women's AC Regattas.	€16,000.00
A Yacht Club whose Invited Teams are participating in both the Youth and Women's AC Regattas.	€24,000.00

10.4. A Branding Contribution fee shall be paid to ACE by 1 May 2024. This fee is:

Entry Type	Branding Contribution
AC Teams in both the Youth and Women's AC Regattas	€0.00

Entry Type	Branding Contribution
A Yacht Club whose Invited Team is participating in one of Youth or Women's AC Regattas.	€16,000.00
A Yacht Club whose Invited Teams are participating in both the Youth and Women's AC Regattas.	€16,000.00

10.5. Bank account details for payment of fees will be provided direct by ACE. Yacht Clubs may email ACE at *youth-women@americascup.com* for the bank account details for the Expression of Interest fee in NoR 10.1.

11. DAMAGE DEPOSIT / DAMAGE BOND

11.1. Each team shall provide to ACE a damage deposit or damage bond of €25,000 prior to the team sailing on any AC40 yacht in the regatta.
11.2. Each person in charge is responsible for the damage or loss to their boat unless responsibility is otherwise assigned by the umpires or jury. The damage deposit / damage bond is the limit of liability of each person in charge for each incident.
11.3. If a deduction is made from the damage deposit / damage bond, the team will be required to restore the deposit / bond to the original value to continue in the regatta.
11.4. Any remaining damage deposit will be refunded to the team within 21 days after the end of the Women's AC Regatta.

12. OTHER COSTS

12.1. Except as otherwise expressly provided in the Rules, each team shall be responsible for all costs and expenses associated with its participation in these regattas.

13. PRE-EVENT COMPETENCIES

13.1. Prior to the first practice at the event, each team shall be responsible for each crewmember completing the following:
(a) safety training; and
(b) AC40 simulator training; to the satisfaction of ACE.
13.2. ACE will prepare and circulate the training standards to be met by 1 May 2024. Teams will be required to provide verification that each crewmember

has met those standards. Teams are responsible for the costs associated with their crew competing this training.

13.3. Crew (including spare crew) shall attend the on and off dock training and the righting of a capsized AC40 training that will be held as part of the initial event briefing.

13.4. ACE may excuse a crewmember from completing this training if ACE is satisfied that the crewmember has completed comparable or higher training.

14. CREW

14.1. Yachts shall be sailed with a crew of 4 people.

14.2. Crew shall be at least 18 years of age before sailing on any AC40 yacht in practice or racing.

14.3. Youth America's Cup crew shall have a date of birth after 10 September 1998 (25 years of age and under).

14.4. Women's America's Cup crew shall be female.

14.5. The total weight of sailing crew dressed in light shorts and top shall not exceed:

(a) 340.0 kg for the Youth America's Cup; and

(b) 280.0 kg for the Women's America's Cup.

ACE intends that crew corrector weights will be used to standardise any crew weight differences. The method ACE uses to standardise this weight shall be approved by the Regatta Director and is not subject to protest nor redress from teams. This may change RRSAC 62.1(a).

Teams shall carry the supplied crew-weight corrector weights as instructed by ACE.

14.6. Unless otherwise determined by the Regatta Director, crew shall be weighed prior to competing. This recorded weight shall be used at any post-race verification of compliance. If a team's sailing crew is re-weighed, a new weight will be recorded and shall be used for any subsequent post-race verification.

14.7. The total mass of equipment worn or carried by each crew member in a race shall not be more than 6.5 kg.

14.8. 100% of the crew at any time sailing on an AC40 yacht and at least one support team member on the chase boat shall have completed a recognised first aid and CPR course as determined by the Regatta Director. It is recommended that all team members who may be on the water complete such a course.

14.9. **Nationality**:

(a) Subject to NoR 14.9(e), the crew sailing each yacht in a race shall be nationals of the country the team represents. All sailing crew shall be nationals of the country that their Youth and Women's Team represents.

(b) a crew member shall be deemed to be a "national" of a country if they satisfy any one (or more) of the following criteria:
  (i) such crew member held a valid passport (or other valid proof of citizenship accepted by ACE) of the country that the team represents as at 17 March 2021; or
  (ii) such crew member was physically present in the country that the team represents (or was outside of that country, representing that country in sailing competition) for a total of 548 days between (but excluding) 17 March 2018 and 18 March 2021. If a crew member is present in the country for only part of a particular day, that day will be counted as a full day.

(c) A prospective team may apply to ACE for:
  (i) a ruling that the country of the team will be considered as an Emerging Nation; and
  (ii) a dispensation from the crew nationality requirements to allow a specific number of approved non-nationals to compete as crew for a team in a race.

(d) Applications for a ruling to be considered an Emerging Nation shall be determined by ACE in its sole discretion.

(e) If a country is approved as an Emerging Nation by ACE, the number of non-nationals approved to compete on the yacht of that Challenger will be determined by ACE based on the following factors:
  (i) the experience and skill level of the team;
  (ii) the experience and skill level of each non-national sailor either engaged or whom the team proposes to engage for the event; and
  (iii) other relevant circumstances of the prospective team.

(f) Approvals under NoR 14.9(e) will be given for specific sailors and may be amended or reviewed by ACE, at their sole discretion at a later date upon application by any team if there is a change of personnel or a change in other relevant circumstances.

(g) It shall be the responsibility of ACE to ensure that the decisions made under NoR 14.9 are as far as possible equitable in relation to other teams.

15. REQUIRED EQUIPMENT

15.1. Each crew member shall wear:

(a) a buoyancy aid that meets the flotation standard of ISO 12402-5 or ISO 12402-6 (CE 50 Newtons) and that is capable of being removed or deflated in the water within five seconds;

(b) a helmet to a minimum standard of CE EN 1077, CE EN 966, ASTM 2040, or Snell S-98 and with at least 300 cm2 of the exterior surface brightly coloured. Competitors shall satisfy the Regatta Director that the brightly coloured region can be seen from above the water with the crew lying face down or face up in the water;

(c) a communication headset or unit acceptable to ACE that is compatible with the communication system on the yacht and can be used without reducing the functionality of the required helmet.

(d) a blade with a length between 50 mm and 150 mm;

(e) at least one personal air supply containing compressed air equivalent to at least 40 litres uncompressed volume each, which does not require the use of hands when in use;

(f) a pocket for carrying crew supplied media equipment with minimum dimensions 80 mm x 200 mm x30mm; and

(g) crew supplied media equipment, which shall be worn in a manner directed by AC Media.

15.2. In regard to headsets detailed in NoR 15.1(e), ACE can put a team into contact with an appropriate vendor representative.

16. LIMITATIONS ON TRAINING

16.1. No team or prospective team shall sail on an AC40 between the date of publication of this NoR and 30 June 2023.

16.2. A team is considered to have sailed on a day when more than one sailor of that team crews on an AC40 yacht at the same time.

16.3. Each team is responsible for making its own arrangements to charter/use an AC40 yacht and any other training equipment or facilities.

16.4. Each team must allow representatives of other teams to observe its sailing on an AC40 yacht, and any observer must stay a safe distance away from the AC40 yacht and support craft and equipment.

17. DISPUTE RESOLUTION

17.1. Races will be umpired. If needed, a jury will be formed from members of the umpire team.

18. CODE OF CONDUCT & SAFETY

18.1. The favourable reputation of the Youth and Women's AC Regattas, events, venue, officials, sponsors, commercial partners and its entrants is a valuable asset and creates financial and other tangible and intangible benefits for all. Accordingly, each team shall not (and shall use its best efforts to ensure that any team member, owner, officer, employee, contractor, affiliate, agent or representative of the entrant shall not) make or cause to be made, or authorize or endorse, any public statement, or engage in any other act or conduct or any activity, in each case, on or off the water, that is prejudicial or detrimental to or against the welfare or the best interests of the Youth and Women's AC Regattas, the America's Cup or the sport of sailing, or that may impair public confidence in the honest and orderly conduct of the Youth and Women's AC Regattas and/or the America's Cup (including all regattas and events forming part of the same in each case) or in the integrity and good character of any entrant, official, selected venue, sponsor or other commercial partner of the Youth and Women's AC Regattas and/or the America's Cup.

18.2. A written safety protocol for the Youth and Women's AC Regattas will be issued by ACE, in conjunction with the Regatta Director, which all Teams are required to comply with.

19. AMERICA'S CUP TRADEMARKS

19.1. Teams shall not be entitled to use in any manner whatsoever any America's Cup trademark without the specific prior written consent of ACE, save as part of any Youth and Women's AC Regattas event logo provided such use is permitted by ACE. Such trademarks include the name "America's Cup" and any image or drawing of the America's Cup trophy.

20. INSURANCE

20.1. **Medical**:

(a) All crew members and team members who go onto the water are required to have medical insurance cover.

(b) It is the team responsibility to assess the level and suitability of the insurance cover based on the circumstances applicable to that team.

(c) A team shall provide details of the medical cover to each crew member and team members who go on the water. A team shall also inform these people of any changes to the insurance cover.

(d) The team shall provide details of medical cover to ACE prior to the start of the regatta.

20.2. **Other personal Insurance**: A team or the individual is responsible for any other form of personal insurance they feel they may need.

20.3. **Hull Insurance:** ACE will have insured each AC40 yacht for this event.

20.4. **Third Party Insurance**: Each supplied yacht will also have third-party liability insurance. The terms of insurance have not been finalised by ACE at the time of publication of this NoR.

20.5. Details of the level of insurance will be supplied to teams prior to the event. This may impact the level of insurance contribution fee or the damage deposit or damage bond.

21. BRANDING AND ADVERTISING

21.1. Branding and advertising at the Youth and Women's AC Regattas venue, on-shore and on-water, shall be controlled by ACE.

21.2. Team branding and advertising may only be displayed on:
(a) crew clothing; and
(b) within the designated team branding area on each side of the mainsail. This area on each side of the mainsails that is visible will be on a removable banner that is attached to the mainsail. The team branding area on the banner shall be 3.03 m in width and 1.14 m in height. Separate to the team branding area will be the country flag of the team on the upper aft corner of the banner. ACE will supply the banners (including the country flags) and teams are responsible for the costs of the banners and any subsequent team branding. A notice detailing how this advertising can be created by a team will be published by ACE no later than 7 March 2024.

21.3. A team shall not display (or cause to be displayed) as advertising or other branding anywhere on its yacht, on the clothing of its crew and/or otherwise in connection with the Youth and Women's AC Regattas:
(a) any name, logo, brand, products and/or services relating to the tobacco industry;
(b) any offensive, obscene, abusive, defamatory and/or illegal image or other content; and
(c) any name, logo, brand, products and/or services of a Media Organization (unless otherwise with the prior approval of ACE).

21.4. ACE may publish a branding manual that forms part of this NoR by 1 July 2024. Teams shall comply with this manual unless they have received prior written approval from ACE.

22. MEDIA RIGHTS

22.1. All rights in and to any audio, visual and/or digital content and data collected by or on behalf of ACE during the course of or in connection with the whole or any part or parts of the Events or the lead up to the Events (including any still and moving, virtual or digital images and any content generated by other technologies) shall vest solely and exclusively in ACE which shall, at its sole discretion, be entitled to use, assign, transfer, licence and/or otherwise exploit any such rights in and to the applicable content and data.

22.2. ACE will establish a media division consisting of independent contractors appointed by ACE ("AC Media") who will be responsible for exercising ACE's media rights and responsibilities, including the delivery of the broadcast and media production (including the race management system), social media and other media related activities for the events, and having the responsibility to deal with each team on media matters in an independent and confidential manner vis a vis all other teams and ACE itself.

22.3. To assist AC Media with the production of the broadcast and media coverage of AC37, teams shall:

(a) provide access as reasonably required by AC Media, following consultation with the team, for AC Media and/or its licensees or authorised agents to take or record still and/or moving images of teams, including (but not limited to) its team training and sailing, and conducting interviews with its team members, during or outside the periods of the events; and

(b) carry and allow the unhindered operation of the television and technical equipment on board their AC40 Yachts, support vessels and crew.

23. OFFICIAL DOCUMENTARY

23.1. In order to broaden the reach and appeal of both the America's Cup and the sport of sailing, AC Media intends to produce an Official Documentary that will include coverage of the Youth and Women's AC Regattas. It is intended that the Official Documentary will provide audiences with behind the scenes access and allow the public to gain a better understanding of what goes into an America's Cup campaign and the America's Cup event.

23.2. As required by NoR 22.3, teams shall comply with all reasonable requests from AC Media in respect to the collection of content for the Official Documentary. This may include content in the lead up to the regattas.

23.3. To protect the exclusivity of the Official Documentary, each team agrees that it will not release or publish a similar 'behind the scenes' style documentary project without the prior written approval of ACE and AC Media.

24. RELEASES

24.1. Broadcasting and digital

(a) All teams acknowledge, and shall (subject to applicable data privacy laws) obtain written acknowledgements and releases from all of their team members, sponsors, licensees and other commercial partners, that

AC Media, its licensees and its authorised agents, including its authorised broadcasters and other content providers, shall be entitled, without payment of fees to any Person including teams or any of their team members, sponsors, licensees or other commercial partners, to reproduce, broadcast, transmit, print, publish and/or disseminate worldwide in any medium the names, logos, images, likenesses, voices and any data of teams, their yachts and other vessels, their team members, sponsors, licensees or other commercial partners and/or burgee for the purposes of broadcasting or otherwise transmitting the whole or any part or parts of any Event or Events in any medium, live or by way of delayed coverage, and in the distribution, exploitation, advertising and promotion of such coverage of the Event(s).

(b) AC Media may also include the names and/or logos of ACE's sponsors, licensees and/or other commercial partners within any Event-related broadcast or transmission.

24.2. Promotion and advertising

(a) All teams acknowledge, and shall obtain written acknowledgements and releases from all of their team members, sponsors, licensees and other commercial partners, that ACE and its authorised agents, sponsors, licensees, other commercial partners and any Host City, shall be entitled, without payment of fees to any Person including Competitors or any of their team members, sponsors, licensees and other commercial partners to reproduce, print, publish or disseminate worldwide in any medium the names, logos, images, likenesses and voices of teams, their yachts and other vessels, their team members, sponsors, licensees and other commercial partners and/or burgee within audio and/ or visual (still and/ or moving) images for the purposes of promoting and advertising the Event(s) and the official merchandising activities of ACE (and/or its appointed retailers, licensees and/or concessionaires) in connection with the whole or any part or parts of AC37, provided that neither ACE nor its authorised agents, sponsors, licensees, other commercial partners or Host Cities place an undue prominence on any single team in connection therewith (except with the approval of such team).

(b) ACE may also include the names and/or logos of ACE's sponsors, licensees and/or other commercial partners in any of its promotion, advertising and merchandising.

24.3. Biometric Data

(a) Teams shall own all biometric data recorded in relation to sailing team performance. Subject to compliance with applicable data privacy laws, teams shall make selected biometric performance data available free of charge to AC Media for use in global broadcast feeds, magazine programmes, preview and review shows, behind the scenes documentary programmes, clips and features, digital and social media content and news content.

(b) Teams, ACE and AC Media shall enter into separate data sharing agreements governing the use and processing of team member personal data.

25. MEDIA ACCESS RESTRICTIONS

Except with the prior approval of AC Media in any case (which AC Media may grant or withhold at its sole discretion), a team:

(a) shall not exclude any accredited media from any media event related to the whole or any part or parts of the event;
(b) may not enter into any exclusive arrangement with any Media Organisation that has the effect of preventing access by any media authorised by AC Media;
(c) shall not provide or permit any media access (excluding AC Media and its appointed production partners) to its competing yacht (being a yacht participating in any given race day of an Event) and/or any of its crew and/or any of its other yachts, tenders and/or chase boats, during the period commencing thirty (30) minutes before the first scheduled race of each race day and ending thirty (30) minutes after the final scheduled race of that race day during any Event;
(d) shall not undertake any media activities that creates any scheduling or other conflict with any of AC Media's media, commercial and/or promotional activities; and
(e) shall not provide or permit media access to telemetry information of or related to its competing yacht or the competing yachts of any other teams on any race day during any event.

26. TEAM MEDIA RIGHTS

26.1. Use by Teams and their sponsors of still and/or moving images:

(a) Teams and their sponsors may use still and/or moving images of their own yachts and crews taken or recorded by them at any time, on and subject to the terms of this NoR, in particular the restrictions contained in NoR 26.2 below.
(b) Where any other team or its yacht or team member also appear in such images, they shall first obtain the written approval of any other team depicted, except where such appearance is incidental and is less than twenty per cent (20%) of the total image. Such approval is intended to also be the approval of all sponsors and suppliers of the relevant team depicted in the approved image.

(c) Each team may also submit requests to AC Media for the prior written approval by AC Media for any specific use by the team on its own official social media platforms, on a royalty-free basis, of up to one hundred and twenty (120) seconds per day of still and/or moving images of its yacht and crew that have been recorded by or on behalf of AC Media. Prior to granting any approval AC Media may amend such terms and conditions of such use at its sole discretion.

26.2. Use of moving images recorded during the Racing Window

(a) In addition to AC Media and its authorised licensees, only a team's internal media team may record moving images of their own yachts and crew racing during the time period commencing thirty (30) minutes before the first scheduled race and ending thirty (30) minutes after the final scheduled race of each race day during any Event (the 'Racing Window').

(b) Except with the prior approval of AC Media, each team shall ensure that all other media personnel that are contracted by or on behalf of or affiliated to any team and/or their sponsors or other commercial partners shall not record any moving images during the Race Window.

(c) Teams, their sponsors and other commercial partners may not without AC Media's prior written approval, sell, broadcast, stream or otherwise publicly distribute (or allow to be distributed) any moving images of any team's yachts or crew recorded by the team during the Racing Window.

(d) Each team agrees to make available to AC Media (for use by AC Media and/or its broadcaster partners) any moving images of its or any other team's yachts and/or crew recorded by the team's Media Team during the Racing Window.

26.3. Not create misleading impression of status

All teams shall ensure their own use and the use by any of their sponsors or other commercial partners of any image does not create a misleading impression as to a sponsorship or association with any Event or Events. In particular, to prevent any misleading impression as to the status of the sponsor or other commercial partner, any team's sponsor or commercial partner using Event- related images shall always include a clear statement as to its designation as sponsor or commercial partner of a particular team.

26.4. Teams' photographers

(a) Photographers contracted to provide photographic services to teams and/or their sponsors or other commercial partners must obtain accreditation from AC Media and will be bound at all times and comply with the provisions of Media Accreditation Conditions.

(b) AC Media may withdraw the accreditation of a team's photographer for failure to comply with the Media Accreditation Conditions imposed by

AC Media, in which case such photographer shall not be further engaged by a team in respect of any Event.

26.5. Teams' media units

(a) Except with the prior approval of AC Media, each team shall ensure that both its own media and all other media personnel contracted by or on behalf of or affiliated to any team and/or their sponsors or other commercial partners:

(i) shall obtain accreditation from AC Media on and subject to any Media Accreditation Conditions imposed by AC Media;

(ii) shall not record any moving images of any racing during any event from the air; and/or

(iii) shall not record moving images anywhere within any Venue, except for:

images of its yachts and/or any of its crew and/or any of its other tenders and/or chase boats whilst afloat within the Venue on any day in which such yachts are not participating in an event and/or at any time on an event race day other than as is restricted pursuant to NoR 26.2 above; and/or within such designated areas of the Venue and at such times as may be permitted pursuant to the Media Accreditation Conditions imposed by AC Media (including, without limitation, at official press conferences and within the designated media mixed zone);

provided always that such media activities shall not create any scheduling or other conflict with any of AC Media's media, commercial and/or promotional activities.

(b) AC Media may withdraw the accreditation of any media personnel contracted by or on behalf of or affiliated to any team and/or their sponsors or other commercial partners for failure by such party to comply with the above conditions or the Media Accreditation Conditions imposed by AC Media, in which case such media personnel shall not be further engaged by a team or their respective sponsors or other commercial partners at any Venue or in respect of any event.

27. MEDIA COMMITMENTS AND PUBLIC APPEARANCES

27.1. Crew comments for broadcast

Teams shall ensure that prior to and after racing, crew on their competing yachts shall be available to provide brief comments for the broadcast and other AC Media programming.

27.2. In the event that a team member of a team swears or undertakes any profane conduct that is captured on any live broadcast by AC Media's licensed broadcasters, the umpires or jury may consider this a breach or sportsmanship or even misconduct.

27.3. Teams will be required to provide team members to attend certain event related media commitments and public appearances. Such commitments may include pre and post-race public appearances within the venue, official post-race press conferences and interviews with media at the media mixed zone.

27.4. AC Media may require specific team members from each team to attend such public and media commitments, including sailing personnel who will be on-board each competing yacht that day or other personnel requested by the host broadcaster.

27.5. Each team will not make available in advance to the media any team members who will be attending a press conference arranged by AC Media on that day, unless approved by AC Media.

28. ACCEPTANCE OF RISK AND DISCLAIMER OF LIABILITY

28.1. By deciding to participate in the Youth and Women's AC Regattas and/or the selection process, each team and prospective team, respectively, acknowledges and agrees on behalf of itself and its crew and team members that each yacht is an experimental vessel and is of an extreme design and propulsion. Use of a yacht or other foiling vessel involves an inherent high risk of damage and/or personal injury. The level of risk is significantly accentuated by use of a yacht or other foiling vessel competitively. Each team and prospective team agrees to assume all risk and liability for damage and/or injury arising from participation in the Youth and Women's AC Regattas, the selection process, and any other use of a yacht or other vessel in relation to the Youth and Women's AC Regattas and/or the selection process. Each team and prospective team agrees that [sponsor], ACE, regatta officials, and each of their respective affiliated entities, and each of the foregoing entities' respective directors, officers, employees and contractors, shall not be liable for any injury, damage, or loss suffered or incurred by one or more teams and/or prospective teams, their crew, employees, officers or other associated persons by direct or indirect entry into or participation in the Youth and Women's AC Regattas, the selection process, or any other use of a yacht or any other vessel.

28.2. The Regatta Director may, in consultation with ACE, terminate an entry at any time for any reason. Once an entry is terminated, that team shall take no further part in any official testing, training, practice or the Youth and Women's AC Regattas.

28.3. Each team and/or prospective team and its team and crew members shall sign before boarding a yacht or any other vessel during the Youth and

Women's AC Regattas and/or the selection process a waiver and release of liability in such form as may be required by ACE and provided to the teams and/or prospective teams.

29. FURTHER INFORMATION

29.1. Refer to the Noticeboard as detailed in NoR 3.1.
29.2. Email communication to ACE can also be sent to youth-women @americascup.com.

APPENDIX A

Background: Youth and Women's AC Regattas

Initial Information Document

This document is intended to provide ACE with contact information from:

Teams representing the Yacht Clubs of the 37th America's Cup Teams; ('AC Teams') and

Teams representing yacht clubs from countries other than countries represented by a Competitor in the 37th America's Cup, who wish to be invited by ACE to enter the regattas ('Invited Teams').

1. OFFICIAL CONTACTS (All teams to complete this section)

Name of contact(s) for correspondence with ACE:

Name	Role in Team	Email Address	Telephone / WhatsApp

2. YACHT CLUB DETAILS (AC Teams do not need to complete this section)

(Every club expressing an interest to be an Invited Team shall complete this section

<table>
<tr><td>Name of Yacht Club:</td><td colspan="2"></td></tr>
<tr><td colspan="2">World Sailing Member National Authority that the club is affiliated to:</td><td></td></tr>
<tr><td>Number of members:</td><td colspan="2"></td></tr>
<tr><td>Club Website:</td><td colspan="2"></td></tr>
<tr><td>The Yacht Club is intending to enter:</td><td colspan="2">☐ Youth America's Cup
☐ Women's America's Cup</td></tr>
</table>

Please attach:	• a letter of authority from club commodore / chairman confirming the contact has authority from the club to express an interest and, if successful, to accept an invitation to enter. • Proof of payment of the Application fee (refer NoR 10.1 and 10.5).

Please send this (and any attachments) to: youth-women@americascup.com.

5.9.2 SAILING INSTRUCTIONS FOR THE YOUTH AND WOMEN'S AMERICA'S CUP INCLUDING AMENDMENT 8

SAILING INSTRUCTIONS for the

Youth and Women's America's Cup

Including amendment 8

1. DECISION TO RACE

With the approval of the Defender and Challenger of Record as well as World Sailing in accordance with Regulation 28.1.3:

1.1 RRSAC 3 is changed to be: 'The responsibility for a boat's decision to participate in a race or to continue racing is hers alone, however, a boat shall not start a race and or continue to race if instructed by the Regatta Director. The Regatta Director shall only instruct a boat to stop racing if he believes there is an unacceptable risk of serious damage to any boat, or injury to people.'

1.2 RRSAC 105 is changed to add a new 105.7: 'In a fleet race, if, prior to the Warning Signal, the Regatta Director instructs a boat not to race due to a failure of a boat system, and the Regatta Director determines this failure was through no fault of the boat, it shall be scored four points for that race.'

1.3 RRSAC 36(b); 43.1(c); 60.3(b); 60.4(g) are changed by deleting the words 'serious damage' and replacing them with 'damage'.

1.4 RRSAC 60.3(b) is changed to be: after receiving a report from the ACE, that a boat has damage or injury, and after consulting with the umpires, may penalize one or both boats for breaking rule 14 without a hearing

2. COMMUNICATIONS

2.1 Boats and their team support vessel shall monitor the Race Committee channel when in the Race Area. A Boat is prohibited from protesting a breach of this SI 2.

3. WIND LIMITS

3.1 The warning signal for a race shall not be given if the Regatta Director decides that the true windspeed falls outside of the range between 7.5 knots and 17 knots.

4. TIME LIMITS

4.1 The Leg 1 time limit will be 10 minutes (refer RRSAC 35.1(a)).
4.2 The "time limit" for a race will be 30 minutes (refer RRSAC 35.1(b)).

5. CREW

5.1 Competitors shall send their intended crew list for each race to the email and/or WhatsApp group as designated by the Regatta Director, two hours before the scheduled start of the first race on each race day that competitor is racing in. Changes to the list can be made up until the Warning signal. The Regatta Director will share the crew list with others for rule and media purposes. A boat is prohibited from protesting a breach of this SI 5.
5.2 Boats shall ensure the crew weight corrector weights are based on the crew on-board in each race.

6. COURSES

6.1 **Course number: 4**

Start - W Gate - L Gate – W Gate - Finish
Course number: 6
Start - W Gate - L Gate - W Gate - L Gate - W Gate – Finish

6.2 The scoring distance shall be at least two legs.

7. MARKS

7.1 The marks are branded autonomous buoys that are approximately 3.0m x 3.5m with a signal mast.
7.2 The starting line will be between the signal masts on the marks used in the starting area.
7.3 The finishing line will be between the signal masts on the marks used in the finishing area.

8. DELAY OF START TIME

8.1 A boat has one delay card in the Fleet Races and one delay card in the Match Race that may be used to delay the starting time of that boat's next scheduled start by 5 minutes, except a boat may not use their card for a race that has already been delayed under this SI 8.1. A boat wishing to use their delay card shall inform the Regatta Director prior to the Warning signal. The Regatta Director will then delay the starting time of that race by at least 5 minutes.

8.2 On the next day, the boat receives their delay card back if, following the delay pursuant to SI 8.1, the Regatta Director is satisfied that the sole reason for the delay was due to a failure of the boat system without fault from the boat.

9. ADVERTISING

Boats shall race with their team branding banner (described in NoR 21.2.(b)) attached to the mainsails. A Boat is prohibited from protesting a breach of this SI 9.

10. HANDLING of BOATS

Boats are prohibited from protesting a breach of this SI 10. At all times during the regatta, boats shall comply with restrictions or instructions that are given by ACE or Race Management, as well as the following:

10.1 **Prohibited Actions**

Except in an emergency or in order to prevent damage or injury, or when directed by ACE or Race Management, the following are prohibited:

(a) Any additions, omissions or alterations to the equipment supplied.
(b) The use of any supplied equipment for a purpose other than that intended or specifically permitted.
(c) The replacement of any equipment without the sanction of ACE.
(d) Modifying or sailing the boat in a manner that it is reasonable to predict that damage, or significant further damage, would result.
(e) Boarding a boat without prior permission.
(f) Taking a boat from its berth or mooring without having permission from ACE or Race Management.
(g) Hauling out a boat or cleaning surfaces below the waterline.
(h) Marking directly on the hull or deck with permanent ink, using duct tape or using any tape that leaves a residue.
(i) Being towed up onto the foil within 4 minutes of a scheduled start.
(j) Crew being out of their cockpits when the boat speed is above 14 knots.
(k) Attempting to sail at greater than 8 knots when the either or both cockpits are significantly full of water.
(l) Crew hanging off, swinging on, or holding on to standing rigging other than to steady themselves.

10.2 **Permitted Items**

Only the following are permitted on board:

(a) Clothing and personal items suitable for the conditions and time on the boat.

(b) Food and drink that will be counted, when full, in the mass of equipment worn or carried as described in NoR 14.7.
(c) basic hand tools
(d) adhesive tape
(e) line (elastic or otherwise of 4 mm diameter or less)
(f) marking pens
(g) handheld compasses, watches, and timers
(h) One small personal video device such as GoPro, to be attached on or near the aft aerial frame as instructed by ACE.
(i) Items with the approval of by ACE or Race Management

10.3 **Mandatory Actions**

The following are required:

(a) To race with the jib as specified by ACE or Race Management
(b) The completion of a written damage report before leaving a boat and submitting it to ACE, even if no damage or loss is recorded. Reports shall include any evidence of matters which could cause damage or disadvantage to the boat in future races. If boat swaps are carried out on the water, the report should be made verbally to the RC as soon as possible.
(c) Pack the boat up at the end of each sailing day, to the satisfaction of ACE.
(d) Complying with any regulations, including speed restrictions and navigation marks, while leaving or returning to the berth or mooring.

Chapter 6 The 37th America's Cup Arbitration Panel Decisions

6.1 ACAP37/01 – CVS' (Luna Rossa) Request for Interpretation in Respect of 'Performance Data' and 'Competitor's Sailing Team': Decision (31 December 2022, 12.30 UT) and Amendment (11 January 2023, 12.00 NZ)

IN THE MATTER
of the Protocol
Governing the 37th America's Cup
AND
IN THE MATTER
of an Application filed by Circolo della Vela Sicilia (CVS) Luna Rossa Challenge for confirmation of its Interpretation of 24.3 of the Protocol

AMERICA'S CUP ARBITRATION PANEL CASE 01

APPLICATION

1. On 7th December 2022 Circolo della Vela Sicilia (CVS) Luna Rossa Challenge Srl, in its capacity as the representative sailing team of CVS (Luna Rossa) made an Application to the Panel requesting an interpretation of Article 24.3 of the Protocol with respect to "performance data" and a "Competitor's sailing team."

DIRECTIONS

2. On 8th December, Graham McKenzie, on behalf of the Panel, emailed those recorded as representatives of each team, and the AC Event Authority:
   (i) setting a time and date by which each of those parties wishing to make an Observation, should do so by 18.00 hours (New Zealand time) on 20th December 2022, with copies to other parties.

(ii) setting a time and date by which CVS is entitled to file a submission in response to any observations: 18.00 hours (New Zealand time) on 22nd December.

(iii) explaining that the World Intellectual Property Organization (WIPO) Electronic Case Facility (ECAF) is not yet set up and that therefore this case will be processed by email exchanges directly between the parties and the Arbitration Panel.

RESPONSES AND REPLIES

3. On 19th December The Challenger of Record and Defender published Protocol Amendment No.8 which, inter alia, amended Article 24.3.
4. On 19th December New York Yacht Club American Magic made a Response, suggesting that the applicant, CVS-Luna Rossa withdraw, or amend their application in view of Amendment 08 of the Protocol and suggested granting a new deadline for the other parties who have received the original directions from the Arbitration Panel to submit observations to the Panel.
5. On 20th December The Panel issued 'Further Directions' noting that the Defender and Challenger of Record published Protocol 'Amendment no.8' inter alia amending Article 24.3 and various definitions that are the subject of the Application. It was also noted that NYYC American Magic, Emirates Team New Zealand (ETNZ) representing the Defender and Athena Racing Limited (ARL) representing the COR all submitted that in view of such Protocol changes the Panel should issue further Directions.

   The Panel invited CVS to state whether they wished to proceed with their Application and should they wish to do so, the Panel may then as it sees fit provide an opportunity for the D, COR and other Competitors to submit further observations.

6. On 21st December Luna Rossa filed a Response acknowledging "that its request of interpretation of the Protocol has been mostly superseded by amendment 08 to the Protocol".
7. On 22nd December the Arbitration Panel issued 'Directions no.3' inviting submissions from other parties and, noting the approaching Christmas period, provided a longer time period than it normally would for responses. The parties may by 18.00 hours (New Zealand time) on 30 December 2022 file a submission/observation in respect of the submission/observations made by Luna Rossa dated 21 December 2022.
8. On 24 December COR/D submitted joint observations asserting that Protocol Amendment No. 8 is not ambiguous. They submitted that the outcome of the amended Article is that Team Members who are not members of the Sailing Team are permitted to sail on third party Surrogate Yachts as individuals, but Article

24.3(c) prohibits the Competitor (and in particular members of its design team) from receiving any performance data which emanates from such sailing. They further submitted that by sailing on a yacht a person does not automatically obtain performance data. They therefore concluded that sailing on a Surrogate Yacht by a non Sailing Team member is permitted.

DECISION

9. The Protocol Changes published on 19th December clarify the points raised in Luna Rossa's Application and do not appear to result in ambiguity. Any further questions would need to be the subject of a new Application, setting out specific facts with reference to the now amended Protocol.

COSTS

10. The norm is that the Applicant should pay the cost of an Application. However in this case, the Application prompted COR/D to issue Protocol Amendments which clarified the interpretation and therefore COR/D should make a contribution.
11. Costs are therefore awarded as follows:
    (i) CVS/LR to pay €5,500
    (ii) COR/D to pay €2,750 each

Payments should made to: KB2323844EUR1AMERICASCUP GB80CITI1850081 4616480

Swift Code CITIGB2L

Citibank, N.A., 25 Canada Square, Canary Wharf, London E14 5LB Payment to be made within 14 days of the date of the Award.

In the case of CVS/LR, the Panel will arrange a rebate of €4,500 (€10,000 paid, less cost award of €5,500)

31st December 2022

America's Cup Arbitration Panel

David Tillett AM, Chairman Graham McKenzie

Bryan Willis

6.2 ACAP37/02 – CVS (Luna Rossa) Request for Relief over Allocation of AC40 Yacht to American Magic: Decision (6 March 2023, 10:50 UTC) and Amendment (6 March 2023, 22:00 UTC)

IN THE MATTER
of the Protocol Governing the 37th America's Cup
AND IN THE MATTER
of an Application filed by Circolo della Vela Sicilia (CVS)
Luna Rossa Challenge (LR) for consideration of the receipt of an AC40 Yacht by the Challenger
New York Yacht Club / American Magic (AM)

AMERICA'S CUP ARBITRATION PANEL CASE 02

APPLICATION

1. On 26th February 2023, an Application dated 25th February 2023 was received by the Arbitration Panel from Circolo della Vela Sicilia (CVS) Luna Rossa Challenge Srl (LR), claiming that the Challenger New York Yacht Club / American Magic (AM) announced on February 24, 2023 on its social media channels the receipt of an AC40 Yacht.
2. The Applicant considered that the receipt by AM of an AC40 Yacht was in violation of the priority order expressly set out by the Protocol and constituted a material unfair competitive advantage for AM, and requested the Arbitration Panel impose appropriate orders and penalties to redress this breach of the Protocol.

DIRECTIONS

3. On 27th February, David Tillett AM, on behalf of the Panel, emailed those recorded as representatives of each team, and the AC Event Authority (ACE):
   (i) Setting a time and date by which each of those parties wishing to make an Observation, should do so by 18:00 (New Zealand time) on 2nd March 2023, with copies to the other parties;
   (ii) Setting a time and date by which LR was entitled to file a submission in response to any Observations, being 18:00 hours (New Zealand time) on 4th March 2023, with a copy to the other parties;
   (iii) Advising that the World Intellectual Property Organization (WIPO) Electronic Case Facility (ECAF) was not yet set up and that therefore this case

would be managed by email exchanges directly between the parties and the Arbitration Panel; and

(iv) Directing that the Application was not suitable for the Fast Track Process as provided for in Article 67.14(b) of the Protocol, as the Panel considered that additional information and further submissions were required but that it had in settling the response times, had regard to the nature of the Application.

RESPONSES AND REPLIES

4. On 1st March 2023 AM submitted a Response, suggesting that ACE allocated the AC40 Yachts as per Article 22.2(d)(iii) of the Protocol and that neither AM nor Alinghi Red Bull Racing ("ARBR") had breached Article 22.2(d)(iii) of the Protocol, nor any other applicable rule in regards to their AC40 Yachts.
5. AM further suggested that it and ARBR had agreed to exchange their allocated AC40 Yachts, thus exchanging the legal ownership of Hull #5 and Hull #7 and AM offered to produce legal evidence of that agreement if ARBR agreed. AM suggested that nothing in the Protocol forbade transferring the property of any AC40 Yacht.
6. On 1st March 2023 ARBR submitted a Response, suggesting that ARBR was allocated Hulls #4 and #5 in accordance with Article 22.2(d) of the Protocol and in accordance with the list published pursuant to Article 13.4 of the Protocol, and suggesting that Hull #5 was never allocated to AM. ARBR contested LR's allegations that Hull #5 was wrongfully allocated to AM or that ARBR's right of allocation was disposed of in favour of AM.
7. ARBR further suggested that it became the legal owner of Hulls #4 and #5 upon payment of the First Instalments as defined in Article 9 and Appendix 1 of the Standardised AC40 Build Contract, and that ARBR had the power to dispose of Hull #5, which it did when it entered into an agreement with AM to dispose of the property of Hull #5. ARBR suggested that such an agreement was a private agreement between private parties and was not forbidden by the Protocol.
8. On 1st March 2023 the Defender (D) and ACE submitted a Response, stating that Competitors were allocated their AC40 Yachts in accordance with the order of priority specified in Article 22.2(d) of the Protocol and that ACE was not involved in any subsequent arrangements that may be made between Teams.
9. On 2nd March 2023 INEOS Britannia sent an email to David Tillett stating that it did not intend to file a Response in relation to Case 002.
10. On 2nd March 2023 LR submitted a Response to the Observations which had been submitted, reconfirming and reinstating the arguments set out in its Application and disputing the arguments contained in the AM Observations and in the ARBR Observations.

THE AM / ARBR AC40 AGREEMENT

11. On 2nd March 2023, with reference to AM in its observations offering to "provide the legal evidence of this agreement" between AM and ARBR with regard to the AC40 Yacht in question and with agreement from ARBR, the Panel directed (noting Protocol Article 67.12(c)) that such agreement be so provided to the Panel. On the same date AM provided a signed copy of such agreement to the Panel. On the same date ARBR advised the Panel it wished to keep the agreement confidential. The Panel made an order on 3rd March in terms of Article 67.12(c) that such agreement would remain confidential to the Panel.

DISCUSSION

12. In The Panel's view, the key aspect of this case is whether ACE met its obligation under Article 22.2(d) of the Protocol to allocate the AC40 Yachts in the order of priority provided for in the Protocol.
13. The arguments that LR advanced that if ARBR chose not to take up its allocation which was for Hull #5 then that meant that LR who had been allocated Hull #6 were then effectively entitled to Hull #5 as of right, are in the Panel's view not correct.
14. The agreement between AM and ARBR does not record a disposal or a private sale, rather it records that they agreed to "exchange Hull #5 with Hull #7 after their respective allocation by Protocol Article 22.2(d)(iii) and upon delivery of the AC40s Build Contracts". The boat builder's contract was unchanged. The same already agreed payment obligations were taken up by the respective parties. For this to be prohibited as LR contends, would require express words under the Protocol. The Panel does however recognise the benefits of as early delivery as possible of an AC40 Yacht.

DECISION

15. ACE met its required obligations under Article 22.2(d) of the Protocol to allocate the AC40 Yachts in the required order of priority.
16. The contract arrangements made between AM and ARBR did not alter the AC40 Yacht Hull allocation obligations that ACE had met.
17. The relief sought by LR is declined.

COSTS

18. This case follows the normal position that the Applicant should pay the costs of an Application. LR is to pay costs of Euros 10,000. As it has already paid this sum in its Application fee, no further costs are payable.

6th March 2023

America's Cup Arbitration Panel

David Tillett AM, Chairman Graham McKenzie

Bryan Willis

America's Cup Arbitration Panel Secretary

Sasha Lines

6.3 ACAP37/03 – SNG (ARBR) Request for Interpretation Regarding Share of AC75 Yacht Design Package: Decision (19 April 2023, 08:30 UTC)

IN THE MATTER
of the Protocol Governing the 37th America's Cup
AND IN THE MATTER
of an Application filed by Société Nautique de Genève (SNG)
Alinghi Red Bull Racing SA (ARBR) for consideration of the
interpretation of several Articles of the Protocol – Share
of an AC75 yacht design package

AMERICA'S CUP ARBITRATION PANEL CASE 03

EMAIL DISTRIBUTION

To: America's Cup Distribution List

Cc: David Tillett, Graham McKenzie, Bryan Willis, Sasha Lines

APPLICATION

1. On 1st April 2023, an Application dated 31st March 2023 was received by the Arbitration Panel ("the Panel") from Sociètè Nautique de Genève (SNG) Alinghi Red Bull Racing SA ("ARBR") ("the Applicant"), seeking the assistance of the Panel to provide an interpretation of Articles 41.2(a) as further developed by the America's Cup Technical Regulations ("TR") TR-10.13(a) and (e), 24.2(h) and 24.3(c) of the Protocol.
2. The Applicant is of the opinion that the Defender ("D") may be or has (or is in the process of) selling (or otherwise sharing) to Orient Express Team ("OET") the complete design, engineering, manufacturing 3D models and 2D drawings, and all related information of D's AC75 yacht that will be raced in the 37th America's Cup (the "Design") and requests the Panel to provide an interpretation of Articles 41.2(a) as further developed by TR-10.13(a) and (e), 24.2(h) and 24.3(c) of the Protocol.
3. The Applicant further requests that the Panel clarify whether an AC75 yacht built by OET as per the Design of D shall be deemed a Surrogate Yacht as defined in Schedule 1 of the Protocol and as contemplated by the TR.

DIRECTIONS

4. On 2nd April 2023 the Panel Secretary, on behalf of the Panel, emailed those recorded as representatives of each team, and the AC Event Authority ("ACE"):

(i) Setting a time and date by which ARBR should produce a translation in English of the You Tube video referred to in paragraph 6(i) of the Application and send the same to all those on the America's Cup Distribution List for the case, by 17:00 hours (New Zealand time) Wednesday 5th April 2023;
(ii) Setting a time and date by which each of those parties wishing to make an Observation, should do so by 17:00 hours (New Zealand time) on Monday 10th April 2023, with a copy to the other parties;
(iii) Advising that the World Intellectual Property Organization ("WIPO") Electronic Case Facility ("ECAF") was not yet set up and that therefore this case would be managed by email exchanges directly between the parties and the Panel; and
(iv) Noting that the Applicant had not requested the Panel to address the Application through the Fast Track Process provided for in Article 67.14(b) and noting that additional information and further submissions were required, and that the Application was not suitable for the Fast Track Process.

CONFIDENTIALITY ORDER AND FURTHER DIRECTIONS

5. On 11th April 2023 the Panel Secretary, on behalf of the Panel, emailed those recorded as representatives of each team, and ACE:
   (i) Ordering that Design Package Agreement between Team New Zealand Limited ("ETNZ") and OET dated 1st February 2023 ("the DP Agreement") should remain confidential as between the parties to the DP Agreement and the Panel;
   (ii) Setting a time and date by which ARBR was entitled to file a submission in response to any Observations, being 17:00 hours (New Zealand time) on Friday 14th April 2023; and
   (iii) Setting a time and date by which each of those parties wishing to make an Observation specifically with regard to the time limit set out in Article 67.10 of the Protocol which requires an application to be filed within ten (10) days from when the Applicant was or could reasonably have been aware of the circumstances justifying the Application, should do so by 17:00 hours (New Zealand time) on Friday 14th April 2023.

RESPONSES AND REPLIES

6. On 3rd April 2023 ARBR submitted a transcript of a podcast "Into the Wind #69" which includes an interview with Bruno Dubois (OET), noting that the relevant sections were at minutes 31'32" to 35'17" and at minutes 36'40" to 39'07". The transcript was provided in both French and English languages.

7. On 9th April 2023 OET submitted a Response, stating that on 2nd February 2023 at its presentation and official challenge announcement, it circulated a press release indicating the existence of a "technological partnership" including "a latest generation design package." OET also stated that on 10th February 2023 Tip and Shaft published the statements referred to in ARBR's Application at paragraph 6(i), and that Multiplast published the statements referred to in ARBR's Application at paragraph 6(ii) on 23rd March 2023.
8. In its Response dated 9th April 2023, OET submitted that given the wide audience of the Official Press Release and the interview published by Tip & Shaft, ARBR could reasonably have been aware of the circumstances justifying the Application before 31st March 2023 and that the 10-day allowance for filing an Application as defined by Article 67.10 of the Protocol had been exceeded.
9. OET further submitted that under the definition of "Reconnaissance" as set out in the Oxford English Dictionary, signing the DP Agreement did not constitute "Reconnaissance" and that by entering into the DP Agreement, OET has not gained information outside the Joint Recon Programme as such term is defined in Schedule 1 and Article 41.1 of the Protocol.
10. OET further submitted that as long as an AC75 Yacht is owned and operated by a Competitor, it cannot be a Surrogate Yacht to another Competitor as such term is defined in Schedule 1 of the Protocol, and that OET has not obtained performance data from a third party sailing a Surrogate Yacht. OET also submitted that it has not been testing in a co-ordinated manner, thereby complying with Article 24.2 of the Protocol.
11. On 10th April 2023 ETNZ submitted a Response stating that ARBR's Application was not lodged in accordance with the time limit set out in Article 67.10 of the Protocol and submitted that ARBR has been aware of the agreement between ETNZ and OET since at least 2nd February 2023 when OET issued a press release announcing its challenge for the 37th America's Cup.
12. ETNZ further submitted that the YouTube video referenced in the Application was published on 10th February 2023, and that both the press release and the YouTube video clearly describe the circumstances on which the Application is based.
13. ETNZ further submitted that the sale of a design package is deliberately permitted by the Protocol, thereby encouraging new entries into the 37th America's Cup.
14. ETNZ further submitted that there is no reconnaissance involved by either Competitor when an AC75 design is sold by one team to another, and no breach of Article 41.2(a) of the Protocol or of Rules 10.13(a) and (e) of the AC Technical Regulations. ETNZ submitted that selling design information is quite distinct from reconnaissance and that the supply of design packages without any subsequent sharing of design or performance information does not breach the reconnaissance provisions of the Protocol or the AC Technical Regulations.

15. ETNZ further submitted that there has been no breach of Articles 24.2(i) or 24.3 of the Protocol and that there is no provision or expectation in the DP Agreement for OET and ETNZ to sail their yachts in a co-ordinated manner, to exchange testing plans, results of tests, or performance data. ETNZ submitted that there are no restrictions in the Protocol on the sharing of designs.
16. ETNZ further submitted that the Protocol does not envisage any AC75 yachts being classified as Surrogate Yachts and therefore that neither OET nor ETNZ's AC75 yachts are Surrogate Yachts.
17. On 14th April 2023 ETNZ filed Observations in accordance with the Panel's Further Directions dated 11th April 2023 and stated that such Observations were supported by the Challenger of Record, the co-authors of the Protocol. Such Observations stated that the 10-day requirement as set out in Article 67.10 of the Protocol is to ensure that Teams do not sit on information they have seen or should have seen, and then later strategically launch an application at a time which could be competitively or financially damaging for another Competitor.
18. On 14th April 2023 ARBR submitted a Response and Observations to the Responses filed by OET and ETNZ on 9th and 10th April 2023 respectively, and the Observations filed by ETNZ on 14th April 2023.
19. In its Response and Observations, ARBR stated that the Application was submitted on time and that the content of the press release issued on 2nd February 2023 is generic and ambiguous with respect to the specifications of the technology package sold and that this did not prompt the interpretive Application lodged to the Panel. ARBR further submitted that Article 67.10 may require refinement or clarification.
20. ARBR further submitted that if the sharing of design of a Yacht and/or components during the 37th America's Cup cycle were deemed to be allowed by the Protocol, compliance with several rules may be put in jeopardy.
21. ARBR further submitted that all Competitors should be entitled to the same quality of information about all other Competitors and that the sale of design between two Competitors would bring them a competitor advantage over all the others. ARBR submitted that the matter which is subject for interpretation is whether Competitors are meant to have access to the same type and amount of information about other Competitors, or whether some other deals may circumvent this prohibition.
22. ARBR further submitted that the word "sailing" in the definition of "sailing in co-ordinated manner" as set out in Article 24.2(h) of the Protocol encompasses the typical actions of what is traditionally called two-boat testing and suggests that "testing… in a coordinated manner" potentially covers a much wider range of activities such as planning, evaluation and discussing the findings of a certain component performance amongst two or more Competitors. ARBR submitted that the co-ordination that exists between two Competitors sharing their designs is far more than comparing two yachts.

DISCUSSION

23. Article 67.10 Application time limits provides:

> "An application to the Arbitration Panel shall be filed within ten (10) days from when the applicant was or could reasonably have been aware of the circumstances justifying the application, unless:
>
> (a) a shorter time limit is specified in the applicable Rules; or
> (b) the Arbitration Panel extends this time limit when it is satisfied that there is good reason to do so, taking into account the desire to expedite disputes and to avoid parties from storing up potential applications."

24. Article 67.10 is broad in its terms and has the effect of requiring applicants to file an application within ten (10) days from when the applicant was or could reasonably have been aware of the circumstances justifying the application. This applies to what may be considered "interpretive" applications as well as "factual" applications.
25. The Panel is of the view that the 10 day limit therefore applies to this case.
26. A press release was published on the 37th America's Cup website on 2nd February 2023, drawing attention to an agreement between ETNZ and OET. The press release referred to "a technological agreement" having been established between ETNZ and OET and further referred to "a fantastic opportunity which makes it possible to erase the debt in time induced by a late entry which places the French on equal terms against talented competition."
27. The press release further referred to securing the fact that OET would be competitive, and that "this partnership technology includes a latest generation design package from which we will work and build our own AC75 made in France. This partnership allows us to start on equal terms with the other Challengers."
28. The effect of this statement makes it clear that a substantial design package was being provided, such that the information was in the public arena for which any Competitor could have made an application relating to same. The Applicant either was aware or could reasonably have been aware of sufficient circumstances on which to make an application. Accordingly, it is considered that the 10 day time limit applied on or about 2nd February 2023 for an application to be lodged.
29. The Application refers to it being "interpretive" in nature and there is clearly sufficient information for a Competitor to make a decision to seek an interpretation in relation to such conduct should they consider it appropriate. It is not directly relevant whether or not there was sufficient information for an applicant to be aware or could reasonably be aware of the circumstances justifying the Application.

30. The Panel is required to give effect to the 10 day application rule and accordingly the Panel considers that the Applicant was or could reasonably have been aware of the circumstances justifying the Application on or about 2nd February 2023. For the Panel to decide otherwise would not be giving effect to the clear intention of the authors of the Protocol that Article 67.10 provides.
31. The Applicant made submissions that "the Applicant's position is that Article 67.10 of the Protocol may require refinement or clarification". The Applicant quite rightly acknowledges that the 10 day time limit applies to all applications to be submitted to the Panel regardless of their nature. The question of amending Article 67.10 is not within the jurisdiction of the Panel, nor does the Panel make any comment on that; such matters are for the Defender and the Challenger of Record.

OTHER COMMENTS

32. Notwithstanding the above, the Panel also notes that the Applicant in its Response and Observations acknowledges that the "Protocol contains no limitations on share of design or freedom of designers to work for more than one Competitor".
33. The Applicant refers to ramifications and implications of such a case; however it is not for the Panel to comment on any such ramifications or implications from the wording of the Protocol.
34. The Panel is of the view that the conduct referred to does not constitute individual Reconnaissance or co-ordinated testing as referred to in the Protocol. Should such breaches be considered in fact to occur, this can be the subject of a separate application.
35. The Panel has had the benefit of being able to review the terms of the DP Agreement between the ETNZ and OET and the Panel is of the view that it discloses no breach of the Protocol.

DECISION

36. The Application is dismissed as it does not comply with Article 67.10 of the Protocol.

COSTS

37. This case follows the normal position that the Applicant should pay the costs of an Application. ARBR is to pay costs of Euros 12,000. As ARBR has already paid

Euros 10,000 in its Application fee, the further costs of Euros 2,000 is to be paid to the Panel account within 7 days.

19th April 2023

America's Cup Arbitration Panel

David Tillett AM (Chair) Graham McKenzie

Bryan Willis

6.4 ACAP37/04 – NYYC (AM) Request to Be Excused from Participation in 2nd Preliminary Regatta Held in Jeddah: Decision (28 May 2023, 14:35 UTC)

IN THE MATTER
of the Protocol
Governing the 37th America's Cup
AND IN THE MATTER
of an Application filed by the New York Yacht Club ("NYYC")
American Magic ("AM") seeking orders to be excused from
participation in the Second AC37 Preliminary Regatta – Jeddah, and to
exclude the application of Article 10.2 of the Protocol
and for no penalty to be imposed for such lack of participation

AMERICA'S CUP ARBITRATION PANEL CASE 004

EMAIL DISTRIBUTION

To: America's Cup Distribution List

Cc: David Tillett, Graham McKenzie, Bryan Willis, Sasha Lines

APPLICATION

1. On 3rd May 2023, an Application dated 3rd May 2023 was received by the Arbitration Panel ("Panel") from New York Yacht Club American Magic ("AM") ("the Applicant"), seeking orders to be excused from participation in the Second AC37 Preliminary Regatta – Jeddah, and to not impose any penalty for such lack of participation.
2. The Applicant has become aware of the announcement made by America's Cup Media (as defined in Article 60.1(c) of the Protocol) on 28th April 2023 stating that the Second Preliminary AC37 Regatta is to be held in Jeddah, Kingdom of Saudi Arabia from 30th November to 3rd December 2023.
3. The Applicant considers that it has reasonable and genuine safety concerns in participating in any of the AC37 Events (as defined in Schedule 1 of the Protocol) in Saudi Arabia including Jeddah and seeks orders from the Panel to excuse AM from participation in the Second AC37 Preliminary Regatta in Jeddah in application of the Protocol including Articles 10.1 and 10.2.
4. The Applicant further requests the Panel to exclude the application of Article 10.2 of the Protocol and therefore to not impose any financial or points penalty on AM for lack of participation in the Second AC37 Preliminary Regatta in Jeddah.

DIRECTIONS

5. On 6th May 2023 the Panel Secretary, on behalf of the Panel, emailed those recorded as representatives of each team, and the AC Event Authority ("ACE"):
   (i) Setting a time and date by which AM must advise whether or not it had asked COR/D to excuse AM from participation in the Second AC37 Preliminary Regatta in Jeddah, by 17:00 (New Zealand time) on Tuesday 9th May 2023, with a copy to the other parties;
   (ii) Setting a time and date by which COR/D may, should it wish to do so, file a submission in response to the submission by AM referred to in clause 5(i) above, by 17:00 hours (New Zealand time) on Saturday 13th April 2023, with a copy to the other parties;
   (iii) Setting a time and date by which each of those parties wishing to make an Observation, should do so by 17:00 hours (New Zealand time) on Wednesday 17th May 2023, with a copy to the other parties; such Observations being limited to whether they considered the Panel to have jurisdiction to make the orders referred to in the Application;
   (iv) Advising that the Panel would review any Submission, Response and Observations that had been filed and would decide if it wished to invite further observations from the Applicant and/or from COR/D and/or from any of the other parties;
   (v) Advising that the World Intellectual Property Organization ("WIPO") Electronic Case Facility ("ECAF") was not yet set up and that therefore this case would be managed by email exchanges directly between the parties and the Panel; and
   (vi) Noting that the Applicant had not requested the Panel to address the Application through the Fast Track Process provided for in Article 67.14(b) and noting that additional information and further submissions were required, and that the Application was not suitable for the Fast Track Process.

RESPONSES AND REPLIES

6. On 9th May 2023 AM sent an email to the Panel and to the Panel Secretary, with a copy to the other parties, stating that it had not at that date, asked COR/D to excuse AM from participation in the Second AC37 Preliminary Regatta in Jeddah as provided for in Article 10.2 of the Protocol.
7. On 10th May 2023 AM sent a letter by email to COR/D, copied to the Regatta Director, the Panel and the Panel Secretary, requesting COR/D to excuse AM from participation in the Second AC37 Preliminary Regatta in Jeddah as provided for in Article 10.2(a) of the Protocol; and further requesting COR/D not to apply to the Arbitration Panel for it to impose any financial or points penalty on AM for lack

of participation in the Second AC37 Preliminary Regatta in Jeddah as provided for in Articles 10.2(a)(i)(B) and 10.2(b)(i) of the Protocol.

8. On 10th May 2023 AM sent an email to the Panel and the Panel Secretary, with a copy to the other parties, stating that it had on 10th May 2023 asked COR/D to excuse AM from participation in the Second AC37 Preliminary Regatta in Jeddah as provided for in Article 10.2 of the Protocol.
9. On 13th May 2023 COR/D submitted a Response confirming that D had received AM's request but that COR had not received AM's request directly and only became aware of such request when it received the email from AM dated 10th May 2023. COR/D further submitted that the Panel has no jurisdiction to grant the orders sought in the Application and that AM's request under Article 10.2 of the Protocol should not affect the Panel's decision on whether it has jurisdiction to determine the case.
10. In its Response dated 13th May 2023 COR/D further submitted that the Application should be dismissed and that AM should be directed to bear the Panel's costs and expenses under Article 67.13 of the Protocol.
11. In its Response dated 13th May 2023 COR/D further submitted that it would review AM's request to excuse non-participation in the Second AC37 Preliminary Regatta in Jeddah under Article 10.2 of the Protocol and would make a decision in due course in accordance with the Protocol.
12. No submissions were received from the other parties served.

CONFIDENTIALITY OF APPLICATIONS

13. On 16th May 2023 it came to the attention of the Panel that there may have been a breach of the confidentiality obligation provided for in Article 67.12(b) of the Protocol in respect of disclosures to outside persons (in this case the media) concerning this Case 004.

FURTHER DIRECTIONS

14. On 18th May 2023 the Panel Secretary, on behalf of the Panel, emailed those recorded as representatives of each team, and the AC Event Authority ("ACE"):
    (i) Setting a time and date by which AM may, should it wish to do so, file a Reply in response to the Response submitted by COR/D referred to in clause 9 above, by 17:00 hours (New Zealand time) on Tuesday 23rd May 2023; and
    (ii) Setting a time and date by which all parties who had been emailed the Further Directions shall use their best endeavours to make enquiries of all persons who may have had access to, or knowledge of, the Application, and to ascertain whether, and if so in what circumstances, any such person communicated in any way with an unauthorised third party, including the

media, in relation to the Application, by 17:00 hours (New Zealand time) on Thursday 25th May 2023.

RESPONSES AND REPLIES

15. On 22nd May 2023 AM submitted a Reply to the Response submitted by COR/D dated 13th May 2023. In its Reply dated 22nd May 2023 AM submitted that it had informed COR/D and the Panel that it had decided not to participate in the Second AC37 Preliminary Regatta – Jeddah due to reasonable and genuine safety concerns of AM, and that it had also advised the COR, the Defender and the Regatta Director.
16. In its Reply dated 22nd May 2023 AM further submitted that it considered the Panel to have jurisdiction in respect of the Application because the Application is a matter of interpretation of several Articles of the Protocol. AM further submitted that the requirement to race under Article 10 of the Protocol and the mandatory participation in Special Events is secondary and subject to, matters of security and safety and at the sole discretion of the Competitor to determine whether or not it is safe to test, train, sail and/or race on any given day.
17. In its Reply dated 22nd May 2023 AM further submitted that if the failure of a Competitor to comply with Article 10.1 of the Protocol is based on reasonable grounds, or circumstances beyond the reasonable control of the Competitor, or reasonable and genuine safety concerns of the Competitor, then COR/D must excuse such competitor from participation and may not apply to the Panel for it to impose such financial penalty as it considers appropriate having regard to the nature and manner of the breach; and the Panel shall not impose the points penalties set out in Article 10.2(b).
18. In its Reply dated 22nd May 2023 AM further submitted reasons as to why it considered the Panel to have jurisdiction to resolve disputes between the Defender and the Challenger of Record, between an individual Challenger and the Defender and between an individual Challenger and the Challenger of Record; and that the Panel has jurisdiction to impose penalties as it considers necessary, and that it has the power to instigate mediation on any dispute it considers appropriate for mediation. AM further submitted that the Application does not fall within any of the situations set out in Articles 47.2 and 67.5 of the Protocol in which the Panel has no jurisdiction.

ADDITIONAL FURTHER DIRECTIONS

19. On 24th May 2023 the Panel Secretary, on behalf of the Panel, emailed those recorded as representatives of each team, and the AC Event Authority ("ACE"):
    (i) Setting a time and date by which COR/D may, should it wish to do so, file a Response in response to the Reply submitted by AM referred to in clause

15 above, such Response being limited only to paragraphs 6 to 14 inclusive of the Reply submitted by AM, by 17:00 hours (New Zealand time) on Friday 26th May 2023; and

(ii) Reminding all parties who had been emailed the Further Directions on 18th May 2023, to use their best endeavours to make enquiries of all persons who may have had access to, or knowledge of, the Application, and to ascertain whether, and if so in what circumstances, any such person communicated in any way with an unauthorised third party, including the media, in relation to the Application, by 17:00 hours (New Zealand time) on Thursday 25th May 2023.

ADDITIONAL RESPONSES AND REPLIES

20. On 24th May 2023 the Defender ("D") submitted its Observations and Findings on the question of confidentiality and stated that the Application was originally received by the five recipients listed on the current Arbitration Panel Distribution List and was circulated internally to five others, including Directors and Legal Counsel. D stated that all recipients had confirmed that they did not further circulate the Application and did not communicate in any way with any unauthorised third party including the media, in relation to the Application. D further submitted that the Application itself was not at that time shared with the Royal New Zealand Yacht Squadron ("RNZYS").
21. In its Observations and Findings dated 24th May 2023 D further submitted that on 16th May 2023 the Commodore of RNZYS received an unsolicited email from James Farmer KC, attaching a copy of the Application, and that the Commodore had circulated it to the four members of an RNZYS Reset Committee. D submitted that the Commodore of the RNZYS and the members of the Reset Committee had all confirmed that they had not passed the Application on to any other third party. D submitted that James Farmer KC was not acting for RNZYS in a professional capacity and was no longer a member of the Club, and nor did he have any association with either the Defender nor with ACE. D submitted that it was not aware if James Farmer KC was acting for any other party on this matter, nor what association he had, if any, with any other Competitor.
22. On 24th May 2023 Alinghi Red Bull Racing ("ARBR") submitted its Observations on the question of confidentiality and stated that it had made enquiries of all persons who may have had access to, or knowledge of, the Application, and that only a limited number of persons in addition to the four recipients listed on the current Arbitration Panel Distribution List had access to or knowledge of the Application, being the four members of the Board of Directors of ARBR and no more than three senior Team Members. ARBR confirmed that the outcome of its internal enquiries was that none of those persons had communicated in any way

with an unauthorised third party, including the media, and had not contravened the confidentiality provisions of Article 67.12(b) of the Protocol.

23. On 24th May 2023 Luna Rossa Challenge Srl ("LR") submitted its Observations on the question of confidentiality and stated that the Application had been received by the Rules Group of LR which comprised of eight persons, and that all members of the Rules Group had confirmed that they had not disclosed nor disseminated information relating to the Application to third parties, including the media.
24. On 24th May 2023 INEOS Britannia ("INEOS") submitted its Observations on the question of confidentiality and stated that it restricted distribution of Panel cases to those within the organisation who had a strict need to know the information for the purposes of responding to directions given by the Panel. INEOS confirmed that all recipients were subject to confidentiality obligations either through their employment contracts, consultancy contracts or professional obligations. INEOS stated that it had reviewed its internal communications regarding the Application for Case 004 and had interviewed all those in receipt of the Application, and had found no evidence that any person from within either the Royal Yacht Squadron Limited or INEOS had communicated in any way with an unauthorised third party including the media, in relation to the Application.
25. On 24th May 2023 AM submitted its Observations on the question of confidentiality and stated that before the start of Case 004 its General Counsel, Luis Saenz Mariscal, had reminded all persons with access to or knowledge of the Application to maintain strict confidentiality of all documents relating to the proceedings. AM further stated that its General Counsel had carried out an internal investigation and had reviewed electronic correspondence and personal conversations and had found no evidence of any member of the New York Yacht Club ("NYYC") or any member of AM as the source of the leak to the media.
26. On 25th May 2023, AM further confirmed that when referring to the media in its Observations dated 24th May 2023, it also implied and meant "any other third person" and that their General Counsel had made enquiries, reviewed email records from the AM servers and conducted personal interviews, and that he had nothing to indicate that anyone related to NYYC or AM had distributed a copy of the Application or made it otherwise available to any third person that did not belong to either NYYC or AM, including the media and by any indirect means. AM confirmed that only a few persons at NYYC and AM had access to the Application and that it was on a "need to know" basis.
27. On 25th May 2025 Orient Express Racing Team ("OERT") submitted its Observations on the question of confidentiality and stated that the Application had been received by eight persons within OERT comprising the internal rules distribution email group, and that OERT had conducted an enquiry into the recipients of the Application and that all recipients had confirmed that they had

not disclosed nor circulated information relating to the Application to third parties, including the media.

28. On 26th May 2023 COR/D submitted a Response to the Reply submitted by AM on 22nd May 2023. In its Response dated 26th May 2023, COR/D submitted that it had observed that AM in its Reply dated 22nd May 2023, had raised various new matters, arguments and grounds which went beyond the relief and arguments raised in its Application dated 3rd May 2023.
29. COR/D further submitted that its position remained that the decision under Article 10 of the Protocol whether or not to excuse a competitor was one for COR/D to make in consultation with the Regatta Director, and not for the Panel to make. COR/D further submitted that no decision had yet been made by COR/D under Article 10 in respect of AM's request to be excused from participation in the Second AC37 Preliminary Regatta in Jeddah and that no dispute currently existed between COR/D and AM.
30. COR/D further submitted that the Panel does not have jurisdiction to pre-emptively determine a dispute that has not yet arisen, and further, does not have jurisdiction to determine the issues raised in the Application, nor to grant the relief sought in the Application. COR/D submitted that if AM wished to raise new matters of interpretation of various provisions of the Protocol, then these should be the subject of a new application.

DISCUSSION

31. The Application from AM dated 3rd May 2023 sought orders from the Panel for AM to be excused from participating in the Second AC37 Preliminary Regatta in Jeddah and for no penalty to be imposed in terms of Article 10.2 of the Protocol. At the time of such Application, AM had not sought the agreement of COR/D to be excused from such Regatta in terms of Articles 10.1 and 10.2 of the Protocol.
32. Following Directions issued by the Panel on 6th May 2023, AM sought the agreement of COR/D to be excused from the Second AC37 Preliminary Regatta in Jeddah. COR/D is currently considering such request with a decision still to be made.
33. The reply from AM dated 22nd May 2023 responding to the COR/D observations dated 13th May 2023 included a broad range of matters including why AM considered the Panel to have jurisdiction, which was a matter of interpretation. AM also included its views on the requirement to race and participate in AC37 Events under Article 10.1 of the Protocol and a "reasonable grounds" test. The Panel considers that much of what was contained in the AM Reply dated 22nd May 2023 was new and very different from what was contained in its Application dated 3rd May 2023. In many respects it was a smorgasbord of multiple arguments. The Panel does not think it appropriate or necessary to address such

a range of arguments. The Panel considers Article 10.2 of the Protocol is clear as to its meaning.

34. The Panel notes that Article 10.1(b) of the Protocol provides that it is "subject to the discretion of COR/D to excuse any competitor pursuant to Article 10.2." Article 10.2(a) of the Protocol provides, "Unless COR/D (in consultation with the Regatta Director) is satisfied...". In the Panel's view, as currently drafted the Protocol is clear that it is only COR/D which has the power to excuse a competitor from an AC37 Event. COR/D has not yet made a decision. COR/D is required to make such decision on "reasonable grounds" in accordance with the Protocol. The Panel is not entitled under the Protocol to make the orders sought in the Application.

COMMENTS ON CONFIDENTIALITY

35. The breach of Article 67.12(b) of the Protocol is a significant concern. An entire copy of the Application has been disclosed to the media whilst these proceedings were continuing. It appears to be a blatant breach of the Protocol, likely intended to cause effect to COR/D. All Competitors have denied any such breach.
36. If such a breach occurs in the future, the Panel gives notice that it intends to take more stringent steps including possible orders of discovery.
37. The Panel notes that significant penalties can be imposed by the Panel under Article 67.4 of the Protocol for breaches of confidentiality.

DECISION

38. The Application is dismissed.
39. When COR/D makes a decision on whether or not to excuse AM from participation in the Second AC37 Preliminary Regatta in Jeddah, if AM considers such decision to be not in accordance with the Protocol, AM may make a new application to the Panel. Such decision by COR/D must be "on reasonable grounds". Such test is subjective.
40. Equally, Article 10.2(a)(i)(B) of the Protocol entitles COR/D to apply to the Panel "to impose such financial penalty it considers appropriate" should COR/D not excuse AM from attending the Second AC37 Preliminary Regatta in Jeddah. What is "appropriate" is within the Panel's discretion.
41. If AM wishes to raise new matters of interpretation relating to the issues raised in Case 004 then AM may make a new application to the Panel. AM should note however, that if it makes an application to the Panel seeking to advance the matters raised in paragraphs 6 to 14 inclusive of its Reply dated 22nd May 2023, prior to COR/D making its decision, for the reasons set out above the Panel would need convincing to deviate from its current position.

COSTS

42. This case follows the normal position that the Applicant should pay the costs of an Application. AM is to pay costs of Euros 14,500. As AM has already paid Euros 10,000 in its Application fee, the further costs of Euros 4,500 is to be paid to the Panel account within 7 days.

28th May 2023

America's Cup Arbitration Panel

David Tillett AM (Chair) Graham McKenzie

Bryan Willis

6.5 ACAP37/05 – SNG (ARBR) Request for Interpretation of Venue, Event and Team Bases, Regarding Retailing and Merchandising: Decision (27 August 2023, 09:10 UTC)

IN THE MATTER
of the Protocol Governing
the 37th America's Cup
AND
IN THE MATTER
of an Application filed by Société Nautique de Genève ("SNG")
and Alinghi Red Bull Racing in its capacity as the representative sailing team of SNG ("ARBR") seeking an interpretation of Article 53.1(a) and several Definitions of the Protocol
with regard to Venue Merchandising and for mediation

AMERICA'S CUP ARBITRATION PANEL CASE 005

In accordance with the America's Cup Arbitration Panel Rules of Procedure, the World Intellectual Property Organisation ("WIPO") electronic ADR case facility ("eADR") is in use for this Application. This Decision will be made available on eADR to all relevant contacts provided by the respective teams.

APPLICATION

1. On 28th July 2023, an Application dated 28th July 2023 was received by the Arbitration Panel ("Panel") from Alinghi Red Bull Racing ("ARBR") ("the Applicant"), seeking an interpretation of Article 53.1(a) of the Protocol, and seeking an interpretation of the definitions of Venue, Event, and Team Bases as defined in the Protocol, regarding the retailing and merchandising activities restrictions in the Protocol.
2. In its Application, the Applicant further requested the Panel to instruct the AC Event Authority ("ACE") to instruct Sportfolio Spain SL ("Sportfolio") to operate the merchandising activities to be carried out at ARBR's Base; or to carve out the exclusivity granted to Sportfolio and approve Sail Racing AB to be the operator of ARBR's retailing or merchandising activities at its Base.
3. In its Application, the Applicant further requested for the Panel to order mediation between ACE and ARBR in order to find an alternative solution to resolve an apparent deadlock situation.
4. In its Application, the Applicant considered that the receipt of a letter from ACE dated 21st July 2023 indicated that ACE had rejected efforts made by ARBR to resolve the matter and had resulted in a deadlock situation.

DIRECTIONS

5. On 29th July 2023 the Panel issued Directions in respect of the Application:
   i) Advising that Article 67.14(a) of the Protocol provided for the establishment of the Arbitration Panel Rules of Procedure and that such Rules of Procedure had been published and that the Application was subject to such Rules of Procedure and would be managed through eADR;
   ii) Directing that the Application was suitable for mediation in accordance with Article 67.3(l) of the Protocol;
   iii) Appointing Graham McKenzie as mediator ("the Mediator");
   iv) Directing that the Mediator would issue separate directions to the Applicant, the Defender and ACE in respect of the mediation; and
   v) Directing that the mediation should remain confidential in all respects to the Mediator, the Applicant, the Defender, ACE, and any other party that the Mediator, in conjunction with the Applicant, the Defender and ACE, determined should be included in the mediation.
6. On 3rd August 2023 the Panel was informed in writing by the Mediator that the mediation between ARBR and ACE had not been successful.

FURTHER DIRECTIONS

7. On 4th August 2023 the Panel issued Further Directions in respect of the Application:
   i) Directing that mediation in respect of the Application had ended;
   ii) Noting that on 1st August 2023 Luna Rossa Prada Pirelli Team ("Luna Rossa") had submitted a request on eADR to join the mediation taking place between ACE and ARBR but that as the mediation had ended, directing that the request submitted by Luna Rossa on 2nd August 2023 was no longer applicable;
   iii) Setting a time and date by which each of those parties wishing to make an Observation, should do so by 17:00 hours (Barcelona time) on Friday 11th August 2023; and
   iv) Setting a time and date by which ARBR may, should it wish to do so, submit a Reply to the observations submitted by the Competitors and/or by ACE, by 17:00 (Barcelona time) on Tuesday 15th August 2023.

RESPONSES AND REPLIES

8. On 11th August 2023, INEOS Britannia in its capacity as the representative of Royal Yacht Squadron Limited and Athena Racing Limited and as Challenger of Record ("INEOS") submitted a Response to the Application, stating that Article 53.1(a) of the Protocol was clear and unambiguous and that only ACE's approved

retailers and concessionaires were authorised to carry on any retailing or merchandising activities at any Venue (as such term is defined in the Protocol).

9. In its Response, INEOS further submitted that the strict wording of Article 53.1(a) meant that ACE had complete discretion to appoint who it wanted as retailers and concessionaries at any Venue and that it was not appropriate to imply into Article 53.1(a) that there was a specific process for approval of any other retailer(s) or concessionaire(s).
10. In its Response, INEOS further submitted that all Competitors agreed to the principles outlined in paragraphs 9 and 10 above when they signed the Protocol and that the principles had not been imposed with the purpose of being anti-competitive.
11. On 11th August 2023 ACE submitted a Response to the Application, stating that the terms of the Protocol were clear and that under Article 3.2 of the Protocol, ACE had the sole responsibility to organise and manage the commercial rights of AC37 and that under Article 48.1, all commercial rights including Event merchandising and brand licensing were vested in ACE and managed by ACE.
12. In its Response, ACE further submitted that Article 48 of the Protocol recorded that each Competitor transferred to ACE their commercial rights related to their participation in AC37 and that Competitors had agreed that their commercial rights were on and subject to the terms of the Protocol. ACE further submitted that no Competitor was authorised as of right to sell its own merchandise from a Team Base and that there was no obligation on ACE under the Protocol to appoint its own retailer, or any other retailer, or to operate a Team Base shop, or to offer any "alternative services".
13. In its Response, ACE further submitted that it had appointed Sportfolio as its exclusive retailer focused in the area of the AC Race Village in Barcelona and that Sportfolio would be selling merchandise supplied by all Teams under the terms of the Protocol. ACE further submitted that Sportfolio had no interest in operating team shops at individual bases and that ACE had no interest in appointing alternative retailers for individual Team Bases, nor did ACE have any obligation to approve other retailers to operate merchandising facilities at Team Bases.
14. In its Response, ACE further submitted that the wording of Article 53.1(a) was clear and unambiguous and that it was doubtful that the Panel had jurisdiction to retrospectively rule that the principles of Spanish or EU anti-competition law administered by local regulators were implied into the wording of Article 53.1(a). Furthermore, that the arrangements had no anti-competitive effect and did not affect trade or restrict competition.
15. On 15th August 2023, ARBR submitted a Reply to the Responses received from INEOS and from ACE. In its Reply, ARBR submitted that by signing and agreeing to the Protocol, Competitors had not relinquished to ACE their own commercial rights over their branded merchandising and that there was nothing in the Protocol prohibiting a Competitor from opening a shop at their Team Base,

nor that Competitors granted ACE exclusive rights over their merchandising activities at the Venue.

16. In its Reply ARBR further submitted that a contract such as the Protocol should not allow ACE to impose on any of the Competitors, conclusions that were contrary to the law and public policy, based on the fact that the jurisdiction of the Protocol was New Zealand and that ACE was not subject to comply with local laws. ARBR further submitted that ACE was obliged to comply with local legislations to the same extent as the Competitors.
17. The Panel noted that ARBR attached as Appendix 1 to its Reply, a Legal Opinion from Law Firm Cuatrecasas dated 15th August 2023 relating to the "Applicability of EU and Spanish competition law to agreements or conducts with effects in the EU or Spain and anticompetitive character of agreements that prevent competitors from accessing a given market".
18. In its Reply ARBR further submitted that ACE, in trying to prevent Competitors from opening shops at their Team Bases, was acting contrary to European and Spanish law, given that the Protocol contained no express prohibition.
19. On 17th August 2023 ACE submitted a Request for Further Filing. In its Request for Further Filing, ACE submitted that the Reply submitted by ARBR dated 15th August 2023 contained new assertions of fact which went beyond the proper scope of reply submissions and that such assertions were incomplete and overlooked certain matters. ACE further submitted that if such factual matters were not addressed, the Panel may be left with an incomplete or inaccurate picture of the circumstances. ACE further submitted that it was in a position to supply information relating to the layout of the Venue's perimeter and the time frames associated and could supply an update on the demarcation of the Venue area.
20. In its Request for Further Filing, ACE sought leave from the Panel to file:
    a. Information showing the size and location of the current Sportfolio store; and
    b. A map of the venue with explanatory notes detailing and explaining the areas either controlled by or on behalf of ACE pursuant to its arrangements with the Barcelona Venue Authorities or those designated as part of the Venue for the Event pursuant to ACE's arrangements with the Barcelona Venue Authorities.
21. In its Request for Further Filing, ACE submitted that it did not seek to file any further reply to the legal aspects of ARBR's Reply dated 15th August 2023.

ADDITIONAL FURTHER DIRECTIONS

22. On 19th August 2023 the Panel issued Additional Further Directions in respect of the Application:

i) Setting a time and date by which ACE shall, by 17:00 (Barcelona time) on Tuesday 22nd August 2023, submit the following:
   a. Information showing the size and location of the current Sportfolio store; and
   b. A map of the venue with explanatory notes detailing and explaining the areas either controlled by or on behalf of ACE pursuant to its arrangements with the Barcelona Venue Authorities or those designated as part of the Venue for the Event pursuant to ACE's arrangements with the Barcelona Venue Authorities; and

ii) Setting a time and date by which ARBR and INEOS Britannia may, if they so wish, submit a Response to the Further Filing made by ACE, by 17:00 (Barcelona time) on Friday 25th August 2023.

RESPONSES AND REPLIES

23. On 22nd August 2023 ACE submitted a Further Filing, setting out further information relating to the Sportfolio Store and Venue.
24. In its Further Filing, ACE submitted that the current Sportfolio Official Store (Botiga Official) had been made available to each of the teams as an outlet for their own Event- related merchandise and currently had stock available for sale supplied by Alinghi Red Bull Racing, American Magic and Emirates Team New Zealand, in addition to the Event merchandise, with other teams' merchandise expected in the near future.
25. In its Further Filing, ACE further submitted a series of slides showing the Venue, and submitted that the area of the delineated Venue was under the ownership and control of the Port Authority of Barcelona (Autoridad Portuaria de Barcelona), one of the Host Venue Authorities under the Venue Appointment Agreement dated 28 Match [*sp. March*] 2022.
26. On 25th August 2023, ARBR submitted a Reply to the Further Filing submitted by ACE on 22nd August 2023.
27. In its Reply, ARBR submitted that the layout of the current Sportfolio store did not show equity between Teams and that that the number of shops set up by ACE would never offer the service expected by Competitors' guests and would never display the full range of Competitors' merchandise portfolio, and that such shops would not compensate the legitimate right of ARBR to have a shop in its base.

DISCUSSION

28. The Application from ARBR dated 28th July 2023 sought an interpretation of Article 53.1(a) of the Protocol, and an interpretation of the definitions of Venue, Event, and Team Bases as defined in the Protocol, regarding the retailing and merchandising activities' restrictions in the Protocol.
29. Articles 3.2 and 48.2 of the Protocol provide for the transfer of "commercial rights" to ACE.

30. Article 48.1 of the Protocol is broadly drafted and allows ACE to exploit all commercial rights of AC37 including "Event branding" and "Event merchandising and brand licensing."
31. Article 48.3 of the Protocol reserves the right for each Competitor to exploit "all commercial rights" (excluding the commercial rights in Article 48.1) including such matters as "the Competitor's branded merchandising and brand licensing."
32. There is a separation in the Protocol between Event branding and Event merchandising under Article 48.1 and Competitor's branded merchandising and brand licensing in Article 48.3.
33. Article 53.1 of the Protocol is titled "Venue Merchandising" and provides that only ACE's approved retailers and concessionaires are authorised to carry on retailing or merchandising activities at the Venue.
34. The Protocol does not expressly state that a Competitor cannot open their own Team Base shop or that there can only be a sole worldwide retailer and concessionaire selling team merchandise.
35. The geographic extent of "Venue" has now been provided in the ACE Further Filing of 22nd August 2023. It stated, "The entire area of the delineated Venue is under the control of the Port Authority of Barcelona ..." (paragraph 7 of ACE's submission). ACE also confirmed that "teams have significant freedom to exploit their own merchandising rights". This includes the ability to set up physical outlet stores outside of each delineated Venue. ARBR in its submission of 25th August 2025 strongly objected to the defined Venue area which it described as "an ad hoc tailor made Venue map." ARBR Also considered it unfair with the existing Sportfolio shop being "not as equal between teams." The Panel recognises the frustration from ARBR but for the reasons that follow, the Panel does not have the power to direct or order Sportfolio to conduct such a retail shop in a specified way.

ARTICLE 53 of the PROTOCOL

36. In ARBR's Application it provided in Exhibit 1 a series of email exchanges between Grant Dalton, Michel Hodara and Russell Green, starting on 18th June 2023. On 20th June 2023, Grant Dalton raised the possibility of a Protocol Amendment if a base shop was to be permitted.
37. In an email dated 10th July 2023 Russell Green stated "I agree with your position that you consider that the Protocol does not actually prohibit a Team from setting up a Team base shop" but then quoted the ACE approval process under Article 53.1(a) of the Protocol. In the same email Russell Green stated, "ACE has approved Sportfolio as its exclusive retailer." The email also stated, "your request for ACE to now approve your own retailer to operate a Team base shop.....has been considered .... but having appointed its retailer on an exclusive basis .... ACE is not prepared to now approve a different retailer."

38. On 3rd July 2023 ARBR by email, made a "formal" request by email for "ACE to operate our retailer". Further emails followed, including on 21st July 2023 an email from Grant Dalton to ARBR giving further reasons as to why ACE would not change its position on the appointment of Sportfolio, "... as ACE does not wish to alter its planned commercial model with its exclusive retailer."
39. The Panel has not seen and does not know what date the agreement was reached with Sportfolio. Sportfolio is not a party to, and therefore not bound by, the Protocol. The Panel has no jurisdiction over Sportfolio.
40. In the Panel's view it is apparent that at least by 10th July 2023, ACE had already decided to appoint Sportfolio as its sole exclusive retailer. The emails that followed, including a formal application, make it clear that the decision was already made and no change could or would be made.
41. Article 53.1(a) of the Protocol means that ARBR requires ACE's prior approval to be permitted to "carry on any retailing or merchandising activities at any Venue". No application criteria or approval process is provided for in the Protocol. The Panel does not have the power to substitute its decision for what ACE decided.
42. Two members of the Panel were concerned that ACE effectively circumvented the approval process provided in Articles 53.1(a) and (c) of the Protocol. There was never any prospect of ARBR being approved under Article 53.1 as it had already been decided that Sportfolio was to be the exclusive retailer. Given what occurred, it is understandable why ARBR filed the Application.
43. The Protocol refers in Article 53.1(a) and (c) to "retailers and concessionaires". This contemplates the possibility of more than one retailer and concessionaire, but does not mean that there must be more than one. However, given that ACE's prior approval is always required under Article 53.1(a), the majority of the Panel can see no point in requiring ACE to reconsider the matter as its decision has already been made. Also, it appears that ACE has already entered into a binding agreement with Sportfolio, and Sportfolio is not subject to the Panel's jurisdiction.
44. The other member of the Panel considers that ACE was entitled to grant the rights that they did, though earlier clarification of the Venue area would have been helpful for Competitors in making their plans. It is noted that ACE provided their reasons for its decision to appoint a retailer/concessionaire, which do not need to be specifically set out. Nevertheless, it was clear that the Team Bases were always included within the Venue.
45. The Panel considers it does not have the power or jurisdiction to make a different decision to that made by ACE with regard to Sportfolio. It is noted that the parties to the Protocol have contractually agreed to the provisions of the Protocol, including the application of New Zealand Law. This does not derogate from the fact, and as recognised in Article 69 of the Protocol, that Competitors (and equally applicable to ACE), must comply with the applicable laws of any city,

state, National or other Governmental authority. It is difficult to see that relevant local law would not apply to commercial contracts. In reaching its decision on a matter concerning the interpretation of the Protocol, the Panel did not consider it necessary or appropriate to further consider the application of local law. The Panel notes that the Venue area as now clarified by ACE is quite specifically identified, and leaves opportunities for merchandising outside this area without the need for approval from ACE.

DECISION

46. In Section F of its Application, the Applicant makes a number of requests of the Panel (numbered (i) to (vi) set out in italic text below):
47. *(i) That the Arbitration Panel confirms the interpretation of Article 53.1(a) submitted in Section B of this Application meaning (i) that the Protocol does not prohibit Competitors from having their own shops at their Team's Base; and (ii) that the Protocol does not prohibit Competitors from selling at their Team's Base their team's merchandise to their guests and to the guests of their sponsors.*
    (i) The Protocol itself does not prohibit Competitors having their own shops at their Team Bases.
    (ii) The Protocol itself does not prohibit Competitors from selling at their Team's Base their team's merchandise to their guests and to the guests of sponsors.
    However, under Article 53.1(a) of the Protocol, only ACE's approved retailers and concessionaires are authorized to carry on any retailing or merchandising activities at any Venue. Any such activities therefore require ACE's approval of the retailer/concessionaire which has been sought by the Applicant and declined.
48. *(ii) That the Arbitration Panel declares that ACE is not entitled to arrogate exclusive rights over the retailing and merchandising activities of a Competitor at their Bases, nor to discretionally refuse the approval of a retailer to operate a Competitor's shop in case Sportfolio (or any approved retailers and concessionaires) would refuse managing the Competitor's retailing or merchandising activities without giving an alternative and reasonable solution to such Competitor.*
    Article 53.1 of the Protocol confers on ACE an absolute discretion to authorize retailers and concessionaires to carry on the subject activities. The Article does not:
    a) contain any specific process for such authorization; nor
    b) contain any specific right for applying for such an authorization.
    The authorization can be by either multiple retailers/concessionaires, or an exclusive authorization.

The use of the plural in Article 53.1(a) is simply permissive of the authorization for ACE to appoint more than one retailer/concessionaire, should they see fit.

It is noted that an authorization was sought by the Applicant from ACE, and this was declined.

Accordingly the Applicant is not entitled to the declaration sought.

49. *(iii) That the Arbitration Panel requests ACE to instruct Sportfolio Spain, SL, to operate ARBR's Team Base from now until the end of the 37AC or at least, until 22 August 2024.*

The request for the instruction is refused (refer to the Decision on question (ii) above).

50. *(iv) Subsidiarily to (iii) above, that the Arbitration Panel instructs ACE to carve out the exclusivity granted to Sportfolio Spain, S.L. and to approve Sail Racing AB as operator of ARBR's Team Base from now until the end of the 37AC or at least, until 22 August 2024, unless ACE replaces Sportfolio Spain SL. by another approved retailer or concessionaire.*

The request for the instruction is refused (refer to the Decision on question (ii) above).

51. *(v) Subsidiarily to (i), (ii), (iii) and (iv) above, that the Arbitration Panel confirms the interpretation of definitions of Venue, Event and Team Bases submitted in Section C of this Application, and declares that restrictions provided for in Article 53.1 (a) shall be effective only during the timeframes set forth for each Event;*

It is further considered that the Venue is a specific area as provided for in the Protocol. ACE has now provided additional information clarifying the areas covered by the definition of Venue. The restrictions contained in Article 53.1(a) of the Protocol are not expressed to be time limited, and accordingly apply notwithstanding whether an Event as defined is occurring or not at the Venue.

52. *(vi) Subsidiarily to (i), (ii), (iii), (iv) and (v) above, that the Arbitration Panel mediates between ACE and ARBR to find an alternative solution to ARBR's request that solves the deadlock situation created by ACE's refusal to approve Sail Racing AB as a retailer.*

Mediation was ordered; it was unsuccessful.

COSTS

53. This Application involved significant commercial issues, and has assisted all Competitors, including the provision of the clarification of aspects relating to the Venue. A mediation also took place. The Applicant was unsuccessful in respect of the remedies sought; however it is recognised that there were good reasons why the Application was lodged.
54. The Panel considers that an appropriate order for Costs is:
    (i) 70% of Costs to be payable by ARBR; and

(ii) 30% of Costs to be payable by ACE.

55. ARBR is to pay costs of Euros 13,667.50. As ARBR has already paid Euros 10,000 in its Application fee, the further costs of Euros 3,667.50 is to be paid to the Panel account within 7 days.
56. ACE is to pay costs of Euros 5,857.50, to be paid into the Panel account within 7 days.

27th August 2023

America's Cup Arbitration Panel

David Tillett AM (Chair)

Graham McKenzie

Bryan Willis

Confirming that cases are conducted via the electronic case management facility "WIPO eADR" made available by the World Intellectual Property Organization.

6.6 ACAP37/06 – Notice Resulting from a Report Received: Decision (14 October 2024, 14:00 UTC)

IN THE MATTER
of the Protocol Governing the 37th America's Cup
AND
IN THE MATTER
of a Report received by the Arbitration Panel
in relation to Rule 69 of the Racing Rules of Sailing – America's Cup Edition
Version 4.07 with
regard to Misconduct

AMERICA'S CUP ARBITRATION PANEL CASE 006

In accordance with the America's Cup Arbitration Panel Rules of Procedure, the World Intellectual Property Organisation ("WIPO") electronic ADR case facility ("eADR") is in use for this Case. This Decision will be made available on eADR to all relevant contacts provided by the respective teams.

REPORT

1. The Arbitration Panel has received information contained in a report claiming that misconduct had occurred in contravention of Rule 69 of the Racing Rules of Sailing – America's Cup Edition Version 4.07 ("Racing Rules AC").
2. At the conclusion of Race 3 on 13th October 2024 in an on-water post-race interview with Sir Ben Ainslie ("Ben"), in a live broadcast:

    Stephen McIvor (Interviewer):
    "Are you still believing you're as close when it comes to performance as I get that feeling coming off your boat?"
    Ben:
    "Well, maybe that's the Kiwi commentator in you, mate."
    Stephen McIvor (Interviewer):
    "Ok, I'll take that one on the chin, thanks buddy."
    After the interview had been completed and as Ben was exiting the cockpit, he said:
    Ben:
    "F*****g W****r"

DISCUSSION

3. The Arbitration Panel has considered Racing Rules AC Rule 69 and in particular Rule 69.2(b) which provides,
   "(b) When the Arbitration Panel, from its own observation or from information received from any source, including evidence taken during a hearing, believes a person may have broken rule 69.1(a), it shall report the matter to the Event Disciplinary Investigating Officer under World Sailing Disciplinary Code 35.4.3 in schedule 3."
4. The Arbitration Panel has listened to a replay of the live broadcast, spoken to two senior TV Host Broadcaster representatives from AC Media, and reviewed other replays of the same Race 3.
5. The Arbitration Panel notes that in the same race, as Emirates Team New Zealand crossed the finish line, Peter Burling ("Peter") said, "F**k we crossed swords there didn't we."
6. The Arbitration Panel understands that all competitors are aware that all times during the broadcast feed, whatever they may say is live and may be broadcast.
7. The Arbitration Panel considers that the comment made by Ben, "Well, maybe that's the Kiwi commentator in you, mate" is not biased. With regard to the words "F*****g W****r", the Arbitration Panel considers that they were made when Ben clearly believed the interview had been completed and he was off-air, and the words were not clearly audible. The Arbitration Panel members were watching and listening to the live broadcast in three different locations and none of them heard such words.
8. With regard to the words used by Peter, the Arbitration Panel also did not hear those words on the live broadcast and no report has been received raising objection before the Arbitration Panel.
9. The Arbitration Panel notes that neither AC Media nor the America's Cup Event Authority have received a complaint about the words used by Ben or by Peter.

DECISION

10. The Arbitration Panel considers that in the particular circumstances of this case, the words used by Ben and by Peter did not break Racing Rules AC Rule 69.1(a).
11. The Arbitration Panel determines that neither Ben nor Peter committed misconduct under Racing Rules AC Rule 69. The broadcast has not caused widespread offence and has not brought the sport into disrepute. Accordingly, the Arbitration Panel has determined that the matter is not referred to an Event Disciplinary Investigating Officer under World Sailing Disciplinary Code 35.4.3.

12. The Arbitration Panel reminds all those competing in the 37th America's Cup Match that what they say on board may be broadcast live and that they have an obligation not to commit misconduct.

14th October 2024

America's Cup Arbitration

Panel David Tillett AM (Chair)

Graham McKenzie

Bryan Willis

Cases are conducted via the electronic case management facility "WIPO eADR" made available by the World Intellectual Property Organization.

Chapter 7 The Jury Decisions

7.1 AC37 Jury Case 01 – Request for Redress by ITA for RR2, Race 29: Decision (10 September 2024)

AC37 Jury

Case 01

Initiator	**Luna Rossa Prada Pirelli (ITA)**
Respondent	**Request for Redress**
Date	**10 September 2024**
Race #	**Louis Vuitton Cup RR2, Race 29**

SUMMARY OF REQUEST:

During Race 29, the supplied FCS software of our AC75 sustained an irreversible error that caused the inability for the crew to operate the yacht.

We believe that our score was made significantly worse through no fault of our own due to the action of a third party, i.e., the supplier of the faulty software. This incident materially affected the outcome of the race by not allowing us to use the FCS and therefore not start the race. It also created a serious safety concern by preventing safe control of the boat forcing the crew to sail through the spectator fleet at high speed.

JURY DECISION:

The Jury interprets from the RRSAC that there is no process nor right for ITA to seek redress.

Redress is instigated by the Measurement Committee reporting serious damage or injury to the Jury and then the requirement under the rules is that the Jury 'shall' consider redress (refer RRSAC 60.3(c)). The Jury Chairman has contacted the Chief Measurer this morning. It was explained that the Measurement Committee was involved in the process in the evening to gain access to the data files. The Measurement Committee has not made any report to the Jury about this issue.

The Jury has used RRSAC 64.1(c) to consider the ITA request to determine if the request can be treated in another manner under the RRSAC. A 'protest' is defined in RRSAC as 'An allegation made under rule 61.2 by a boat, the Regatta Director or the Jury that a boat has broken a rule.' The request received from ITA has no allegation that any boat has broken a rule, therefore the Jury is unable to proceed with this case as a protest. RRSAC 63.1 requires that the Jury hears all protests, however, in this instance the request for redress sent by ITA is not a protest (as defined).

In this case, there is no rule that allows the Jury to hold a hearing on this matter. The Jury will not be proceeding any further.

37th America's Cup International Jury

Richard Slater (Chairperson), Miguel Allen, Arnaud Mante, Craig Mitchell, and Sofia Truchanowicz

7.2 AC37 Jury Case 02 – Jury Interpretation of 'Serious Physical Damage' and 'Action by a 3rd Party': Decision (14 September 2024)

37th America's Cup International Jury

Case 02

14 September 2024

Following Jury Case 01, the Measurement Committee and Regatta Director have asked the Jury two questions. As provided in Protocol Article 45 (c) and RRSAC N2.1, the Jury provides the following interpretations.

Preface:

This interpretation is based on The Racing Rules of Sailing AC edition ('RRSAC') v4.06.

The RRSAC states in the Introduction that '*Other words and terms are used in the sense ordinarily understood in nautical or general use.*'

If the use of such words and terms conflict with schedule one of the Protocol or the Oxford English Dictionary ('OED'), then Protocol Article 1.4 requires that schedule one or the OED definition shall be referenced.

When a person or body is required to make a determination, RRSAC 64.1(a) provides guidance that the decision is based on a balance of probabilities.

Question 1:

What is 'injury to the crew or serious physical damage to a boat' in relation to the RRSAC?

Answer 1:

The 'crew' are the human beings who were on the yacht in the race when the incident happened.

A crew member is injured when they are harmed, damaged, or impaired to an extent that is greater than any normal injuries crew members experience when racing on the boat. Fatigue is not an injury.

'Damage' is physical harm that impairs usefulness, or normal function of something.

For damage to be 'physical' the damage shall be tangible or concrete. For example, impairment to the normal function of software is not physical damage.

Damage is 'serious' when it is:

(a) worrying because of possible danger or risk. Racing on an AC75 Yacht or AC40 Yacht already involves increased danger and risk. The person or body making the determination has decided that the damage substantially increases the danger or risk; or
(b) significant. Being that the person or body making the determination has decided that the damage did impact, or could impact, a race result.

Question 2:

What is meant by 'an action by a third party' in relation to the RRSAC 62.1(e)?

Answer 2:

A third party referred to in RRSAC 62.1(e) for AC37 is a person or group other than those directly associated with a boat in a race.

An action is a thing done, an act. It is not an omission.

The last part of the sentence in (e), limits that the third party must do something while the boat is racing which then causes injury to the crew or serious physical damage to the boat.

7.3 Youth America's Cup Jury Case 01: Decision (18 September 2024)

Youth America's Cup Jury

Case 01

Initiator	**Alinghi Red Bull Racing ('SUI')**
Respondent	**Youth America's Cup Jury**
Date	**18 September 2024**
Race #	**Youth America's Cup Qualifying Series Group A Race 4**

SUMMARY OF REQUEST:

SUI lodged the following:

On the last downwind leg we were close to the finish in a solid 2nd position, we gybed from starboard to port and the foil arm begins to low and raise without our control.

We stop foiling and we crossed the finish line in 3rd position.

We request redress, our position has been significantly worsen through no our fault and clearly because of a one design part.

In addition, we saw also what happen to the other yachts it's a clear issue. We ask to consider this redress.

JURY DECISION:

The Jury interprets from the RRSAC that there is no process nor right for SUI to seek redress.

RRSAC 60.1 allows a boat to protest another boat for certain rules but it does not allow them to seek redress.

RRSAC 63.1 requires that the Jury hears all protests, however, in this instance the request for redress sent by SUI is not a protest. A 'protest' is defined in RRSAC as 'An allegation made under rule 61.2 by a boat, the Regatta Director or the Jury that a boat has broken a rule.'

In this case, there is no rule that allows the Jury to hold a hearing on this matter. The Jury will not be proceeding any further.

Youth America's Cup International Jury

Richard Slater (Chairperson), Miguel Allen, Svenja Huensch, Arnaud Mante, Katie Maxim, Craig Mitchell, Ryan Parkin and Sofia Truchanowicz.

Index

A

AC40 Class Rule, 277-300
AC40 yacht,
  allocation, 400-403
  transfer of property, 16, 401
AC75 Class Rule, 188-276
AC75 yacht,
  selling/sharing of design package, 404-410
ACE (America's Cup Event Authority), 4, 5, 13, 16, 18, 39-48, 50-55, 57, 60, 63, 64, 67, 69, 72, 73, 76-95, 98, 103, 105-107, 109-112, 116, 118, 121-123, 126, 128, 141, 299, 359, 360, 363, 366, 371-373, 375-384, 386, 389-393, 395, 396, 400, 401, 402, 404, 405, 412-415, 420-429, 431
AC Technical Regulations, 301-358
Action by a third party, 171, 436
ADR Case Facility, 135, 420, 430
America's Cup
  background, 3
  future of, 19-20
  36th edition, 1, 11
  38th edition, 7, 19, 20, 58-59, 118
America's Cup Event Authority (ACE), 4, 5, 13, 16, 18, 39-48, 50-55, 57, 60, 63, 64, 67, 69, 72, 73, 76-95, 98, 103, 105-107, 109-112, 116, 118, 121-123, 126, 128, 141, 299, 359, 360, 363, 366, 371-373, 375-384, 386, 389-393, 395, 396, 400, 401, 402, 404, 405, 412-415, 420-429, 431
Arbitration Panel
  37th America's Cup Arbitration Panel, 11-20
    composition, 11-13
    decisions, 14-19
    jurisdiction, 13-14
    mediation, 14
    power to substitute, 426
    Rules of Procedure, 14
    seat, 136
Arbitration proceedings
  confidentiality in, 140-141
Assignment and Acceptance deed, 3
Audience and economic impact of AC37, 7-10

B

Balance of probabilities, 173, 435
Barcelona, 2, 5, 7-9, 60, 360, 363-366, 372, 421-425
Branding and Advertising, 82, 84-85, 383

C

Challenger Selection Series ('CSS')
  Notice of race and conditions (Louis Vuitton Cup Conditions), 2, 359-362
  schedule, 360
Commercial rights
  ACE's role, 82

Commercial rights (cont'd)
responsibility to organize and manage, 39, 422
transfer of, 424
Competitors sailing team, 5
Confidentiality
in arbitration, 108, 140-141, 145
breach of, 111, 413, 418
of an application, 108, 141, 413
order, 108, 140, 405
'Constructed in country' requirement, 62-63
Co-ordinated testing, 17, 409
Cost containment and limitations, 6, 59-62

D

Deadlock situation
Deed of Gift, 21-32
amendment of, 21
current version of, 2
commentary of, 24-25
Deed of Assignment and Acceptance, 3
original (handwritten) version, 22-23
Disrepute,
to bring the sport into, 175

E

Economic impact of AC37, 7-10
Electronic Case Facility (ECAF), 14-15, 110, 130, 398, 400, 405, 412
Event Disciplinary Investigating Officer (EDIO), 18, 19, 176, 431
Events,
AC37 Events
37th America's Cup Match, 41
interpretation of, 420-429
Jeddah, Saudi Arabia, 5
Louis Vuitton Challenger Selection Series (CSS), 5
Louis Vuitton Cup Round Robin Series, 5
Louis Vuitton Preliminary Regattas, 5
safety concerns in participating in, 17, 411
Vilanova i La Geltrú, Spain, 5, 8

G

Governing rules (of AC37), 5, 69-70

H

Hydrogen powered support vessels (HSVs), 6, 66, 67, 121
Hypothetical question, 139

I

Inability to operate a yacht, 433
Individual Reconnaissance, 17, 409
Injury to the crew, 171, 435, 436

J

Jury
37th America's Cup Jury Decisions, 2

L

Law
applicable law, 30-32, 112, 113, 116, 325, 326, 426
compliance with all applicable laws and legally binding regulations of any city, state, national or other governmental authority, 112, 426-427
EU and Spanish competition law, 423
New Zealand law, 426

Louis Vuitton Cup Conditions (Race Conditions – 37th America's Cup Challenger Selection Series), 359-363

M

Match, 7, 364-366, 369-370
Match Conditions – 37th America's Cup Match – Barcelona, Spain, 364-366
Measurement Committee, 10, 15, 62, 63, 77-82, 122, 124-126, 130, 169, 170, 174, 185, 186, 195, 202-204, 206, 210, 211, 223, 237, 238, 242, 244, 247, 251, 255-259, 264-265, 267, 269-273, 275, 282-284, 286-291, 295, 296, 298, 306, 307, 310-318, 322, 323, 328, 335, 350, 360, 365, 433, 435
Media
  coverage, 9, 66, 85, 92, 275, 384
Mediation
  cases, 15, 18, 135
  confidentiality of, 421
Merchandising and brand licensing, 82, 83, 422, 425
Misconduct
  Rule 69, 169-171, 187, 430, 431

N

Nationality, 17, 19, 46, 63-65, 115, 130, 131, 186, 359, 379-380

O

Orders of discovery, 418

P

Penalty
  financial penalty, 17, 47, 60, 97, 414, 418
  point penalty, 47, 173, 335, 411, 412, 414
Performance data, 15, 61, 93, 335, 385, 397-399, 406, 407
Power to excuse a competitor from an Event, 17, 18
Preliminary Regattas
  Jeddah, 5, 8, 17, 18, 183, 411-419
  Vilanova i La Geltrú, 5, 8
  lack of participation, 17, 411
Protest, 151, 155, 165, 169-173, 175, 178, 179, 186, 367-370, 379, 393-395, 434, 437
Protest Committee, 19
Protocol
  breach of, 16, 400, 409, 418
  change of / amendment of, 15, 33, 88, 111-112, 398, 399, 425
  interpretation of, 11, 13, 37, 38, 105, 117, 398, 427
Protocol of 37th America's Cup, 33-133
Protocol of 38th America's Cup, 19, 20, 118

R

Race Conditions – 37th America's Cup Challenger Selection Series, 359-363
Reasonable grounds test, 417
Redress
  applicable rule
    RRSAC, 433
  entitlement to request, 433
  relevance of foil arm deficiency

Redress (cont'd)
relevance of software deficiency, 433
request of, 433
role of the Measurement Committee, 433
serious damage or injury, 433
Regatta Officials
Jury, 80-81
Measurement Committee, 79-80
Regatta Director, 78-79
Rules Committee, 79-80
Umpires, 80-81
Regatta Director
jurisdiction, 10, 13, 79, 105
Retailing and merchandizing activities
restrictions of, 420, 424
Rules Committee
jurisdiction, 10, 79-81

S

Safety concerns
reasonable and genuine, 17, 47, 411, 414
Sailing Instructions for the 37th America's Cup Match, 2, 4, 369-370
Sailing Instructions for the Louis Vuitton Cup Challenger Selection Series, 2, 367-368
Sailing Instructions for the Youth and Women's America's Cup, 2, 393-396
Serious physical damage to a boat, 171, 435, 436
Support Vessels, 6, 65, 66, 87, 92, 178, 367, 369, 384, 393
Surrogate Yacht, 15, 16, 60, 61, 79, 124, 130-133, 305, 355, 398, 404, 406, 407

T

Team Bases,
interpretation of, 420-429
Time-limits, 17, 108, 137-140, 143, 163, 166, 171, 179, 361, 366-370, 394, 405, 406, 408, 409, 428
Starting point, 408-409

U

Umpire, 10-12, 19, 77, 79-81, 123, 124, 126, 148, 154-156, 160, 164-167, 169-171, 180, 271, 361, 378, 381, 389, 393

V

Venue
interpretation of, 420-429
Venue merchandising, 18, 89, 420, 425

W

Wind limits, 71-72, 361, 365, 393
WIPO, 14-15, 135, 138, 398, 400, 405, 412, 420, 430, 432
WIPO eADR, 429, 432
World Sailing International Jury, 10, 77, 121, 148
World Sailing Racing Rules of Sailing – America's Cup Edition, for use in the 37th America's Cup, 2, 147-187

Y

Youth and Women's America's Cup regattas, 5-6, 45-46

Youth and Women's America's Cup Agreement, 2

www.ingramcontent.com/pod-product-compliance
Lightning Source LLC
LaVergne TN
LVHW020002031026
849161LV00023B/835

* 9 7 8 9 4 0 3 5 2 9 6 9 1 *